PENSION FUNDS AND ECONOMIC POWER

BY PAUL P. HARBRECHT, S.J.

PENSION FUNDS

AND

ECONOMIC POWER

THE TWENTIETH CENTURY FUND

NEW YORK · 1959

HJ 7106
U5
H 25 p

FOREWORD

For several years the Trustees of the Twentieth Century Fund have been interested in certain financial institutions which seem in a deep way to be altering the nature of American capitalism. Included in these institutions are mutual funds, insurance companies and pension trusts. The latter, because of their comparatively recent development and their rapid rate of growth, as well as because of their intrinsic importance, offers a particularly tempting field for research and evaluation. This volume by Father Harbrecht is part of a project which the Fund hopes may result in further studies in the same area.

The subject of pension trusts has a good deal more significance than might seem apparent at first glance. That such a device should have arisen within the private sector of the economy, with the promise of giving to increasing numbers of Americans a more secure future, is in itself striking. But the hope for a higher degree of economic independence after retirement is only one aspect of the drive behind the growth of pension funds. In addition there has been a steady and increasing pressure toward a wider diffusion of the benefits of the modern industrial system. With such a diffusion there has come also a subtle alteration in the nature of that system and in many of the concepts — such as those of property and power — which underlie it.

Father Harbrecht in this volume gives close attention to the facts of today's pension trusts; but it is to be hoped that the larger significance of his theme will not be overlooked. He writes in his final chapter of what he calls the "Paraproprietal Society," drawing together the implications of this and other developments in contemporary capitalism. He suggests that we are in a period when property once again, as at other important periods of history, is undergoing a change in its basic character. The ownership of property begins to take new forms, and power is exercised under conditions and limitations which are effective even though still only imperfectly understood.

It is frequently recognized that American capitalism is a quite different thing from what it was conceived to be by the classical economists. A theory adequate to comprehend its modern dimensions has not yet been even sketched. Father Harbrecht would not claim to have added more than a few stones to the structure which will ultimately be found capable

Foreword

of containing so dynamic, complex, and mysterious a system. Perhaps it would be best to say that in focusing on the institution of pension trusts he has been like the physicist who, in isolating a new element, impels a basic reconsideration of the whole theoretical framework.

AUGUST HECKSCHER

Director, The Twentieth Century Fund

41 East 70th Street, New York
September 1959

ACKNOWLEDGMENTS

THIS BOOK began as a doctoral dissertation which was presented to the Faculty of the Columbia University School of Law. My thanks are therefore in the first instance due to the University which enabled me to pursue advanced studies in law and to the officials who accorded me the privileges of Visiting Scholar during the year 1956–1957. I am most grateful for the inspiration and orientation toward this study which came originally from Professor Adolf A. Berle, Jr., and continued in frequent discussions until the book evolved to its present form. The reader who is familiar with Professor Berle's work will be aware of the extent of my indebtedness to him in the following pages. The responsibility for my conclusions is, of course, my own.

To Professor William L. Cary of the Columbia Law School go my thanks for performing so generously the ungrateful task of criticizing my initial efforts to set down on paper the results of my researches. I am also grateful to Mr. Jonathan Brown of the New York Stock Exchange, Mr. Jean Lindberg and Mr. Esmond Gardner of the Chase Manhattan Bank, Mr. Ralph Hemminger of the Bankers Trust Company, Mr. William Brennan and Mr. Edward Feldman of the New York State Banking Department, Mr. Benjamin Tenzer of the New York Insurance Department, and Mr. Paul O'Keefe, all of whom were very helpful in the early stages of my research. I have also received valuable assistance from pension officials of the General Motors, the Ford and the Sears, Roebuck companies and from the legal and economics departments of the United Auto Workers.

That this study now appears in print and in its present revised and expanded form is due to the support and encouragement of the trustees and staff of the Twentieth Century Fund, for which I am deeply grateful. I wish particularly to thank the Director of the Fund, Mr. August Heckscher, for his generosity and interest, and Mr. Thomas R. Carskadon for his timely encouragement.

To Mrs. Louise Field of the Fund staff I am indeed greatly indebted. Whatever virtues of intelligibility and accuracy this book may have are due in great part to her patient insistence upon clarity and attention to detail; her personal contribution to this work is second only to the author's.

Acknowledgments

I am grateful also to Mrs. Ruth Rocker and to Mrs. Elizabeth Blackert for performing so expertly all the difficult tasks required to transform a manuscript into a book. In preparing the manuscript I was fortunate in having the competent help of Miss Jane Coyle and Mrs. Frances Roesch. I am grateful to them both.

Finally I wish to thank my Superiors in the Society of Jesus for the understanding they have shown in enabling me to devote so much time to the studies that have gone into this book. In particular, I wish to thank Father Leo Brown, Director of the Institute of Social Order, of which I am a member, for his ready cooperation in so many matters connected with this publication. Father Edward Duff was also very generous with his editorial talent.

To the others who have given me their assistance and encouragement I am no less grateful though they remain nameless here.

PAUL P. HARBRECHT, S. J.

CONTENTS

APPENDICES

TABLES

Tables

Tables

CHART

PENSION FUNDS AND ECONOMIC POWER

CHAPTER 1

THE ADVENT OF
THE PENSION TRUSTS

The forces that move economic man are various and often difficult to predict, but no motive in man's history has been more constant or more obvious than his quest for security. Pension trusts are but the most recent attack human society has made upon its age-old problem. There is nothing new or startling about the fact that man, like the ant, lays up stores for the future. But the pension trusts are new and startling because they bear all the marks of the newest age of man and reflect the unique social and economic organization of mid-twentieth century America. The wealth of the pension trusts is great, their growth is nothing less than explosive and their economic powers have only begun to be exploited.

At present one quarter of the nation's working population is covered by all types of pension plans which have amassed assets of over $33 billion. During the 1940s the pension plans more than quadrupled their assets and they will have done so again by 1960. Their assets are now growing at a rate of well over $4 billion a year and it is unlikely that this rate will diminish before 1970. The pension trusts are currently buying nearly as much common stock as all individual purchasers together, and their acquisitions of corporate bonds are even greater in amount than their stock purchases. These trusts are even now in a position to affect the balance of forces in our economy by their influence on the level of savings, the capital markets, and the buying power of millions of workers. And in the immediate future their economic impact is certain to grow.

The pension trusts as the unique product of their times tell us a great deal about the social system which has produced them. There is nothing new in the concept of personal savings, nor is there anything original in the concept of a government pension. But the pension trusts are new, wholly new, because they are neither personal savings nor are they state-controlled funds. They are vast aggregations of wealth upon which many have claims but of which no one can call himself an owner. This is, to say the least, an unusual situation, but the formation of the pension trusts is the latest step in the organization and control of productive property which has aptly been called the twentieth century capitalist revolution.

Pension Trusts and Social Property

Today the notion that ownership has been divorced from control of productive property has become commonplace. Though it is not so clearly known, the evidence is now before us that, with the advent of the pension trusts, the mutual funds and the large accumulations of corporate stock in the hands of bank-trustees, ownership itself as an operating reality is diminishing. Indeed, such an evolution, once control of property was divorced from ownership, was all but inevitable. In the process of the evolution of property relationships the concept of ownership has been gradually stripped of the rights and prerogatives that once made ownership desirable. We have reached a stage in the evolution of property — and here we are speaking only of productive property — where the individual is an owner because he possesses a piece of paper which says he is. The sole advantage left to the possessor of the paper, however, is the right, under certain circumstances, to receive income.

But another type of owner has emerged in the evolutionary process of property organization. This is the financial institution. Through the acquisition of stock in corporations for income purposes the financial organizations have begun to gather to themselves the atomized rights of control that have always been attached to shares of stock. This the institutions have not sought, but a real power of control over property has coalesced in the large financial institutions as their holdings of corporate stocks have gradually mounted. Even so, the concept of ownership is meaningless since the "ownership" resides in the legal fiction, the financial corporation. A bare title held by a legal fiction is an inert concept. In the financial institution the concept of ownership has reached a dead end and no longer has any functional meaning, whereas the control over property which resides in the managers of these institutions is a dynamic and powerful force.

Property and Power

From an economic point of view, then, we may say that our society has passed from a property system to a power system. In the economic sphere rights are now attached to men and not to things. This has always been true in the political sphere. The novel element that private property introduces into systems of social organization is that it sets up a sphere in which power is derived from a source independent of political power. Within the confines of our economic life the property system brought about a dispersion of power over men by attaching rights to material things which are themselves divisible. Thus, with a wide distribution of material wealth, there were widely divided rights and powers. But now that control over wealth has become concentrated in large blocs, power over men has again become centralized. What remains from the era when the property system was the dominant institution in our society is the separation of political and economic powers.

Indeed, the rise of the property system may be interpreted as a struggle for the division of power over men. The material goods of this world are a natural source of social influence and power since control of them enables one man to dictate to another. But power over their *use* is the necessary means of producing the fruits that material resources can provide. As modern society began to demand things which could be provided only through large aggregations of wealth it became necessary to constitute centers of power to organize and exploit these resources to serve the needs of society. Thus in the mid-twentieth century we find our society highly organized on two broad lines of influence, one economic and the other political. The last possible amalgamation of power in our society would occur if the political power became united to the economic power.

The pension trusts are becoming one of the primary centers of power in the newly emerging social system. The concentration of power they represent is not the result of a drive for power itself but of social forces that have been at work for other purposes. The pension trusts are the product of the molding influences of our major institutions: the corporation, the government and the labor unions. Only in their relationship to these other institutions will we be able to understand the role they will play in our society. A brief view of the origins of the pension funds and the reasons for their growth will point up some of these relationships.

Why the Pension Funds Grew

The early attitude of employers toward pension plans was that pensions were gifts to their workers in recognition of "long and faithful service" and that no legal rights were thereby given to employees who became beneficiaries of a plan. Plans at this period were extremely informal, often consisting of mere statements that the employer expected to pay certain benefits to those who fulfilled certain service requirements. In general the employer did not set up a special fund to provide pension benefits and the text of the plan was carefully worded to relieve him of all liability.

The earliest lawsuit concerning pension rights, *Pennie* v. *Reis*, reached the Supreme Court of the United States in 1889. In this case the court denied a police officer's plea that his pension was being unfairly withheld. Contributions to a pension fund had been taken from the officer's salary at the rate of two dollars a month. But although the contributions had been called part of his compensation, the Court ruled that the money was not his since he had never received or controlled it nor could he prevent its being contributed to the fund. The Court's reason for denying the officer's right to his contribution was simple: "He had no such power of disposition over it as always accompanies ownership of property."[1]

Significant growth in the pension movement in the United States began about 1915 and by 1925 an estimated 4 million employees were covered by approximately 400 plans. These figures do not indicate very wide coverage of private pension plans, however, since over half of the workers covered were employed by thirteen corporations each of which had at least 50,000 employees, and more than 40 per cent worked for railroad corporations. Further analysis shows that a third of the covered employees were in four corporations, the U. S. Steel Corporation, the American Telephone and Telegraph Company, the Pennsylvania Railroad System and the New York Central Lines.[2]

Pension plans grew slowly until after the depression, but by 1940 in a wartime economy pension plans began to show a remarkable proliferation in kind, number, size and employee coverage. By 1949 an estimated 6.2 million employees were covered by private pension plans.

This advance in employee coverage under private pension plans is even more impressive when we recall that most railroad employees were no longer covered by privately established plans whereas in 1925 they made up a large proportion of the membership of such plans.

By this time many of the pension funds were being put upon a sound actuarial basis with trust funds to support pension obligations. In most

---

[1] 132 U. S. 464, 470 (1889). Other cases of this period were decided in similar fashion.

[2] Rainard B. Robbins, *Pensions in Industry*, 1952, p. 98 (Mimeographed. Distributed by Teachers Insurance and Annuity Association of America).

of the earlier plans pension funds were simply set up as "balance sheet reserves" on the books of companies and no attempt was made to make use of the experience gained in England and on the Continent. In the cases where trusts had been created for employees much of the reserves were invested in the company's own securities and in practically all cases the trustees were given wide latitude in deciding on investment policies. As a result many unwise investments were made and the accumulation of book assets did not guarantee that these plans were secure. Among 307 companies studied in 1928 little more than a third had accumulated any reserves for pension benefits. Of these, only 41 had trust funds, while 67 were of the book-reserve type.[3]

By the end of 1958 approximately 16.5 million employees were covered by all types of private pension plans with about two-thirds included under agreements reached through collective bargaining. The most rapid period of growth occurred during the period 1951–1954. An SEC survey indicates that the number of corporations with self-administered plans rose by about one-third and that assets increased by 75 per cent during those years.[4]

Formative Influences

An analysis of this rapid growth reveals the influences at work in shaping the private pension plans. In a report on welfare and pension plans the subcommittee of the Senate Committee on Labor and Public Welfare gives the following reasons for the recent growth of pension programs:[5]

1. During and since World War II, high corporation taxes coupled with tax reductions for contributions to pension funds permitted the establishment of these programs at low net costs.

2. Wage stabilization programs during and since World War II and the Korean conflict froze wage rates but permitted increased employee compensation in the form of these "fringe" benefits.

3. Court decisions in the years 1948–1950 made welfare and pension matters a bargainable issue.

4. Since 1948 the labor unions have put on a drive to obtain welfare

---

[3] Martin S. House, *Private Employee Benefit Plans: A Public Trust*, State of New York Insurance Department, 1956, p. 48.

[4] SEC Statistical Series, Release No. 1335, October 12, 1955. Another study, by the U. S. Bureau of Internal Revenue, indicates a 200 per cent growth in the six-year period 1946–1952. *Private Employee Benefit Plans*, p. 51. This latter estimate is on a basis of contributions.

[5] Senate Report No. 1734, 84th Cong., 2d sess., 1956, p. 12.

and pension programs. Labor spokesmen state that another reason for the development of these programs has been the inadequacy of benefits under the government programs.

A survey of corporate pension funds published by the Securities and Exchange Commission in October 1956 finds essentially the same reasons for their growth. But the SEC study goes on to say: "The chief impetus to pension fund growth, however, was the establishment of Old Age and Survivors Insurance in the middle thirties; at about that time railroad pensioners also came under the Railroad Retirement System of the Government."[6] It has often been remarked that the government's program to provide social security benefits made Americans "security conscious." The insurance industry vigorously opposed the social security program in the beginning, but its representatives soon began to realize that the program operated very much to their advantage by selling people the idea of the need for security.

With the country's social security program providing the psychological setting for the growth of private pension funds, the federal tax policy added a strong inducement to set up these plans. A brief history of the federal tax treatment of pension funds will indicate the formative influence of government policies upon the development of the pension movement.

Federal Tax Policy

From 1913 when the income tax was inaugurated until 1921, employers could treat pension liabilities accruing in the current year as ordinary business expenses. Amounts contributed to pension funds could be deducted from gross income. The income from pension trusts, however, was subject to the same taxation as any other trust. At the same time retired employees were subject to tax on the pension payments they received. Employees were also taxed during their years of active service on the amount of their employer's contribution to a pension trust for their benefit. Furthermore, there was no exemption of an employer's payments to fund liabilities for past service benefits.

The situation, then, was that the employee was being taxed on contributions made by the employer for pension benefits which might never be received. The plan itself might be terminated at any time or the worker might leave his job and thereby forfeit all rights to a pension. In

[6] SEC, *Survey of Corporate Pension Funds, 1951–1954,* 1956, p. 1.

these circumstances, employers were discouraged from funding pension plans to meet future liabilities and were also deterred from funding past service liabilities.

The first exemption favoring pension trusts was incorporated in the Revenue Act of 1921. This act exempted the income of pension and profit-sharing trusts from income tax and relieved employees from the tax on current contributions made to a trust for their benefit by the employer. There was still no relief given for funding of past service liabilities. The provision enabling an employer to deduct a reasonable contribution for past service liabilities over a ten-year period was not made until 1928. At that time employer's contributions to a pension fund were allowed as a deduction from gross income because they constituted a business expense, even though a company could at any time amend or revoke a plan and divert pension funds to its own uses. The Revenue Act of 1938, however, provided for an exemption only if the wording of the plan made it impossible to divert pension funds from uses other than the exclusive benefit of the employees.

Advances previously made were preserved in the 1942 Revenue Act in which the pension tax provisions were completely rewritten. The new statute contained much more specific provisions for regulating employee benefits and methods of deduction.

These successive liberalizations of the tax law clearly provided a great incentive to establish pension plans. With corporate excess profit taxes as high as 82 per cent during and after the war many employers concluded that they could provide pension plans at a cost to their companies of about eighteen cents on the dollar. We shall consider the merits of this conclusion in Chapter 5, which discusses at length the molding influence of the tax laws on pensions.

Further Reasons for Rapid Growth

Recent economic developments have also given impetus to the pension movement. During the 1950s, the period in which the private pension funds have been growing most rapidly, their assets have been invested to an increasing extent in a rising capital market. As a result, the earnings performance of the funds has been rewarding and has justified the employers' hopes in establishing and maintaining pension trusts. The growing desire of employers to put the plans for retirement of their workers on a steady and predictable basis has also played a part.

Finally, as the economy has moved upward toward a situation in which skilled labor is at a premium and efficiency is in greater demand, employers feel that they must provide inducements to keep their trained employees on the job. The pension plan with its promise of rewards for long service is an excellent device to insure the continued services of valued employees. These factors will doubtless become an even more important guarantee of the growth of the private pension system in the foreseeable future.

Role and Potentials of the Pension Trusts

As we have already remarked, the pension trusts are one of the primary centers of power in the newly emerging social system. From our cursory review of their origins and the reasons for their growth, it is obvious that they are institutions that ramify deeply into the nation's economic structure. But we can know little about their social import until we know the sources of their power, who controls it and how control is exercised.

In the following chapters we shall examine the role they play in a transition that is now going forward whereby the power to control property is passing from the hands of individuals, where it is ineffective, into large financial institutions where it can become effective. The organization of the pension trusts themselves will be examined to determine where the authority over them resides and what rights are granted to their beneficiaries. Further, an examination of the theories that guided their formation, their actual operation and the objectives they seek to accomplish will help to explain why the pension trusts are structured as they are.

After dealing with these questions we shall turn to the external forces affecting the organization and operations of the pension trusts. The foremost of these is the government, which has had a great formative influence on the pension trusts mainly through its tax policy. Various specialized state and federal agencies have also had some impact on the rise of these new institutions, but until recently they have exercised only a limited amount of supervision.

One of the anomalies of the pension trusts is the difficulty of identifying any proprietary interest in them. An examination of the legal rights of the beneficiaries will show that the courts have been so slow to recognize that the beneficiaries have any rights in the pension funds that the state itself has had to step in and constitute itself the custodian of pensioners' rights. Thus, where proprietary rights could exist in individuals their powers are being assumed by the public authority and an opportunity for economic influence is lost to the private person.

At this point in our study the complex relationships that go to make up a pension trust will have been defined and we shall attack the problem of the extent of their economic power. For power, if it is real, is always exercised by someone and in certain quantities. After attempting to weigh the economic power of pension trusts we shall explore the possibilities of their future growth and influence, offer recommendations for their improvement and finally try to give some intimation of their role as forerunners of a new type of social organization.

In general this book reports the facts about the nature of the pension trusts and the control of property. We should point out here, however, that some of the observations in this introductory chapter and the final chapter are of a rather speculative nature. Such speculation is the result of reflection on the fact that only in a society as highly organized as the twentieth century capitalist society could such institutions as the pension trusts become possible. They are vast aggregations of wealth, neither public nor private (except in the sense that they are not owned or controlled by the state). They are "owned" by no one in any meaningful sense of the term. Such a phenomenon in a capitalist society, which has traditionally considered the distinction between public and private ownership to be adequate and complete, challenges us to find a rational framework to accommodate it. The old conceptual framework has no room for the pension trusts. The old bottles are now bursting with new wine.

PROPERTY IN

TRANSITION

Ownership and Control of Corporations

The Transition of Control

Since our study is mainly concerned with the impact of the pension trusts on the institution of private property we shall begin with an analysis of the dominant system of property tenure in the United States today. In our society status and power in the economic and, to a large extent, the social sphere of life derive from the control of productive property. It is true that what we might call "possessory property" is a flourishing institution in our midst. But this type of property, i.e., a man's house, his automobile, his television set, is a very limited source of influence and power in a society primarily geared to the economic process of production.

The dominant form of property tenure in the United States today is corporate ownership. In 1955 the book value of the assets of business corporations was $888.6 billion, or 70 per cent of the estimated total national wealth.[1] In 1956 the payroll of nonfarm and nonfinancial corporations was $135.5 billion, about 60 per cent of the nation's payroll and over 72 per cent of the nation's nongovernmental payroll.[2]

The corporate system of ownership is itself a method of concentrating property ownership to carry on enterprises beyond the scope of the in-

[1] *Statistical Abstract of the United States, 1958,* pp. 323, 491.
[2] *Ibid.,* p. 310.

dividual proprietors. But in the present stage of the evolution of property organization there is within the ranks of the corporations themselves a high degree of concentration of ownership. Seventy per cent of all productive property in the United States is owned by corporations large enough to be called concentrates, and 45 per cent of all productive property is owned by 135 corporations.[3] These corporate giants, generally speaking, control the productive property of the greatest strategic importance, the oil, steel, aluminum, chemical, electronic, transportation, motor and other industries.[4]

OWNERSHIP AND CONTROL
OF CORPORATIONS

Since productive property is so extensively owned by the corporations, it is important to know who controls the corporations themselves. Here we find that while, formally or legally, control is designed to be in the hands of the stockholders, it has in fact been turned over to a class of managers who in theory represent the stockholders. But actually, and to an extent autonomously, these managers exercise the owners' powers of direction and control. Management has acquired this power because shareholdings are so widely dispersed that the stockholders do not have a significant voice in the direction of their companies. An analysis of stock ownership will show why corporations are beyond the control of their owners.

[3] M. A. Adelman, "The Measurement of Industrial Concentration," *Review of Economics and Statistics,* November 1951, p. 289. Reference to this is made in *The 20th Century Capitalist Revolution* by A. A. Berle, Jr., Harcourt, Brace, New York, 1954, p. 26. In January 1952 corporations constituted 13 per cent of all business firms but accounted for more than 70 per cent of all business. In manufacturing one-third of all firms were corporations which accounted for over 90 per cent of all manufactures. Erwin W. Boehmler, *Financial Institutions,* Irwin, Homewood, Illinois, 1956, p. 216 (based on data of the U. S. Department of Commerce, Office of Business Economics).

[4] *Concentration in American Industry,* Report of the Subcommittee on Antitrust and Monopoly to the Senate Judiciary Committee, 85th Cong., 1st sess., 1957. See also Adelman, *op. cit.,* note 2; Berle, *op. cit.;* Berle and Means, *The Modern Corporation and Private Property,* Macmillan, New York, 1932, *passim;* A. D. H. Kaplan, *Big Enterprise in a Competitive System,* The Brookings Institution, Washington, 1954; George W. Stocking and Myron W. Watkins, *Monopoly and Free Enterprise,* Twentieth Century Fund, 1951; "Business Population by Legal Form of Organization," *Survey of Current Business,* April 1955; "Recent Business Population Movements," *ibid.,* January 1954; and "Size Characteristics of the Business Population," *ibid.,* May 1954.

Table 1

DISTRIBUTION OF ASSETS OF 2,991 CORPORATIONS
AS OF THE CALENDAR YEAR 1950
OR THE FISCAL YEAR ENDED IN 1951

Size of Corporation (*Assets in Millions*)	Number of Cor- porations	Per Cent of Total Number	Amount of Assets[a] (*Millions*)	Per Cent of Total Assets
Total	2,991	100.0	$292,508	100.0
Under $1	163	5.4	71	[b]
$1–$5	507	17.0	1,503	.5
$5–$10	471	15.8	3,490	1.2
$10–$20	473	15.8	6,906	2.4
$20–$50	537	18.0	18,118	6.2
$50–$100	291	9.7	21,606	7.4
$100–$200	252	8.4	36,643	12.5
$200–$500	189	6.3	60,209	20.6
$500 and over	108	3.6	143,961	49.2

Source: Lewis H. Kimmel, *Share Ownership in the United States,* The Brookings Institution, Washington, 1952, p. 9.

[a] For a small number of companies the assets figures used were estimates.
[b] Less than one-tenth of one per cent.

OWNERSHIP BY INDIVIDUALS

In 1952 the Brookings Institution published an analysis of corporate ownership in the United States.[5] The study was sponsored by the New York Stock Exchange to determine how widespread the ownership of American corporations might be. There was great interest at this time in testing the notion that American enterprise was truly owned by the American people. There were then about 156 million people and about 50 million families in the United States.[6] The results of the study showed a large number of small investors but not enough to establish a claim that the stock market is the agent of a "people's capitalism." In the population as a whole, an estimated 6.5 million individuals representing 4.75 million family spending units owned shares of public stock at the end of 1951.[7]

The nearly 3,000 corporations studied included most of the largest corporations as well as many smaller ones. As Table 1 shows, less than 4 per

[5] Lewis H. Kimmel, *Share Ownership in the United States,* The Brookings Institution, Washington, 1952.
[6] *Ibid.,* pp. iii, 87.
[7] *Ibid.,* p. 126.

cent of the companies — those of the largest size — owned 49 per cent of all the assets represented in the survey and 10 per cent owned as much as 70 per cent.

This evidence of concentration becomes particularly important when we relate the assets to shareholdings, as we have done in Table 2. Such a comparison shows that dispersion of share ownership is markedly greater in the companies controlling 70 per cent of all assets than it is among the smaller companies. Our arguments showing the dispersion of shares among individual owners are thus most valid for the largest and most important companies in our economy.[8]

Table 2, showing the number of shares outstanding and the number of shares per holding, bears out this conclusion. As the size of corporations increases, the number of shares outstanding is greater but the number of shares per holding is smaller. Thus, while the smallest-sized corporations had a total of 113 million shares outstanding as of 1952, the largest had a total of 964 million, but the average number of shares per holding in the smallest corporations was nearly nine times the number in the largest corporations.

These statistics were based on a survey of 3.7 billion shares of stock, or 76 per cent of the estimated total of all publicly owned stocks. The high degree of dispersion may be gathered from the following statement from the same report: "Approximately two-thirds of all shareholdings in these stocks consists of less than 100 shares. For individual owners the median or middle shareholding is well below 100 shares."[9]

This finding is closely tied in with the fact that individuals as a group own the bulk of the stock in publicly owned corporations. The Brookings study estimated that individuals owned 70.8 per cent of all publicly

---

[8] We are justified in extending our conclusions based on this study to the whole economy since the companies included are estimated to have issued 76 per cent of all publicly owned stocks. *Ibid.*, p. 8.

The 1,200 U. S. companies with stocks and/or bonds listed on the New York Stock Exchange earn about half of all the net profits after taxes reported by all United States corporations. They also account for about half of all goods produced in the United States.

Corporations listed on the Exchange provide jobs for more than 11 million workers. Of the national total, these companies:

Produce about 99% of all passenger cars;
Perform 93% of our domestic airline transportation;
Produce 93% of all steel ingot tonnage;
Provide 87% of all telephone service;
Generate 85% of the electric power produced by private companies.

(1956 *Fact Book*, New York Stock Exchange, p. 9.)

[9] *Ibid.*, p. 126.

Table 2

DISTRIBUTION OF SHARE OWNERSHIP
IN 2,991 CORPORATIONS, END OF 1951

(*Shareholdings of Record [Common and Preferred Stocks] in*
Reporting Corporations Classified by Size of Total Assets)

Size of Corporation (*Assets in Millions*)	Num- ber of Issues	Shares Out- standing (*Thou- sands*)	SHAREHOLDINGS OF RECORD			
			Num- ber (*Thou- sands*)	Average Number of Shares	Market Value, Dec. 1951 (*Millions*)	Average Value per Share- holding
Total	3,954	3,695,279	20,321	181.8	$132,087	$6,500
Under $1	173	112,984	92	1,231.0	119	1,300
$1–$5	611	162,987	501	325.2	1,589	3,166
$5–$10	583	213,528	820	260.6	2,724	3,324
$10–$20	607	243,613	1,071	227.4	5,073	4,736
$20–$50	737	457,092	2,170	210.7	10,723	4,942
$50–$100	435	450,785	2,209	204.0	12,694	5,746
$100–$200	372	463,287	3,030	152.9	14,569	4,808
$200–$500	281	626,516	3,575	175.3	28,282	7,912
$500 and over	155	964,487	6,854	140.7	56,318	8,217

Source: Lewis H. Kimmel, *Share Ownership in the United States,* The Brookings Institution, Washington, 1952, p. 27.

Note: Some explanation of terms is necessary with regard to the Brookings study. Its author offers this explanation: "Each holding by an individual or other owner counts as one shareholding; a person who owns shares in five stock issues has five shareholdings" (p. 124). Thus, in reading this table, one cannot conclude that the "average number of shares" applies to the total number of shares owned by a single stockholder since a stockholder may own shares in more than one issue. However, the force of the argument for dispersion is not vitiated since the number of issues decreases in inverse proportion to the size of the corporations, there being only 107 common stock issues in the largest size group. Kimmel also tells us that 62 per cent of all individual shareowners own two issues or less (p. 110).

Furthermore, in the Brookings study the reader is cautioned not to take the number of shares per holding as applying only to individuals. The large average holdings of nominees, brokers, dealers and institutions weight the average heavily. The average number of shares of stock (preferred and common combined) held by men was 139; by women, 98; and in joint accounts, 91 (p. 18). These figures are worth noting here as they are not available in later studies discussed below.

owned stock issues in the United States, including stocks held for them, while fiduciaries held slightly more than 11 per cent and institutions and foundations, 2.5 per cent. Miscellaneous shareowners (insurance companies, investment companies and business corporations) held the remaining 15 per cent.[10]

The average number of shares per holding of the fiduciaries was estimated at 159, of institutions at 471, of miscellaneous owners at 1,339.[11] In comparison with the much smaller average holdings of individuals these figures indicate that the fiduciaries, institutions, foundations and miscellaneous holders showed a smaller degree of dispersion in their holdings. Furthermore, the miscellaneous group, which probably included the pension trusts, accounted for only about 2 per cent of the total shareholdings but held 15 per cent of the total shares.[12] These percentages indicate, in another way, that this group tends to concentrate its purchases of stock within a rather narrow range of companies, a conclusion that is verified by a Senate Committee Staff Report analyzed in Chapter 4.

We have now established the characteristics of stock ownership: individual investors, as a class, have created a wide *dispersion of ownership and control;* larger, institutional types of owners tend toward *concentration of ownership and control.*

Increase in Individual Shareholders

In a recent census of shareholders, the New York Stock Exchange found a similar picture of stock ownership. Comparison with the earlier Brookings study revealed a similar dispersion of ownership. The Stock Exchange estimated that more than 8.6 million people owned shares in publicly held corporations by the end of 1955 as compared with the estimate of 6.5 million individual shareholders reported by Brookings as of early 1952. In these few years, then, the number of individual owners of American corporations had grown by one-third.[13]

The Stock Exchange census also revealed that individuals in the

10 *Ibid.*, p. 124. Publicly owned stocks are issues traded on the organized stock exchanges and over the counter.

11 *Ibid.*

12 *Ibid.*

13 *Who Owns American Business?*, 1956 Census of Shareowners, New York Stock Exchange, 1956, pp. 5, 6, 8. Eighty per cent of the share-owning population owned stocks listed on the New York Stock Exchange. In addition to the 8.6 million owners of public corporations, approximately 1.4 million individuals owned shares *only* in privately held corporations, bringing total ownership to over 10 million people.

United States owned 56.9 per cent of the nearly 8 billion shares representing ownership of publicly held businesses.[14] At first glance this percentage seems to present a markedly different picture from the Brookings estimate of 70.8 per cent for individual ownership in 1952. But the Brookings' totals include "adjusted holdings"; that is, the authors of the study attempted to "take into account the beneficial holdings of shares registered in the names of nominees and brokers and dealers."[15] On the basis of "shareholders of record" the percentage of ownership by individuals in 1952 would be 57 per cent,[16] which is closely in line with the Stock Exchange estimate for 1955. The wider coverage of the later study and, perhaps, slightly different methods of analysis make the two studies difficult to compare, but insofar as they are comparable they indicate that the percentage of ownership by individuals was about the same.

But while they owned about the same proportion of all shares, the number of individual owners increased by about 33 per cent between 1952 and 1956. This probably does not represent much change in the dispersion of corporate ownership and control even though the number of shares outstanding increased 55 per cent, from 4.9 billion to 7.6 billion, in the same period,[17] since the corporations themselves probably expanded only a little more than their ownership. The assets of U. S. corporations increased by 37 per cent in the period 1951 to 1955 (the latest year for which statistics are available).[18] But these general figures tell us very little about the more important factor of the concentration of share ownership and the use of share voting powers among individuals. In the absence of direct information on these points we shall examine the economic status and market activities of individual shareholders to determine how much control they exercise over corporations.

Economic Status of Individual Shareowners

The economic status of most of the individual stockholders indicates that they are financially unable to acquire sufficient stock to exercise effective control of their corporations. The Stock Exchange study showed that about two-thirds of all shareowners were in households having incomes of less than $7,500 in 1956.[19] Over half the adult shareowners were

[14] *Ibid.*, p. 26.
[15] Kimmel, *op. cit.*, p. 63.
[16] *Who Owns American Business?*, p. 27.
[17] Kimmel, *op. cit.*, p. 124; *Who Owns American Business?*, p. 26.
[18] *Statistical Abstract of the United States, 1956,* p. 491; *1958,* p. 491.
[19] *Who Owns American Business?*, p. 14.

in households having incomes ranging between $3,000 and $7,500 a year.

The median income of shareowners is also decreasing. In 1956 it was $6,200, as compared to $7,100 in 1952.[20] But the information of greatest significance, that is, the value of the individual shareholdings, is not available. It would be useful to know what percentage of the total number of shares outstanding is in the hands of the low-income groups. Probably a large majority of the shares are actually owned by the higher income groups. If so, since there are fewer individuals in these income brackets, greater control may be in the hands of certain individuals than the median statistics would indicate.

A suggestion that this is true may be gathered from the estimate in the Brookings study that 27.6 per cent of the individual shareowners are in the more highly paid occupational groups, such as administrative executives, operating supervisory officials, professional persons and sales personnel.[21] It is also significant that the percentage of shareowners earning $5,000 and over declined from 68 per cent of the total number in 1952 to 62 per cent in 1956.[22]

Stock Market Activity of Individuals

We shall turn now to an analysis of the activity of individuals in the market to find out whether their motivation in purchasing stocks is for speculative or for investment purposes. The length of time shares are held is indicative of how much corporate control individuals are likely to exercise. Those who intend to hold a stock for a short period of time are almost certainly not interested in participating in the policy decisions of a corporation. Study of the volume of transactions according to income groups will also serve as a rough indicator of the extent of corporate control possible to individuals. The small investor, at least, is not likely to own enough shares in any one corporation to have any element of control over its policies.

In a study of market transactions for two days in October 1957 the New York Stock Exchange reported that almost 54.3 per cent of the volume of all shares traded was for individuals. This was a rather low percentage compared with previous years when transactions for individuals averaged in the neighborhood of 59 per cent of the volume of trading and rose as high as 63.3 per cent in 1954. In 1957, however, institutions, com-

20 *Ibid.*
21 Kimmel, *op. cit.*, p. 98.
22 *Who Owns American Business?*, p. 15.

Table 3

INVESTMENT MOTIVATION OF INDIVIDUALS' TRANSACTIONS
ON THE NEW YORK STOCK EXCHANGE DURING TWO-DAY
PERIODS IN EACH OF THE YEARS 1952–1957

(*Per Cent*)

For Two Days in:	Total Trans- actions	Trading Trans- actions ("30–day")	Short-Term Investment (1 to 6 mos.)	Long-Term Investment (Over 6 mos.)
Sept. 1952	100	7.5	19.0	73.5
Mar. 1953	100	11.6	23.1	65.3
Mar. 1954	100	11.5	21.1	67.4
Dec. 1954	100	16.6	27.8	55.6
June 1955	100	14.5	28.5	57.0
Mar. 1956	100	13.0	26.6	60.4
Oct. 1957	100	13.6	19.7	66.7

Source: A Picture of the Stock Market, Seventh Public Transaction Study, October 9 and 16, 1957, New York Stock Exchange, 1958, p. 5.

mercial banks and trust companies accounted for about 20 per cent of the transactions, while stock brokers and dealers accounted for about 26 per cent.[23] The volume for institutions and intermediaries in 1957 was higher than usual but not very much out of line with previous years.

Investment Motivation

In their study of the motivation behind individual transactions, the stock exchange analysts found that nearly 14 per cent of the transactions were for trading, that is, shares were purchased and sold that were to be kept or had been kept for less than 30 days. Another 20 per cent of all the individual trading was for short-term investment (shares held from one to six months). Thus as much as one-third of all purchases and sales for individuals were for purposes that could be accomplished by holding the stock less than six months. The remaining two-thirds of the transactions by individuals fell under the category of long-term investment (shares held longer than six months). (See Table 3.)

These proportions may be taken as a rough indication that only about two out of three individual stock purchasers could be interested in influ-

[23] *A Picture of the Stock Market,* Seventh Public Transaction Study, New York Stock Exchange, 1958, p. 2.

encing the policy of their corporations. Of course it does not follow that the individuals making long-term investments would actively participate in the affairs of the corporations in which they hold shares. These figures simply indicate that not more than two-thirds of the individual share-owners are at all likely to take an interest in the direction and management of their corporations.

Income Groups

The Stock Exchange transaction study also reported on the income of individuals for whom purchases and sales were transacted during two days in each of the years from 1952 to 1957. Table 4 indicates that the most active individuals in the market came from the class of shareowners with annual incomes of $10,000 to $25,000. These individuals, together with those in the $25,000 and over income brackets, have consistently accounted for more than two-thirds of all the market activity of individuals. When we speak of these percentages of market activity we are talking about the proportions of all shares bought and sold. If, then, more than two-thirds of the shares traded belong to individuals whose income exceeded $10,000, we might conclude that about this same proportion of all the shares of individuals were owned by this group. Certainly the two-thirds proportion is one of long standing and there must be some ex-

Table 4

PERCENTAGE DISTRIBUTION OF INDIVIDUALS' TRANSACTIONS,
BY SIZE OF INCOME, DURING TWO-DAY PERIODS
IN EACH OF THE YEARS 1952–1957

For Two Days in:	Total Transactions	ESTIMATED ANNUAL INCOME			
		Under $5,000	$5,000– $10,000	$10,000– $25,000	$25,000 and Over
Sept. 1952	100	8.9	26.1	31.1	33.9
Mar. 1953	100	8.4	26.1	34.1	31.4
Mar. 1954	100	8.0	26.6	34.0	31.4
Dec. 1954	100	7.0	26.5	33.8	32.7
June 1955	100	5.9	25.5	36.0	32.6
Mar. 1956	100	5.1	25.7	36.2	33.0
Oct. 1957	100	4.3	25.4	38.4	31.9

Source: A Picture of the Stock Market, Seventh Public Transaction Study, October 9 and 16, 1957, New York Stock Exchange, 1958, p. 6.

planation for such consistent performance. In support of this conclusion we may also point out that the individuals' share in the total volume of trading, about 59 per cent, closely corresponds to their proportion of stock ownership, 57 per cent.

While this conclusion is only an inference, there are no apparent facts to refute it, since the Stock Exchange does not report what proportions of all stocks outstanding are owned by the different income groups. But if we combine our inference based on the volume of market activity with the information from the 1956 Census of Shareowners that 35.9 per cent of all shareowners earn more than $7,500,[24] we may conclude that something like one-third of all individual shareowners own two-thirds of the outstanding stocks. This argues for more concentration in share ownership than we might otherwise suspect.

The argument for wide dispersion of ownership and consequent dissipation of control power among individuals might seem to be weakened by this conclusion. Still, there are almost 3 million shareowners earning more than $7,500 and, as we shall see, not all of them have a continuing interest in their corporations.

Individual Stockholders Have Little Control of Corporations

To sum up the position of corporate ownership by individuals, a combination of three factors leads us to conclude that for the 57 per cent of the shares in American corporations held by individuals control is effectively separated from ownership.

1. A significant proportion of individuals purchase shares with no intention of taking a permanent interest in the management of their corporations.

2. The economic status of shareowners is such that the majority of them do not and cannot expect to gain sufficient proportions of corporate ownership to exercise a voice in management.

3. The average number of shares per holding of individuals is so small that control is too widely dispersed for effective mobilization.

INSTITUTIONAL OWNERSHIP AND THE CONTROL OF PRODUCTIVE PROPERTY

Our analysis of property ownership has thus far been devoted to an aspect of the corporate system that has long been the subject of comment —

[24] *Who Owns American Business?*, p. 15.

the separation of ownership from control.[25] We have only added new data on dispersion of ownership. This dispersion places corporate control sometimes in a strategically placed stockholder minority or, more often, in a well-entrenched management group. But a new tendency toward concentration of control in financial institutions has appeared. What is meant by institutions here is well defined by Raymond W. Goldsmith as follows:

... institutions that receive funds from other economic units as creditors, stockholders, or trustees and use these funds to make loans to, or to buy securities of, other economic units which they do not control, rather than to acquire tangible assets for operation as most nonfinancial enterprises do.[26]

In these institutions, which have been entrusted with the capital of millions of small savers and investors, control of productive property tends to coalesce. Ownership and control are again converging, but with the tremendous difference that these two components of property are now vested in trustees. Effective control of productive wealth is now at one more remove from the individual contributor who has become only a beneficiary without even a vestigial right of control. The individual may give his money to these institutions or not, but if he does, he has no claim to any voice in their management. In the case of most pension trusts he may not even refuse to participate.

Size of Institutions

A glance at the growth and present size of institutional holdings is enough to convince one that there is a new element of considerable magnitude in the picture of property control in the United States. In a study of financial intermediaries from 1900 to 1952, Raymond Goldsmith found that financial intermediaries have grown at a faster rate than other segments of our economy. Their share of intangible assets rose from one-fourth in 1900 to approximately 40 per cent in 1952, while their holdings of long-term claims increased from three-tenths to about six-tenths. Similarly, the proportion of individuals' total assets entrusted to them grew

[25] This situation was canvassed by A. A. Berle, Jr., in 1928 in *Studies in the Law of Corporation Finance,* Callaghan, Chicago, 1928, and again in 1932 in *The Modern Corporation and Private Property,* and by other authors, e.g., Harold G. Reuschlein, *The Schools of Corporate Reform,* University of Pittsburgh, 1950, and F. D. Emerson and F. C. Latcham, *Shareholder Democracy,* Western Reserve University Press, Cleveland, 1954. These books have excellent bibliographies on this subject.

[26] R. W. Goldsmith, *The Share of Financial Intermediaries in National Wealth, 1900–1949,* National Bureau of Economic Research, New York, 1954, p. 19.

from one-tenth in 1900 to one-fourth in recent years. During the 1930s and 1940s about one-half of net personal savings (excluding consumer durables) flowed through the financial intermediaries; in the 1940s and early 1950s about two-thirds of all personal savings flowed through them.[27]

Role of Pension Trusts

If the trend toward institutionalization of ownership is impressive, the pension aspect of institutions is even more so. Raymond Goldsmith tells us that, while the aggregate assets of all financial intermediaries increased 3.3 times from 1929 to 1952, private noninsured pension funds grew 18 times larger.[28] Self-administered pension plans are probably also the largest current purchasers of common stocks.[29] Furthermore, 1954 purchases of securities by these pension funds accounted for almost 29 per cent of the new capital raised through corporate securities[30] and for 27 per cent of the new money obtained by the sale of common stock.[31] For the five years 1951–1955 the pension funds accounted for new purchases amounting to 24 per cent of the net issues of corporate business exclusive of the investment companies.[32]

Institutional Ownership of Corporate Securities

In order to define the position of financial institutions as owners and controllers of productive wealth in corporations we turn now to the total picture of the ownership of corporate securities. Table 5 shows that in 1957 institutions owned 26 per cent by value of all corporate securities outstanding while individuals owned 72 per cent. The table indicates also that individuals and institutions differ in their investment preferences. While individuals invest more heavily in stocks, owning in this form two-

[27] These figures are taken from Simon Kuznets' Foreword to Raymond W. Goldsmith, *Financial Intermediaries in the American Economy since 1900,* Princeton University Press, Princeton, 1958, p. x.

[28] *Suggestions for Research in the Economics of Pensions,* National Bureau of Economic Research, New York, 1957, p. 33.

[29] *Institutional Investors and the Stock Market, 1953–1955,* Staff Report to the Senate Committee on Banking and Currency, 84th Cong., 2d sess., 1956, p. 53, Table 2.

[30] *New York Times,* May 6, 1957. See Chapter 7 for a more thorough and up-to-date treatment of this question.

[31] *Institutional Investors and the Stock Market, 1953–1955,* p. 53, Table 2.

[32] *Ibid.* Including issues of investment companies, the percentage is about 19, but it is logical to exclude them since it is unlikely that a banker-trustee would buy any of these shares. Furthermore, this type of stock does not represent direct sharing of corporate control.

Table 5

OWNERSHIP OF ALL U. S. CORPORATE SECURITIES,
END OF 1954 AND 1957

	1954		1957	
Ownership	Market Value (*Billions*)	Per Cent	Market Value (*Billions*)	Per Cent
Total value	$353.5	100	$375.0	100
Institutions	75.0	21+	97.1	26
Stocks	22.0	6	29.4	8
Bonds[a]	53.0	15	67.7	18
Individuals (domestic)[b]	272.9	77	271.4	72
Stocks	242.8	69	247.4	66
Bonds[a]	30.1	8	24.0	6
Foreigners	5.6	1+	6.4	2

Source: Data provided by the Securities and Exchange Commission, October 8, 1958 and SEC, *Survey of Corporate Pension Funds, 1951–1954,* 1956, p. 36.

[a] Includes quasi-government debt issues for which separate data were not available.

[b] Includes personal trust funds and nonprofit organizations.

Note: The figure for individual stockholdings given here is not strictly comparable with the estimates derived from the Brookings study of 1952 and the Stock Exchange Census of Shareowners in 1956. These two studies contain a more elaborate division of stockowners. For example, the 1956 Census of Shareowners (*Who Owns American Business?*, p. 27) shows the shareholdings of the following groups which, for the purposes of the SEC, are probably classed as individuals (per cent of all common issues):

Fiduciaries (individuals)	3.9
Brokers and dealers	9.4
Nominees	9.9
Total	23.2

These percentages represent the ratios of holdings among all domestic stockholders. If these holdings are taken from the percentage assigned to individuals above, the resulting estimate for individual holdings is roughly comparable to the 57 per cent estimate by the Stock Exchange.

thirds of all corporate securities, institutions own only 8 per cent. The tendency is reversed in the case of bonds, with institutions owning three times as much as individuals.

Comparison of the division of ownership in 1954 with that of 1957 shows the growing importance of institutional ownership. Over-all ownership of corporate securities by the institutions increased by 5 percentage points while that of individuals fell off in the same proportion. Individuals lost ground to the institutions in their share of both stock and bond holdings.

Ownership of Stocks

Thus far we have used the term "ownership" loosely, but we must make use of a stricter meaning of the term to obtain an accurate knowledge of how the rights to control corporate wealth are disposed through securities. The figures given for individual ownership include personal trust funds and nonprofit organizations. As a result, individuals appear to have a greater proportion of corporate control through stock ownership than they actually possess. The titles to personal trust funds are in fact legally vested in banks or corporate trustees, in other words, financial institutions.

What is more important, these trustees usually control the voting rights to the stocks which they hold for beneficiaries. Thus, when we speak of the division of corporate control through stock ownership it would be more informative to assign personal trust funds to financial institutions. The same is true for the assets of nonprofit institutions, which usually leave the management of their funds to the discretion of a corporate trustee. Such institutions, for example colleges and universities, commonly have as much as 55 to 60 per cent of their capital invested in stocks.

Some adjustment in stock ownership figures must therefore be made to reflect the fact that institutions own and can vote more stock than we have thus far indicated. Table 6 incorporates the most recent available estimate of beneficial stockholdings in an effort to reapportion stock ownership figures to reflect the true location of voting control. Thus, with personal trust funds, nonprofit institutions and the like assigned to the institutional category, we find that institutions own 27 per cent of all shares outstanding.

If all the sources of institutional ownership of stocks could be determined, their proportion of stockholdings might be even higher. Rough as these estimates are, we have sufficient evidence to show that the financial institutions have acquired shares of stock in great enough quantities to have a considerable impact on the control of productive wealth.

New York Stock Exchange Estimates

The figures just presented refer to all stocks outstanding. Reports on the distribution of ownership of shares recently made by the New York Stock Exchange confirm the suspicion that institutional ownership is greater than the SEC figures indicate. In March of 1955, G. Keith Funston, president of the Exchange, testifying before the Fulbright Commit-

Table 6

ESTIMATE OF OWNERSHIP OF ALL U. S. CORPORATIONS,
BY CLASS OF OWNER, DECEMBER 31, 1957

Class of Owner	STOCKHOLDINGS Value (*Billions*)	Per Cent
All classes	$283.0	100
Domestic individuals	247.4	87
Minus personal trust funds and nonprofit organizations	−45.2[a]	16
Domestic individuals, adjusted	202.2	71
Institutions	29.4	10
Plus personal trust funds and nonprofit organizations	+45.2[a]	16
Institutions, adjusted	74.6	27
Foreigners	6.1	2

Source: Data provided by Securities and Exchange Commission, October 8, 1958.

[a] Since current data on stockholdings are unavailable, the estimate of $45.2 billion for personal trusts and nonprofit organizations was arrived at by taking the SEC's estimate for 1954 ($44 billion; see *Survey of Corporate Pension Funds, 1951–1954,* p. 18) and determining what percentage it was of the total stocks outstanding. This percentage, 16.3, was then applied to the total stock value figure for 1957 to yield the estimate of $45.2 billion. The total stock value figure for 1957 includes preferred stocks while the estimate of $44 billion referred only to common stocks. Thus our estimate for common stocks of personal trust funds and nonprofit organizations could be slightly higher. There are also indications that nonprofit institutions are increasing the percentage of their portfolios invested in common stocks.

tee, which was then investigating the stock market, outlined the position of institutions as stock investors as follows:

At the end of 1954 it is estimated that insurance companies, pension funds, investment companies, foundations and endowment funds, and mutual savings banks own stock valued at $28 billion, and personal trust funds administered by banks own stock worth another $38 billion — for a total market value of $66 billion held by institutions compared with $32 billion in 1949. About 80 per cent of this increase is accounted for by a rise in market value, with the balance representing net additional purchases. Of this $66 billion in stock owned by institutions, approximately $48 billion are common and preferred stocks listed on the New York Stock Exchange.[33]

[33] *Stock Market Study,* Hearings before the Senate Committee on Banking and Currency, 84th Cong., 1st sess., March 1955, p. 97.

Testifying before the same committee Mr. Funston estimated that institutional investors owned 28 per cent of the total value of the stocks listed on his own exchange,[34] which is a slightly higher percentage than the adjusted estimates of 27 per cent based on SEC data. (See Table 6.) In October of the same year, 1955, the Stock Exchange revised its estimates of institutional ownership upward to 31 per cent.[35] The proportion of shares owned by institutions may be higher on the New York Stock Exchange because, as we shall see in Chapter 4, the institutional investors tend to concentrate their purchases among the higher-priced stock issues and these are generally registered on the New York Exchange.

CHARACTERISTICS OF INSTITUTIONAL STOCK PURCHASES

In addition to purchasing large amounts of stocks, the financial institutions exhibit certain other tendencies which operate to place them in a position to control our economic wealth. For example, they tend to concentrate their purchases in shares of the largest corporations and they are long-term investors.

Equities of the Largest Corporations

In a supplement to its 1956 Census of Shareholders the Stock Exchange broke down the common shareholdings of institutions in a way that roughly indicates the size of the corporations in which the institutions interest themselves. This analysis shows that institutional median holdings range from a low of 4.8 per cent in issues with less than a million shares outstanding to a high of 8.2 per cent in issues in the 3–10 million size class. (See Table 7.) The significance of this finding becomes clear when we refer to Table 2, which shows that the largest issues of stock are those of the largest corporations. Actually, institutional preference for the shares of these corporations is greater than a cursory examination of Table 7 would indicate because a much greater amount of capital is required to purchase a given percentage of a large issue than to purchase the same amount of a smaller issue. And yet, as the table shows, the institutions own higher percentages of the larger issues.

We may conclude, then, that their purchases of common stocks are tending to place the institutions in a position of control in the most influential U. S. corporations.

[34] *Ibid.*, p. 8.
[35] *New York Times*, October 5, p. 48.

Table 7

PER CENT OF COMMON SHARES HELD BY INSTITUTIONS, BY SIZE OF COMMON ISSUE, AT END OF 1955

Per Cent of Shares Held by Institutions	SIZE CLASS: TOTAL NUMBER (MILLIONS) OF SHARES OUTSTANDING			
	10 and Over (49 Issues)	3–10 (120 Issues)	1–3 (181 Issues)	Under 1 (213 Issues)
Median	7.8	8.2	5.7	4.8
Total	100.0	100.0	100.0	100.0
30.0 and over	8.2	7.5	7.8	13.1
25.0–29.9	–	1.7	1.1	1.9
20.0–24.9	–	5.0	6.1	1.4
15.0–19.9	10.2	9.2	3.3	4.2
10.0–14.9	14.3	15.8	9.9	8.0
5.0–9.9	38.7	30.0	25.4	18.8
0.0–4.9	28.6	30.8	46.4	52.6

Source: 1956 Census of Shareowners, Special Supplement, New York Stock Exchange, 1956, Table X.

Market Activity of Institutions

Institutional investors show a set of characteristics peculiar to themselves in the market. In addition to their preference for "blue chip" investments, they are long-term investors. Winthrop H. Smith, managing partner of Merrill Lynch, Pierce, Fenner & Beane, made this observation about institutional investors in testifying before the Fulbright Committee:

> Among those institutions that I am familiar with I find that they very seldom make sales. When they make a purchase, they are pretty apt to stay with it for a long time, almost an indefinite time.[36]

At the same hearings, Dorsey Richardson, chairman of the executive committee of the National Association of Investment Companies, had this to say:

> Institutional holdings of common stocks have, in my opinion, a most desirable stabilizing effect. Institutional investors are cash buyers, not margin buyers. They have long-term investment objectives and are not subject to panic

[36] Senate Report No. 376, 84th Cong., 1st sess., 1955, p. 8.

selling in the face of market decline and not harried by short-term fluctuations. Their approach is professional. They do not follow stock-market prices up.[37]

In fact, the continuing stock purchases of institutions were frequently mentioned in the course of these hearings as one of the factors responsible for the stock market rise. It was asserted that the institutions are increasingly investing in stocks, that they influence the demand price, and that as semipermanent investors they reduce the "floating" supply, particularly of "blue chips."[38]

In its Seventh Public Transaction Study, published in 1958, the New York Stock Exchange noted, as one of the most salient findings, "the importance of institutional investors and intermediaries now accounting for about one out of every four shares bought and sold."[39] In its study of the total volume of trading for individuals, institutions and intermediaries on two days in October 1957, the Stock Exchange found that 30 out of 100 shares bought and sold were either for, or through the account of, the institutions and intermediaries.[40] Within this group the most important institutions were commercial banks and trust companies, the same institutions that manage pension fund assets.

Further light was cast on institutional activity and its effect on the market at the time of the Fulbright hearings on stock market activity when the chairman said to G. Keith Funston: "If I understand you correctly, something a little under $3 billion of new equity securities were issued last year and about $2 billion are presumed to be taken off by what you call institutional investors."[41]

A little later, in summing up its findings of the hearings, the Senate Committee expressed some concern over the net effect of institutional investment:

> One fundamental long-range issue came sharply to focus during the hearings, namely, that continuation of the rapid increase in stock buying by institutional purchasers may result in financial institutions having a dominant influence over the managerial policies of industrial enterprise.[42]

The committee explicitly mentioned the case of the Sears, Roebuck & Company pension fund, which in 1955 owned 26 per cent of the equities of that company.[43]

[37] *Ibid.*
[38] *Ibid.*, p. 7.
[39] *A Picture of the Stock Market*, p. II.
[40] *Ibid.*, p. 11.
[41] *Stock Market Study*, Hearings, March 1955, p. 75.
[42] Senate Report No. 376, p. 8.
[43] *Ibid.*

FUTURE OF INSTITUTIONAL INVESTMENT

The growing activity of institutional investors in the stock market was dramatically described in a recent address by Mr. Funston when he said, *"during the average business day,* and on the basis of 1954 figures, U. S. institutions make net purchases of common and preferred stock of about $6 million. I am intrigued by the thought that this is equivalent to $750,000 *every working hour."*[44] He added that these figures represented only *net* purchases. Looking to the future we must conclude that institutional investors will play a large role in America's development. In the same address, Mr. Funston estimated that between 1955 and 1965 total institutional stockholdings would almost double and would reach a total of approximately $60 billion.[45] He also predicted that new equity purchases by institutions would rise 200 per cent but that the nation's over-all equity needs would rise by 350 per cent.[46]

If the pattern of growth established by the financial institutions in the first half of this century continues, the financial institutions will surely play an increasingly important role in corporate ownership. Raymond Goldsmith reports that in 1900 financial intermediaries held about 6 per cent of all stock outstanding and that this ratio had increased to about 12 per cent by 1929 and to 20 per cent by 1952.[47]

The noninsured pension funds, which were a negligible factor in this trend until the late 1940s, have become the major influence in institutionalizing corporate ownership.[48] Since the early 1950s they have been the leading purchasers of stock among the financial institutions,[49] and we shall see in Chapter 8 that they are likely to continue increasing their stock purchases for some time to come.

THE TRANSITION OF CONTROL

The preceding investigation of security ownership indicates that individuals own about 57 per cent of all corporate stocks outstanding and financial institutions about 27 to 30 per cent. Since the remaining stocks are registered in the names of brokers, dealers and nominees, we cannot determine who controls the voting power they represent. Examination

[44] "Institutional Investors" (Address), October 14, 1955, p. 4.
[45] *Ibid.*, p. 5.
[46] *Ibid.*, pp. 6 and 7.
[47] *Financial Intermediaries in the American Economy*, p. 322.
[48] See Table 34, p. 238 for pension fund growth since 1920.
[49] See Table 32, p. 230.

of the two major types of stockholders, however, makes it clear that a major shift of power is taking place within our property system.

Dispersion of Control

The wide dispersion of corporate control among individuals is immediately evident from the statistics of share ownership. But, as we have pointed out, any possibility of effective control by individuals is cut down by one-third because corporate shares in that amount are held for so short a time that the owners could not be interested in corporate policy, which involves long-term planning. Such holdings are obviously acquired for profit on sale and not for capital appreciation. Furthermore, effective control cannot be exercised without a substantial stockholding, and the annual income of the great majority of individual shareholders is so limited that they could not possibly purchase any more than a tiny fragment of control.

We suspect that about one-third of all shareholders own about two-thirds of all shares held by individuals, but even so they are so numerous that effective control is out of their reach. Some idea of the high cost of control may be gained from the fact that acquisition of 2.64 per cent of the common stock in the Socony Mobile Oil Company cost New York banks, purchasing it for pension trusts, $50 million by 1954.[50] In other instances small amounts of control were bought at the following costs: .98 per cent of General Electric, $39.6 million; 2.58 per cent of IBM, $38.3 million; 2.67 per cent of National City Bank of New York, $11.6 million. Similarly, if an investor had been buying American Gas and Electric for some years before 1954, an outlay of $9.6 million would have brought him only 1.75 per cent of control. And, of course, all the prices are higher now.

There is probably no further need of proof, even for those most difficult to convince, that corporate control is so widely dispersed among individual stockholders that to the extent of 57 per cent of corporate ownership there is no effective control at all. But with regard to a large portion of ownership entrusted to financial intermediaries the story is somewhat different.

Convergence of Control

The institutional investors now controlling 27 to 30 per cent of all stock issues exhibit characteristics in marked contrast to individual own-

[50] See Table 14, p. 198.

ers. They tend, in the first place, to invest more heavily in larger corporations, that is, precisely in the corporations which otherwise have the widest dispersion of ownership. Second, experts testify and market activity seems to indicate that institutions are interested in more or less permanent ownership in the corporations in which they invest. Third, they are large purchasers of stock, buying an amount equal to nearly two-thirds of the new issues in 1954. Fourth, the president of the New York Stock Exchange has indicated that he expects this trend to continue.

It is extremely important, too, to realize that while dispersion is characteristic of the individual owners, concentration is typical of the financial institutions. *The Fortune Directory of the 500 Largest U. S. Industrial Corporations* informs us that among the 50 largest commercial banks:

> 5 banks had $30 billion, or 38 per cent, and
> 10 banks had $44 billion, or 55 per cent of all assets.

A similar picture emerges from a review of the distribution of the assets of the 50 largest life insurance companies:

> 5 companies had $45 billion, or 56 per cent, and
> 10 companies had $58 billion, or 72 per cent of the assets.[51]

Later in this study we shall point out the high degree of concentration among the noninsured pension funds themselves and demonstrate that their assets are in turn concentrated in the largest banks. Among the investment companies the concentration is similar though not as great. The largest investment company at the end of 1954 held assets of $791 million,[52] and in 1953, 53 per cent of the mutual companies did 78 per cent of the business.[53]

The Meaning of Institutionalization

Comparison of the 1952 and 1956 stock ownership studies indicates that while the number of stockholders has increased, actual dispersion of ownership probably has not. Stock ownership among institutions, however, has increased. Institutional purchases of stocks have limited the trend toward fission of control into small elements and have set up a countertrend toward fusion of control.

These forces necessarily affect the property structure of our society in

[51] *Fortune,* Supplement, July 1956, pp. 12 and 15.
[52] *Stock Market Study,* Hearings, p. 708.
[53] *Ibid.,* p. 726. As of the end of 1954 there were 115 mutual funds (open-end companies) with assets of $6.1 billion and 30 closed-end companies with assets of $1.2 billion (*ibid.,* p. 719).

two vital ways which tend to reinforce one another. First, the funds shunted through institutional intermediaries would otherwise be employed by individuals in a proprietary way. But by contributing their capital to financial institutions, individuals are cut off from even the paper ties to property control which they might have as stockholders in corporations owning productive wealth.

Secondly, the corporations themselves, as they evolved, became instruments for the institutional control of property. Salaried managers exercised the control over property that the so-called owners could not mobilize. But the power to control through ownership of shares of stock was still there though dormant. Now that institutions have begun to concentrate stockholdings in large units, they may begin to exert the influence they have acquired. Indeed, as the institutional intermediaries become more deeply interested in the equities of corporations, their very obligations to the individuals they represent will force them to exercise the control powers that have come to them as the result of their investments.

The impact of this development upon the property system becomes evident when we realize that as property becomes institutionalized it will not be individual income producers but salaried managers who control productive wealth. More and more the individual is losing his proprietary interest in the most significant kind of property in our economic system.

At this point the behavior of the institutions becomes very interesting. As candidates for a position of major influence in our society it is important to know how their power is divided among them. What are the mechanics of control within the institutions? Whence do they draw their capital? What claims do individuals have on them? What are the checks on their powers?

We shall not try to answer these questions for all of the financial institutions but take one of them, the pension trusts, for careful scrutiny. The pension trusts, as the most dynamic of all the financial institutions, provide a prime example of the tendencies which lead to the institutionalization of property.

WHAT ARE THE

PENSION TRUSTS?

The Pension Plan and Labor Agreements

The "Plan" and Its Administration

Financing the Pension Program

The foregoing analysis of United States capital assets has roughly defined the place of pension trusts in the American system of property ownership. The present chapter will discuss the incidence of the property ownership in these funds. In other words, we shall be answering these two questions: What are the powers of pension plan administrators and trustees? What are the property rights of pensioners?

As they are typically set up today, the structure and operation of pension plans are defined in a document called the "Plan," which is usually supplemented by a trust indenture granting to a corporate trustee the authority to manage and invest the assets of a pension fund. Furthermore, since the pension plans of about 60 per cent of all covered employees have been affected by collective bargaining agreements, the union agreement is very important in any adequate discussion of the rights of employees to receive pensions.

But the fact is that the pension funds have made use of legal devices, particularly the trust, for purposes beyond the scope of their traditional application. As the final report of the Senate Subcommittee on Welfare and Pension Funds observes:

The application of well-established doctrines of trust law to the field of employee benefit funds is a most difficult task. To an ever-increasing extent these funds are leaving the realm of usually understood trust principles and are posing an entirely new concept for dealing with property that has no parallel elsewhere in law.[1]

Because of the rapid growth of these funds, the law has not had time to grow apace with the institution it is to serve. The courts and legislatures are now faced with the problem of evolving a coherent body of law which will reconcile traditional property rights with new forms of property organization involving millions of workers and billions of dollars. Since these new forms of property are already in being and form the bases of the future support for so many, the courts are faced with a *de facto* situation which in substance must be preserved.

We shall therefore begin with an analysis of how pension trusts are actually organized and in a later chapter deal with the concepts that have been applied to define their legal structure.

THE PENSION PLAN AND LABOR AGREEMENTS

While the section of the collective bargaining agreement pertaining to pensions is not, strictly speaking, part of the pension plan itself, it is extremely important in that certain essential features of the pension plan will be determined by the contract between the employer and the union. In some industries labor unions have inaugurated their own pension plans, but the usual pattern has been for the union to persuade management to institute and administer the pension program.

Coverage under Union-Negotiated Agreements

The Senate subcommittee investigating welfare and pension funds revealed that most of the covered employees are in pension plans administered by a single employer. Less than one per cent of the workers are in plans administered by a single employer jointly with the union, while 13 per cent are under plans managed by many employers jointly with the union.[2] These figures would be misleading on the point of union influence upon pension plans if we did not consider that "approximately 60

---

[1] Senate Report No. 1734, 84th Cong., 2d sess., 1956, p. 67.
[2] *Ibid.*, p. 14.

per cent of the workers who are covered for pension benefits and about 40 per cent of those covered by the various welfare programs are under programs which are collectively bargained."[3] This means that the union has a voice in the determination of the level of benefits, requirements for inclusion in the plan, and so on, for two out of three workers in pension programs. The nature of the union's interest in pensions is pointed up by the following statement of Arthur J. Goldberg, general counsel of the CIO:

> The union and management come to the bargaining table with some appraisal of how much money there is in the "kitty" for an increase. The appraisals are, naturally, different. But it is the *total* cost of improvements which provides the framework within which the union and management bargain. If the 5 cents, for example, does not go into a health and welfare fund, it can go into a wage increase or two extra holidays or double time for overtime on Saturdays. This is what collective bargaining is all about.[4]

These agreements, according to an analysis made by Rainard B. Robbins, run from a year to five years and contain no guarantee of benefits beyond their expiration period other than that pensions already being paid out will be continued until the pensioner dies.[5] The commitments of the employers range from a maximum promise to fund both past and current service liabilities according to actuarial calculations to mere promises to fund pensions already granted or to agreements which leave the employer free to determine how he will meet his responsibilities. Union-negotiated agreements rarely contain provisions which vest an interest in the fund for the employee before the normal time of retirement. Such provisions are usually found only in contracts covering a small group of employees, although a trend is developing toward more widespread coverage by vesting provisions.

Pension Provisions of Union Contracts

The formative period for these contracts was during 1949–1950, following the Supreme Court decision in the *Inland Steel* case.[6] The Court then declared pensions subject to collective bargaining and opened the

[3] *Ibid.*, p. 12.

[4] State of New York Insurance Department, *Welfare and Pension Funds, Public Hearing*, 1955, Exhibit 4, p. 11 (mimeographed).

[5] *Pensions in Industry*, 1952, p. 133 (Mimeographed. Distributed by Teachers Insurance and Annuity Association of America).

[6] Inland Steel Co. v. NLRB, 170 F. 2d 247 (7th Cir. 1948), *cert. denied*, 336 U. S. 960 (1949).

way to agreements in the coal mining, steel and automotive industries. These contracts are summarized here because they set the pattern for future pension plans:

While agreements have differed in important details the composite provides a flat pension of $100 a month including the primary OASI benefit, available at age 65 after twenty-five years of continuous service, with proportionally smaller pensions for shorter service periods, not shorter than fifteen years of continuous service, paid for by the employer alone who is solely responsible for method of financing, and with benefit questions determined by joint committee action. Retirement is usually automatic at age 68, with service after age 65 at the option of the employer, but little emphasis seems to have been placed on service after age 65. Under a number of plans the pension is, in form, proportioned to wages — 1 per cent of average salary during the last 10 years of service for each year of continuous service — with a minimum benefit of $100 a month after twenty-five years of continuous service. A correspondingly lower minimum is applicable after a shorter service. Usually fifteen years of continuous service is required for receipt of any benefit, but in one prominent agreement, only ten years are required.[7]

Such contracts, where they exist, provide the basis for the pension plan itself which is usually drawn up in detail by the employer in consultation with actuaries and pension consultants. The legal effects of these agreements upon the rights of pensioners will be discussed in Chapter 6, and the policy objectives of union bargaining in Chapter 4.

Impact of Collective Bargaining Agreements

While the foregoing summary of pension provisions gives a good idea of what goes into a pension plan as a result of collective bargaining negotiations, two important observations should be made with regard to the impact of these agreements on pension rights. First, the employee whose pension plan is based on a union-management contract has greater assurance that pension promises will be met than an employee under a non-negotiated plan. And secondly, even when pension rights are bargained, many important areas in the plan are not subject to union influence.

Protection under Collectively Bargained Plans

As we shall see in subsequent sections of this chapter the employer usually reserves to himself the right to amend or terminate the pension plan whenever he sees fit to do so. Thus, under the pension plan itself, the

[7] Robbins, *op. cit.*, p. 134.

employee often has little guarantee that his pension will not be reduced or cut off entirely. But when the pension plan is the result of a collective bargaining agreement, union members among the employees will be protected by the pension promises contained in the agreement,[8] and about 60 per cent of all covered employees are so protected.

In this connection an objection may be raised that collective bargaining agreements seldom run longer than a few years. In actual practice, however, these contracts are more in the nature of continuing agreements and no union is going to abandon pension concessions it has previously won.

Limitations of Negotiated Plans

Despite the protection that union-management pension agreements provide, the statements of certain witnesses before the Senate subcommittee investigating welfare and pension funds indicate that collective bargaining on pensions leaves much to be desired. In a conference of labor representatives it was said, for example, that the unions wanted joint administration of funds, disclosure of all necessary pension information and investment of funds in areas where they would benefit workers "while they are actively at work."[9]

Joint administration of the pension fund is the most fundamental of these recommendations, and it would greatly help to solve the other difficulties. Short of this provision, sufficient information to bargain about pensions would seem to be a requisite. Indeed, it was held in *Aluminum Ore Co.* v. *NLRB* as far back as 1942 that it is the duty of the employer to provide sufficient information to a union to bargain about pensions.[10] Despite this ruling, labor representatives feel that legal remedies to guarantee disclosure are far from adequate.

Since the cost of a trusteed pension plan is a variable sum, it is important to a union to have current actuarial information and data on pension fund earnings. Typically, negotiation is carried on about payments on a cents-per-hour or level-of-benefits basis, with the union having little or no information about the cost of a plan. Lacking these figures, the employees' representatives do not know what demands an employer can be forced to meet.

[8] Senate Report No. 1734, p. 40.
[9] *Ibid.*, p. 302. See also pp. 97 ff.
[10] 131 F. 2d 485 (7th Cir. 1942).

Such disclosure would involve a knowledge of the earnings of the trust supporting the fund. But management's attitude is probably typified by U. S. Steel's position in hearings before the Senate Subcommittee on Welfare and Pension Funds that its bargaining contract merely required the company to pay benefits and left it free to decide how to provide the necessary funds. Thus, the company's general counsel could say: ". . . since the determination of whether or not to create a trust is a matter of internal policy, we believe that the operations are of a like nature."[11]

General Motors' attitude was similar. Its spokesman declared that the company would be at a competitive disadvantage at the bargaining table if complete disclosure of the operations of its fund were required. The scope of bargaining is clearly expressed in the following statement: ". . . the entire cost of the hourly rate pension plan is borne by the corporation. We negotiate with labor organizations only the benefits to be provided under the pension plan."[12]

A minority of collective bargaining agreements contain a provision that the agreed benefits will be financed by a pension trust or by insurance. But even this provision gives the union little or no control over employee pension funds. As a result, the employee really has little to say about the actual conduct of a pension trust even through the most powerful instrument of which he could make use.

Thus, to sum up, the principal effects which the unions have had on pension funds through collective bargaining is, first of all, to force certain companies or industries to provide these funds and, secondly, to add their weight to enforce fulfillment of pension promises. In both of these functions the unions are hampered by insufficient information and by lack of any voice in the actual operations of the funds. The possible effect of state disclosure statutes on the problem of information will be treated in Chapter 4.

In the following discussion of the provisions of the pension plan it will be important to remember that certain clauses in the plan document which give the employer wide latitude in such matters as termination and amendment may, in fact, be restricted by collective bargaining obligations assumed by the employer. This feature of the pension picture makes the right of the union to enforce collective bargaining agreements, discussed in Chapter 6, a matter of great importance.

[11] Hearings on S. Res. 40, 84th Cong., 1st sess., 1955, Part 3, p. 1170.
[12] *Ibid.*, p. 1135. See also the discussion of disclosure in Chapter 4.

THE "PLAN" AND ITS ADMINISTRATION

The pension plan, which must be completely in writing and communicated to the employee in order to qualify for tax exemption, usually contains the following types of provision:

(1) General statement of company policy with regard to retirement.
(2) Details on the administration of the pension plan.
(3) Requirements for eligibility to receive pension benefits.
(4) Description of a formula to determine the amount of benefits.
(5) Provisions for early, compulsory and disability retirement.
(6) Provisions covering the costs of the pension programs, whether the plan shall be contributory or noncontributory, include past service liability, future service liability, and so forth.[13]

This document forms the basis of the employee's rights to receive the benefits promised him under the plan. (See Appendix A.)

Generally speaking, four types of pension plan administration are to be distinguished: the single-employer-administered plan; the single-employer–jointly administered (employer-union) plan; the multi-employer–jointly administered plan; and the wholly union-administered plan.

Single-Employer-Administered Plans

Administration of the pension plan by the employer, either by himself or through a pension committee, is typical of most pension programs. As previously noted, the 1956 report of the Senate Subcommittee on Welfare and Pension Funds estimated that 86 per cent of all covered employees were in pension plans administered by a single employer. Most of these pension programs are noncontributory, that is, the employer pays the whole cost; under some, the employees make contributions.[14] If a pension plan of this type is the result of a collective bargaining agreement, the contract may specify whether or not the plan is to be insured or self-administered and, if self-administered, whether or not an independent trustee is to manage the assets. But if no such specification is made in the agreement or if the program is initiated by the employer, it is up to the employer to choose whether or not the plan will be insured or self-admin-

[13] For a check list of pension provisions, see Robert E. Sibson, *A Survey of Pension Planning*, Commerce Clearing House, 1953, p. 169.
[14] Senate Report No. 1734, p. 14.

istered, who will be the insurance carrier, or who will act as trustee of the funds. Determination of these matters, if not specified in collective bargaining agreements, is also within the power of the administrators in the three other types of pension programs.

Single-Employer–Jointly Administered Plans

This type of plan is similar to the single-employer-administered plan in that only the employees of a single company are involved in or covered by the pension program. The main point of difference is that real control of the plan is the joint concern of the employer and the union as provided by Section 302(c) of the Labor-Management Relations Act of 1947.[15] Under such a plan the company usually agrees to contribute so many cents per employee-hour worked, or a specified percentage of its payroll, to a fund managed by a committee of trustees chosen by the company and the union. Each party to the agreement usually has an equal number of representatives.

Multi-Employer–Jointly Administered Plans

This type of fund differs from the preceding type in that many employers are involved in the administration of a single plan established by contract with a union or unions. Contributions are usually made on the same basis as in the plans administered by a single employer and the union, and the fund is managed by trustees representing the employers and the union, in equal numbers, as required by the Taft-Hartley Act. In addition, one or more neutral or public trustees are appointed. The Senate Subcommittee on Welfare and Pension Funds makes the following comment on this type of plan:

> These multi-employer types of programs are found mainly in industries marked by small or numerous employers such as are found in the construction, coal mining, men's and women's clothing, cleaning and dyeing, laundry, trucking, restaurant, small scale retail merchandising, and other service industries. Frequently these funds are established on an area basis. However, some teamsters' funds cover many States and some funds, such as the United Mine Workers, are on a national scale.[16]

The New York State Insurance Department survey states that "Nearly all of the multi-employer plans resulted from collective bargaining."[17]

---

[15] 61 Stat. 157 (1947), as amended, 29 U. S. C. § 186(c) (1952).

[16] Senate Report No. 1734, p. 15.

[17] Martin S. House, *Private Employee Benefit Plans: A Public Trust*, State of New York Insurance Department, 1956, p. 83.

Wholly Union-Administered Plans

Relatively few pension funds are administered solely by the unions. Such plans are managed by a local or international union, and participation in them may or may not be required of the members. These funds usually derive their income from dues and assessments paid by the union membership, although there are a few wholly union-administered programs based upon employer contributions.

SCOPE OF ADMINISTRATIVE POWERS

In employer-administered plans the management is usually vested in a pension committee or board consisting solely of representatives appointed by the employer. A few include employee representatives appointed by the employer. In some plans which have been collectively bargained, provision is made for labor-appointed representatives, usually on grievance committees, but their activities are restricted to such matters as eligibility, termination of benefits and interpretation of plan provisions. The New York State Insurance Department report indicated that only 5 per cent of the 271 single-employer plans studied provided for union representation in their management.[18]

The scope of activity in the administration of a pension plan may be roughly described under five headings:[19]

(1) To develop and enforce rules and regulations for the operation of the plan.
(2) If funded on an actuarial basis, to adopt appropriate funding methods and to engage actuarial services for this purpose.
(3) To invest and hold the plan's assets, if any, or to delegate such responsibilities, in whole or in part, to a bank or trust company.
(4) To grant pensions.
(5) To maintain accounts and other records.

Many of the negotiated plans in the iron and steel industry are in accord with this general description of plan administration. An examination of the provisions of thirty-one pension agreements for the wage earners in this industry in 1951 revealed that the typical collectively bargained agreement provided for administration of pension plans along these lines.[20]

[18] *Private Employee Benefit Plans,* pp. 92, 93, Table 5.
[19] George A. Mooney, *Pension and Other Employee Welfare Plans,* New York State Banking Department, 1955, Tables 123 and 124. These tables summarize the administration of New York pension plans covering 2.5 million employees.
[20] *Classified Provisions of Thirty-One Pension Agreements for Wage Earners in the*

Nearly all pension plans grant the pension committee broad powers such as those outlined in the pension plan of the American Cyanamid Company and subsidiaries:

. . . the Pension Committee shall have the exclusive right to interpret the Plan and to determine any question arising hereunder or in connection with the administration thereof, and its decision or action in respect thereof shall be conclusive and binding upon all past, present and future employees of the company and its subsidiaries, and their contingent annuitants . . .[21]

The Senate subcommittee report previously referred to notes that since 1946 a considerable number of multi-employer–jointly managed plans have been negotiated. It lists as the principal plans of this type: the United Mine Workers Welfare and Retirement Fund, the pension plans of the International Ladies' Garment Workers' Union, the Amalgamated Clothing Workers of America, the International Brotherhood of Electrical Workers, and the Teamsters Central States, Southeast and Southwest Areas pension fund. These, together with a small number of plans wholly administered by labor unions, cover possibly 2 million workers, with total contributions in 1954 estimated at about $140 million. The bulk of this amount, $120 million, was contributed by employers and the remainder by employees.[22] However, despite the provision for joint administration of these funds, the New York State Insurance Department found that "while the plan instrument or collective bargaining agreement may provide for joint administration, there is no assurance that such joint administration will in fact take place."[23]

Although the employer or his representative has the last word with regard to pension benefits in most types of pension programs, a number of plans give the employee some kind of right of appeal from the decision of the administrator. While it is difficult to determine how many employees enjoy this privilege, the New York State Banking Department's report of 1955 indicates that, except for jointly administered or collectively bargained plans, relatively few plans contain provisions for appeal. Only 77 out of 556 plans studied in New York had set up procedures for this purpose. In the case of jointly administered plans, however, 65 out of 69

Iron and Steel Industry, American Iron and Steel Institute, New York, 1951, pp. 129 ff.

[21] Fleming Bomar and others, *Handbook for Pension Planning,* Bureau of National Affairs, Washington, 1949, p. 302.

[22] Senate Report No. 1734, p. 49.

[23] *Private Employee Benefit Plans,* p. 92.

plans contained provisions for arbitration and 3 others for appeal.[24] It must be remembered, also, that in the country as a whole two out of every three employees covered by pension programs are in plans negotiated by union-management agreements which give the unions a right to enforce certain guarantees of pension benefits for their members.

In summary, we may conclude that, in seeking to vindicate rights they may feel are being violated, nearly two-thirds of the employees covered by pension plans may have recourse to action on the part of their unions. But only in a very small percentage of the pension plans in force will the grievance of an employee be handled according to some kind of formally established grievance procedure. In the other cases his remedy will be sought by the usual form of union representation, and in the case of over one-third of the employees under pension plans the only recourse is direct procedure against the management or its representative.

TERMINATION

The significance of the employer's power to amend or terminate the pension plan is clearly illustrated by the classic case of the liquidation of the Morris & Company contributory pension plan.[25] This company was acquired by Armour & Company in 1923 without assumption of pension liabilities, although contributions by officers and employees had been made at the rate of 3 per cent of their salaries. The Morris pension plan limited the company's pension liabilities to $500,000, to which the company had voluntarily added sums amounting to $980,000.

The committee in charge of the fund decided to liquidate it at the time of the dissolution of the business. It was determined that all contributions from employees would be returned in full together with interest at 4 per cent. But at the time this action was taken some 400 persons were receiving pension allowances under the plan. The result of liquidation was to cut off their funds. To insure continuance of their allowance a reserve of over $7 million would have been needed, as this was the actuarial value of the accrued liabilities at the time. A group of the disappointed pensioners brought suit against Morris & Company to require the establishment of a sufficient reserve fund out of the assets of the liquidated corporation. Their claim was based on the fact that they had been induced to contribute to the fund, to remain employees of the company in spite of

[24] New York State Banking Department, *op. cit.*, Table 123.
[25] *Private Employee Benefit Plans*, p. 97.

other employment opportunities, and to make similar sacrifices in reliance upon promises that they would enjoy the protection of a pension as a reward for continuous employment. Judgment was given against the employees on the ground that there was no evidence of conspiracy between the pension committee and Morris & Company to end the liability for pensions or to destroy the fund.[26]

The Morris case is thus a graphic example of the large sums of money needed to realize pension promises and of the dangers of failing to fund a pension plan.

Dorrance C. Bronson, a leading pension consultant, describes the circumstances which may lead to termination of a plan as follows:

. . . plans may terminate by business necessity, by union-management agreement or disagreement, by dissolution or merger of companies, by encroachment of Social Security, etc. . . . A plan may terminate, or splinter, in respect of a part of its coverage, by the closing of a plant, by the dissociation of a subsidiary, by the withdrawal of a union group, by separation of a once common plan into hourly or salary categories, etc.[27]

In general, Mr. Bronson finds the provisions for termination of pension plans extremely inadequate. He speaks of three varieties of termination provision. The first is very general and indefinite, i.e., that the interests and allocations are "to be determined" by the employer, the trustee, the pension committee, the actuary, or a combination thereof, without any details on the "how" of doing it. Another method of termination is described by the phrases "in an equitable manner" or "on an accepted actuarial basis." The third method attempts a definite establishment of employee categories of priority or allocation ratios for the distribution of fund assets.

It is evident that very serious legal and ethical problems may arise as to the relative equities of various groups participating in a pension plan, for example those who have already retired, those close to retirement and the younger active employees. Certainly, some provision for termination is to be highly recommended for inclusion in the plan, but at present the employer is left in the dominant position to determine what is to happen to a pension fund on termination of the program.

We can see from the Morris case what a serious business it can be to

[26] The case is discussed in *Industrial Pensions in the United States*, National Industrial Conference Board, New York, 1925.

[27] "Pension Plans — Provisions for Termination of Plan," *Transactions of the Society of Actuaries*, Vol. VIII, June 1955, cited in *Private Employee Benefit Plans*, pp. 96 and 97.

enter into a pension program for employees. As a result of experiences like this, most pension documents reserve to the employer the right to terminate the plan at any time. Single-employer plans generally contain provisions limiting the obligations of the employer to the amount of the accumulated assets and require him to pay out only those contributions already made to the pension fund.

Pension programs have been terminated from time to time, usually because of business downturns or failure or the merging of companies. In New York, according to the Banking Department study, a total of 111 plans were terminated during the years 1936–1954. At termination, the assets of these funds, amounting to less than $4 million, were almost entirely distributed among the 3,634 active members and the 93 retired participants. The principal reasons given for liquidating the 111 pension plans were "adverse business conditions" (37); "discontinuance of employer's business" (26); "failure to meet Internal Revenue requirements" (10); "merger or absorption of employer" (7); and "absorption of employees by a new plan" (7).[28]

The data contained in Table 8, based on nationwide reports submitted to the Internal Revenue Service, suggest that termination of ordinary pension trusts and pension plans based on profit sharing is more common than the New York experience indicates. Of 94 such plans terminated in three months of 1957, one-fifth ended because of financial difficulties and another fifth because of dissolution of the corporation. Sales and mergers of companies may have resulted in the transfer of some employees to other plans, but no doubt there were others who lost their pension rights. It is not mere alarmism to point out that pension expectations depend on the solvency and continued existence of the employer.

AMENDMENT

Even greater latitude is enjoyed in amending the plan through provisions granting to the employer the explicit right to reduce or suspend contributions at any time at his own discretion without a requirement to make a corresponding modification in the benefits structure of the plan. We find in the New York Banking Department survey of corporate trusteed pension plans that most of the 643 plans reporting contained a provision permitting amendment at the sole discretion of the employer. Many of the plans specifically permitted the employer to reduce or suspend con-

[28] New York State Banking Department, *op. cit.*, pp. xii, xiii, 81.

Table 8

TERMINATION OF PENSION TRUSTS, SEPTEMBER,
OCTOBER AND NOVEMBER 1957, AS REPORTED
TO THE INTERNAL REVENUE SERVICE

Reason for Termination	Total Number of Plans	Pension	Profit-Sharing Type
Total	94	49	45
Merger	25	14	11
Sale of company	12	6	6
Financial difficulties	19	13	6
Corporation dissolved	20	5	15
Death of employer	1	–	1
Automatic termination	1	–	1
Lack of employee participation	3	1	2
Establishment of new pension plans:			
Collective bargaining	1	1	–
Noncollective bargaining	1	1	–
Change to a profit-sharing plan	8	5	3
Substitution of a salary increase	1	1	–
Loss of bargaining rights by the union			
participating	1	1	–
By agreement with union	1	1	–

Source: IRS Form 517–T, Statistics Division, Internal Revenue Service, November 26, 1957.

tributions to the plan. However, the survey found that very few employers had exercised such a right.[29] A similar pattern of limiting liability is disclosed by the New York State Insurance Department survey of pension plans.[30]

In the case of plans related to collectively bargained agreements, however, employers are frequently required to continue their contributions and to guarantee pension benefits for the duration of the collective bargaining agreement.

In the large majority of the so-called "New York" plans included in the Banking Department survey, the employer or his representative de-

[29] *Ibid.*, pp. 58–61.
[30] *Private Employee Benefit Plans*, pp. 94 and 95, Tables 6 and 7.

termines in practice the dollar amount of the periodic contributions to be made by the company to the pension fund.[31]

ELIGIBILITY REQUIREMENTS

"Eligibility requirements" refer to the conditions which must be fulfilled before an employee may be covered by a pension plan, for example, whether or not the employee must make a contribution to be included under the plan, what class or classes of employees will be covered, whether a plan will cover only "salaried employees" or include "wage earners." Usually participation in a pension program is made dependent upon completion of a certain number of years of continuous service, the age of the employee and/or the accumulation of a certain amount of earnings. These and other provisions have for their purpose the exclusion of employees who may not be expected to remain members of the plan for any great length of time.

Noninsured trusteed plans are likely to have less restrictive eligibility provisions than the typical insured plan. The Insurance Department of the State of New York has this to say about requirements under the two types of plans:

In general, eligibility requirements for participation in self-administered trusteed pension plans, particularly multi-employer plans, are less restrictive than those found in insured plans because a greater proportion of self-administered plans are noncontributory. Moreover, many self-administered plans do not "vest" in the employee any right, on termination, to receive part or all of the employer's contribution. This permits the use of turnover rates in calculating future pension obligations.[32]

The problem of a maximum age for participation in a pension plan is a serious one. Eligibility for a pension is almost universally dependent upon conditions of age and continuous employment with the corporation. The usual age of retirement is 65 years and the usual span of service, twenty to twenty-five years. Some plans specify a maximum age for eligibility; others allow the employers an upper age limit in their hiring policy for the purpose of excluding employees for whom the purchase of pension benefits would be too costly. The high cost of funding a pension plan for an older employee has been thought by many commentators to result

[31] New York State Banking Department, *op. cit.*, p. 124.
[32] *Private Employee Benefit Plans*, p. 138.

in the creation of a class of unemployables, generally persons of 45 or over.

The most recent tendency in pension planning, however, is to liberalize eligibility requirements for employees, increasing the classes of workers covered and reducing the requirements which must be met before an employee becomes eligible for coverage under a plan. This trend is well illustrated by a comparison of eligibility requirements in a study of industrial plans established during the period 1948–1955. The plans initiated during the last two years of this period definitely tend toward more liberal requirements for plan membership. (See Table 9.)

Table 9

ELIGIBILITY REQUIREMENTS IN CONVENTIONAL PLANS SET UP DURING 1948–1955

(Per Cent)

Eligibility Requirements for Plan Membership	1948–1950 Plans	1950–1952 Plans	1953–1955 Plans
Total plans	100	100	100
No eligibility requirements	14	21	29
Age only	5	1	5
Service only	30	35	30
Age and service	51	43	36

Source: A Study of Industrial Retirement Plans, Bankers Trust Company, 1956, p. 8.

A similar trend toward more comprehensive coverage by pension programs emerges from the study of "New York" pension funds. More than two-thirds of the 643 plans surveyed were set up to include all employees, except temporary, seasonal or part-time employees. About a third of the plans specified minimum age and service requirements for eligibility and many included a maximum age requirement. The absence of any minimum age and service provision was much more characteristic of the plans covering large employee groups than of the plans established for small companies. The plans in general did not require that participation in the plan or enjoyment of benefits was to be contingent on continued good standing in a union. Less than 4 per cent of them included such a requirement for eligibility.[33]

[33] New York State Banking Department, *op. cit.*, pp. 49, 50, 51, 54.

VESTING

"Vesting" is a feature of modern pension planning which is much discussed by the experts. A vested plan is one in which an employee receives a benefit from the fund although he has not reached the full requirements of age or service before separating himself from the plan or the employer who established it. Only a limited number of pension funds have this so-called vesting feature. In one type of vesting, the employee is given the proportion of retirement benefit that he has earned at the date of separation from the company. In the other, or "deferred benefit" type, receipt of the benefit is delayed until the employee reaches retirement age. Thus, through the device known as vesting the employee enjoys an equitable interest in the pension fund as soon as he begins to be covered by a plan.

Vesting is more common in funds to which the employee must make a contribution than in noncontributory plans, where it is provided for rather rarely. Apparently the thinking behind this is that once an employee has turned some of his own money over to a pension fund, he should be able to get it back again. But if we follow the theory that a pension is really a deferred wage and admit that pensions are paid for out of funds an employee has earned, then even under a noncontributory plan an employee would seem to have a vested right in a certain part of the fund.

Since the great majority of employees are covered by noncontributory rather than contributory plans, the really critical question becomes one of vesting in the employee the contributions made to a pension plan for him by the employer. To simplify the discussion of vesting we shall use the definition given in the New York State Insurance Department study: "Vesting refers to an employee's right, on leaving employment before retirement, to receive all or part of the benefits purchased in his behalf by the employer's contributions."[34] The study goes on to say that under contributory plans vesting of the employer's contribution is usually made contingent upon the employee's leaving his contributions with the pension fund or the insurance company to be applied for the purchase of a paid-up deferred pension. Not all vested plans provide for complete vesting. Vesting may be partial or progressive, that is, a certain percentage of total benefits may vest at age 40, with increasing percentages up to age 65 when the employee receives 100 per cent of the benefits.

It is usual to have some requirements of age, service or membership in

[34] *Private Employee Benefit Plans,* p. 141.

the plan as a requisite for vesting of contributions made for the employee. The purpose of these requirements is to exclude casual or transient employees and to keep the cost of financing the program from becoming unduly high. Whatever justification there may be for these limitations, it would seem unjust to deny benefits to employees who have a faithful and long service record even though they do not fully complete the requirements for pension benefits. Many social thinkers advocate widespread vesting provisions as a device to counteract the adverse effect on labor mobility that pension plans now have. To a limited extent this problem is solved without vesting in the case of industry-wide collectively bargained plans which cover all the employees in the industry whoever their employer may be. But, as we have seen, only 13 per cent of the employees under pension coverage had this protection as late as 1954.

Cost of Vesting

The principal obstacle in the way of vesting provisions is, of course, the increased expense of providing such benefits. In the face of the large number of unpredictable factors in the cost of vesting, it is difficult to give any accurate figures on what it actually does cost. It has been estimated that vesting can as much as double the cost of a pension plan. But this much may be said with certainty: the increase in cost as a result of vesting will be in proportion to the labor turnover. Vesting may, therefore, be undertaken more readily in those industries which have a relatively small labor turnover, but this is hardly an answer to those who wish to secure greater labor mobility than the pension plans seem to permit. To evaluate the beneficial effects of pension programs it would be very desirable to have statistics on labor turnover since so many pension funds provide benefits only for those employees who remain under a given plan for a relatively long period of time. While such data are extremely sketchy, OASI records provide some helpful information. They show that in each of the four years 1944 to 1948 from 25 to 30 per cent of all covered employees were employed *in more than one industry*.[35] Dan M. McGill, executive director of the Huebner Foundation for Insurance Education, makes this comment on the OASI figures:

Presumably the movement from employer to employer would be even higher. This is indicated by the fact that within the steel industry in 1947, 38 per cent of all employees worked for at least two different employers, while in

[35] Dan M. McGill, *Pensions: Problems and Trends,* Huebner Foundation for Insurance Education, University of Pennsylvania, Irwin, Homewood, Illinois, 1955, p. 33.

the same year 40 per cent of all employees in the automobile industry worked for two or more employers. In the age bracket where job mobility should be at its lowest — age 45 to 65 — 23.4 per cent of the workers changed employers at least once in 1948.[36]

Reliable conclusions are difficult to draw from these statistics on labor turnover because adequate allowance must be made for the fact that the same workers — marginal employees — may be changing employers from year to year. The rate of turnover is also distorted in the OASI records by the inclusion of certain industries and occupations having unusually high rates of labor mobility, such as the construction industry, farm workers and others. But if in each of the four years included in the OASI statistics as many as 25 per cent of all covered workers were employed in more than one industry, how many employees may we expect to fulfill a twenty-year continuous employment requirement? McGill estimates that, because of lack of vesting, "no more than 40 per cent and certainly no more than 50 per cent of employees *presently covered* under private pension plans will ever receive a cash benefit from the plan."[37] He adds that unless vesting provisions are liberalized, it is unlikely that more than 20 to 25 per cent of persons 65 and over will ever receive benefits from private pension plans.

There is no question that private pension plans do have an effect on labor turnover. The January 1957 issue of the *Monthly Labor Review* reported the findings of a study of labor turnover in six areas based on data for the twelve months preceding June 30, 1955. This study showed that turnover rates were notably lower — for both younger and older workers — in firms that had private pension plans than in those that did not. It also revealed that job seekers 45 and over stood better chances of employment in companies that did not have pension plans and, further, that firms which did provide pension coverage hired older workers for protected jobs at only one-third the rate of younger workers seeking similar jobs. Pension plans were found to have a very definite effect on hiring policy: ". . . hires of workers aged 45 and over constituted 14 per cent of all hires where a plan was in effect, as against 25 per cent where there was no coverage. The same pattern applied uniformly in all six areas for which data were available."[38]

[36] *Ibid.*, p. 34.
[37] *Ibid.*, p. 40.
[38] John I. Saks, "The Older Worker — II, Status in the Labor Market," *Monthly Labor Review*, January 1957, pp. 15, 20, 21.

Although these are the best figures available on this subject, this type of analysis is open to the objection that the enterprises having pension plans tend to be more stable and probably have an otherwise more favorable labor policy. A more reliable comparison would be one made between the hires and separations in the same businesses before and after pension plans were instituted. Even so, it will always be difficult to rule out extraneous factors affecting hires and separations.

A concrete example provided by one pension expert illustrates what vesting may mean in terms of added cost. In a hypothetical pension program covering 610 employees, costing $166,700 a year and providing vesting on a basis of benefits of one per cent a year, the additional cost for 25 per cent deferred vesting of accrued benefits is $4,600. Under the same terms, the additional cost for 50 per cent deferred vesting of accrued benefits would be $9,200, and for 100 per cent deferred vesting, $18,500.[39]

RESTRICTIONS ON PENSION RIGHTS

"Restrictions" on an employee's right to a pension may be distinguished from eligibility requirements in that they refer to conditions which may arise *after* retirement. A possible exception to this definition is the restrictive requirement stating that membership in the plan is not to be construed as a guarantee of continuing employment. Many pension plans also contain a "competitor" clause which provides for forfeiture of pension rights after retirement if the retiree works in a competing firm or engages in any activity in competition with the employer from whose pension plan he expects benefit payments. Some plans provide employers with full discretion to suspend or terminate a pension for so-called "misconduct." The further definition of "misconduct" is left to the discretion of the pension committee or the firm's board of directors.

Multi-employer pension plans have a slightly different pattern of restrictive provisions, as may be expected from the nature of this type of program. In many such plans the pensioners are prohibited from engaging in any employment within the same industry either as employee or employer. Other restrictive conditions include contingencies as broadly stated as "fluctuation of income to the fund due to unemployment conditions."

In the New York State Banking study similar grounds for suspension, modification or revocation of benefits were found in more than one-third of the 643 plans analyzed. About 10 per cent of the plans prohibited re-

[39] Bomar, *op. cit.*, pp. 185 and 196.

employment by the same company or, in the case of industry-wide plans, in the same industry, while more than 20 per cent prohibited employment with a competitor or activities detrimental to the interests of the company. A few conditioned the payment of the pension upon the absence of misconduct by the employee. In addition, a small percentage (5.5 per cent) provided for reduction of the pension in proportion to salary received from other employment, other benefits received from the plan, increase in social security benefits, and benefits received under public programs. All of the plans contained a provision that benefits may be suspended upon termination of the plan itself or the employer's contributions, or upon failure of the employee to furnish required information or to comply with other procedural requirements.[40]

The reason for the restriction on employment with a competitor may be that employers do not want to make it possible for competitors to employ retired workers at lower wages. They argue that since the retired employee is receiving a pension from one employer, he might be willing to work for another company at less than the going rate. This contention ought to be tested for whatever basis it may have in fact. Furthermore, such a provision is not consistent with the developing policy of considering pensions to be deferred compensation actually earned by the employee. At any rate, the existence of this restriction in a pension plan ought certainly to be classed as a benefit to the employer in any attempt to determine whether or not a pension is a mere gratuity on the part of an employer. Court decisions have already demonstrated that "misconduct" provisions will be tested according to the "rule of reason" should a claim of capricious or arbitrary denial of pension rights be brought into court.[41]

Analysis of these and other escape provisions clearly indicates that membership in a pension plan may give far less assurance of continuity of benefits for the retired employee than may appear at first sight. Wide coverage of employees under pension programs is a matter of fairly recent experience, and during the life of most of the plans economic conditions have been very favorable. In a period of prolonged depression, however, it is questionable how many employees would realize the expected benefits from existing pension funds.

[40] New York State Banking Department, *op. cit.*, pp. 113 and 114.
[41] Clark v. New England Tel. & Tel. Co., 229 Mass. 1, 118 N. E. 348 (1918) (death benefits); Wilson v. Rudolph Wurlitzer Co., 48 Ohio App. 450, 194 N. E. 441 (1934); George A. Fuller Co. v. Brown, 15 F. 2d 672 (4th Cir. 1926) (bonus); Forrish v. Kennedy, Pa., 105 A. 2d 67 (1954) (pension); Montgomery Ward & Co. v. Reich, 131 Colo. 407, 282 P. 2d 1091 (1955) (bonus).

COMMUNICATION OF PENSION PROVISIONS

One basic reason why a pension program should be thought of as creating a fiduciary responsibility is that participants in the plan rely on pension promises in planning for old age. Examination of many pension plans shows quite clearly that the typical pension plan is subject to devastating effects from severe economic reverses. Employers have felt that safeguards such as the various escape clauses described in the preceding pages are necessary, and it is unquestionably true that many of these provisions, if not all, provide an "out" for the employer who finds it extremely difficult or impossible to carry out the intended benefits of his program. These protective devices cannot be placed under a blanket condemnation inasmuch as the accrued obligations of a really effective pension plan can become so enormous as to subject an employer to possible bankruptcy.

At the same time, it is not fair to allow the employer to reap the benefits of a pension program through the device of holding out exaggerated promises of economic security. This raises the problem of publication and disclosure of pension provisions and assets, a subject of great concern in pension investigations and of criticism of the pension movement. It is simply a question of communicating to the employee an accurate picture of what he may expect a pension program to do for him. While the objective may be simple, its execution may be quite difficult since a pension program is often a very complicated matter. The New York State Insurance Department study points out that many employers and trustees of multi-employer plans have failed to inform workers about important limitations of the plans:

> Where given to employees, such information was frequently cloaked in elaborate or legalistic terminology or in such ambiguous language that even persons skilled in the law or with special competence in pension matters would have difficulty in understanding it. As a result, employees were often lulled into a false sense of security.[42]

The problem of communication is often complicated by poor draftsmanship in drawing up the pension document and by its complex terms. The provisions of a plan are usually communicated to the employees by means of a booklet which the New York Insurance investigators found in many cases to be oversimplified and to give an exaggerated impression of security. The lack of a guarantee of pension benefits, the fact that they

[42] *Private Employee Benefit Plans,* p. 102.

are payable only out of available funds and that an employer's liability may be limited only to past contributions, are often omitted or glossed over. The investigation disclosed this sorry state of affairs:

Only 84 out of 188 plans analyzed for this purpose clearly stated that pension benefits were not promised or guaranteed. Contrary to the facts, 70 plans out of 188 expressly stated or implied that the benefits were guaranteed or promised without reservation. An additional 34 plans were completely silent on the conditional nature of the pension "promise."[43]

In the many cases where pension payments are limited to available funds it is extremely important for the plan participant to know the financial condition of the fund.

Reports of the official and semiofficial investigations and hearings on private pension plans, despite some disagreement upon nearly all points, have come close to unanimous agreement that public disclosure of the conditions and financial status of pension plans should be required by law. While opinions differ on the extent of this disclosure, as, for instance, whether or not the trustees should be required to reveal the composition of their portfolios, a balance sheet of pension assets would seem to be a minimal requirement for any effective disclosure of pension plan operations. Such a regulation would go far in itself to promote the actuarial soundness and the balancing of current assets with accrued liabilities that pension experts have been urging for some time. At least in some of the extreme cases of misrepresentation such as those uncovered by the New York Insurance Department study, a court might be justified in employing the doctrine of estoppel to support a claim by a pensioner who can show that he has relied on the promises in a pension plan booklet. One of many such cases turned up by the insurance investigation was described as follows:

Despite the provisions of the pension plan that all contributions by the employer are "voluntary" on its part and non-contractual and that "there shall be no liability on the part of the company for failure to make any contributions to the trust," the booklet contains the following unqualified statement:

"TRUST FUND ASSURES PAYMENT OF BENEFITS.
To carry out the provisions of the plans, X Company has set up a trust fund of which the Y Trust Company is Trustee. The Company will make contributions into this trust fund in the *amounts determined by the actuaries* as being necessary to maintain the plan on a sound financial basis and assure the payment of all benefits under the plan."[44]

[43] *Ibid.*, p. 105.
[44] *Ibid.*, p. 108.

A representation as misleading as this, especially if the plan document itself has not been made available to the prospective pensioners, should provide an excellent case for the argument that the pension plan should be required to pay the employee the promised benefit despite the fact that escape clauses in the plan might discharge the employer from pension liability.

A mere discrepancy between the plan and the booklet, however, would probably not afford sufficient grounds for a successful action on the part of an employee. In the case of *Gallo* v. *Howard Stores Corp.*,[45] an insurance contract governing a pension plan expressly stated that an employee could retire early (before 65) only with the employer's consent, but the booklet explaining the pension plan did not mention that early retirement was conditioned in this way. In a suit to enforce his alleged right to retire before age 65 without the employer's consent, an employee claimed that the distribution of the booklet and his payment of contributions thereafter established a new contract. He claimed, further, that the publishing of the booklet estopped the employer from setting up the original insurance contract as a bar to his claim. The Court of Appeals for the Third Circuit upheld a lower court in finding that the employee had not proved his claim. The booklet, it said, would not lead a reasonable man to assume that the employer intended to amend the original contract. The court held, moreover, that since the employee had been warned before leaving his job that the employer's consent was necessary, he could not claim that he had changed his position to his detriment by relying on the employer's representation in the booklet.

In cases of this sort, if the employee is specifically told of the contract provision, or has a copy of the plan or contract, or if the booklet states that the provisions of the plan or contract will govern in case of discrepancy with the booklet, the employee would probably not be able to recover.

A recent action in which an employee successfully urged promissory estoppel was *Frebank Co.* v. *White*.[46] In this case the employee alleged a verbal promise by his employer of a Christmas bonus of $5,000 to $6,000. Furthermore, when the employee was negotiating an FHA loan, the employer signed a statement to the effect that the minimum annual bonus was $4,000. However, when Christmas came, the amount the employee received was only $200. The employer's defense was that the minimum

45 145 F. Supp. 909, 250 F. 2d 37 (3d Cir. 1957).
46 152 Cal. App. 2d 522, 313 P. 2d 633 (Dist. Ct. App. 1957).

bonus set forth in his signed statement was a gratuity and not binding. But the court held that the employer's conversations were either a promise of a bonus or a misrepresentation to induce the employee to remain with the company. In allowing recovery for the plaintiff, the court said that a promissory estoppel is a promise which the promisor should reasonably expect to induce action or forbearance of a definite and substantial character, and which does induce such action or forbearance, and that it is binding if injustice can be avoided only by enforcement of the promise.

FINANCING THE PENSION PROGRAM

As we have already seen, the methods of financing pension plans may be roughly divided into insured and noninsured types of funding. The noninsured type has been called an employer-managed fund. This term is not entirely accurate since the actual management of fund assets of noninsured plans is usually in the hands of a corporate trustee appointed by the employer. But here we shall use the term "noninsured plans" to indicate all pension plans which are financed by any method other than insurance. In the case of the so-called "insured plans," the pension assets are not segregated but are made a part of the undivided assets of the insurance company and invested along with funds from other sources in a single portfolio.

In this study we shall discuss only the general investment policies of the insurance companies and bypass a detailed analysis of the various types of insurance plans which have been devised to finance pension programs. As we are interested primarily in the question of control of the large blocks of capital represented by the pension funds, it is sufficient in considering this question to know what part of insurance company assets are derived from pension programs as sources. But to complete the picture of control of noninsured pension financing, the following description of the common methods used by both types of funds will be useful.

METHODS OF FINANCING

Probably the oldest of the noninsured methods is the so-called *pay-as-you-go* plan. Under this type of plan, in which the employer usually reserves the right to reduce or discontinue payments, pension benefits are paid on an informal year-to-year basis. Pay-as-you-go plans are conducted with varying degrees of formality, but under all of them benefit payments are a current charge against operating expenses and the benefits may be expected to continue only as long as the employer is able to meet payments as they fall due unless, of course, the rights of the employees are protected by a collective bargaining agreement. The importance of this point is obvious when we realize that such a method of financing will have a relatively low cost at the beginning when few pensioners are claiming benefits but that, as time goes on and the number of pensioners builds up, the current costs of such a plan will greatly increase. For this reason pension experts frown on this type of financing for companies of larger size.

The difference between the so-called formal and informal plans is that in the first type the employer makes a formal communication of the provisions of the plan to his employees; in the second, he may leave the pension program no more fully enunciated than in a memorandum in the company's files, the contents of which may not be known to the employees. But in either instance the employer may promise the employees definite pension or retirement benefits. The employer may also draw up a modified pay-as-you-go plan under which he may accumulate a partial reserve either on his books of account or in a segregated fund.

The *balance sheet* or *book-reserve* method of funding is a step nearer to the true funding procedure. Under this system, reserves are maintained only on the employer's books and may be accumulated by regular additions or any other method the employer may choose. In effect, under this kind of financial arrangement the pension fund is invested in the employer's assets, his plant, equipment, inventory, and so on. This fund may be maintained with an eye to an actuarial computation of prospective obligations and in such cases it is credited annually with an estimated rate of interest. The reserve balance is regulated by actuarial valuation of obligations, and pension payments are charged against this reserve. While some pension plans are financed in this manner, their number is kept down by exclusion from immediate tax-exemption privileges.

Among the noninsured types of plans the *trusteed pension plan* is by far the most common. Under such an arrangement the pension funds are turned over to a third party, other than an insurance company, to conserve and invest against the future obligations of the pension program. The trustees may be a group of individuals or, more commonly, a bank or trust company. The trust indenture governing this arrangement will spell out the responsibilities to be borne by the plan committee and by the trustees. The divisions of responsibility are so various, however, that it is difficult to generalize about them. At one extreme the employer or his committee may assume full responsibility for making investments, disbursements and collections and, at the other, the trustee may perform all of these functions and be subject to the direction of the employer or committee only in the designation of the beneficiaries and the amounts they are to receive.

The New York Insurance Department study notes a recent tendency among larger employers to use a combination of insured and trust plans: "For example, the insured plan may be used for benefits accruing from current service and the trust fund for past-service benefits. The trust fund approach may also be used to provide a cost-of-living supplement to an insured plan."[47]

In the most comprehensive survey of pension statistics published to date, the Securities and Exchange Commission reported that 39 per cent of the companies filing reports with the Commission had noninsured funded plans while 29 per cent had insured plans. Only 6 per cent of the companies indicated that their plans were unfunded, or on a pay-as-you-go basis, while 26 per cent had no retirement plans at all.[48] Further evidence of the widespread use of noninsured plans is provided by the Senate subcommittee report of 1956, which states: "Of 12,500,000 covered employees, 3,915,000 were under insured plans, about 1 million were under pay-as-you-go plans, and the remainder, 7,585,000, under funded trusteed plans."[49]

TRUSTEED PLANS AND THE TRUST INDENTURE

According to the SEC, private pension and retirement funds amounted to $33.3 billion in 1957.[50] Of this sum $19.3 billion, or 58 per cent, was in the hands of corporate noninsured funds. Looking back to September 1955, the New York State Banking Department estimated that banks in its state held $7.5 billion in pension and other welfare funds and that this constituted almost three-fifths of all such trusteed funds in the United States.[51] Furthermore, the funds held by New York banks had been growing at a rate of over $1 billion a year. The position of the bank trustee in

[47] *Private Employee Benefit Plans,* p. 87.
[48] *Survey of Corporate Pension Funds, 1951–1954,* 1956, p. 3.
[49] Senate Report No. 1734, p. 48.
[50] Based on statistics developed by the SEC to update *Survey of Corporate Pension Funds, 1951–1954,* November 1958.
[51] New York State Banking Department, *op. cit.,* p. i.

the pension picture is aptly described by the Senate Subcommittee on Welfare and Pension Funds as follows:

> Some 80 to 90 per cent of all pension plans of this type use a bank as corporate trustee to hold and invest the funds in accordance with the trust agreement. In most other cases a committee appointed by the employer performs this function. In some cases — a minority — the bank merely serves as custodian of the fund's securities or other holdings and has no discretion as to investments, the employer directing all investments.[52]

Authority of the Trustee

The powers and responsibilities of a pension trustee are usually established by an indenture or deed of trust in accordance with the terms under which the plan is administered. In many pension plans, especially those that are collectively bargained, the plan requires that a corporate trustee be placed in charge of the funds. A trustee usually holds title to the assets of the pension fund, which may consist of securities, cash and other property. The amount of investment authority given to the trustee varies from plan to plan, but according to the Banking Department study, nearly seven out of ten of the plans in New York State gave full authority to the trustee. In most of the other plans studied the trustee had either severely limited or no authority over the funds, being allowed to invest them only with the approval or under the direction of the plan's administrators.[53] Even in the plans in which the trustee is given full investment authority, a large amount of residual power remains in the hands of the pension committee which appoints the trustee. This committee, usually the employer or his representative or representatives, will almost always have the authority to change the trustee at any time.

It is certainly the most common arrangement, however, to give the corporate trustee full investment powers in the management of pension funds. This arrangement seems to be both logical and efficient since by this means the pension committee is able to call upon some of the best investment experience available. Moreover, a well-planned and fruitful investment policy is of the greatest importance to the success of a pension fund, for the ability of a trusteed pension plan to fulfill its promises rests to a large degree on the prudent conservation of accumulated funds. The plan may be economical in the long run in direct proportion to the shrewdness of its investment management.

[52] Senate Report No. 1734, p. 48.
[53] New York State Banking Department, *op. cit.*, p. 30.

Provisions of Indenture

In the usual trust indenture, the trustee undertakes to receive any contributions paid into the pension fund in cash or in other acceptable property, together with the income derived from it, according to the terms of the agreement with the pension committee. The fund is furthermore held in the hands of the trustee without distinction between principal and income and without liability for the payment of interest. The trustee does not undertake the responsibility for the collection of contributions to the plan or for the distribution of the trust funds to such persons as may be the beneficiaries of the fund. Once the pension committee has authorized distribution of pension benefits, the trustee's liability ceases.

The corporate trustee usually surrounds itself with immunities spelled out in the indenture. This provides that no part of the trust fund is to be used for, or diverted to, purposes other than the exclusive benefit of the members under the plan or their beneficiaries. Further, the indenture may state that in distributing benefits as authorized by the committee, the trustee may accept the direction of the committee as a certification that such payment complies with the provisions of the indenture and that no further investigation is required.

In the enumeration of powers given to the corporate trustee, such provision is made, in most instances, for the management and administration of trust funds and securities that in effect trustees have powers over the trust corpus amounting to the control that a private individual would have over his own investment portfolio. A complete text of the investment powers of corporate trustees will be found in Appendix B, but in the present discussion it is worthwhile to note some of the principal provisions. The financial trustees are usually given the following powers in the standard form of trust agreement:

To purchase or subscribe for any securities or other property and to retain in trust such securities or other property.

To sell for cash or on credit, to grant options, convert, redeem, exchange for other securities or other property, or otherwise to dispose of any security or other property at any time held by it.

To exercise any conversion privilege and/or subscription right available in connection with any securities or other property at any time held by it . . .

To exercise, personally or by general or by limited power of attorney, any right, including the right to vote, appurtenant to any securities or other property held by it at any time.

To borrow money from any lender including the trustee in its individual capacity in such amounts and upon such terms and conditions as shall be deemed advisable or proper to carry out the purposes of the trust and to pledge any securities or other property for the repayment of such loan.[54]

Other powers of the corporate trustee include the management, administration, operation, leasing for any number of years, development, improvement, repair, alteration, mortgaging, etc., of any real property in the name of the trustee or of a nominee, with or without the addition of words indicating that such property is held in a fiduciary capacity. To make, renew or extend mortgages is also within the purview of the trustee. The corporate trustee may also hold part or all of the capital trust fund invested, or may form corporations and create trusts to hold title to any securities or other property, and may make, execute and deliver any and all deeds, leases, mortgages, conveyances, etc., which may be necessary for the accomplishment of the enumerated powers.

Checks on the Trustee

While these powers may be, and often are, completely untrammeled and left to the discretion of the trustee, it is not unusual for the pension committee to retain some control of the investment policy of the corporate trustee. This control may take the form of a veto power giving the committee the power to disapprove retention of any particular asset by the trustee. The corporate trustee in such cases is usually protected by a provision that "the trustee shall not be liable for any loss sustained in connection with any such disapproved asset."

Another possible arrangement is to make the exercise of certain enumerated powers of the financial trustee subject to the written approval of the committee. In such cases provision is made that the trustee shall not be held liable for any loss sustained by the trust fund by reason of the failure of the committee to approve any action proposed by the trustee under any of the powers granted in the instrument.

Still another arrangement provides that the corporate trustee shall be directed by the pension committee in all its functions. The instrument may read that "the trustee shall be under no duty to question any direction of the committee, to review any securities or other property held in the trust fund, or to make suggestions to the committee with respect to the exercise or non-exercise of the said powers." (In at least one standard form of indenture, used by one of the largest banks, this provision *must* be used when a security is purchased of the company for whose employ-

[54] See Article Fourth of specimen form of Trust Agreement, Appendix B.

ees the pension plan is designed.) In such cases the trustee is really a mere depository for the trust fund, and provision is then made that the trustee is under no liability for any loss resulting from an action taken by it in accordance with the direction of the pension committee. Further, the terms of the trust may limit investment to the so-called "legal lists," that is, securities approved by state statute for purchase by trustees and fiduciaries.

Exculpatory Clauses

In the course of the previous account of the powers of financial trustees, we have noted certain clauses in the indenture designed to protect the trustee. A further attempt to protect the trustee from extensive liability is found in this typical wording: "No person other than the company or the committee may require an accounting or bring any action against the trustee with respect to the trust or its action as trustee."

With regard to disbursements from the funds in favor of beneficiaries, the trustee disclaims all liability and seeks to protect itself by a clause in the indenture to the following effect: "Neither the trustee nor any member of the committee shall be liable hereunder except for its own negligence or willful misconduct."

Another provision in the trust indenture aimed at insulating the trustee from action by third parties or beneficiaries refers to any action or proceeding for the settlement of accounts or questions of construction which may arise under the indenture: ". . . the only necessary parties defendant to such action shall be the Company and the Committee, except that the trustee may, if it so elects, bring in as parties defendant any other person or persons."

These and other exculpatory clauses, if upheld by the courts, provide the trustees of pension funds with a sweeping immunity. They bring to mind the Federal Trust Indenture Act of 1939.[55] This act was aimed at the frequent use of trust indentures which failed to provide security holders with essential protections and absolved trustees from minimum obligations. Some of its provisions could with profit be incorporated into a statute applicable to pension trusts. The act requires that the trustee be free from conflicting interests; imposes high standards of conduct; provides for reports and notices by the trustee to security holders; prohibits impairment of the security holder's rights to sue individually; and

[55] Trust Indenture Act of 1939, 15 U. S. C. § 77aaa–bbb (1952).

requires the maintenance of a list of security holders which may be used by the security holders themselves to communicate with each other regarding their rights. The application of such provisions to the pension situation is obvious.

The Trust Indenture Act was thought to be necessary because the courts upheld many exculpatory clauses. Similarly, the New York legislature sought to prohibit in the Decedent Estate Law any provision attempting to exculpate lack of due care.[56] Certainly the "prudent man" rule of investment, discussed in Chapter 5, exacts a higher standard of care than that to which the financial trustees commonly admit in their indentures, and there is no reason for a lower standard here than in the other aspects of a trustee's business.

Obligations of the Trustee

A provision in the trust indenture such as a requirement that the trustee make an accounting only to the company or pension committee clearly seeks to make the trustee and the company or committee the only parties in interest to any litigation which may arise over the conduct of the trust. Such provisions raise the vital question whether or not this kind of arrangement, now universally designated as a "trust," is really a trust in fact or a mere contractual agreement the provisions of which govern the rights of the intended beneficiaries of the fund. These so-called indentures have many if not all of the earmarks of an agreement which would establish a true trust. The document is so referred to in its text and the custodian of the fund is termed a trustee. Further evidence that these arrangements are thought of as constituting a trust is indicated by such a provision as the following, which is always to be found in the trust indenture:

> It shall be impossible, at any time prior to the satisfaction of all liabilities with respect to the members under the Plan or their beneficiaries, for any part of the Trust Fund . . . to be used for, or diverted to, purposes other than for the exclusive benefit of the members under the Plan or their beneficiaries.[57]

This same question was raised during the Senate subcommittee hearings when the United States Steel pension fund was under discussion. The fund in this case is the result of a negotiated collective bargaining agreement under which the Steel Corporation agreed with the union to

---

[56] N. Y. Decedent Estate Law § 125.1.
[57] See Article Third of Trust Agreement, Appendix B.

pay a certain level of benefits to its employees. Enders M. Voorhees, as spokesman for the company, made the point before the subcommittee that U. S. Steel did not, under the bargaining agreement, have to set up a pension fund. Its contractual requirement was merely to pay the benefits stipulated in the contract. The trust fund was established merely as a convenient way of providing for the pensions that the company could foresee it would have to pay. On this point the following colloquy took place between Paul J. Cotter, chief counsel and staff director for the subcommittee, and Mr. Voorhees:

Mr. Cotter.   Is that an irrevocable trust?

Mr. Voorhees.   As far as the United States Steel Corporation is concerned, it is irrevocable. We can't put a finger on that money.

Mr. Cotter.   Is it certain that those employees, who reach 65 after working a given number of years, become eligible for retirement or for benefits out of that trust?

Mr. Voorhees.   I think that depends upon our contractual relationship insofar as the union is concerned, sir. Whatever the contract relation is, we live up to it.

Mr. Cotter.   But there is nothing outside the contractual relationship which requires United States Steel, as a result of setting up this trust, to pay a pension to an employee who has worked 35 years and is 65 years old?

Mr. Voorhees.   If the employee retires while the contract is in effect, he gets his pension.

*   *   *

Mr. Cotter.   I was trying to speak of employees without respect to the union. I was wondering whether there is any direct obligation between the company and the employee as the result of setting up this trust.

Mr. Voorhees.   No, sir.

Mr. Cotter.   What is meant is that the money is put irrevocably out of the hands of United States Steel?

Mr. Voorhees.   It is for the use of employees.

*   *   *

Mr. Cotter.   Do they have any type of interest? Do they have some equitable interest, not a particular interest, but a joint interest in the fund?

Mr. Voorhees.   I can't see that they have because the obligation first is on the trust fund — that is, the Pennsylvania Corp. — and if the funds there are not sufficient to pay the contractual relationship with the union, then the obligation rests on United States Steel Corp.[58]

From this and other comments made by Mr. Voorhees, we may conclude that the position of U. S. Steel in this matter is that the employees

[58] Hearings on S. Res. 40, Part 3, pp. 1171 and 1172.

of the company have no legal interest in the pension fund for two reasons: (1) they were not direct parties to the collective bargaining agreement, nor (2) are they common-law beneficiaries of the trust because the corporation on its own motion established the trust as a convenient way of meeting its own future obligations. Furthermore, it would seem that the only reason why the funds are irrevocably separated from the control of the company is to make the company pension plan conform to the requirements of the income tax law.

Thus, the status of the U. S. Steel pension trust, as described by Mr. Voorhees, is anomalous in the truest sense of the word, for this is a trust without a beneficiary. According to the company representative, the employees have no equitable interest in the trust fund. U. S. Steel "can't put a finger on that money" and so it can hardly be the beneficiary. Though called a trust, it would seem that the company is attempting to treat the reserves set aside for pensions more like a fund set up to take advantage of the tax laws which favor pensions.

What U. S. Steel is attempting by this is to retain complete control of the trust fund by maintaining that all its obligations to pay pensions arise out of and are contained in the collective bargaining agreement.

Yet let us suppose that the so-called trust is seriously mismanaged or looted, a thing quite unlikely in the case of U. S. Steel but quite possible in a smaller fund. With the disappearance or shrinking of the trust fund would go the pension expectations of the employees. The company could plead inability to pay on its promise to the union or even declare itself bankrupt. The point becomes clear that the operations of the trust vitally affect the future security of the employees since they come to rely on it. Furthermore, the trust money is in fact set aside for them, and through their representatives at the bargaining table they have undoubtedly given up the advantage of a pay increase in order to gain the economic advantages of tax exemption and long-term investment. Though no case has yet been decided on this point, a court might well declare that this kind of trust is a true trust.[59] The result would be that the employees have equitable interests which they could enforce in court. Certainly the doctrines of implied and resulting trusts extend far enough to cover such a situation, though it should not be necessary to invoke them. In

---

[59] The nearest any court has come to deciding this question was in *Hurd* v. *Illinois*, discussed in Chapter 6 (p. 178). In this case the question was only referred to by way of *dictum*. See also Chapter 6 (p. 174) for a discussion of the *Booth* case on union pension funds.

this and in similar cases the employer does not admit that his employees have an equitable interest, but in every other way he behaves as a trustee.

If the courts should refuse to recognize this theory, however, the collective bargaining agreement would be the sole bulwark guaranteeing pension rights. U. S. Steel, for example, takes the position that if there is no contract with the union there is no legal obligation to pay pensions.

To sum up, then, we have noted that for about 60 per cent of the employees covered by so-called pension trusts the pension plan is a result of collective bargaining. Furthermore, many of these plans expressly stipulate that the form in which the fund will be reserved will be that of a pension trust. But many other collectively bargained plans, such as that of U. S. Steel, contain no such provision. Several million additional employees covered by pension trusts are under plans voluntarily initiated and set up in this form by the employer. If the logic of the U. S. Steel Corporation, as expressed before the Senate subcommittee, is correct, then there is no equitable interest in the funds which can be claimed by the employees. It is a safe prediction, however, that by whatever logic the courts may choose to travel, they will not conclude that the employer may reject his own promise to provide pensions, at least in cases where a pension fund is already established.

Summary

In the typical pension trust the worker's hopes for security are based on three documents — a labor agreement providing for the pension plan, the plan itself, and an agreement between the plan administrators and a trustee of the funds.

Union-negotiated contracts usually specify a level of retirement benefits and require that pensions once begun be continued. Enforcement by the union of its contract presents the best guarantee of pension rights, but even these agreements leave something to be desired. The union contract may or may not require full funding of past and future service liabilities. Often enough it does not. Vesting provisions are less frequent for employees who are union members. In any case, the negotiated agreement does not last longer than five years and seldom runs that long. Finally, about a third of all covered employees are not under negotiated contracts.

The pension plans themselves contain inherent limitations on the security they offer. First, nearly all plans limit the employer's liability to the extent of the funds reserved for pension payment, and not all plans are fully funded. Second, it is quite common for the employer to reserve the right to determine the amounts of periodic contributions. Rights are also reserved to terminate, modify or amend the plan. Third, the actual receiving of pension benefits is often dependent upon restrictive conditions. Fourth, most plans are administered by the employers alone and in only a minority of cases are employees represented on the pension committee or board which passes on eligibility requirements, violations of restrictive conditions, and so forth. And usually the plan contains a clause stating that the board's decision in all matters is final.

Taken together, these contract provisions leave the employee very much dependent upon the continued solvency and good will of the employer. Conditions written into the plan allow the employer plenty of room for escape. It may be argued that more binding commitments upon the employer might put him in danger of bankruptcy because pension liabilities can become enormous. But whatever the merits of this argument, there is no excuse for failing to inform the employee of the conditional nature of his pension prospects.

Similarly, the trust indenture contains sweeping escape clauses making it impossible for the beneficiaries to call the financial trustee to account for stewardship. The trustee is protected from a charge of anything short of gross negligence in handling funds and cannot be blamed if reserves are inadequate to meet liabilities.

This is the way pension trusts are. In the chapters immediately following we shall see why.

CHAPTER 4

OBJECTIVES, THEORY

AND PRACTICE

Employer Policies

Employer Objectives

Union Attitudes and Objectives

Investment Policies of Financial Trustees

Passive Role of the Beneficiaries

Our preoccupation throughout this study is with the effect of pension trusts upon the ownership and control of productive property in the United States, but an adequate understanding of these problems cannot be gained without an examination of how these trusts operate. Similarly, to understand their impact upon the capital structure of the United States we need to know what purposes the pension trusts are designed to serve and what policies have been adopted to serve these ends.

In considering the objectives of pension planning it would be valuable to determine what the objectives of all of the interested parties are and ought to be, including the opinions of the economists and the sociologists on this subject. We shall discuss the impact of the pension movement upon our society later and examine here only the objectives as seen by the parties most concerned with the operation of pension plans: the employer, the employee or his union, and the fund manager or financial trustee. Our attention will be further concentrated on the policy considerations that bear directly upon the acquisition and deployment of pension fund assets; those problems which are of greater interest to the labor consultant and the sociologist will be treated only insofar as they have a bearing upon the ebb and flow of the capital represented by pension trusts.

EMPLOYER POLICIES

Thus far we have seen something of the history and rise of the pension movement. We have noted that in the early period such benefits were widely considered to be a move on the part of the employer to share some of his returns with his employees. Pensions were regarded as a free gift of the employer, an expression of his largess. Of late we have come to recognize that management also derives definite advantages from a pension program, yet it is extremely difficult to give a concise and accurate description of the motivation in providing these benefits. To be sure, the desire to do "the right thing" by the employee is not absent today, whatever may have been the attitude of the employer in the past. Still, business being what it is, it would be naive to think that this is the sole or even the principal motivating force behind the employer's interest in a pension program.

Advantages which can accrue to the employer run a wide gamut. Among the benefits he derives from a pension program are the undoubted increased efficiency in orderly retirement of superannuated personnel as well as the much more indefinite "improvement of good will." A well-devised and established pension plan may also help to develop and retain a superior work force and to serve as a means of reducing strikes and promoting loyalty to the company.

Conflicting Concepts of Pension Programs

As early as 1912 pension experts argued that

... from the standpoint of the whole system of social economy no employer has a right to engage men in any occupation that exhausts the individual's industrial life in 10, 20, or 40 years; and then leave the remnant floating on society at large as a derelict at sea.[1]

[1] Lee Welling Squiers, *Old Age Dependency in the United States,* Macmillan, New York, 1912, p. 272.

The same philosophy was espoused by the President's Steel Industry Board in 1949. But if this "human depreciation" view of pensions has been adopted to any extent by employers, it has escaped the notice of most of the reliable pension commentators.[2] In general these observers have explicitly rejected the Steel Board's attempt to compare the worker to a machine which needs to be cared for when its useful life is over. In arguing this point before the President's Steel Industry Board, Enders M. Voorhees, chairman of the finance committee, U. S. Steel Corporation, expressed his company's view as follows:

U. S. Steel takes care of and replenishes its materials and machinery because it owns them, just as you and I care for our homes and clothes. Machines are not paid current wages which they can freely elect to spend or to save . . . U. S. Steel "cares for" — cooperates with — its employees by paying money to them representing full value of services rendered, as judged by the public as customers.[3]

An alternative idea has been advanced that pensions ought to be considered "deferred wages." Since pension payments must ultimately be regarded as a cost of doing business, it may seem to make little difference on what theory a pension program is grounded. But both the "human depreciation" and the "deferred wage" theories involve the issue of who shall control the operations of the pension program. If the ruling concept is that a pension represents a depreciation cost, it is the concern and the prerogative of the employer to decide how to meet that cost. If pensions are considered a deferred wage, then it becomes the legitimate concern of the worker to see that his expectancy is safeguarded and preserved. Management has recognized that the pension is a cost of doing business, but it has not embraced the view that it should assume the responsibility for old-age provision. Nor has management appeared ready to admit all the consequences of considering pension payments as a deferred wage. In his testimony before the Senate Subcommittee on Welfare and Pension Funds, Mr. Voorhees said:

In the first place, as a service is performed, there is a question of cost, and, therefore, the cost of the product that the employee works on, should bear that cost.

[2] Rainard B. Robbins, *Pensions in Industry*, 1952 (mimeographed); Dan M. McGill, *Pensions: Problems and Trends*, Huebner Foundation for Insurance Education, University of Pennsylvania, Irwin, Homewood, Illinois, 1955; Charles L. Dearing, *Industrial Pensions*, The Brookings Institution, Washington, 1954.

[3] The Steel Industry Board, "Report to the President of the United States on the Labor Dispute in the Basic Steel Industry," September 10, 1949, p. 10.

In the second place, insofar as that employee is concerned, you don't know whether he is going to eventually get a pension or not, but based on the actuarial amounts, the actuarial determination, some of those people who are working presently are eventually going to be retired and pensions are going to be paid to them.[4]

Yet U. S. Steel regards the problem of pension payments as a matter for its own determination. Under its noncontributory pension plan, the company believes itself to be under a contract obligation to pay certain benefits to the employee. Thus its general counsel could say: "Under these circumstances, since the determination of whether or not to create a trust is a matter of internal policy, we believe that the operations of the trust are of a like nature."[5]

The position of U. S. Steel might be regarded as a refinement of the deferred wage theory in that by contract the employee has the right to a specified benefit which does not mature until certain conditions of age and service are met. Even in such a case it would seem that the employee should be able to take action to see that his expectancy is protected. Since a trust fund has been established to provide for his pension benefits out of funds representing part of the price of his labor, some legal recourse ought to be available to him, or some protection by law, to insure that his expectations will materialize.

The law has traditionally been realistic enough to recognize that a person having a material interest in a benefit not yet due him should have a right to take whatever measures are necessary to preserve that interest, especially when and if a certain *res* or corpus of property is destroyed, the expectancy is also extinguished. The case for such a right was clearly advanced in a formal statement submitted by the U. S. Steel Corporation itself to the Senate Subcommittee on Welfare and Pension Funds:

> The funding of current service costs starts out by recognizing that the cost of an employee's service is greater than the amount currently paid to him as wages because, as he works, he concurrently establishes a possible claim to a pension. In a sense this is a claim to more pay for the same work; it is therefore deemed to be a part of the cost of that work and hence a part of the cost of the product resulting from that work.[6]

U. S. Steel is thinking in terms of costs, but what is a "cost" to the company is, to the worker, a "wage" and therefore his by right.

---

[4] Hearings on S. Res. 40, 84th Cong., 1st sess., 1955, Part 3, p. 1171.
[5] *Ibid.,* p. 1170.
[6] *Ibid.,* p. 1171.

Perhaps the most accurate summary of the employer's attitude toward pensions was given by H. W. Anderson, vice president in charge of the personnel staff of General Motors, testifying before the same Senate subcommittee:

We have long recognized that GM employees and General Motors both stand to gain when they take advantage of the employment relationship to secure group insurance and other types of group plans which will help our employees to meet the individual hazards of life.[7]

If there is an American way of doing things, it is well described by the Biblical "sufficient for the day is the evil thereof." Here as elsewhere in the American economy and business we find an unwillingness to be bound by the strictures of a single theory. And since management does not know all of the possibilities for loss and gain in the pension movement, it has not yet adopted a theory which consistently covers all the problems raised by pension funds.

Broad Characteristics

Certain characteristics of the employer's attitude can be discovered from the broad outlines of the pension movement. The first is that American business has recognized pensions as a cost of doing business and, by the form of financing it has adopted, business has in effect committed itself to dedicating a significant portion of its income to the provision of pensions for its workers. The vast majority of pension funds are in the form of irrevocable pension trusts or insurance contracts in which employers' contributions are placed beyond the power of recall. Furthermore, since the majority of these funds are handled by large investment banks and insurance companies, the control has passed into hands which will administer them impartially for the benefit of the workers. The financial advantage in utilizing these institutions lies in reducing the ultimate cost of the pension program as a result of expertly controlled investment policies.

It is not surprising that pension funds are irrevocably separated from the employer as owner since there are great tax advantages in such an arrangement. Even so, management could conceivably do what in fact one large corporation has done: it can retain control of the administration of pension funds and use this large accumulation of capital to advance the interests of the corporation. No particular investment vehicle has as

[7] *Ibid.*, p. 1083.

yet been forced upon management. In the typically bargained pension program, for instance, the unions have not generally insisted upon a provision specifying the type of financing to be employed.

The second broad characteristic of the pension movement which reveals the mind of employers is the absence of vesting in most pension programs. The limited number of plans providing vesting privileges suggests that employers have not been boundless in their generosity toward prospective pensioners. It is also an indication that pension funds are not universally regarded as the property of the employee. Such conclusions must be tempered by an understanding of the difficulty and cost involved in providing for vesting. But the very existence of a growing number of programs which do vest the funds in the employees indicates that it can be done and that if the desire to give this security to employees were strong enough, the way would be found in nearly all cases to provide it. In fact, successive studies made by the Bankers Trust Company of the large number of pension accounts they handle reveal a consistent trend toward liberalization of pension provisions.

EMPLOYER OBJECTIVES

In deciding on what type of pension program best suits the interests of the employees and the company, management may have several, somewhat conflicting objectives. Granted that the primary purpose of inaugurating a pension program is to provide for the security of the workers, management must consider the advantages and disadvantages of insured versus trusteed types of plans as to costs, investment policies and public relations.

MEETING THE WORKERS' NEEDS

The management of a company may choose between several different types of benefit programs according to its conception of the particular needs and wants of its employees. For example, there is the broad question of whether to fund a pension program by means of an insurance corporation or to set it up as a pension trust in which an investment bank or independent board of trustees manages the fund. In general, an insured type of program will be chosen where the needs or the preferences of those concerned run to a fixed dollar benefit and the trusteed type will be more appropriate when greater investment flexibility and a high rate of return are desired.

The principal feature distinguishing insured programs from the non-insured types is that, once a pension program is arranged with an insurance company and the costs have been determined, the insurance company itself undertakes to guarantee a certain level of benefits for the employees upon retirement. In the case of noninsured pension funds, however, the level of the pensioners' benefits will depend upon the amount of money in the fund or trust when the benefits become due upon retirement. The security of a pension expectation under a noninsured plan thus depends on the solvency of the pension trust. And this, in turn, will depend upon whether or not the pension trust has been fully funded and well administered during the active employment period of the pensioner.

There is, moreover, a wide range of choice within the insured type and the trusteed type of plan, and many corporations choose a combination of both types. The decision on the method of funding is a matter for the consideration of experts, but the choice between insured and trusteed plans is of significance here in that the trusteed type will result in a flow of capital for purchase of common and preferred stocks, that is, into channels of investment which will bear corporate control.[8]

DETERMINATION OF INVESTMENT POLICY

Another type of special objective of direct interest to the employer concerns the placement of the capital of a pension fund. Here we find a broad range of policy. Certain large corporations have attempted to diversify the portfolio of their funds so as to avoid the charge of attempted market control. Others have concentrated fund investment in the securities of the employing corporation for the purpose of conscripting capital or of insuring the tenure of the board. Perhaps in some cases there has even been an attempt at manipulating the securities of the corporation.

An example of an attempt of a corporation to avoid market control or the appearance thereof was presented to the Senate Subcommittee on Welfare and Pension Funds in a letter which a corporation had addressed to the seven trustees holding the assets of its two pension trust programs. The letter sets forth, in part, the investment policy favored by General Motors:

[8] A statistical survey of capital distribution resulting from a preference for one or another type of funding will be attempted in Chapter 7.

An investment up to 35 per cent of the combined trust funds for each plan in common stocks, exclusive of the stocks of banks and insurance companies, and an investment up to 15 per cent of the combined trusts in the discretion of the trustees in preferred stocks and in common stocks of banks and insurance companies appear to be satisfactory to all the trustees and ourselves. There would be a balance of at least 50 per cent of the combined trusts for each plan for investment in fixed income securities.

Certain limitations on investments in common stocks also appear to all to be desirable at this time. Investments in the common stocks of any one industry should be limited to 7 per cent of the combined trust funds for each plan. In addition, it appears desirable to limit the investments in stock of any one company to 2.5 per cent of the combined trust funds for each plan. If a trustee has any doubt as to the industry classification of any common stock, it may consult with the coordinator, hereinafter referred to, and his determination shall be conclusive.

❖   ❖   ❖

The limitations suggested herein with respect to the combined trust funds for each plan should be applied in the same pattern to each trust fund. However, investments by one or more trustees well within these limitations may make it possible for another trustee or other trustees, upon notice to the coordinator, to exceed such limitations in the management of their respective trust funds and still maintain the combined trust funds within the overall limitations.

❖   ❖   ❖

Also in order to insure that the trustees and the corporation will avoid any possible charge that control or management responsibility is being acquired in any company through the pension funds, investments of each trustee in the voting stocks of any one company should not exceed three-fourths of one per cent of any company's voting stock. A higher percentage limitation of this type of investment may be established by any trustee or trustees, with the approval of the coordinator, to the extent that any other trustee or trustees do not wish to take full advantage of an investment, with their respective trust funds, of three-fourths of one per cent in the voting stocks of any company and accept a lower percentage limitation . . . provided that the investments of the combined trust funds in the voting stocks of any one company do not exceed 5 per cent of such company's voting stock.

All of the limitations set forth above will apply, of course, to investments in the stocks of General Motors Corp. or its subsidiaries.

❖   ❖   ❖

In view of the general understanding of the trustees and ourselves with respect to investment policies and practices, which will guide the trustees in the management of the respective trusts, the trust instruments confer broad investment powers on the trustees.[9]

[9] Hearings on S. Res. 40, Part 3, p. 1137.

As of September 1955, General Motors had assets of $260,931,000 in its pension trusts, distributed among seven banks acting as trustees for the management of the funds. Of the total, 32.8 per cent was invested in common stocks of manufacturing companies (0.7 in General Motors) and 7.1 per cent in the common stocks of banks and insurance companies. Thus, close to 40 per cent of the pension portfolio was in common stocks.[10]

DISCLOSURE OF PORTFOLIO

Attitude of General Motors

Apropos of the issue of disclosing the current status of the pension fund to employees, the General Motors' representative stated at the Senate subcommittee hearings that the only information provided for the employees is given to the union in the form of a statement of the total amount in the fund and a statement by actuaries that as of a given date the amount is not less than that required by the labor contract.[11] The union is periodically given detailed reports on the number of people who have retired, the conditions of retirement and other information such as the age and sex frequency distribution.

At the Senate hearings General Motors raised serious objections to disclosure of its trust portfolio. The company maintained that disclosure is unnecessary because the investment of the funds is in the hands of reliable banking institutions subject to federal and state examination. It was also argued that publication of specific investment policies would mislead the individual investor because of the special nature of the pension fund investment. Even stronger was the company argument that

Disclosure to other investors of these decisions would have the undesirable effect of undermining or destroying the value of such decisions. Knowledge of the selections would permit other investors to purchase the same investments. As a consequence this might cause higher prices for these investments, which the trustee, by reason of his judgment, could have purchased at lower prices, had their selections not been disclosed.[12]

General Motors felt that it would be at a competitive disadvantage at the collective bargaining table if complete disclosure were required. Moreover, the statement of policy set forth by its executive vice president implies that it is none of the employee's business how the pension plan is invested: "The entire cost of the hourly rate pension plan is borne by the corporation. We negotiate with labor organizations only the benefits to

[10] *Ibid.*, p. 1135.
[11] *Ibid.*, p. 1132.
[12] *Ibid.*, p. 1134.

be provided under the pension plan."[13] The General Motors' representative went on to say that requirements for financing the pension plans as contained in the labor contracts are examined by independent actuaries and that the assurance given to the union from time to time that the requirements are being met should be satisfactory to them.

Attitude of U. S. Steel

During the same hearings before the Senate subcommittee, representatives of U. S. Steel presented arguments against full disclosure of the corporation's investment policies. U. S. Steel had built up a pension trust fund amounting to about $728 million by October 1955.[14] Its investment policy is similar to that of General Motors in providing for wide dispersion of the holdings of the fund:

> The maximum investment in any one common stock is about one-half of 1 per cent of the total investments. The trusts seldom own more than 1 per cent of the common stocks of any company, and as a matter of policy they do not aim to hold more than 5 per cent of the stock of a company, except in the case of a few small industrial enterprises where risk capital may be provided.[15]

The three trusts set up by the corporation did not have any holdings of U. S. Steel common or preferred stock although their holdings included $67.7 million of U. S. Steel Corporation serial debentures and $12.2 million of subsidiary railroad company mortgage bonds. About 17 per cent of the investments were in common stocks, exclusive of common stocks of banks and insurance companies.[16]

U. S. Steel was also opposed to disclosure of its investment policy with regard to individual securities. The first reason offered for secrecy was that, since the corporation was under no obligation to set up a trust and did so of its own volition, the trust should be regarded as similar to a corporate reserve fund to cover expected obligations. The trustee should be accountable to U. S. Steel and to no one else "except in accordance with general law." Secondly, the company felt that the investments of pension trusts should be confidential in nature because the business of investing funds is highly competitive. The advantage of employing expert financial skills would be lost if the decisions respecting investments were publicized. It was feared that if the holdings of such a fund were

---

[13] *Ibid.*, p. 1135.
[14] *Ibid.*, p. 1166.
[15] *Ibid.*, p. 1163.
[16] *Ibid.*

generally known, other investors might follow the same policy and force up the market before a long-range program could be completed. The company gave as its final reason that the buying and selling of securities in the investment portfolio "could be improperly construed as an expression of confidence or lack of confidence in a particular company or investment." Its representative argued that this would lead to disturbing influences in the market.[17]

In the course of the Senate subcommittee hearings, Senator Gordon Allott pointed out a significant distinction between pension trusts and investment trusts regarding disclosure: "Investment trusts are in the competitive market for money for investment and, of course, no one is going to invest unless he has a chance to see what is in them."[18] Thus it is logical to require by law that the portfolios of investment trusts be made public. Pension trusts are of course dissimilar since shares in these funds are not offered on the public market. But efforts have been made to liken them to investment trusts, and reference was made in the course of these hearings to an attempt to assimilate pension trusts to investment trusts in Section 505 of the 1954 tax bill.

"SELF-DEALING" INVESTMENTS

Another special objective of an employer setting up a pension program may include advantages he may seek by investing pension funds in the securities of his own corporation. This practice has been scanned with unfriendly eyes and has been given the title "self-dealing," although it cannot be and has not been condemned universally. The obvious objection to self-dealing investments was stated by C. Canby Balderston, vice chairman of the Board of Governors of the Federal Reserve System, as follows:

First of all, it violates the principle of diversification of investments, and secondly, it places employee funds that they should be able to rely upon in "rainy seasons" in the same company on which they depend for their jobs and livelihoods.[19]

In the course of its investigation of welfare and pension plans, the Senate subcommittee staff surveyed the operations of 66 large banks known to hold the bulk of the assets of all pension trusts for which banks serve as trustees. Of the 5,053 pension and other employee trust accounts

[17] *Ibid.*, pp. 1165, 1166.
[18] *Ibid.*, p. 1167.
[19] Senate Report No. 1734, 84th Cong., 2d sess., 1956, p. 53.

held by 64 of these banks, 63 per cent (3,191 funds) were noninsured pension plans handled under trust agreements. On the matter of investment in the assets of the employing companies, about 30 per cent of the trust agreements specifically permitted such investment of the funds while 20 per cent expressly prohibited it. The remaining 50 per cent were silent on this point.

Further analysis of the actual investments made by the banks showed that while only 6 per cent of the 3,191 funds included any securities, obligations or other property of the employer among their holdings, in 65 cases employer's assets amounted to more than 10 per cent of the total holdings in the portfolio. This led the Senate subcommittee to arrive at the following conclusion:

... the perusal of this list of pension plans raises a number of disquieting questions. It seems obvious to us that there are a number of instances in this list in which the heavy investment in the assets of the employer may not be in the interests of the beneficiaries and in which the investment may have been motivated, at least in part, by ulterior considerations.[20]

The SEC and the New York State Banking Department have also looked into the extent of "self-dealing" in the investment policies of pension programs. Their studies reveal that the practice is limited to a small percentage of the funds.

The SEC survey found, for example, that at the end of 1954 less than 3 per cent of the total assets of all noninsured funds were invested by the funds in the stock of their own companies. Of this small proportion, 85 per cent was held by the funds of retail trade companies and was accounted for almost entirely by the holdings of the Savings and Profit-Sharing Pension Fund of Sears, Roebuck employees. But with the Sears plan excluded, the percentage of total assets invested in own company stock was only one-half of one per cent. Similarly, the SEC's analysis of a sample of 695 trusteed plans showed that 17 per cent had investments in own company stock, but that Sears alone accounted for approximately 85 per cent of these holdings. The great majority of such investments (95 per cent) were made by only 11 per cent of the funds including Sears.[21]

In its 1955 survey of 1,024 pension trust funds, the New York State Banking Department found a similar pattern. Only a little over one-half of one per cent of the total assets ($315 million out of $4.9 billion) were held in the stock, obligations or other property of the employing com-

20 Senate Report No. 1734, p. 52.
21 SEC, *Survey of Corporate Pension Funds, 1951–1954*, 1956, p. 13.

panies, their affiliates or subsidiaries.[22] A rating of these investments showed that only a quarter of one per cent of these securities were of substandard quality. This seems to provide ample evidence that pension assets are not being exploited for the business advantage of the employers.[23] The same study found no transactions in the 1,024 funds between the trustee acting for itself and the trust. And in only twenty-seven instances had there been any transaction (purchase or sale) between the trust, on the one hand, and the employing company or any of its subsidiaries or its affiliates on the other.

These studies are based, for the most part, upon bank-trusteed pension programs. We may expect that the employment of a banker-trustee would have a deterrent effect upon the practice of investment in own company securities. The Senate Subcommittee on Welfare and Pension Funds quotes a representative of the banking industry to the effect that "Banks attempt to prevent such self-investments and seek to insert clauses in the trust agreements prohibiting it."[24]

A further check on the "self-dealing" practice comes from the tax-exemption provisions applied to these funds by the Internal Revenue Service. These provisions require a full disclosure of all stock or securities investments in the assets of the employer or of loans made to him. If the Internal Revenue Service discovers that investment in the obligations of the employer results in a benefit to any other party than the employees exclusively, it may revoke a favorable determination of tax exemption.

The Remarkable Sears, Roebuck Plan

The statistics thus far cited indicate that the policy of investing in employer assets is not sufficiently widespread to be of major significance in the securities markets with, however, the possible exception of the Sears program. The savings and profit-sharing plan of Sears, Roebuck & Co. is especially interesting, though atypical in many respects, because we can find in it many of the potentialities of pension programs in a more highly developed state. As pension plans go, the Sears plan has been in effect for a relatively long time, having been instituted in 1916. In that year there were 6,064 members in the profit-sharing fund, and the total assets were $554,000. Nearly four decades later, at the end of 1954, 123,800 em-

---

[22] George A. Mooney, *Pension and Other Employee Welfare Plans,* New York State Banking Department, 1955, p. xvi.
[23] *Ibid.,* p. 29.
[24] Senate Report No. 1734, p. 298.

ployees were covered by total assets of nearly $633.6 million. In 1916 the fund contained 2,473 shares of Sears stock, compared to 6,331,814 shares in 1954.[25]

At the committee hearings on the condition of the stock market, held in March 1955 under the chairmanship of Senator J. W. Fulbright, General R. E. Wood, chairman of the finance committee of Sears, Roebuck & Co. and chairman of the board of trustees of the Sears Savings and Profit-Sharing Pension Fund, testified, with perhaps justifiable satisfaction, that

> In the 38 years the fund has been in existence the employees have put in $191,536,061 and the company has contributed $312,268,568. Through these 38 years members have withdrawn $351,165,749 in stock and cash and this, together with the balance of $633,596,766 in the fund at the end of last year, equals $984,762,515, or five times what the employees put in.[26]

Under the provisions of the plan, each member deposits 5 per cent of his compensation up to a maximum of $10,000 a year, or a maximum deposit of $500, and the company contributes 10 per cent of its profits before taxes. In the five years up to 1955 the company contributed a yearly average of $31 million. All Sears employees who have been with the company over one year are eligible for participation in the plan, and of the 157,000 employees in 1955, 116,000 were participating.[27]

The benefits available to a long-term employee at Sears are remarkable. General Wood was able to say before the same Senate committee: "In fact, every employee who has been with us over 30 years gets out, no matter how humble their position, with a minimum capital of $50,000, which may go up to $150,000. In other words, we are making capitalists every year."[28]

General Wood further cited the case of a woman who began working at Sears for $6 a week and after thirty-seven years was earning about $80 a week. During the thirty-seven-year period she put $4,800 into the profit-sharing plan and took out $4,500 to buy a house, leaving $275 as her net contribution in the fund. But the net benefit accruing to her as a result of company contributions to the fund included 1,380 shares in the fund worth $104,000 and $17,000 in cash, a total of $121,000. The directors of the Sears fund may regard this case as somewhat exceptional, yet it does illustrate the advantages that may be derived from such a plan.

But if the Sears plan is of great benefit to the employees, they are not

[25] *Stock Market Study*, Hearings before the Senate Committee on Banking and Currency (Fulbright Committee), 84th Cong., 1st sess., 1955, p. 496.
[26] *Ibid.*
[27] *Ibid.*, pp. 495–496, 506.
[28] *Ibid.*, p. 505.

the only ones to achieve a measure of security from it since it is entirely controlled by the company. From its beginning the rules of the fund have provided that the members should share as largely as possible in the success of the company by means of ownership of Sears capital stock. As a result of this policy, by the end of 1954 the fund represented about 26 per cent of the ownership of the voting stock in the corporation, which then had a total of 24.8 million shares outstanding.[29]

The fund until 1958 was managed and the stock was voted by five trustees appointed by the board of directors of the company. Of these five, one of the trustees was an officer and director of the company, two others were directors of the company, and the remaining two were employees who were neither directors nor officers of the company. In the course of the Fulbright hearings, General Wood said that before an election for directors of the company, the trustees met to decide upon which board of directors they would support. Senator Fulbright then asked if there was ever any difference of opinion among the trustees. General Wood replied:

No. In 30 years during which I have been connected with the company, and 26 years in which I have headed the company, we have never had a dispute. We have never had any controversy, and we have never had any proxy fight. It has been very peaceful. There is, of course, the danger at some time trustees might seek to perpetuate a man for their own selfish purposes.[30]

The fund was reported to be having difficulty in purchasing enough shares in Sears to continue its policy and was being forced to buy shares in other companies. General Wood testified that the new stock purchases were mostly all in Sears subsidiaries, though not yet amounting to as much as 50 per cent of the stock of any one of them. He mentioned six companies in which the Sears fund had substantial interests, the largest being the Whirlpool Corporation and the Seager Corporation. He added that the fund did not control either corporation because "family" interests held large blocks of the stock. During the hearings it was pointed out, however, that the Sears fund would be likely to buy out these family interests as it had the holdings of the Rosenwald family, which at one time owned 4.8 million shares of Sears, Roebuck stock. It would seem that the Sears fund would be the logical purchaser of the shares in the companies in which it already had such large interests.[31]

General Wood attributed the phenomenal growth of the fund to the

[29] *Ibid.*, p. 504.
[30] *Ibid.*
[31] *Ibid.*, pp. 512, 513.

policy of investment in Sears stock, which, he said, has the wholehearted approval of fund members. In addition to the 26 per cent of Sears stock in the pension fund, the management and employees held about 7 per cent of the stock of the company in their own names. Thus a third of the assets of the corporation were owned by Sears employees or by their pension fund.[32]

How long the policy of purchasing Sears' own stock will be feasible is a matter of doubt, for "in the last 3 years [up to 1955] the supply of floating stock has been so limited that even moderate purchases tend to cause the price of the stock to rise. As the objective of the trustees is naturally to purchase the stock at as low a price as possible for the benefit of the employees, it has become more and more difficult to purchase the stock on this basis."[33] As a result of this embarrassment the purchase of Sears stock by the fund has been decreasing and in 1954 amounted to only 20 per cent of the 750,000 shares traded in that year.

In General Wood's opinion the fund will reach a leveling-off point within ten years, that is, a point at which as much will be taken out of the fund as is put in. He stated that the net addition in shares was 24,000 in 1954 while employees took out $45 million in stock and cash.[34] The size of the fund is still increasing, however, because the retail section of the company is as yet relatively young, having been set up in 1925. In the mail order section, as many employees are retiring as are going in. But at present General Wood and his associates find themselves with a true embarrassment of riches. As he stated in the hearings: "[We] have found ourselves confronted with the problem of what we are going to do with . . . $90 million in cash which belongs to our employees."[35]

There is no reason to doubt General Wood's testimony that the operations of the pension fund are entirely beneficial to the employees of Sears, Roebuck, and there is every reason to believe that he is correct in stating that the outstanding performance of the fund is due to its policy of purchasing stock in the company. This has been true because the management of Sears and that of the pension fund have behaved responsibly and wisely, and General Wood assured the Senate committee that present policies would be continued for at least ten years. But suppose it had not acted wisely, or does not in the future? What would an employee or

32 *Ibid.*, p. 504.
33 *Ibid.*, p. 497.
34 *Ibid.*, p. 515.
35 *Ibid.*, p. 502.

stockholder of Sears do about it? The management and trustees were obviously in an impregnable position, since the board of directors appointed the trustees and the trustees voted the controlling block of stock. Some serious questions were raised about the consequences of such a policy. Senator Fulbright asked General Wood: "Have you thought through to the logical end of the development which you have now started?"[36]

Apparently the investigations of the Senate subcommittee did give rise to some serious second thoughts. On May 12, 1958 the stockholders of Sears, acting on a recommendation of the board of directors, authorized the board of trustees of the fund to amend the fund rules to provide:

(1) that, in connection with each meeting of stockholders of the Company, each Group of B, C, and D members be furnished with a proxy statement and a form on which he could give instructions as to voting the stock credited to his account,

(2) that the stock be voted in accordance with such instructions by a committee consisting of Trustees who are not directors, officers or candidates for election as directors,

(3) that the stock not credited to such members or as to which instructions are not received within the designated time shall be voted in accordance with the discretion and direction of the committee, and

(4) that reasonable means be employed to provide secrecy respecting each Fund member's voting instructions.[37]

This change in the rules will mean that by the time of the 1959 annual meeting of the stockholders, members of the fund will be able to vote approximately 95 per cent of the shares of common stock of the company held by the fund. The employees can now control the corporation since, in addition to their 25 to 26 per cent ownership of common stock through the fund, they are estimated to own in their own names from 7 to 10 per cent of all stock outstanding.

The Senate investigation undoubtedly had an effect on the thinking at Sears. The chairman of the board of the corporation, T. V. Houser, subsequently remarked to a group of employees: "More and more attention is being paid to employee trust funds by the Government. The recent investigation of union funds has centered even more scrutiny on this subject."[38] Chairman Houser told the same group that it was not the employ-

---

[36] *Ibid.*, p. 514.

[37] Prospectus, offered to the members of the Savings and Profit-Sharing Pension Fund of Sears, Roebuck & Co. Employees, June 30, 1958, p. 5.

[38] *Sears News-Graphic*, April 10, 1958, p. 9.

ees who had raised the voting issue, but that the move was made to forestall any criticism by government or outside stockholders of the possibility that management might vote the stock for its own advantage.

Though the Sears fund bears very little similarity to the pension plans typical of other large corporations, especially with regard to the profit-sharing feature, it is well worth studying since it offers so many suggestive possibilities for the future development of pension plans. In the first place, the willingness of the Sears management to give voting rights to its employees might well be imitated by other pension trusts in allowing their employees some voice in the management of their funds. Secondly, the outstanding success of the profit-sharing feature of the plan and the investment of pension funds in the employing company's stock present a real challenge to other industries. Investing pension assets in the securities of the employing company is one of the traditional caveats in pension financing. The 42-year success story of the Sears fund raises the question whether the "all your eggs in one basket" caveat is a sound principle of pension investment or merely an outmoded taboo. We shall return to this question in a later chapter in a discussion of the broader social impact of pension trusts.

SUMMARY OF EMPLOYERS' OBJECTIVES

In general, we may say of the employers' objectives in the pension movement, first, that employers are quite aware and willing to admit that they derive definite advantages from a pension plan. Secondly, employers are sincerely interested in seeing that the promised benefits of a pension program will actually be realized by the employees. Concrete evidence of this objective is provided by the form in which most of the pension funds are invested. Thirdly, it must be said that management is not yet sufficiently interested in providing economic independence for employees to have worked out the problem of vesting of interests in pension funds. Furthermore, although managers of large corporations will often speak of the costs of pension benefits as a deferred wage, they are not yet prepared to accept all of the consequences of this theory. They will not even admit that the employee has a right to full disclosure of the operations of the fund. The subcommittee of the Senate in its final report on the subject of welfare and pension plans in 1956 had this to say apropos of the information to which the employee is entitled: "The attitude that a pension program, even though a noncontributory one, is the sole proprietary interest of the employer is fallacious. Tax laws, court decisions and even the employer's willingness to bargain on pension benefits refute the assumption of such arbitrary policies."[39]

Misapplication of Funds

It sometimes happens that the pension fund device is used in the manner of a bribe between employer and union officials. In such cases the employer simply turns the requisite funds for employee benefits over to union officials who manage the pension fund in such a way that they derive considerable advantage from the monies entrusted to them. Instances of these practices have been uncovered and deplored by various investigations of employee pension funds. Each such study, however, is careful to point out that this sort of misapplication happens only in the minority of cases. Certainly, it is not practiced on a scale large enough to affect the broad stratification of property control in which the present study is interested.

UNION ATTITUDES AND OBJECTIVES

For a considerable time after it had begun to come of age, organized labor remained indifferent to pensions as an objective for its members. Certain unions actually opposed employer-sponsored programs because they saw in them an attempt to weaken the power of the union and win the loyalty of the workers to management. Wage stabilization and taxes during World War II had a great influence upon the spread of the pension movement, but after the war organized labor again took advantage of its freedom to bargain over take-home pay and working conditions generally. The year 1949 marked the beginning of labor's active interest in providing pension programs. The case of *Inland Steel Company* v. *NLRB* had established the rule that pensions were within the scope of collective bargaining,[40] and the report of the President's Steel Industry Board, issued in that year, strongly supported the pension movement. Other developments made 1949 a logical time for the unions to begin their drive for old-age security. Two years before, John L. Lewis had obtained for the United Mine Workers an industry-financed welfare fund which must certainly have stimulated the interest of union leaders in this type of benefit for workers. Also, 1949 saw a temporary leveling off of

[39] Senate Report No. 1734, p. 55.
[40] 170 F. 2d 247 (7th Cir. 1948).

the upward movement of prices, and pensions provided a better arguing point than wage increases.

Although the AFL and CIO have since merged, we shall discuss their policies separately for two reasons. First, it was as separate policy-making bodies that the two organizations had their impact upon pension programs during the formative years of the pension movement. Secondly, the two policies show interesting contrasts of theory behind pension programs, and it is not yet apparent that the combined AFL–CIO has formed a unified policy.

OBJECTIVES OF THE CIO

According to Charles L. Dearing, the pension drive of the CIO set the pace in the unions' campaign for pensions.[41] Whether or not this opinion is universally accepted, the statement of CIO objectives gives us a clear idea of the philosophy of labor on the subject of social security. The private pension drive of the CIO in 1950 was part of a much larger over-all objective based on the assumption that "an adequate program of social security is a basic human right and need as fundamental as the need for food, clothing and shelter, and a way, therefore, must be found to meet the cost."[42]

The CIO leadership had long maintained that its effort to get increased benefits from the federal government had been blocked by groups representing employers and insurance companies which argued that governmental security programs were unnecessary. Walter Reuther and others felt that pressure applied to the individual employers would have the effect of bringing them down to Washington to back labor's plea for increased social security benefits.[43] Thus the pension movement was really a two-pronged advance with the single objective of security for its members. In the opinion of the CIO, collective bargaining for pensions was not a substitute for governmental programs but was meant to "fill the gaps."[44] Nor was the drive for collectively bargained pensions to be a haphazard affair; the CIO had devised over-all standards for pension plans, and each plan had to be approved by a union regional director.

[41] *Op. cit.,* p. 45.

[42] Harry Becker, Director, UAW–CIO, Social Security Department, "Organized Labor and Social Security," in *The Quest for Economic Security,* University of Michigan, Ann Arbor, 1950, p. 4.

[43] *Social Security Revision,* Hearings before the Senate Finance Committee, 81st Cong., 2d sess., 1950, Part 3, p. 1908.

[44] UAW–CIO, *Collective Bargaining Handbook for Workers' Security Programs,* rev. ed., 1949, p. 4.

Basis in "Human Depreciation" Theory

The objectives of the CIO were translated into practical demands when the UAW–CIO pension program was presented in memorandum form to the Ford Motor Company in 1949. The basic contentions of the CIO can be reduced to the following five propositions, of which the second is the most important since it expresses the "human depreciation" theory underlying CIO thinking.

1. Federal old-age insurance benefits were inadequate. The government programs supplied an average benefit in 1949 of $39 a month for a worker aged 65 and his wife, whereas the Federal Security Agency estimated that $148 was the minimum monthly requirement for a "decent standard of living."[45]

2. The worker's need for additional security must be supplied by industry. This proposition was based on the union's conclusion that the security of workers is a responsibility of management, which in turn was based on the analogy already used by John L. Lewis in his drive for mine workers' pensions.[46] The argument was the now familiar one that management has always regarded the cost of repair and replacement of machines as part of the cost of doing business. The worker, too, had a claim for "repair and retirement" as a legitimate cost of doing business.[47] Since the union based its claim upon the *need* of the worker, it could argue logically that the level of benefits should be determined by the worker's "need" rather than by his earnings. Thus the benefit formula proposed by the union, consistently with its position that industry benefits were supplemental to governmental aid, provided for a $100 minimum monthly pension, including federal old-age insurance benefits, for all employees aged 65 with thirty years of service.

3. Workers could not finance the cost of security themselves.

4. All workers must be included.

5. The union must be allowed to participate in the management of pension programs. This proposition was based on the union's claim that pension money really belongs to the workers and that the union therefore has the right to share in the management of pension programs. Thus the union stipulated that pension programs should be in the form of a pension trust and that the employees should have equal representation with

[45] *Ibid.*, p. 1.
[46] United Mine Workers of America Welfare & Retirement Fund, "Pensions for Coal Miners" (no date), p. 4.
[47] UAW–CIO *Handbook,* p. 11.

management on the board of directors of the fund. This proposition is a matter of serious contention at the present time.

Results of CIO Program

The CIO–UAW philosophy does not represent the thinking of all of organized labor, nor has the CIO been completely successful in promoting its entire program. The UAW succeeded, however, in negotiating some 260 pension plans covering more than 1.1 million workers as of 1955.[48] These plans covered about 80 per cent of the UAW membership but less than 20 per cent of the plants organized by the union. In nearly all of the plans, benefits are determined on the basis of a specified monthly amount times the number of years of service, regardless of the level of earnings. Most of the plans are funded and provide that the company pay into a fund a sum equal to the full current costs of benefits earned plus additional sums required for past service liability. A few of the funds are terminally funded and about 10 per cent are of the insured type.

Plans of the Big Three

The pension plans of the "Big Three" — General Motors, Ford and Chrysler — are of special interest because they represent such a large proportion of the workers in the automobile industry. These plans provide a monthly pension of $2.25 multiplied by the years of service on retirement at age 65.[49] (This benefit is exclusive of social security benefits.) In the light of the argument that vesting is too expensive, it is significant that vesting is provided for the employee leaving service after age 40 with at least ten years of service credit. He then becomes eligible for a deferred pension, payable at age 65, equal to at least $2.25 a month times his years of service after age 30. It may be argued that if vesting is possible here, it ought to be possible in other industries.

Under the "Big Three" plans joint committees, set up for each plant and for the company as a whole, authorize pensions, but the union does not participate in the administration of the fund and has no voice in the selection of the trustee, the terms of the trust agreement or the investment of the funds. Certain information concerning the operation of the fund is given to the union, but financial control is closely held in the hands of management.[50]

[48] Senate Report No. 1734, p. 99.
[49] *Ibid.*, p. 100. Now $2.50. See Art. II of the General Motors Plan in App. A.
[50] *Ibid.*, pp. 100 and 101.

OBJECTIVES OF THE AFL

The attitude of the AFL toward pension plans showed some interesting similarities and contrasts with that of the CIO. On one basic premise the two labor groups were in agreement from the beginning: they both maintained that "the Federal Social Security system, even after recent improvements, still remains pitifully inadequate."[51] Like the CIO, the AFL did not regard private pension plans as a substitute for social security and warned against allowing the drive for privately negotiated plans to divert unions from "the more important basic objective of promoting the improvement and expansion of the Federal Old-Age Insurance program."[52] Summing up its position the AFL stated:

The Social Security system accomplishes the aims of vesting, continuity of coverage, adequate guarantees, and equity of treatment much more economically, effectively, and efficiently than is possible through a system of scattered, fragmentary, limited and unrelated private pension systems. A private plan should be regarded only as a supplement to the Social Security program. It is not, and never can be, a substitute for it.[53]

The AFL–CIO does not seem to have abandoned this position, though a clear policy statement on this point is lacking. If we are to construe policy from action we may conclude that it now regards the private pension plan as a permanent supplement to federal old-age insurance, seeking to get as much as possible for its members from both systems.

Basis in "Deferred Wage" Theory

While the AFL and the CIO were thus in complete agreement on a very basic issue of pension planning, in another matter of policy there was a divergence of views from the start. The AFL staked its entire claim for pensions upon the principle that "A pension plan is not . . . a conditional or discretionary gift by the employer, but a *deferred wage* earned by current labor services, and required by the terms of the contract."[54] In contrast, the thinking of the CIO is based on the analogy between the older worker and the depreciation cost of a machine, a view rejected by the AFL in the following terms:

It [the deferred wage theory] means, first, that the worker's interest in the pension fund is not established solely by reason of advanced age and "long and

---

[51] AFL, *Pension Plans Under Collective Bargaining, A Reference Guide for Trade Unions* (no date), p. v.
[52] *Ibid.*, p. 86.
[53] *Ibid.*
[54] *Ibid.*, p. 1.

faithful" service with an employer. That interest is established by reason of the work performed by all the members during the term of the contract.[55]

Consequences of the AFL Position

The AFL's statement of policy went on to say that the employer has a right to expect no more in return for his contributions to a pension fund than the performance of an employee's work and that therefore payments to a pension fund should be irrevocable and as far beyond the employer's reach as are cash wage payments. The AFL took the further logical step of making the claim that the union representatives have as much right to a voice in the management of the fund as if the workers had set up the fund entirely through their own resources.

Nor did the AFL seem very anxious to claim that the workers cannot finance the cost of security themselves. It regarded payments to a pension fund as simply a wage increase which could be paid in cash to the worker and turned over to a union fund or be paid directly by the company to a fund which was union-managed.[56]

The AFL policy statement was equally consistent in its strong insistence upon vesting of pension funds: it characterized the nonvested plan as one that benefits the management more than it does the employee. This argument followed logically from the AFL's premise that a pension plan is a form of deferred wage payment. It therefore concluded that allowing the employer to deprive an employee of this deferred wage would make it possible to use the workers' income to keep the most valuable and experienced members of the company's work force tied to their jobs at lower rates of pay.[57]

A final point of major difference between AFL and CIO policy was the interest which the AFL took in providing a pension scale related to the level of the worker's income. However, it did not pursue this policy when it would result in providing low-paid workers already close to the subsistence margin with benefits only sufficient for the bare necessities of life. In such cases the AFL recommended "a minimum benefit provision, guaranteeing that the pension will not be less than a certain flat dollar amount," which was to be included as part of a pay-related formula.[58] Another suggested alternative was a variable formula providing low-

---

[55] *Ibid.*, p. 2.
[56] *Ibid.*, p. 3.
[57] *Ibid.*, pp. 69–71.
[58] *Ibid.*, p. 53.

paid workers with a pension based on a higher percentage of their work-ing wage.

Other labor groups have pursued different policies depending upon the various circumstances in which they find themselves. A small union in a weak bargaining position will settle for a far less satisfactory pension plan than will a larger and more powerful union. Even the policies of the large unions will vary from time to time with changes in the cost-of-living index, technological advances, inflation, and so forth.

CURRENT OBJECTIVES OF LABOR

As part of its hearings on welfare and pension plans, the Senate subcom-mittee conducted a panel discussion by labor representatives. These men, who represented a cross section of the labor movement, were in agreement on several basic points. They maintained that whether or not a pension program is jointly or unilaterally administered, money paid into the fund belongs to the worker and the benefits the employer agrees to provide at the bargaining table are due to the worker in return for his services. The labor representatives further agreed that joint administra-tion was to be desired. They also unanimously desired disclosure of all pension plan information and felt that the remedies presently provided by law to guarantee disclosure were inadequate. They wanted a full annual report on pension plan operations to be furnished to all employees and members individually, and most of them agreed that this information should also be made public.

Several of the union representatives further stated that the unions were interested in having the reserved pension funds invested in projects which would (1) benefit their members incidentally through earnings of interest or dividends, or (2) be of wide social advantage. Loans to aid union members with housing problems, bonds for low-cost housing guaranteed by the government, and housing projects themselves were cited as useful channels of investment. The reason given for such a policy was that "the workers should receive some benefit from the funds while they are actively at work."[59]

The UAW Proposal

A step was made in this direction during the contract negotiations in the automobile industry in the spring and summer of 1958. Walter P.

[59] Senate Report No. 1734, pp. 302–307.

Reuther, president of the UAW, proposed to the Ford Motor Company that their workers' pension funds be invested in housing and other community facilities in areas where Ford workers lived so that they and their families might share more fully in the benefits of the fund. Mr. Reuther argued that the money in the pension fund belongs to the employees and is held in trust for them. He pointed to other soundly financed pension funds that have demonstrated the feasibility of investing in housing for workers. He further noted that a portion of the Ford pension fund was already invested in housing facilities in other parts of the United States not accessible to Ford workers. At the same time he requested information on the relationship between the Ford Motor Company and its financial trustee, copies of the annual reports of the trustee along with specific information on the investment of the funds, and information on the policy in effect for voting common stock held by the pension trust fund.[60]

These were specific points in the union's over-all proposal to amend the retirement plan in order to establish "a limited degree of joint control by the company and the union of the selection of the trustee and of the form and terms of the trust agreement."[61]

The company's position was that the function of the pension fund under the plan was to provide a secure means of financing benefit payments to those who become eligible to receive *retirement* benefits. Any use of the fund for other purposes would be a departure from this basic principle and would be improper and unwise from the standpoint of both the employees and the company. In justification of this position Mr. Bugas quoted Article V, Section 9 of the Ford pension plan in a letter to Mr. Reuther as follows: "No employee shall have any vested right under the plan except such rights, if any, as may accrue to him upon retirement as provided in the plan."[62] He closed his letter with the following words: "Legal considerations aside, we remain fully opposed, as we have been consistently in the past to broadening the scope of our negotiations with the UAW to embrace the broad social fields that you envision."

During the debate Mr. Bugas argued that one of the strongest features of the Ford plan lay in placing the funds under the management of a completely independent trustee. This, he argued, was done to insure maximum safety of investment and to guarantee that the fund could not

[60] Letter of Walter P. Reuther to John S. Bugas, vice-president in charge of Industrial Relations, Ford Motor Company, June 27, 1958.
[61] Letter of Walter P. Reuther to John S. Bugas, July 29, 1958.
[62] Letter of July 18, 1958.

be exploited either by the company or by the union. At the same time he affirmed that the principle that the trustee has sole investment responsibility had been strictly observed both by the company and the trustee. Under the trust agreement governing the investment of the Ford fund, the trustee has uncontrolled power to vote the stock held by it under the trust agreement, and the company does not enter into discussions with the trustee as to how such votes shall be cast.

The exchange of views was carried on with some acrimony on both sides, and the issue remained unsettled at the end of negotiations. The collective bargaining agreement which resulted throughout the industry contained substantial increases in pension benefits and liberalization of policy. But on the issue of pension fund investment the only result was that much more data on the trust fund and on active and retired workers would be made available to the joint board of administration so that the union could better verify the value and safety of the program. The management also promised cooperation in developing special reports for use of the local pension committees. Finally an informal understanding was reached by the parties that, after the contracts were ratified, there would be further discussions relating to investments in areas where the employees lived.

INVESTMENT POLICIES OF
FINANCIAL TRUSTEES

The individuals who actually make the investment of pension reserves fall into one or another of three groups: employers, union officials or corporate trustees. Since most of the pension trust assets are invested by corporate trustees, our main concern will be to investigate their policies. Still, it will be worthwhile to note in passing the contrasting characteristics of the other two classes of investors of pension funds.

Pension trust investments which are under the control of union trustees and in which the corporate trustee is either absent or acting only in a ministerial capacity show a remarkable degree of conservatism in investment policy. It is a characteristic of union-directed investment policy to include little or no holdings of common stocks. Yet most of the innovations in trust investment policy that do appear in the pension investment field are attributable to the labor unions, for example, the substantial investments which have been made in low-cost housing by union-dominated pension programs.

Since employer investment policies vary widely, little generalization is possible. It is within this class of investors, however, that we usually find the practice of investing pension funds in the employer's own securities. The Sears program provides the outstanding example of this policy, of course, but if its investments are excepted, "self-dealing" investments comprise a negligible proportion of total pension trust investments.[63]

RESPONSIBILITIES OF CORPORATE TRUSTEES

In conducting the business of a pension trust the corporate trustee brings to the task the traditional principles and ideals of fiduciary relationships. The statement of principles issued in 1933 by the American Bankers Association is an excellent expression of the basic policy with which a corporate trustee approaches the administration of a pension trust:

> It is the duty of a trustee to administer a trust solely in the interest of the beneficiaries without permitting the intrusion of interest of the trustee or third parties that may in any way conflict with the interests of the trust; to keep and render accurate accounts with respect to the administration of the trust; to acquaint the beneficiaries with all the material facts in connection with the trust; and, in administering the trust, to exercise the care a prudent man familiar with such matters would exercise as trustee of the property of others, adhering to the rule that the trustee is primarily a conserver.[64]

In the same statement, the bankers affirm that the principles of trust institutions are a matter of public interest, but one looks in vain for any indication that the trust itself is affected with a public interest. In interviews and in the published articles and speeches of the trust officers of banks, for example, there is no loyalty acknowledged to any interest other than that of the beneficiaries of a trust. Yet the pension trusts administered by pension officers of banks are becoming so large that their management cannot fail to have a significant effect on the general welfare.

Whatever one may think of the weight of this consideration, the pension trust undoubtedly presents a new, and in some respects an anomalous, situation for the corporate trustee. This is readily apparent if we ask the question, who *is* the beneficiary to whom the trustee is responsible? Under the common trust arrangement, the banker-trustee is subject to replacement by the employer at any time. Furthermore, the trustee

---

[63] SEC, *Survey of Corporate Pension Funds, 1951–1954,* p. 13.

[64] Statement adopted by the Executive Committee of the Trust Division, American Bankers Association, April 10, 1933, and approved by the Executive Council of the American Bankers Association, April 11, 1933.

makes his accounting to the employer, but the right of the employee, the ultimate beneficiary, to demand an accounting and enforce his interest at law is still a matter of doubt. Finally, the prospective beneficiaries of these trusts are often so many and their number so subject to change that some courts have decided that pension trusts should be classified as charitable trusts.[65]

From these considerations, it becomes apparent that the pension trust differs from the classic form of the private trust in some very important respects. The clear statement of loyalties made by the Bankers Association is adequate for private trusts but leaves something to be desired when applied to pension trusts.

Conflicting Loyalties

If the corporate trustees are embarrassed by their anomalous position, however, they give very little evidence of it. Practically, the banker-trustee can do little else than to consider the employee who is ultimately to receive the benefits accruing from the funds entrusted to the bank's care to be the party to whom he owes undivided loyalty. This certainly is the attitude of mind of the trust officers of banking institutions interviewed in the course of this study. It is safe to conclude, then, that the activities of corporate trustees are directed solely toward obtaining the maximum return on the funds entrusted to them consistent with a high degree of safety, ". . . adhering to the rule that the trustee is primarily a conserver." Investment policy will be carried out, therefore, to enhance the value of the monies in trust, without considering the interests of the employer, or broad social interests, or stability in the securities market, except as these considerations may benefit the fund itself more or less directly.

Here again we find one of the anomalies of the situation. Actually, the beneficiary of any advantage a corporate trustee may gain by prudent investment will usually be the employer, the "settlor" of the trust. This is true because the employer usually commits himself to providing a certain level of benefits for the employee and the costs remain his concern. Investment gains will reduce the cost of providing pensions but will not increase the amount given to an individual employee. In a larger view, of course, it may be argued that as the cost of pensions decreases, the level of benefits to which an employer will commit himself can be increased.

[65] Union Pacific v. Artist, 60 Fed. 365 (8th Cir. 1894); Van Horn v. Lewis, 79 F. Supp. 541 (D. C. 1948); Upholsterers International Union v. Leathercraft Furniture Co., 82 F. Supp. 570 (E. D. Pa. 1949). See also cases cited in Chapter 6.

UNIQUE FEATURES OF PENSION
TRUST INVESTMENT

While the management of pension funds is subject to the principles of prudent investment which are applicable generally, these funds exhibit certain unique characteristics which have a profound effect upon investment policy:

1. Since pension trusts are built up by steady accumulation of regular contributions and reinvestment of earnings, even a slight increase in investment rates of return can have a considerable effect upon costs. Table 10, based on a study by Esmond B. Gardner and C. Jerome Weber, indicates the reductions in contributions that are possible from a constant realization of investment returns in excess of a rate of 2½ per cent. The savings are large in comparison with relatively small increases in investment earnings because of the cumulative effect of these increases over a period of time. The possible reduction in contributions is smaller in the case of accrued liability than for current liability because funding to meet this obligation is usually carried out over a shorter period of time.

Table 10

EFFECT OF INVESTMENT EARNINGS ON PENSION COSTS

(*Per Cent*)

| | Reductions in Contributions to Meet Liability | |
Investment Yield	Current	Accrued
2.75	6	5
3.00	12	10
3.25	17	14
3.50	22	18

Source: Esmond B. Gardner and C. Jerome Weber, "Comparison of Common Stock and Fixed Income Yields: Effect on Pension Funding," *Journal of Commerce,* New York, June 12, 1952.

2. No distinction is made in the trusts between principal and income. The entire trust corpus is committed to pension benefits for employees who have the same rights in both principal and income. This gives the trustee great liberty in the disposition of the various types of assets in his portfolio.

3. There is a continuous inflow of cash contributions from the em-

ployer and, if the pension plan is contributory, from the employee. This places a substantial amount of new capital at the disposal of the trustee periodically.

4. The trustee need not provide for liquidity in his investments since the yearly contributions to the fund will be in excess of the disbursements until the hypothetical point of full funding is reached. After that time, the continuing contributions and the income from investments will equal disbursements.

5. The pension trust is exempt from taxes on both income and capital gains.

6. In the case of most pension funds, the amount of capital at the trustee's disposal is usually so large that he can take advantage of investment devices such as dollar-averaging, and of certain investments, such as private placements, which are not available to small investors.

These, then, are the principal features of pension trusts from an investment point of view, and every one of them represents an advantage in the quest to maximize investment earnings. With the safeguards of low liquidity requirements, a continuous inflow of new capital and a long term in which to manipulate the trust portfolio, it is little wonder that corporate trustees have accepted and even sought considerable freedom to invest the funds committed to their care despite the added responsibilities this authority entails.

One of the largest investment banks in this field enjoys full investment control in 88.6 per cent of its accounts while in only 4.8 per cent is it subject to company approval of investments.[66] In the remaining 6.6 per cent of its accounts its duties are merely ministerial. A further breakdown of the accounts which the trustee alone controls shows that no restrictions are placed on the type of investments permitted under the trust agreement in well over one-third (38.7 per cent) of the accounts. Nearly 10 per cent (9.5 per cent) restrict investments to securities legal for life insurance companies or fiduciaries, with common stock purchases limited to 25–40 per cent of the fund. About 6 per cent of the accounts provide for a miscellaneous investment category which usually permits the purchase of some common stocks.

The same banking institution reports that new accounts and revisions of old accounts show a trend toward no investment restrictions. Thus, in less than 15.5 per cent of the pension accounts it handles, does this trustee

[66] Unpublished report of a large New York bank.

lack the flexibility to enable it to take full advantage of all investment opportunities consistent with a prudent caution.

HOW INVESTMENT GOALS ARE REALIZED

In an address before the Mortgage Bankers Association in 1956, Esmond B. Gardner, vice president of the Chase Manhattan Bank, made the following statement:

> Most professional trustees seem to believe that such a trust should have a diversified portfolio of investments. A typical distribution at this time might be 60–65 per cent in fixed income investments — 10–15 per cent in preferred stocks, and 20–35 per cent in common stocks.[67]

The SEC's continuing survey of corporate pension funds shows that in 1957 their assets, estimated at book value, were invested as follows: 67.8 per cent in fixed income investments, 3.2 per cent in preferred stocks, 24.7 per cent in common stocks and 4.3 per cent in other assets. Based on market value, the distribution would be respectively: 62.7 per cent, 2.8 per cent, 30.3 per cent and 4.2 per cent. (See Table 13, p. 196.)

Higher Concentration in Common Stocks

Compared with the traditionally conservative attitude of the fiduciary toward common stocks and with the practice of the insurance companies of keeping investment in common stocks under 2–3 per cent of portfolio, the striking feature about the distribution of pension fund assets is the high percentage now being invested in common stocks.

Furthermore, the tendency with regard to common stock purchase is upward. The SEC surveys reveal a continuous growth in the percentage of total assets of corporate pension funds invested in common stocks — from 11.4 in 1951 to 24.7 in 1957. Further evidence of this trend was found by the staff of the Senate Committee on Banking and Currency in a special analysis of the activities of the pension trusts of thirty companies representing about 35 per cent of all the assets of corporate pension funds from 1951 to 1954.[68] Although, according to the SEC, the number of corporations having noninsured pension funds increased about one-third during this period,[69] the assets of the thirty pension trusts studied by the Senate committee staff constituted approximately the

[67] Esmond B. Gardner, Address, Chicago, Ill., October 9, 1956 (Mimeographed. Chase Manhattan Bank).

[68] *Institutional Investors and the Stock Market, 1953–1955,* Staff Report to the Senate Committee on Banking and Currency, 84th Cong., 2d sess., 1956, p. 20.

[69] SEC, *Survey of Corporate Pension Funds, 1951–1954,* p. 5.

same proportion of all pension fund assets in these years, indicating that these funds were growing at a faster rate than the others. Apparently, these leaders in the pension trust field are also showing the way to increased investments in common stocks, for

at the end of 1951, the 30 companies had 18.7 per cent of their assets in common stocks, while all corporate pension funds had only 11.4 per cent. At the end of 1954, the 30 companies held 26.7 per cent of their assets in common stocks, while all non-insured funds had 18.4 per cent so invested.[70]

The Senate committee report also revealed what categories of the portfolio of these pension funds decreased to make way for greater investment in common stocks. While common stock investment rose until it represented more than a quarter of the assets in 1954, investment in U. S. government securities and preferred stock declined:

The rise between 1951 and 1954 in the percent of assets in common stocks of the 30 companies was accompanied by a marked decline in the percent invested in United States Government securities — 34.2 percent in 1951 and 18.2 percent in 1954. Preferred stock and cash account deposits represented a decreasing proportion of the assets in the 4 years. Corporate bond holdings of the 30 companies rose from 34.7 percent in 1951 to 44.1 percent in 1954.[71]

Corporate pension funds are investing an increasing amount of their assets in common stocks because they are a source of appreciably higher return upon investment. Furthermore, to offset the risk of a downturn in the market, pension trusts have certain characteristics which protect them in such a contingency.

Higher Yields

In their comparison of common stock and fixed income investment yields previously referred to, Gardner and Weber found a marked difference in the average yield from life insurance company investments and an assumed investment in stock issues included in one of the common stock averages. These authors claim their statistics prove that "The yields on Common Stock Averages over a period of time have exceeded the yield from the life insurance companies by about 2 percentage points per annum."[72] They further point out that it is reasonable to expect that a group of investment specialists would have achieved a result at least

[70] *Institutional Investors and the Stock Market, 1953–1955,* p. 20.
[71] *Ibid.,* pp. 20–21.
[72] Esmond B. Gardner and C. Jerome Weber, "Comparison of Common Stock and Fixed Income Investment Yields: Effect on Pension Funding," *Journal of Commerce,* New York, June 12, 1952.

equal to that of the averages and probably would have done better. Gardner and Weber conclude, therefore, that if 25 per cent of a pension trust were invested in common stocks over the twenty-two-year period studied and the remaining portion of a pension trust (consisting of bonds, mortgages, preferred stocks and lease-backs) were invested at a yield equivalent to that of a life insurance company, the over-all yield of a pension trust over a period would then be increased by one-half of a percentage point per annum. Likewise, the differential would be 0.8 of a percentage point if 40 per cent of the fund were invested in common stocks. The significant conclusion is that "Such increases in investment earnings would decrease costs by about 11 to 12 per cent and nearly 20 per cent respectively."[73]

Detailed comparison of yields reveals that in 1928, 1929 and 1930 the cash income of the investments of life insurance companies exceeded that from the common stock averages. However, in the remaining twenty-two years, yields from common stocks were greater and the cash income, not compounded, on $100 invested each year for the life insurance companies was $1,113.83 compared to $1,815.76 for the common stock averages.[74] They add: "It is significant that the yields to the life insurance companies have receded gradually from 5.09 per cent in 1926 to 3.09 per cent in 1950, while the common stock yields have varied from 5.07 per cent in 1926 down to 3.23 per cent in 1929 and then up to 6.96 per cent in 1950." The authors note that tables prepared on a basis of the Dow-Jones Industrial Averages show a similar pattern but a result even more favorable to the common stock averages.

An extremely interesting study by Professors Eiteman and Smith of the University of Michigan points out that over the period 1897–1951 the Dow-Jones averages of stock prices showed an upward trend of 3.19 per cent a year.[75] Obviously, this average would be improved by including the years 1952 to 1957. To avoid the objection that investors do not buy averages but specific securities, these authors made an arbitrary choice of a list of stocks, selecting the period 1937–1950 in which the Dow-Jones average of industrial prices was approximately the same at the end as it

[73] *Ibid.* The statistics which form the basis of this study were taken from William C. Greenough, *A New Approach to Retirement Income,* Teachers Insurance and Annuity Association of America.

[74] In making this and other comparisons, Gardner and Weber made statistical corrections which make insurance company yields comparable to pension trust yields, i.e., common stock yields were converted to an inventory value basis.

[75] W. J. Eiteman and F. P. Smith, *Common Stock Values and Yields,* University of Michigan, Ann Arbor, 1953, p. 1.

was at the beginning. The common stocks selected for this study were chosen by including all those stocks listed on the New York Stock Exchange with a trading volume of one million shares or more during the calendar year 1936. This resulted in a list of 92 stocks used to make up a portfolio which was kept intact during the fourteen-year period. It was assumed that on January 15, 1937, $1,000 was invested in each issue on the list and an equal sum was invested in each of the following years on the same date. Furthermore, the increments in the portfolio were considered to be made up in the following ways: (1) the balance of cash remaining, if any, from the previous investment; (2) cash dividends received since the previous investment date; and (3) cash received from the sale of stock dividends.[76] Stock dividends were held in the portfolio only if identical with the stockholding on which the dividend was issued. Different types or classes were sold at the low price for the year in which the stock dividends were received. Proceeds from the sale of such stocks were added to the cash fund of the portfolio to be invested the following January. Rights to purchase additional shares were exercised at the earliest possible date, even though such purchases were inadvisable from the point of view of the investor. In other words, wherever possible the authors exhibited an intentional bias to rule out any advantage of hindsight and refused a great many of the advantages which any ordinarily prudent investor would have taken in the management of his portfolio.

The results of this study were, in part, as follows: During each of the first five years (1938–1942), the market values of the portfolio were less than the amount of investment funds contributed. There was a decline of approximately 40 per cent from January 15, 1937 to January 15, 1942 in the market. But in January of 1942 the portfolio was only 12 per cent less than the amount of cash contributions of the investor. The losses, of course, were in large part offset by dividends.

By January 15, 1950, the market value of the portfolio equaled what the investor would have earned had he invested his $92,000 ($1,000 in each of 92 stocks) each January for fourteen years at a compound interest rate of 12.2 per cent. At the end of this period the investor's total contribution was $1,288,000 and the market value of the portfolio was $3,028,855, or two and a third times his investment.

A further comparison was made by supposing an annual investment of $1,000 in the stocks of the test portfolio and the same investment annually

<hr />

[76] *Ibid.*, p. 14.

in the list of stocks which go to make up the Dow-Jones Industrial Average. This comparison showed that the test portfolio realized 127 per cent of what was gained by the Dow-Jones stocks.[77]

Common Stocks as Inflation Hedge

Investment in common stocks has often been recommended as a hedge against inflation. Professors Eiteman and Smith made a further comparison between the appreciation of an annual $1,000 investment required to keep pace with the Consumer Price Index and the appreciation of $1,000 invested annually in the test portfolio. The appreciation of the value of the portfolio did not keep pace with the rise in the Consumer Price Index until 1943. But by 1950 the ratio of the portfolio to purchasing power requirements was 172 per cent, that is, the annual sums invested would have to be worth $19,175 to preserve the purchasing power of the dollars committed over the period, but the market value of the stocks in the portfolio was $32,922.[78] These figures are not perfectly comparable in aggregate because in addition to the $14,000 invested in the portfolio by 1950, dividends were reinvested. Still, a portfolio with a market value of 172 per cent of that necessary to maintain the purchasing power contributed by the investor is a strong argument that common stocks are a successful hedge against inflation.

The results of the Eiteman-Smith study make very interesting reading in connection with pension trust investments because it is concerned with the intrinsic merits of common stocks as long-term investment media. The assumptions made for the hypothetical investors are very similar to those which actually apply in the case of pension trust investment, with the exception that the hypothetical investor had none of the advantages of inside knowledge, market analysis, trend techniques and so forth. We can reasonably expect that a corporate trustee with long experience and access to market information could do as well or considerably better than the hypothetical investor. The results of this program of steady, regular purchasing of common stocks at given intervals were exceptionally good, but they would have been even better if the investment program had been carried further. As of January 15, 1951 the test portfolio would have had a market value of $4,566,813, or 331 per cent of the investment.[79] For 1952 and later years the percentage would have been even higher. This record is a reflection of our expanding economy which

[77] *Ibid.*, pp. 15, 16 and 18.
[78] *Ibid.*, p. 19.
[79] *Ibid.*, p. 35.

has produced an upward trend in common stocks for fifty years or more. Furthermore, there is good reason to presume that this trend will continue.

This is certainly the opinion of Paul L. Howell, financial consultant, who maintains that it is possible for a pension fund to realize a 6 per cent return on its investment through purchase of common stocks.[80] Mr. Howell also points out that in addition to their high rate of earnings common stocks also produce income in the form of capital gains. He reports that the earnings of the pension funds for 1955, 1956 and 1957, as reported by the SEC, were 3.58 per cent, 3.68 per cent and 3.84 per cent and, with capital gains added, would be 4.22 per cent, 3.92 per cent and 3.90 per cent, respectively.[81]

Security of Stock Investments

With such clear evidence of the long-term advantage of investment in common stocks, the only objection to this type of investment would be that circumstances might force a sale in an unfavorable market. The pension trust is, however, peculiarly well protected against such a contingency. It is characteristic of pension funds that for a considerable period of time the contributions exceed the amount of pensions being paid so that the size of the fund keeps on increasing for many years. During this period of growth there is little danger to the common stock portion of the portfolio. But at some future time a pension fund will, at least in theory, reach a point at which its net earnings plus the current contributions of the company will equal the pensions being paid, plus expenses. Even at this point, or at a future time when the fund may contract, selling of common stocks in order to pay pensions may be postponed until after the trustee has exhausted the company's annual contribution, the income of the fund, the fixed interest obligations and the preferred stock.

These arguments were made by Frederick T. Burrows and James J. O'Brien in a recent article on investment policies for pension funds in which they drew the following conclusion: "In view of the relatively small size of the annual pension obligation to the total value of the trust fund, it can readily be seen that the liquidation of common stocks except for investment purposes should not ever be necessary."[82]

[80] Paul L. Howell, "Common Stocks and Pension Fund Investing," *Harvard Business Review*, November–December 1958, p. 93. This article also contains an excellent summary of the literature on stock investment and a number of case studies of pension fund investment.

[81] *Ibid.*, p. 98.

[82] Frederick T. Burrows and James J. O'Brien, "New Pension-Welfare Plan Policy

The arguments in favor of investment in common stock have weight particularly for large pension funds which are or will be fully funded. They should be used with greater caution, however, in the case of many pension funds which are not yet receiving large enough contributions to match accruing liabilities. Yet the argument in favor of such a policy is so forceful, and the over-all performance of the market, at least at present, is such that corporate trustees may be expected to continue their present rate of investment in common stocks and even to increase it.

In a statement concerning its pension trust investment policy, the Chase Manhattan Bank says: "In embarking upon an investment program for a pension fund, we would be governed in regard to the amount to be invested in stocks by the size of the fund, the nature of the business, the attitude of the company management, and a number of other factors."[83]

As a final comment on the safety of common stock investments, the conclusion reached by Professor G. Wright Hoffmann in a volume of studies of the investment of life insurance funds is apposite:

The evidence and reasoning . . . indicate that life insurance companies can invest to their economic advantage substantially larger amounts in common stock — perhaps a minimum of 10 per cent to a maximum of 25 per cent of admitted assets. Moreover, if they believe in the wisdom of such a move and advocate it, it is altogether likely that state laws will be amended to permit it.[84]

The logic inherent in the objectives of the pension trust and the condition of the investment market has led corporate trustees to invest to an increasing extent in corporate stocks to obtain the maximum investment yields consistent with a high degree of safety. The possible control of corporations that may result from this tendency is of great significance for the structure of ownership and control of property in the United States.

PERFORMANCE OF TRUST PORTFOLIO

Now that we have considered the investment policies followed by corporate trustees, what has been the actual performance of pension trust managers? The following discussion of their investment record is based on

Problems," a special issue of *Journal of Commerce*, New York, June 19, 1950, p. 2 (Mimeographed. Chase Manhattan Bank).

[83] Chase Manhattan Bank, *Investing A Large Pension Fund* (no date), p. 3.

[84] David McCahan (ed.), *Investment of Life Insurance Funds,* University of Pennsylvania, Philadelphia, 1953, p. 212.

the Staff Report of the Senate Committee on Banking and Currency referred to previously.[85]

Investment Record

In reviewing the investment activities of the thirty pension trusts which were the subject of the Senate Committee's study, we should point out that their holdings of common stock (at market value) increased from $856.5 million on January 1, 1953 to over $2.2 billion on October 31, 1955. This rate of growth — 158 per cent in less than two years — was by far the largest increase in stockholdings of the seven types of institutions studied. (The next largest increase was 87.2 per cent for open-end investment companies.) These thirty leading pension funds provide us with an excellent picture of the market activity of pension trusts in general. Their assets of $4.1 billion (book value) at the end of 1954 represented a third of the $11.8 billion assets of all noninsured corporate pension funds. Moreover, the common stock holdings of the thirty funds accounted for half of the common stock held by all private noninsured pension funds at that time.

Pension funds are, on the whole, cash purchasers. The Senate Committee found that three-fourths of the increase in the number of shares held by corporate pension funds for the period under study, January 1, 1953 to October 31, 1955, resulted from cash purchases. It would seem, further, that these purchases were expended for the higher-priced stocks since corporate pension funds led all the other institutions in value per share at the beginning and at the end of the period of study.[86] The common stock holdings of pension trusts at the end of October 1955 were valued at $68.81 per share as compared with the average price of $54.16 for listed stocks on the New York Stock Exchange. The record of purchase and sales prices for the year 1954 in particular, when stock prices rose spectacularly, would suggest that the pension trusts were heavy investors in "blue chip" stocks. This is further indicated by the fact that the pension trusts were selling cheaper stocks to buy more valuable ones. The difference in average purchase price over average sales price was $4.55. For the following year (the first ten months of 1955) the spread was $4.35. In fact, the average spread for the corporate pension funds was the greatest of any group with the exception of the fire-insurance companies. Since the spread for pension trusts was only $2.09 in 1953, the yearly differ-

[85] *Institutional Investors and the Stock Market, 1953–1955,* pp. 4, 6, 7 and 8.
[86] Value per share was not available for the life insurance companies. *Ibid.,* p. 7.

ences between 1953 and 1954 seem to indicate a change in the distribution of pension trust portfolios as the stock market rose.

The accompanying graph presents a record of the aggregate monthly
purchases and sales of the pension trusts over the thirty-four-month period of study. During this time the pension funds were seldom sellers:
they purchased $4.50 worth of common stock for every dollar of stock
they sold. This was not true, however, of all the other categories of institutional investors. Some of them showed a high percentage of selling
activity, for example, the open-end companies, which sold $100 worth of
stock for every $1.50 that they purchased. The records of closed-end in-
vestment companies and bank-administered personal trust funds also
showed a dollar volume of sales substantially exceeding their purchases
during this period.

Relation to Market Influences

While the graph of purchases and sales speaks for itself, a better view
is obtained by relating pension trust sales and purchases to Standard and
Poor's Index of Industrial Stock Prices, which is also indicated on the
graph. We may conclude from the graph that pension purchases and
sales do not follow the fluctuations of the market. Trustees buy in a declining market, as in the second and third quarters of 1953 and the fourth
quarter of 1955. They also buy in a sharply rising market, as in the second
quarter of 1955, or shift their holdings in a period of gradual rise, as in
the first quarter of 1955. Market levels undoubtedly affect the buying and
selling policies of the pension funds, but the market does not determine
their activity.

If we turn our attention to the impact of the pension trusts themselves
upon the market, our conclusions must be more speculative. The graph
of pension trust activities as compared with Standard and Poor's prices
might lead us to the conclusion that the trustees were good prophets of
what the market would do. At the same time it is inevitable that heavy
selling or buying by these institutions will have an effect on general market levels. Thus, if a trustee begins to sell or ceases to purchase shares on
the basis of his prediction of a market decline he may succeed in making
his own prediction come true. Conclusions now must be tentative, but
these possible effects will become increasingly real as the pension funds
increase their equity holdings.

Comparison of the activities of corporate pension funds with the other
investor groups shows that the growth of the trusts was their most dis-

STOCK MARKET ACTIVITIES OF CORPORATE PENSION FUNDS,
MONTHLY, JANUARY 1953 THROUGH OCTOBER 1955

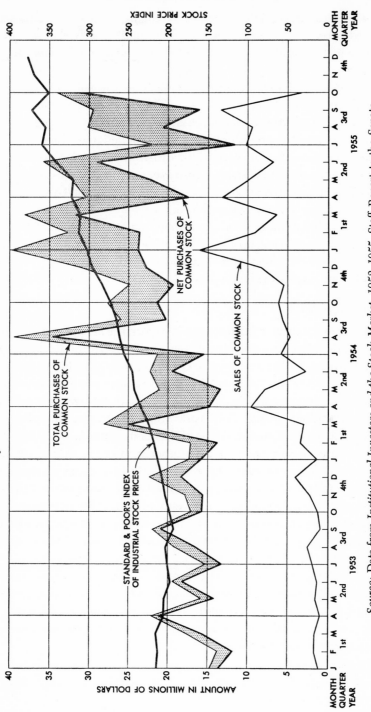

Source: Data from *Institutional Investors and the Stock Market, 1953–1955,* Staff Report to the Senate
Committee on Banking and Currency, 84th Cong., 2d sess., 1956, pp. 8, 10, 11, 14.

tinctive feature. The staff of the Senate committee concluded that "non-insured corporate pension funds were unquestionably the institutional group with the highest rate of withdrawal of stocks from the market; with allowance for differences in coverage for each group, it would appear that the dollar volume of their net acquisitions was substantially greater than that of any of the other groups."[87] The corporate pension funds also showed less fluctuation in net purchases than any of the other groups.

In addition to the growth factor as an explanation of the high volume of stock purchases, a shift in portfolio distribution also took place during the period of study. As we have already seen, common stocks represented 18.7 per cent of total assets of the thirty leading pension trusts in 1951 as compared with 26.7 per cent at the end of 1954. Net income for the thirty funds was $605 million in 1953 and the same in 1954, but net purchases of common stock went up from $195 million in 1953 to $236 million in 1954.[88] Thus corporate trustees have been steadily increasing the proportion of common stocks in their portfolios.

Stocks Preferred by Pension Trusts

As part of its study of institutional investors, the Senate committee staff made a detailed analysis of changes in the institutional holdings of twenty-five carefully selected stocks during the same thirty-four-month period in 1953–1955. The stocks selected represented seventeen industries and were of top rank in dollar volume of sales and capitalization and in active trading on the New York Stock Exchange. They were also among the favored issues in the portfolios of institutional groups.

Corporate pension funds led the other institutions in the number of stocks traded continuously over the thirty-four-month period. They traded in fifteen of the stocks for at least thirty months, and only two stocks were traded in in less than twenty months. The corporate pension funds were net buyers in nearly 90 per cent of the months in which the stocks were traded and in only two stocks were they net sellers.[89]

Purchases. Pension funds purchased nearly one-fourth of all of their common stocks from this list of twenty-five. The Senate committee staff report concludes from this and from the activities of the other institutional investors that pension funds "concentrate their purchases in a relatively small proportion of the approximately 1,100 common-stock issues listed on the New York Stock Exchange."[90]

[87] *Ibid.*, pp. 16–17.
[88] *Ibid.*, pp. 20 and 21.
[89] *Ibid.*, p. 22.
[90] *Ibid.*, p. 25.

Sales. Sales of the twenty-five stocks by the corporate pension funds amounted to 17 per cent of the total stock sales made by these companies. This and other data led the Senate investigators to conclude that the institutional investor, especially the open-end investment, corporate pension and life insurance groups, tended to favor the stocks in the list of twenty-five for increasing their common stock holdings.

Net Acquisitions. Corporate pension funds made 26 per cent of their total net purchases from the selected list of twenty-five stocks. All institutional investors studied showed a definite preference for relatively few stocks in their trading, but the pension funds showed a concentration on even fewer stocks when making additions to their portfolios.[91] The Senate committee staff also noted that in the rapidly rising market of 1954, net acquisitions of the twenty-five stocks accounted for an especially high proportion of total acquisitions. In six of the twelve months of that year more than 30 per cent of pension fund acquisitions were in this list of stocks.

This is interesting when compared with pension trust investments in a falling market. During the nine-month decline in 1953 the sharpest drop in stock prices was in the second quarter. In April, the month of the greatest decline in prices, corporate pension funds showed their largest monthly increase in purchases of the twenty-five stocks and recorded no sales. In relation to total stock purchases, acquisitions of the twenty-five stocks were at their highest point in May and December of that year. Finally, reference to the graph of stock prices shows that for the period under study, stock prices were reaching their peak in September of 1955. In this month, more than one half of the pension fund sales, which were at a relatively high level, were from the list of the twenty-five stocks.[92]

PROXY VOTING POLICIES OF BANKER-TRUSTEES

As we might expect, very little accurate information is published on the voting policies of banker-trustees that control the voting rights of the stocks for which they are fiduciaries. We find, however, that the portion of the stock market study by the subcommittee of the Senate Committee on Banking and Currency devoted to corporate proxy contests has thrown some light on this subject. The Senate hearings in connection

[91] *Ibid.*, pp. 26 and 28.

[92] As may be expected, from what we have seen of the laws governing investments of fiduciaries, the corporate pension funds trade mostly on the New York Stock Exchange. For the full list of thirty companies the median percentage of trading in common stocks on the exchanges was 85.0 per cent for the New York Stock Exchange, for all other exchanges 2.0 per cent, and for the over-the-counter market, 12.4 per cent. *Ibid.*, p. 81.

with this study took place shortly after the Montgomery Ward and New York Central Railroad proxy fights. Both of these struggles were widely reported in the press and became subjects of no little interest on the part of the senators.

Montgomery Ward Contest

In the course of queries put to John A. Barr, chairman of the board and president of Montgomery Ward & Co. during the Senate hearings, Senator Herbert H. Lehman made the following statements concerning the voting of proxies by Montgomery Ward shareholders:

> In the case of banks, virtually 92 per cent, 91.9, was voted for the management, and only 8.1 was voted for the opposition . . . The same thing is true of investment trusts, in which there is a close association between relatively few people, of 92.8 per cent voted for the management, and only 7.2 per cent voted for the opposition. Whereas for individuals there was a very much larger percentage voted, and as far as brokers are concerned, a very much larger percentage voted for the opposition.[93]

In explanation of this Mr. Barr pointed out that no pressure had been placed on the banks and that to a substantial extent stockholding banks did not hold Montgomery Ward's deposits. He also pointed out that investment trusts voted only 10,000 out of 6½ million shares of the company's stock. About the size of bank-held stock he was silent.[94]

Case of the New York Central

The same ground was covered with Robert R. Young, leader of the proxy fight for control of the New York Central Railroad. He stated that in the proxy contest of the New York Central about half the shares of stock voted were registered in individual names and the other half were held for individual accounts by brokers and banks, trust companies and other organizations. Approximately 6.6 million shares were voted in the contest, with the custodian and trust accounts totaling 423,717 shares. Of this block of 423,717 shares, approximately 10 per cent were voted for the challengers, and 90 per cent for the New York Central management.[95]

In the course of his testimony Mr. Young said, "My 1938 experience

---

[93] *Stock Market Study* (Corporate Proxy Contests), Hearings on S. 879, 84th Cong., 1st sess., 1956, Part 3, p. 1358.

[94] *Ibid.*, p. 1359.

[95] *Ibid.*, p. 1481.

and my 1954 experience in proxy fights just shows that those trustees just vote down the line." By this he meant that banker-trustees always voted in favor of management. He further testified that at one time the Chesapeake & Ohio Railway, of which he was chairman, owned 800,000 shares of New York Central stock. At the direction of the Interstate Commerce Commission this stock was placed in the trusteeship of the Chase Bank, the trustee Mr. Young had chosen, and he and his associates were to have the power to vote the stock for anything except New York Central directorships. Later, when Mr. Young was engaged in his proxy fight for control of the New York Central, the question of how the shares held by Chase would be voted became extremely important. According to Mr. Young he was informed that the president of the Chase Bank would "probably be neutral." He claimed, however, that as a result of pressure the Bank then decided to vote with the management of the New York Central.[96]

Can a Trustee Be "Neutral"?

Mr. Young's story is presented here not so much as an account of the actual facts relating to any decision the Chase Bank might have made, but as an illustration of the dilemma in which a large corporate trustee may find itself. It is certainly an anomaly of the so-called democratic corporate system that a large and powerful block of stock should be in a position where it would have to be "neutralized." As a matter of fact, the 800,000 New York Central shares in question wound up in the "Young" column when the votes were tabulated, but had those shares still been in the control of Chase, the very decision to remain neutral could have had tremendous consequences. The withdrawal of a large block of shares inevitably results in making the remaining shares of greater strategic value.

It was Mr. Young's contention at the Senate hearings that the bank-trustee was prepared to sacrifice his interests as beneficial owner of 800,000 shares of New York Central stock to its own interests or the interests of others. Had the bank had to defend such a decision, it undoubtedly would have contended that it was in the interests of the New York Central to retain the incumbent management.

This was a somewhat special situation in that the ICC directed the separation of the power to vote for directors from the beneficial ownership of the shares in contemplation of just such a situation as later arose.

[96] *Ibid.*, pp. 1471, 1483–1485, 1496.

Presumably, the ICC wished to have the power to vote for management in hands which could exercise that power contrary to the wishes of Mr. Young. This certainly weakens if it does not demolish Mr. Young's claim that the bank had violated a trust, but in normal circumstances a bank-trustee would be expected to consult the interests of the beneficial owner in voting shares of stock.[97]

Supposedly, the reason for "neutrality" is that the trustees may avoid the unpleasant accusation that they control business. But if this is the reason for a decision not to vote shares, as sometimes happens, it would seem that the trustee is acting out of loyalty to itself instead of serving the interests of the owners of beneficial interests in the stocks. Further-more, the law of corporations has progressed to the rule that where a stockholder is in a dominant position, he is required to act with the same degree of fiduciary responsibility toward the rest of the stockholders as he would have to exercise if he were in fact a director of the corpora-tion.[98]

If, then, a corporate trustee should find itself in the position of "domi-nant stockholder," it might be presented with a nice question of loyalty divided between the beneficial owners of a particular block of stock and the other shareholders of a corporation. The increasing amounts of equi-ties in corporations which the pension trusts are acquiring may some day bring corporate trustees face to face with such a dilemma. What is still more likely is that corporate trustees will find themselves refusing to in-vest in certain valuable securities merely to avoid becoming dominant stockholders. This is particularly true for large banks which are trustees for many pension funds. A bank may find it impossible to do for all the funds what it could do for one fund alone.

Case of the Teamsters' Union

During the same Senate hearings, the activities of the Teamsters' Un-ion welfare fund were discussed in a similar connection. According to

---

[97] *Ibid.*, pp. 1496–1497.

[98] Farmer's Loan and Trust Co. v. New York and N. Ry. Co., Ct. App. N. Y., 150 N. Y. 410, 44 N. E. 1043, 34 L. R. A. 76 (1896), in which the court said: "But when the New York Central and Hudson River Railroad Company purchased the stock and bonds in question, thus obtaining a controlling interest in the affairs of the New York & Northern Railway Company, . . . it becomes clear that, as such stockholder, it owed a duty to the minority stockholders, that the law implied a quasi trust upon its part . . ." See also cases cited therein. All of these cases involved fraud, but the same court in 1886 interpreted Ervin v. Navigation Co. (27 Fed. 625, 630) to the effect that, ". . . when a number of stockholders combine to constitute themselves a majority, to

testimony before the investigating committee, the Teamsters' Union welfare fund acquired 13,500 shares of Montgomery Ward common stock in the course of that company's proxy fight.[99] The committee counsel cited a news magazine to the effect that the union influenced 100,000 shares through its various bank and other connections. The stock owned by the union and other shares allegedly influenced by it were voted in favor of the incumbent management.

The committee counsel further revealed that shortly thereafter Montgomery Ward signed a union contract which had been a matter of bitter dispute for some eighteen months before that time. Furthermore, this contract contained a clause to which the president of Montgomery Ward had previously declared himself to be unalterably opposed. These statements are related here, again not with the intention of accepting the implications as facts, but merely to illustrate the potential power of a union welfare fund. Whatever the ethics of such a transaction, it is clear that control of the large assets of a pension fund places considerable economic power in the hands of union leaders.

PASSIVE ROLE OF THE BENEFICIARIES

The real parties in interest in the pension trust system are, of course, the employees. Their interest is greater than that of any other party because their security is the ultimate object of the pension system and dictates the stable and fiduciary character of the entire operation. Furthermore, we may presume that in planning for their security the ultimate decisions as to the type of fund, whether it shall be of fixed dollar benefit or tied to the expanding economy, will be based on the circumstances of their needs and wants. As yet, however, the beneficiaries are the group who have the least influence upon formulation of pension trust policy.

The employee is least influential in policy determination because his role in the pension trust system is primarily passive. In the first place, he is seldom free to make his own choice of what benefit suits him best. Most often his employer or his union will make the decision for him and the employee will merely be told that he can expect a certain level of benefits at a certain time in his life. In some cases, as with the Sears plan, he

control the corporation as they see fit, they become, for all practical purposes, the corporation itself, and assume the trust relation of a corporation towards its stockholders . . ."

[99] *Stock Market Study,* Hearings, Part 3, p. 1367.

may be free to join the plan or not, but more often not even this choice is open to him because he will be covered by a noncontributory plan which he accepts along with the other conditions of his employment.

Secondly, the employee seldom has any way of knowing whether or not his benefits are being adequately provided for. In most cases he has very little access to the type of information that will enable him to judge whether or not sufficient funds are being supplied to the pension trust. And further, the financial operations of the fund are so complex that it is difficult for even the trained actuary or accountant to assess liabilities and reserves properly.

The legal rights of an employee in a pension fund, discussed in Chapter 6, have not yet been fully defined, especially such rights as he may have as beneficiary of a true trust. But practically speaking, the employee's rights are limited to his claims after he has reached age 65 and has worked for some twenty to thirty years for his company. He has no effective source of control over the pension fund as such during his term of employment — only a claim upon it after he has reached retirement age. As a worker grows older the net capital built up to provide for his future becomes considerable, but to the extent that his capital worth is represented by pension expectations he is not a free agent. So far as the pension fund is concerned he is not free to continue or to stop saving nor may he determine the form his savings will take. More than that, he becomes tied to a certain corporation or industry and is, as it were, "locked" into a certain place in the economic system.

The Employee's Growing Dependence

The private pension trust system has thus forged new links of dependence for the employee. He is also more closely tied to his union in many instances because its contract with the employer may establish the level of pension benefits, and more closely tied to the employer because the success or failure of the business will affect the size of the pension fund backing the employee's expectation of old-age benefits.

The welfare of the individual employee is, furthermore, now more than ever dependent on the general level of the economic welfare of the United States because his hope for enjoyment of a good life at the time he retires is linked by the pension fund to the interest rates of bonds and mortgages, the dividends of stocks and the value of the dollar. Thus the decisions made by the financial community and fiscal officials in government are matters of much greater impact upon his future. Similarly, the decisions made by his union limit the worker's freedom of choice. The union official can influence the channeling of large sums into current consumption or savings by his decision that a wage package shall be divided up, so much into the weekly envelope, so much into the pension fund. The union official may also have a hand in determining, by his preference for a method of funding a pension plan, whether the fixed securities of insurance investments will grow or whether risk capital will expand because he prefers a noninsured trust fund. It is quite evident, then, that the power or, to use a more limited and less frightening word, the capacity for making decisions which the employee does not have or has lost under the present system does not thereby become nonexistent. The burden — or the power to make decisions about the economic welfare of the employee — is taken up by the employer, by the union, and, for the employee's protection, by the government in its regulatory capacity.

Whether the average employee is more or less dependent upon the decisions of others than he was before the rise of the pension systems may be hard to determine. But we do know, at least, that there is a new alignment of the powers controlling him and that certain decisions he once could make are now no longer under his control. In many cases, the most evident decision-making power he has lost is whether or not he will save. With this have gone the consequent decisions as to his rate of savings, the form his savings will take and the amount he will save. Certainly it is true that the worker has lost the power of decision he would have had if his salary increases had appeared in his pay envelope rather than on the credit rosters of some pension fund. If the effect of the pension funds is to make the employee a capitalist, as many have said, he has only one of the prerogatives that make it desirable to be a capitalist — security. He gains little in the way of economic power or the freedom that economic power carries with it. Capitalist he may be, but certainly not in the sense that Marx and Adam Smith used the term.

IMPACT OF

GOVERNMENT POLICIES

Role of the Federal Government

Influence of State Governments

Taxation of Insured Pension Plans

Summary

The form that pension trusts have taken and will take is significantly shaped by influences from government and from private organizations. In the closely knit economy of 1959 no major institution can fail to feel certain effects from the operations of other large organizations, and the pension funds are no exception. Perhaps the greatest formative influence on the pension trusts coming from an external source is the effect of the tax policy of the federal government with regard to the exemption of pension fund income.

Besides the impact of the provisions of the Internal Revenue Code of 1954, the Taft-Hartley Act and the federal banking laws have also influenced the development of private pension programs. Finally, in the past few years state governments have shown a growing interest in the need for some kind of regulation and public disclosure of the activities of employee retirement and other benefit plans, and several states have taken the lead in enacting legislation to provide a measure of supervisory control and information about the plans and their financial operations.

ROLE OF THE FEDERAL GOVERNMENT

We have already seen something of the historical development of the present tax policy as it concerns pension and welfare funds. At present the operative law affecting pension trusts is the Internal Revenue Code of 1954. We shall attempt to analyze here only those sections of the code that have an important influence on the form and operations of trusteed pension plans. The basic provisions of the 1939 Code, as amended by the Revenue Act of 1942, form the substance of the 1954 Code.[1] The major change in the 1942 Act was the provision that a pension or profit-sharing plan must not be discriminatory if it is to be tax exempt. The code provisions which we are about to analyze were all in effect during the period of greatest growth in the pension movement and have had a formative influence upon it.

TAX TREATMENT OF PENSION PLANS

The provisions of the 1954 Code became effective in August of that year.[2] But it was not until September 1956, two years later, that the Internal Revenue Service issued its regulations interpreting the pension exemption provisions of the 1954 Act.[3] We may presume that in establishing its regulations the Internal Revenue Service made extensive use of previous experience with the 1939 Code, the deliberations of the House Committee which proposed extensive amendments to the pension trust provisions, the hearings of the Senate Subcommittee on Welfare and Pension Funds,[4] and other sources of information in this field.

Contributions made by an employer to welfare and pension plans are deductible as an ordinary and necessary business expense, under Section 162(a)(1) of the Code. This type of deduction is always open to the employer, but a deduction taken under Section 162 would still be taxed to the employee as part of his income for the current year. Under Section 402 of the Internal Revenue Code of 1954, however, the employee is

---

[1] Internal Revenue Code of 1954, § 401.

[2] Pub. L. No. 591, 83d Cong., 2d sess., Aug. 16, 1954.

[3] T. D. 6203, 21 Fed. Reg. 7269, Sept. 25, 1956; 26 C. F. R. § 1.401; also reported in *U. S. Code Congressional and Administrative News* (1956), p. 7284.

[4] Harold T. Swartz, Director, Tax Rulings Division, Internal Revenue Service, testified before the subcommittee that the Senate Finance Committee eliminated the extensive changes proposed in the House bill because it desired to make a further study of the problems. He stated that "there were no substantial changes in the statute other than the fact that the prohibited transactions provision and the unrelated business activities provisions were made applicable to pension trusts in the 1954 Code." Hearings on S. Res. 40, 84th Cong., 2d sess., 1955, Part 3, p. 864.

specifically exempted from taxation on current contributions made for him by the employer. The advantages of a pension system are further enhanced by exemption of the earnings of pension funds until such time as the trust pays out pension benefits to the employees.

The net results of these deductions and exemptions are illustrated by the following examples. One expert has estimated that an employee who at age 65 wished to buy himself an immediate annuity of $100 a month would have to pay a premium of about $15,000. An annuity of $500 a month would cost an executive about $75,000. The same annuities bought by a corporation able to deduct the cost from excess profits taxed at a rate of 80 per cent would cost about $3,000 and $15,000 respectively. The same authority adds:

> And when it is considered that the net earnings of a corporation are usually not available to the stockholders except upon payment of a second tax (on the dividends distributed to them), it will be seen that the net cost of the expenditures to the ultimate owners is even smaller than these figures.[5]

Requirements for a "Qualified" Plan

Section 404 of the Internal Revenue Code of 1954 provides for deductions for employer contributions to an employees' trust or annuity plan and compensation under a deferred-payment plan and places certain limitations on the amount of deductible contributions. Section 402 covers taxability of beneficiaries of employees' trusts, and Section 403, taxation of employees' annuities. In general these sections provide that benefits distributed to pensioners are taxable as annuities at the time they are received. Requirements for the exemption of employees' pension funds are treated in Section 401 of the Code, which also covers stock-bonus and profit-sharing funds.

The 1956 regulations interpreting the Code set forth a definition of the kind of pension plan that may qualify for tax deduction and exemption under Section 401(a) of the Code. It is requisite (1) that there be a plan, "established and maintained by an employer primarily to provide systematically for the payment of definitely determinable benefits to his employees over a period of years . . ."; and (2) that "the determination of the retirement benefits and the contributions to provide such benefits are not dependent upon profits." According to the regulations, "benefits are

---

[5] Dan M. McGill, *Pensions: Problems and Trends,* Huebner Foundation for Insurance Education, University of Pennsylvania, Irwin, Homewood, Illinois, 1955, p. 64.

not definitely determinable if funds arising from forfeitures on termination, or other reason, may be used to provide increased benefits for the remaining participants instead of being used to reduce the amount of contributions by the employer."[6] Benefits are determinable if "the employer contributions under the plan can be determined actuarially on the basis of definitely determinable benefits."[7]

These requisites, which at first sight would appear to be merely a definition of the meaning of a pension plan, have the effect of making otherwise vague and formless plans very clear in their commitments. Doubtless many plans have been formalized to meet the qualification requirements. It would seem that the requirement that forfeitures be used to decrease employer contributions rather than to benefit the remaining participants is part of the policy of nondiscrimination since the more highly salaried employees would not be as likely to leave the employ of a company as would those in the lower wage brackets.

The regulations further require that the "plan" be a permanent program as distinguished from a temporary arrangement. Abandonment of the plan after a few years for any reason other than business necessity would be evidence that from its inception it was not a bona fide program for the exclusive benefit of the employees in general. This requirement of permanency has undoubtedly been efficacious in bringing about the establishment of more soundly backed pension plans, especially when the matter of permanency is as broadly investigated as the following statement implies: "The permanency of the plan will be indicated by all of the surrounding facts and circumstances, including the likelihood of the employer's ability to continue contributions as provided under the plan."[8]

Pension programs set up as a device for the distribution of profits to shareholders do not qualify. The regulations are explicit on the point that "the plan must benefit the employees in general, although it need not provide benefits for all the employees."[9] Thus, according to the rules, if a plan discriminates either in eligibility requirements, contributions or benefits in favor of officers, shareholders, supervisors or other highly compensated personnel, it cannot qualify for tax exemption. The broad scope of the inquiry made by the IRS into pension plans is indicated by

[6] 26 C.F.R. § 1.401–1(b)(1)(i); *U. S. Code Cong. & Ad. News* (1956), p. 7287.
[7] *Ibid.*
[8] 26 C.F.R. § 1.401–1(b)(2); *U. S. Code Cong. & Ad. News,* p. 7288.
[9] 26 C.F.R. § 1.401–1(b)(3); *U. S. Code Cong. & Ad. News,* p. 7288.

its policy statement that the law is concerned not only with the form of the plan but also with its effects in operation.

The law contains no specific limitations on the type of investments permitted to a pension trust and the regulations rely on local law for protection of the beneficiaries. However, a trust is subject to a tax under Section 511 of the Code with respect to any "unrelated business taxable income" and the tax-exempt status of the trust may be forfeited if the investments made by the trustees constitute so-called prohibited transactions within the meaning of Section 503 of the Code.[10] In general these transactions would include any negotiations that would serve to divert a substantial amount of securities or property in the trust to the creator of the trust or a related person. An allied restriction requires full disclosure of investments in the employer's stock or securities, or loans to him or other persons so situated as to be able to take advantage of self-serving management of the trust.

Another important regulation applies to Section 401(2)(2) of the Code and requires that under the trust instrument no part of the trust can possibly be used for purposes other than for the exclusive benefit of employees or their beneficiaries. This regulation permits the employer to retain the power to modify or terminate the rights of certain employees covered by the trust, but requires that funds once in the trust may be used to benefit employees only.

The only funds that an employer may recover from the trust upon its termination are those represented by "any balance remaining in the trust which is due to erroneous actuarial computations during the previous life of the trust."[11] A surplus resulting from a change in the benefit provisions or the eligibility requirements of a pension plan could not revert to the employer because it would not be the result of an "erroneous actuarial computation." It seems evident that the Internal Revenue authorities consider a "pension trust" to be a true trust for, in order to make it impossible for the employer to recover pension funds, they require that "the trust instrument must contain a definite affirmative provision to this effect, irrespective of whether the obligations to employees have their source in the trust instrument itself, in the plan of which the trust forms a part, or in some collateral instrument . . ."[12] Thus, for example, in the U. S. Steel Corporation plan, although the company regards its obliga-

---

[10] 26 C.F.R. § 1.401–1(b)(5)(i); *U. S. Code Cong. & Ad. News*, p. 7289.
[11] 26 C.F.R. § 1.401–2(b)(1); *U. S. Code Cong. & Ad. News*, p. 7290.
[12] 26 C.F.R. § 1.401–2(b)(2); *U. S. Code Cong. & Ad. News*, p. 7290.

tion as stemming from its labor contract, the pension funds must be irrevocably dedicated to the benefit of the employees.

In order to guarantee that a pension or other tax-exempt plan will in fact operate for the benefit of the employees in general, a trust will not be qualified unless it is part of a plan which satisfies the coverage requirements of Section 401(a)(3) of the Code. These requirements are as follows: 70 per cent of all active employees or 80 per cent of the eligible employees (provided that 70 per cent of all employees are eligible) must participate in the plan. But it is permissible to limit eligibility by a waiting period of not more than five years. In the example given by the authors of the Internal Revenue regulations, a plan with 462 participating employees out of a total of 1,000 may qualify when all legitimate conditions of eligibility are considered.[13]

Even broader latitude is possible under an alternative provided by the statute to the effect that a plan may win qualification if it covers only such employees as qualify under a classification set up by the employer and found by the Commissioner of Internal Revenue not to be discriminatory. The code and rules further proscribe any discrimination on the basis of contributions or benefits in favor of officers, shareholders, employees whose principal duties consist in supervising the work of other employees, or highly compensated employees as against other employees *whether within or without the plan.*[14]

Limitations on Deductions

Section 404 of the Code covers deductions for contributions to pension plans. The limitations on deductions are of importance in the light of arguments that the government is really paying the greater portion of the cost of benefits under pension programs. The first important limitation for our purposes is that

In no case is a deduction allowable under Section 404(a) for the amount of any contribution for the benefit of an employee in excess of the amount which, together with other deductions allowed for compensation for such employee's services, constitutes a reasonable allowance for compensation for the services actually rendered.[15]

In other words, deductions for contributions to a pension fund, plus other

---

[13] 26 C.F.R. § 1.401–3(a)(2); *U. S. Code Cong. & Ad. News,* p. 7291.

[14] 26 C.F.R. § 1.401–1(b)(3); § 1.401–3(a)(1)(b); § 1.401–4(a)(1)(i)(ii); *U. S. Code Cong. & Ad. News,* pp. 7290, 7291, 7294.

[15] 26 C.F.R. § 1.404(a)–1(b); *U. S. Code Cong. & Ad. News,* p. 7310.

compensation to the employee, may not exceed the reasonable value of his services.

An employer's contribution need not be limited to services which are performed within the current tax year and may represent additional compensation for services performed in prior years. The amount that an employer may deduct annually must be determined on an acceptable actuarial basis. Further, an employer may not allege costs which exceed those based on assumptions and methods that are reasonable in view of the provisions and coverage of the plan, the funding medium, and reasonable expectations as to the effects of mortality and interest and other factors. This, in the opinion of one expert observer, has resulted in the adoption of definite commitments and the conversion of many voluntary or discretionary programs into more or less fixed obligations.[16]

Several methods are available to the employer for computing his deductions for contributions to pension funds, but the aim of all these formulas is to limit the employer's deductions to contributions for current liabilities and for funding of past service liability. Past service costs may be apportioned over the remaining service of the employees or may be funded at a rate of not more than 10 per cent a year. An important provision allows any amount paid in excess of the amount deductible in any year to be carried forward and deducted in future years.

Taxation of the Beneficiary

Of equal importance is the matter of taxation of the employee. In the case of a qualified trust the amount received by each pensioner is taxable to him in the year in which he receives payment, as if it were an annuity. Prior to 1954, the employee in a contributory plan paid a tax of 3 per cent on the amount of his own contributions and charged off the rest of what he received against his cost until it was recovered; after that his receipts were taxed in full.[17] But under Section 72 of the 1954 Code the employee may spread his cost over the periodic payments of the annuity, and the difference between the annual prorated costs and the amount actually received is taxed as income. An exception is made where the employee's total cost is not greater than the annuity payments of the first three years. In this case the first payments are charged off against cost until completely recovered; subsequent payments are taxed as income.[18] As may

[16] McGill, *op. cit.*, p. 76.
[17] *Ibid.*, p. 70.
[18] Internal Revenue Code of 1954, § 72(d).

be expected, in noncontributory plans all payments are taxable as received. Another exception occurs when the employee or his estate receives the total amount of his benefits in a single year. In this case the benefit, less the employee's contributions, is taxed as a long-term capital gain.[19]

Taxation of a Nonexempt Trust

The tax policy applicable to nonexempt trusts points up the great advantage to be gained by establishing a trust which will qualify for exemption. In nonexempt trusts, the employer's contributions, to the extent that they represent remuneration for services, are, of course, deductible for the employer, but these contributions are immediately taxable to the employees in plans in which their interests are nonforfeitable. Where the employee's interests are forfeitable, they are not taxed to him until the benefits are received or become nonforfeitable. But in such a case the Treasury has held that contributions are not deductible by the employer. The law thus places the nonqualified trust at a distinct tax disadvantage.[20]

EVALUATION OF TAX POLICY
ON PENSION FUNDS

From the preceding survey of the tax provisions, it should be evident that the ultimate advantages to be derived from the tax treatment of pension trusts depend on timing. All funds flowing into pension trusts are taxed eventually, but the question of when they shall be taxed is of the highest importance. For the employer there is the advantage of paying the cost of future pensions out of income which would otherwise be subject to taxation at current rates and he further has a degree of latitude in selecting the year in which to make a contribution and claim deduction. For the employee there is the advantage of paying the tax on a portion of his income after retirement when he will be taxed at a lower rate.

Noncontributory Plans Favored

The tax structure which we have been examining also results in a cost advantage to noncontributory plans over contributory plans. In a plan in which the employee contributes to the cost, he is taxed currently for the amount of his contribution. Even though this income is withheld from

[19] McGill, *op. cit.*, p. 70.
[20] *Ibid.*

his wages and paid into the trust, it remains taxable to the employee. The net effect of this system is that an employer can provide a larger pension by contributing directly to the pension fund from his own pocket and by-passing the employee. Since the total sum required to purchase pension benefits comes ultimately from the employer anyway, in most cases the tax advantages to the employee in a noncontributory plan will outweigh the advantages of a contributory plan.[21]

Effect on Over-all Tax Structure

Thus far we have been discussing the statutory and regulatory provisions governing the establishment and operation of pension plans. These, to a large extent, have provided the mold which has given the pension system its form. We might further say that the tax rates have provided much of the pressure to force the pension system into its mold. We have already seen how the most rapid expansion of pension plans took place when labor was in great demand and wages and salaries were frozen during World War II. At this time, according to the Brookings Institution study, the excess profits tax structure created the impression that the federal government would be paying as much as 85.5 per cent of pension expenses. After a brief enough lapse, the enactment of the 1950 excess profits tax provisions resulted in a marginal rate of 82 per cent for many corporations during 1952 and 1953.[22] When we add to these factors the intensive sales efforts of banks, insurance and trust companies, all making full use of the arguments presented by the tax structure, we have strong incentives for the rapid build-up of the pension system.

Lewis Kimmel, who prepared the section on tax problems in the Brookings study, maintains that the federal government bears a considerable portion of pension costs only in the *short run*. He argues that

in the *long run* the one most important factor influencing the incidence of employer contributions is that they constitute costs . . . Few businesses will accept

[21] This point is made by Haddad (McGill, *op. cit.*, p. 76) and by Lewis Kimmel in the Brookings study. Kimmel gives an example of this situation in which there would be an increase of $1.43, representing taxes, for each $10 allotted for pensions under a contributory plan where employer and employee each paid half. But he makes the point that "it cannot be assumed, however, that employee's contributions — or any other continuing expenditure — are covered from marginal income in all circumstances. The marginal or 'last-in' approach is not valid in the case of long established pension plans." See Charles L. Dearing, *Industrial Pensions*, The Brookings Institution, Washington, 1955, p. 301.
[22] Dearing, *op. cit.*, p. 300.

indefinitely a new cost item that is substantial in amount, without attempting to recoup it through their price schedules.[23]

Mr. Kimmel further points out that to the cost accountant the price of pensions is no different from the wages that go into pay envelopes and that they are a category of expense which must be covered before any profit can be realized. He admits that certain industries, for example those in which demand may be uncertain and fairly elastic, and those in which business is declining or is temporarily depressed, may find it difficult to recover the cost of past service credits — or even current costs. Thus, while it may not be safe to make an inclusive statement, it is generally true that insofar as possible an employer will seek to pass the expenses of pension programs along to the consumer. It is difficult to refute Mr. Kimmel's final argument:

It must not be forgotten that it is the economy as a whole, including employees in the governmental sector, which finances the services performed by government. Considered as a long-range proposition, the converse — that government covers the cost of programs and activities that are privately financed — is not defensible.[24]

While it may be indefensible to say that government covers the major cost of privately financed pension programs and activities, the effect of taxation may be to distribute the expense of these programs inequitably among the taxpayers. Although all of the income represented by pensions is ultimately subject to taxation, the delay in taxing pension income works very favorably for the employee. For the average retired employee who enjoys a pension, the benefit or annuity probably constitutes the greater part of his income and the taxable portion of this income will be greatly reduced by deductions and personal exemptions. Retired employees are entitled to personal exemptions and persons over 65 may claim two exemptions.[25] A pensioner aged 65 with a wife aged 60, for example, would pay no tax on an income of less than $2,000 before exemptions. The advantage of paying income tax at future reduced rates would seem to be even greater in the case of highly compensated employees who may expect to find themselves paying taxes on pensions which were earned at a time when they enjoyed the dubious honor of being in a relatively high tax bracket. Kimmel points out in the Brookings study that "as the coverage of tax favored private pension plans expands, the revenue nec-

23 *Ibid.*, p. 303.
24 *Ibid.*, p. 305.
25 *Ibid.*, p. 298.

essary to support the federal government must be obtained from other tax sources or by raising the rates for the corporate income tax or other taxes."[26]

We can see that in part, at least, the cost of pensions is now being borne by doctors, lawyers and other professional and self-employed workers who do not benefit from the tax exemptions enjoyed by the pension trusts. It is this apparent advantage of the employed worker over the self-employed individual that the proponents of H.R. 10 in the present Congress point to. Legislation to remedy this inequity has been introduced in every Congress since 1951 and a bill granting tax relief to the self-employed individual was actually passed by the House of Representatives in the 85th Congress only to die in the Senate rush for adjournment. Similar legislation has been introduced into both the Senate and the House of Representatives in the 86th Congress and proponents of H.R. 10, which has already been reported out of the House Ways and Means Committee, predict early passage in the House.[27]

H.R. 10 allows tax deductions of amounts paid into approved retirement funds up to $2,500 or 10 per cent of the year's net earnings, whichever is smaller. No deductions are to be allowed to an individual for such payments after the age of 70½, and a lifetime limit of $50,000 is placed on the amount of income on which taxes may be deferred. For those aged 50 or over before January 1, 1959 the annual limit is increased by one-tenth for each year of age in excess of 50. The lifetime limit is reduced for those who have acquired nonforfeitable rights in employee benefit plans. The bill would apply to those individuals who are subject to the tax on self-employment under the Social Security law along with certain other classes of self-employed individuals, such as doctors and ministers, who are not subject to the self-employment tax. Payments for retirement will not be deductible after age 70½. Withdrawals of benefits may start at 65 and must begin by 70½, at which time the funds become subject to income taxation.

Payments for retirement benefits may be made to buy a restricted retirement policy from an insurance company, or funds may be placed in a bank-trusteed retirement fund. We can thus expect a new flow of wealth

[26] *Ibid.*, p. 257.

[27] H.R. 10, 86th Cong., 1st sess., introduced by Rep. Keogh. H.R. 9, introduced by Rep. Simpson, and S. 944, introduced by Sen. Kefauver, are identical with H.R. 10 and differ very little from the bill which passed the House in July 1958. Other bills, H.R. 1286, H.R. 2889 and H.R. 3389, are similar but allow a higher ceiling on yearly contributions for retirement. Cf. 66 Harv. L. Rev. 1105 (1953).

into the hands of the insurance companies and the corporate trustees. That the amount will be considerable may be gathered from the estimate of United States Treasury officials that passage of this bill may reduce tax revenues by $365 million.

The estimated $365 million drop in tax proceeds is one of the reasons why the proposal is receiving opposition in certain quarters. But proponents of the measure maintain that this figure is merely a measure of the discrimination which results from granting favored tax treatment to the employee at the expense of the self-employed individual.

Limited Role of Internal Revenue Service

Since federal tax exemption is of vital importance to a pension plan and since the enabling statute and operating rules give broad powers of discretion to the Internal Revenue Service, it is evident that the federal authorities, through the tax laws, could exercise strong regulatory powers over the pension system. As far as may be determined, however, the tax authorities have not made extensive use of these powers. The representative of the Internal Revenue Service who testified before the Senate Subcommittee on Welfare and Pension Funds emphasized the point that the principal function and interest of the IRS is the collection of federal taxes. He pointed out that the Service was responsible for the collection of over seventy different internal revenue taxes and that this involved the processing of nearly 95 million tax returns. He concluded: "Accordingly, only a small portion of our time can be devoted to examining into the annual information returns filed by exempt organizations."[28]

Thus, the formative influence of the federal tax laws on pension trusts derives mainly from the structure of those laws and the general rules for application which we have been discussing. It is highly impractical to expect a continuing supervision of pension trusts from the Internal Revenue Service even though such supervision might be justified on the grounds of the federal power to tax.

EFFECT OF LABOR LEGISLATION
ON PENSION PLANS

Section 302 of the Labor-Management Relations Act of 1947, the Taft-Hartley Act, deals with pension funds by way of restrictions on payments to employee representatives.[29] The pertinent provisions of the act permit

[28] Hearings on S. Res. 40, Part 3, p. 847.
[29] 61 Stat. 157 (1947); 302(c)(5); 29 U. S. C. 186(c)(5) (1952).

payment of funds to employee representatives only when such funds are used exclusively in employee benefit programs. In estimating the effect of the Taft-Hartley provisions upon the pension movement it is well to remember that at most 13.5 per cent of all employees participating in pension plans are covered by a Taft-Hartley type of administration.[30] Paragraphs (a) and (b) of Section 302 make it unlawful for the employer to pay or deliver money or other things of value to a representative of any of his employees in an industry affecting commerce. Paragraph (c)(5) makes the prohibition inapplicable, however, "with respect to money or other things of value paid to a trust fund established by such representative, for the sole and exclusive benefit of the employees of such employer, and their families and dependents." But the proviso clause of Section 302 lays down certain further conditions under which such payments are lawful and thus prescribes the form of an employees' trust:

Provided That (A) such payments are held in trust for the purpose of paying, either from principal or income or both, for the benefit of employees, their families and dependents, for medical or hospital care, pensions on retirement or death of employees, compensation for injuries . . .

(B) The detailed basis upon which such payments are to be made is specified in a written agreement with the employer, and the employees and employers are equally represented in the administration of such fund, together with such neutral persons as the representatives of the employers and the representatives of the employees may agree upon . . . and shall also contain provisions for an annual audit of the trust fund, a statement of the results of which shall be available for inspection by interested persons at the principal office of the trust fund and at such other places as may be designated in such written agreement; and

(C) Such payments as are intended to be used for the purpose of providing pensions or annuities for employees are made to a separate trust which provides that the funds held therein cannot be used for any purposes other than paying such pensions or annuities.

In effect, Section 302 of the Taft-Hartley law is an attempt to determine that pension plans will be trust funds administered jointly by union and management representatives. Its purpose is to prevent bribery between an employer and union officials. The statute is penal in nature and lays down prohibitions against paying funds to an employee representa-

---

[30] Senate Report No. 1734, Senate Subcommittee on Welfare and Pension Funds, 84th Cong., 2d sess., 1956, p. 14.

tive for any purpose other than to support a trust fund for the benefit of employees.[31]

Furthermore, the National Labor Relations Board has refused to admit responsibility for enforcement of Section 302. The Board has adopted the position that its exclusive province is unfair labor practice jurisdiction and claims that Congress established criminal prosecution and injunction to be sought by the Attorney General as the only method of enforcing this section.[32] Since pension and welfare plans are subjects for collective bargaining, as determined by the NLRB, the Board will deal with matters covered by Section 302 only to the extent that they constitute unfair labor practices under the act.[33]

Within the scope of this jurisdiction, the Board has held that an employer must furnish information necessary for intelligent collective bargaining.[34] The Board has also held that the discrimination in hiring, discharge and other matters prohibited by Section 8a(3) includes discriminations in pensions.[35] Furthermore, it has held that a pension or welfare plan may not be used to coerce or restrain employees.[36]

Court Interpretations of Section 302

Two judicial interpretations of Section 302 led the Committee on Labor and Social Security Legislation of the Association of the Bar of the City of New York to state in 1955 that the courts had ". . . to a substantial extent freed the welfare funds from Federal control since trust funds are not covered by the Act."[37] The Bar Committee felt justified in issuing this statement on the grounds that federal decisions had put pen-

---

[31] Senate Report No. 1734, p. 57.

[32] Local 1664 (Dock Division), 103 N.L.R.B. 1217 (1953); New Orleans Laundry, Inc., 100 N.L.R.B. 966 (1952); Crown Products Co., 99 N.L.R.B. 602 (1952).

[33] Inland Steel, 77 N.L.R.B. 1 (1948); *enforcement granted,* 170 F. 2d 247 (7th Cir. 1948); Black Clawson Co., 103 N.L.R.B. 928 (1953); Allied Mills, Inc., 82 N.L.R.B. 854 (1949).

[34] Jacobs Manufacturing Co., 94 N.L.R.B. 1214 (1951); *enforcement granted,* 196 F. 2d 680 (2d Cir. 1952); Aluminum Ore v. NLRB, 131 F. 2d 485 (7th Cir. 1942); Phelps Dodge Copper Products Corp., 101 N.L.R.B. 360 (1952); Reed & Prince Manufacturing Co., 96 N.L.R.B. 850 (1951).

[35] Bedding and Drapery Workers Union, 34 L.R.R.M. 1332 (1954); Jandel Furs, 100 N.L.R.B. 1390 (1952); Rockaway News Supplies Co., 94 N.L.R.B. 1056 (1951).

[36] Burns Brick Co., 80 N.L.R.B. 389 (1948); Hazen and Jaeger Funeral Home, 95 N.L.R.B. 1034 (1951). The union's unfair labor practices are also forbidden. See Pennello v. International Union, UMW, 88 F. Supp. 935 (D. C. 1950).

[37] New York State Insurance Department, *Welfare and Pension Funds, Public Hearing,* Exhibit 3, Report of Association of the Bar of the City of New York, 1955, p. 3 (mimeographed).

sion trustees outside the scope of Section 302 by declaring them not to be "representatives" as intended in that section.

In *United Marine Division* v. *Essex Transport Co.* the plaintiff was seeking to compel the payment of money by an employer to a pension trust for employees. The employer's defense was that such payments were prohibited by Section 302. The Court of Appeals for the Third Circuit reviewed the legislative history of the section and stated what the legislators were attempting to do: "They were forbidding money to be paid to representatives of unions unless through a trust fund, the requirements for which were set up in some detail."[38]

It would seem, however, that in the court's view the trustees in this case did not need the exception provided in Section 302, for:

> These trustees were not, in our judgment, representatives of the employees. They were trustees of a welfare fund. It is true that they were chosen half and half by the employer's association and this union. But we think that when set up as a board . . . these individuals are not acting as representatives of either union or employers. They are trustees of a fund and have fiduciary duties in connection therewith as do any other trustees.[39]

The case of *Rice-Stix Co.* v. *St. Louis Institute* strengthens this view.[40] The Court of Appeals for the Second Circuit held a similar doctrine in *United States* v. *Ryan* until it was reversed by the Supreme Court.[41] The defendant was indicted under Section 302(b) for receiving money from an employer. The Court of Appeals held that the term "representative" in the act was limited to "the exclusive bargaining representative of employees." In its disagreement, the Supreme Court gave a broad interpretation of the term to the effect that ". . . in using the term 'representative' Congress intended that it include any person authorized by the employees to act for them in dealings with their employers,"[42] and again, ". . . 302 prohibits payments by employers to individuals who represent employees in their relations with employers."[43]

The decision in the Court of Appeals had resulted in exempting the president of the union from application of the act because it was the union itself which was the bargaining representative. The Supreme Court

[38] 216 F. 2d 410, 412 (3d Cir. 1954).
[39] *Ibid.*
[40] 22 L.R.R.M. 2528 (E.D. Mo. 1948).
[41] 350 U. S. 299, 307 (1956), *reversing* 225 F. 2d 417 (2d Cir. 1955); 69 Harv. L. Rev. 386 (1956).
[42] 350 U. S. at 302.
[43] 350 U. S. at 307.

held that such an interpretation would unduly restrict the application of Section 302 prohibitions. Thus, the explicit limitations on welfare funds would be easy to evade and payments made directly to union officials, or to other individuals as trustees, would apparently be excluded from Section 302.

But in eschewing the narrow construction in order not to allow the primary intent of Congress to be frustrated, the Court may have raised other problems. Is the Court's definition so broad that it covers employer-administered funds, for example, so that trustees of such a fund and the fund itself become subject to the provisions of the act? It is not likely that the Court had such far-reaching effects in mind. Yet the language "individuals who represent employees in their relations with employers" could, in logic, include the trustees of employer-managed funds.[44]

The first distinction that suggests itself for narrowing the application of the *Ryan* rule is that in many employer-managed pension funds the so-called pension committee or trustees (i.e., the committee or trustees as distinguished from the fiduciary) are not in fact the representatives of the employees but rather represent management. Such was the case in *Ball* v. *Victor Adding Machine Co.*,[45] in which the court held that since the committee was subject to the absolute power of removal by the employer, the court could determine whether the ruling of the committee was an independent decision or one dominated by the employer's wishes.

Since the Supreme Court has held that the provisions of Section 302 are intended to prevent bribery of employee representatives, it would seem reasonable and consistent to limit the application of Taft-Hartley restrictions to those funds in which payments to a welfare fund actually leave the control and supervision of the employer and are placed unreservedly within the power of the employee representatives.

Limitations of Taft-Hartley Provisions

The extreme limitations of Section 302 are well illustrated in a letter from the Assistant Attorney General sent to the Senate Subcommittee on Welfare and Pension Funds in August 1955. It refers as follows to an earlier hearing in the House of Representatives investigating welfare and pension funds:

The hearings did produce considerable evidence of deliberate mismanagement of large welfare funds brought about by payments of excessive fees and

[44] See Note, 70 Harv. L. Rev. 490, 503 (1957).
[45] 236 F. 2d 170 (5th Cir. 1956).

premiums for insurance, excessive costs of administration, failure to keep adequate records and other improper practices. However, the funds were established in conformity with the requirements of Section 302(c)(5) of the Labor Management Relations Act.[46]

Enforcement of Section 302 is left to the Attorney General, whose representative before the Senate subcommittee reported that as of July 1955 there had been no prosecutions under Section 302(c)(5).[47] Although prosecution has occurred since that date, the main defect of the provision is still present. The section contains no requirement that funds be efficiently managed and no prohibition against exorbitant salaries and expenses, and it is not a federal offense to ransack or loot the trust corpus.

The disclosure provisions of Section 302 might have produced a good result if its requirement of an annual audit had been specific enough to require disclosure of the names of persons to whom payments are made and the actual amounts paid. But the annual audit need not furnish sufficient information to determine whether or not the fund is being looted or whether there is self-dealing by administrators of the funds. Moreover, the statute's requirement that the audit be available for inspection at the principal office of the fund does not make disclosure widespread enough to insure any significant influence on fund activity on the part of its beneficiaries.

Question of Federal Pre-emption of Legislation

Finally, although nearly every investigative body has found the application of Section 302 of the Taft-Hartley Act inadequate,[48] its very existence has raised doubts as to whether or not the area of pension legislation has been pre-empted by federal law. The question arises from two Constitutional principles: (1) that a state may not legislate contrary to a law of Congress in a matter involving interstate commerce; and (2) that if Congress intends by its statute to claim exclusive federal jurisdiction in a given area, state legislatures may not touch even those questions within the prescribed area not explicitly provided for in the federal legislation. The pertinent question here is whether or not Congress intended to pre-empt the entire field of employee benefits in interstate commerce.

---

[46] Hearings on S. Res. 40, Part 3, p. 905.

[47] *Ibid.*, pp. 902–904; Senate Report No. 1734, p. 58.

[48] Senate Report No. 1734, p. 59; *Private Employee Benefit Plans — A Public Trust*, State of New York Insurance Department, 1956, p. 287; Siskind, "Employee Benefit Plans," 1955 Wash. U. L. Q. 112.

On this point the New York State Insurance Department argues that

> State regulation of welfare funds to protect the rights of employees and to prevent waste and corruption can be so designed that it does not conflict or interfere with any of the provisions of section 302 of the Taft-Hartley Law, but, rather, implements them.[49]

The Insurance Department makes the point that the statutory provisions concern "the mode of donation and the permissible recipients of money ... paid to a 'representative' of employees."[50] An even stronger argument could be made that the provisions of Section 302 are primarily intended to prevent the bribery of employee representatives and that the exceptions contained in (c)(5) merely find their way into the statute in order to prevent the prohibitions of the section from being too wide in their application.

Justice Frankfurter has had occasion to refer to questions similar to this as "... this delicate problem of the interplay between state and federal jurisdiction touching labor relations."[51] In the same case he gives a summary of Supreme Court rulings on the matter. His fourth classification of cases includes those in which the Court has held that the authority exercised by the state was not exclusively absorbed by the federal enactments. Among these the case of *United Construction Workers* v. *Laburnum Construction Corp.* offers a most interesting parallel to the problem we are considering.[52] This was an action for damages for violent conduct which a state court found to be a common-law tort. The Court assumed that an unfair labor practice under the Taft-Hartley Act had occurred but sustained the state judgment on the ground that there was no compensatory relief under the federal act and no federal administrative relief with which the state remedy conflicted.

As we have already pointed out, the NLRB takes the position that its jurisdiction does not extend to enforcement of Section 302 and that it will deal with matters falling under that section only to the extent that they constitute unfair labor practices. Furthermore, the Department of Justice adopts the view that "its jurisdiction is limited to mismanagement or theft of trust funds."[53]

It would seem, then, that the holding of *United Construction Workers*

---

49 *Private Employee Benefit Plans*, p. 276.
50 *Ibid.*, p. 277.
51 Weber v. Anheuser-Busch, Inc., 348 U. S. 468, 474 (1955).
52 347 U. S. 656 (1954).
53 Hearings on S. Res. 40, Part 3, p. 902.

v. *Laburnum Corp.*, along with the narrow jurisdiction of the NLRB and the Department of Justice in pension matters, leaves a fairly large area for state legislation. This conclusion is re-enforced by the Supreme Court's statement in *Garner* v. *Teamsters Union* that the Labor Management Relations Act "leaves much to the states, though Congress has refrained from telling us how much."[54]

The New York State Insurance Department's argument that "by applying the law of trusts to welfare fund administrators, the Federal statute places the burden of regulating the funds upon the states under their fiduciary laws" appears to be in line with this view.[55] The conclusion of the Department, that a state statute can pick up regulation at the point where federal coverage ends, would seem to be correct. Certainly, it is by no means clear that Congress intended to pre-empt this field of legislation. The New York Bar recommends federal legislation but urges that "the Federal act should provide that jurisdiction shall be ceded to the State . . . in a State which has enacted a statute containing provisions substantially the same as those contained in the Federal act."[56]

IMPACT OF FEDERAL BANKING LAWS ON PENSION TRUSTS

The federal government exercises supervisory power over the corporate trustees of pension plans through the Board of Governors of the Federal Reserve System. This supervision is confined, however, to national banks and to such state banks as are members of the system. The Federal Reserve Act authorizes the Board of Governors to determine what national banks may act as trustees and to issue regulations governing their operations. At the present time about 1,500 national banks are permitted to engage in trust activities.[57] The actual supervision of trust activities is carried out by the Comptroller of Currency through periodic examinations of national banks according to the specifications of Regulation F issued by the Federal Reserve Board.[58] The Comptroller of Currency further ascertains whether or not a bank's trust business is being conducted in conformity with the provisions of the individual trust instruments.

[54] 348 U. S. 485, 488 (1955).
[55] *Private Employee Benefit Plans*, p. 277.
[56] Report of the Association of the Bar of the City of New York, p. 19, note 40.
[57] Hearings on S. Res. 40, Part 3, p. 864.
[58] *Ibid.*, p. 865. Regulation F, Trust Powers of National Banks, as amended, effective Feb. 5, 1951, and amendment to Regulation F, effective June 13, 1955.

In addition to the national banks, state banks that are Federal Reserve members are examined by the federal as well as by the state authorities. There are 636 state banks exercising trust powers which must be in conformity with the regulations of the Federal Reserve Board. A certain amount of federal regulation of state banks is also conducted by the Federal Deposit Insurance Corporation in the banks insured by the Corporation.

Trustees' Responsibilities under Federal Reserve Regulations

Regulation F of the Federal Reserve Board, which sets forth the acceptable practices and standards for trust departments of banks, contains only one specific provision regarding pension trusts. The provision states that if a pension trust is exempt from federal income taxes, its funds may be invested collectively with those of other pension trusts provided this is authorized by the trust instrument.[59] Other than this regulation, the provisions of Regulation F treat pension trusts like other trusts. We shall therefore limit the present discussion of federal regulation of trust activities to a few features of federal influence on the pension system through regulation of banking activities.

Section 6(b) of Regulation F makes the bank's board of directors responsible for the investment of trust funds by the bank, the disposition of trust investments, and the supervision of the trust department. Paragraph (c) requires the board of directors to appoint a trust investment committee to make periodic reviews of all trust investments. Section 10(a) requires that every trust be carried out in strict accordance with the instrument creating the trust, and when the bank is so authorized it may invest the trust funds in its discretion but only with the approval of the trust investment committee. If the instrument is silent on the subject of allowable types of investment and does not give discretion to the officers and directors, investments are limited to those permissible by state law for fiduciaries.

Section 11 prohibits trust investments that involve conflict of interest or self-dealing when no explicit authorization for such activities is contained in the trust instrument itself. The limitations of federal supervision of pension trust investments by banks was well expressed by C. Canby Balderston, vice chairman of the Federal Reserve System, as follows:

> The regulation and supervision of trust business by Federal banking authorities cover pension trusts, like all other trusts, only to the extent of ascertaining

[59] Amendment to Regulation F, effective June 13, 1955, subsection (c).

whether the bank conducts its operations in accordance with the governing trust instruments, statutes, regulations, and sound principles of trust administration. The responsibilities of bank supervisory authorities do not include any control over investment or other important discretionary actions.[60]

Extent of Federal Reserve Regulation of Trust Assets

Some idea of the amount of pension fund assets now held in banks which are subject to federal regulation can be gained from the hearings of the Senate Subcommittee on Welfare and Pension Funds.[61] The report of these hearings states that as of the end of 1954, about 3,100 of the 13,840 commercial banks in the United States were exercising trust powers for pension, health and welfare fund accounts. The bulk of these funds were held by 65 banks large enough to have personal trust accounts exceeding $100 million. In the opinion of the vice chairman of the Board of Governors of the Federal Reserve System these trusts depended primarily on pension funds rather than on welfare funds.

Among the 65 banks with the largest trust accounts, 20 were national banks handling 2,029 pension and other employee trust accounts with assets aggregating more than $2 billion. We should point out here that nonpension assets represent only a small portion of this total since these types of benefit funds depend only on current contributions and have no need for the capital accumulation characteristic of pension trust funds. According to testimony before the subcommittee, this group of 20 national banks had investment responsibility for about 60 per cent of the accounts administered by them — those including $1.6 billion of the total assets — and acted only in a custodial capacity for the remaining 40 per cent of the accounts.

The 65 large trust institutions also included 38 state banks which as members of the Federal Reserve System are subject to federal regulation. These state member banks were estimated to be holding roughly $6 billion in some 2,800 pension and other employee benefit trust accounts, over which they exercised varying degrees of investment power.

The remaining large personal trust accounts were managed by a small group of state-chartered banks which were not members of the Federal Reserve System.

In consolidating the information gleaned from this testimony, the Senate subcommittee report estimated that the 65 banks in which the bulk of the bank-administered trust funds were concentrated in 1954 held

[60] Hearings on S. Res. 40, Part 3, p. 888.
[61] *Ibid.*, pp. 888, 889, 890.

5,269 pension and other employee benefit trust accounts with total assets of $8.3 billion. The subcommittee further estimated that more than $6 billion of these assets were in trust accounts for which these banks had investment responsibility.[62]

Finally, there is evidence that the high degree of fiduciary responsibility required by the federal statute and regulations is being met by the corporate trustees of the pension and other trust funds. The chief examiner for the Federal Reserve System testified before the Senate subcommittee that

. . . in our examination of the administration of these funds we are concerned with those where the investment responsibility rests with the bank as trustee and we test administration against the requirements of the instrument which controls the account. We do not find abuses of the provisions of these trust instruments.[63]

Before leaving consideration of Regulation F, it would be well to take note of Section 17 relating to common trust funds because the following limitations, as stated in Paragraph (c)(5), may prove to be desirable for pension trusts generally:

No investment for a Common Trust Fund shall be made in stocks, or bonds or other obligations of any one person, firm or corporation which would cause the total amount of investment in stocks, or bonds or other obligations issued or guaranteed by such person, firm, or corporation to exceed 10 percent of the value of the Common Trust Fund . . .

No investment for a Common Trust Fund shall be made in any one class of shares of stock of any one corporation which would cause the total number of such shares held by the Common Trust Fund to exceed 5 percent of the number of such shares outstanding. If the bank administers more than one Common Trust Fund no investment shall be made which will cause the aggregate investment for all such Common Trust Funds in shares of stock of any one corporation to exceed such limitation.[64]

INFLUENCE OF OTHER FEDERAL AGENCIES

In addition to the impact of federal tax policy and labor and banking laws on the pension movement, other governmental agencies have had a direct or indirect influence in shaping its direction and scope. Some of the activities of such agencies as the Labor Department, the Health,

---

[62] *Ibid.*, p. 890.
[63] *Ibid.*, p. 896.
[64] Regulation F, Sec. 17(c)(5); Hearings on S. Res. 40, Part 3, p. 874.

Education and Welfare Department, and the Securities and Exchange Commission have a bearing on pension plans and their development.

Department of Labor

In the course of studies which the Department of Labor makes of labor-management relations, it has published statistics of undoubted value to both union and management in framing pension plans. The Department's files of current agreements and employee benefit plans and its reports and studies measuring the prevalence and characteristics of specific types of agreements provide a clearinghouse of information on pension matters.

As part of the work in the field of labor-management relations, the Bureau of Labor Standards through its Division of Union Registration maintains a file of annual reports from unions. These cover, among other matters, financial reports which include the unions' interest and participation in insurance and other benefit plans. Since this information is accessible to members of a particular labor organization and to the national and international organization of which the reporting union is an affiliate, it provides a source of widespread disclosure of union activities in the pension field. In its administration of the Fair Labor Standards Act in the application of Section 7(d)(4), the Department of Labor has determined that contributions made irrevocably to the trustee of an employee benefit plan must be excluded from the regular rate of wage.[65] Some determinations of pension matters are also handled by the Department in its administration of the Davis-Bacon Act and the Copeland Anti-Kickback Act.[66]

Department of Health, Education and Welfare

As directed by the original act of 1935, the Social Security Administration has been making continuous studies of private and public social security programs. Besides its regular publications of industry statistics in the *Social Security Bulletin*, the Bureau has made special studies requested by various industries. These findings and statistics are a valuable source of information to employers and labor organizations in developing private benefit plans.

[65] 52 Stat. 1062, 29 U. S. C. 206 (1952).

[66] Other federal statutes of occasional application are those concerning veterans' re-employment rights and bankruptcy and reorganization laws.

Securities and Exchange Commission

The SEC, in particular, has played a considerable role in providing a continuous flow of information about the activities and finances of corporate pension funds. The Commission administers the Securities Act of 1933, the Securities Exchange Act of 1934 and the Investment Company Act of 1940.[67] In view of the long experience of the SEC with the administration of disclosure statutes, the Senate Subcommittee on Welfare and Pension Funds recommended that the Commission be assigned the task of "administration of disclosure, factfinding, detecting frauds, and irregularities in complicated financial operations."[68]

In this field the Commission already has some degree of familiarity with pension plans since many companies have had to file plans as part of their registration statements. Furthermore, the Commission has undertaken to publish a series of annual releases presenting estimates of financial data on noninsured pension funds. The first release appeared on October 12, 1955.[69] This was followed by the comprehensive *Survey of Corporate Pension Funds, 1951–1954,* issued in October 1956, which the SEC has supplemented annually. This survey and the subsequent releases contain the most comprehensive and probably the most competent estimates of the over-all financial aspects of corporate pension fund activities. However, the SEC has already expressed its reluctance to assume the task of regulation and other responsibilities in regard to pension programs.

Some few pension plans are registered with the SEC because they have undertaken to sell securities, usually those of the employer, to the employees. To date, however, it cannot be said that the SEC has had any direct influence on the pension trust system.[70]

---

[67] Securities Act of 1934, 48 Stat. 74, as amended, 15 U. S. C. 77a–aa (1952); Securities Exchange Act of 1934, 48 Stat. 881, 15 U. S. C. 78a (1952). Contributory funds which do not meet the requirements of section 401(a) of the Internal Revenue Code are subject to the Investment Company Act of 1940, 3(c)(13), 54 Stat. 799, as amended, 15 U. S. C. 80a–3(c)(13) (1952).

[68] Senate Report No. 1734, p. 75.

[69] SEC Statistical Series, Release No. 1335, Oct. 12, 1955.

[70] Shortly after the establishment of the SEC the Commission made an effort to cope with mismanagement of pension funds by making the funds subject to its regulation on the theory that they were investment contracts. It would seem that nothing has come of this. See 56 Colum. L. Rev. 251, 265 (1956) and 96 U. Pa. L. Rev. 549, 551 (1948).

INFLUENCE OF STATE GOVERNMENTS

We turn now to the role of the state governments in providing for regulation or public supervision of pension fund and other employee benefit operations. Although many states have passed legislation which grants corporations the necessary powers to conduct employee benefit plans and exempts pension trusts from the rule against perpetuities and the rule against accumulations, the Senate Subcommittee on Welfare and Pension Funds was able to state in its 1956 report "that almost without exception the States do not regulate the administration of these programs."[71]

But since the publication of the Senate subcommittee report, the number of exceptions has grown. As of the end of 1958, six states had statutes ordering supervision of retirement programs — California, Connecticut, Massachusetts, New York, Washington and Wisconsin. In addition, Alaska and Nebraska have passed laws making it a crime for an employer to fail to make payments to a pension fund or other fund for the benefit of his employees if he has an agreement with his employees or a collective bargaining contract to do so.[72]

STATE LAWS

The substantive provisions of the six state laws pertaining to welfare and retirement programs are outlined here in some detail as they will have a formative influence on the spread of regulatory legislation in this field.

California

All health and welfare programs created by contracts between labor organizations and employers for the benefit of employees or their dependents are subject to the supervision and investigation of the insurance commissioner, with the exception of funds or insurance policies placed

---

[71] Senate Report No. 1734, p. 61. The following states exempt pension trusts from the rules against perpetuities and accumulations: Alabama, California, Connecticut, Delaware, Florida, Georgia, Hawaii, Illinois, Indiana, Kentucky, Louisiana, Maine, Massachusetts, Michigan, Minnesota, Mississippi, Missouri, New Jersey (only for corporations), New York, North Carolina, Ohio, Oklahoma, Oregon, Pennsylvania, Rhode Island, South Dakota, Tennessee, Texas, Virginia, Washington, West Virginia and Wisconsin. Prentice Hall, *Pension and Profit Sharing Service*, ¶ 6206 (1957).

[72] Alaska, H.B. 40, approved, March 1, 1957; Title 43, Chapter 2, Article 13, Alaska Compiled Laws Annotated 1949; Nebraska, CCH, Pension Plan Guide, ¶ 10,442.

with a corporate trustee which are subject to the jurisdiction of the California Superintendent of Banks, the Board of Governors of the Federal Reserve System, or the Comptroller of Currency of the United States.

Every health and welfare program covering persons employed in the state must register with the insurance commissioner. The commissioner may except from regulation and reporting any program which (a) covers less than 25 persons employed in the state, (b) is of a type that contains no potential detriment to the beneficiaries, or (c) involves nonresident trustees who are subject to and comply with the requirements of the law of any other state or of the United States.

The insurance commissioner may examine any employee program as often as he deems necessary, and must do so at least once every three years. However, if the program has been audited by a certified public accountant, the commissioner may dispense with this examination.

Each program must file an annual report with the commissioner.

The commissioner may address to any program, or to its agents or officers, any inquiry in relation to its transactions or condition.

The management of every such program must make an annual report to every contributing employer or employee covered by the program if they so request.[73]

The powers of investigation given to the insurance commissioner are very broad, but in excepting funds placed with corporate trustees, the California law suffers from a serious omission. From the analysis of the supervisory powers of the superintendents of banks which follows, and of the powers of the Board of Governors and the Comptroller already discussed, it becomes apparent that in many cases important areas of pension fund operation will not be supervised. In the first place, the majority of pension plans (if California plans conform to the national pattern) are placed with corporate trustees and so will not be subject to the supervision of the insurance commissioner. Of course the activities of the banks will remain subject to the powers of the banking authorities and the usual state regulation. But this means only that the activities of the banks will be examined for sound investment policies, conformity with the trust instrument, and so forth. The administration of the fund itself, for example in supplying information, avoiding discrimination, etc., will go unsupervised.

One important area of fund activity is, however, wisely covered by

[73] A.B. 1773 (appr. July 8, 1957, eff. Sept. 11, 1957) added to Insurance Code of California, §§ 10640–10655.

another statute requiring that a retirement trust must create and maintain reserves calculated to cover its liabilities adequately.[74] The state commissioner of corporations may require reserves to be calculated at an interest rate not in excess of 4 per cent. Mortality, disability and other experience tables may also be subjected to his approval. Furthermore, the documents setting forth the retirement system must provide for contributions to create, within a reasonable time, sufficient reserves to fund the benefits payable to an employee at the time of his retirement. Fifteen years is considered a reasonable period, but it is within the discretion of the commissioner to require funding within a shorter time.

When benefits are underwritten by an insurer authorized to do business in California they are exempt from this funding requirement. These insurers will, of course, be subject to the California insurance law. Although this measure closes an important part of the gap left by the statute, it is difficult to see why all funds without exception are not made subject to the general supervisory law.

Connecticut

As of 1957, the trustees of any "employee welfare plan" which receives contributions from an employer located in the state of Connecticut, or which pays benefits to persons employed within the state, are required to register the fund with the insurance commissioner.

The commissioner may examine the affairs of any such fund if requested by (1) 30 per cent of the contributing employers or 30 per cent of the labor unions involved, (2) 10 per cent of the employees or 100 employees (whichever is less) covered by the fund, or (3) a majority of the employee or employer trustees.

An annual statement must be filed with the insurance commissioner showing the status of the fund as of the end of the preceding calendar year.

A fund not located in Connecticut which is required to register and complies with the laws of another state may be excused by the commissioner from complying with the Connecticut statute.[75]

The Connecticut law is at once stricter and more lenient in its requirements than the California law. It is stricter in admitting no exceptions to

---

[74] S.B. 1969, Ch. 2043 (appr. July 8, 1957); California Corporations Code, § 28403.

[75] H.B. 983 (appr. May 28, 1957, eff. Oct. 1, 1957); General Statutes of Connecticut, Revision of 1958, §§ 31–78 to 31–89.

the registration and filing requirements. On the other hand, the powers of the commissioner are more limited, reports need not be made available to those participating in welfare funds and the law does not require full funding. From one point of view, this leniency may appear to be a defect, especially in not requiring full funding. One of the principal arguments in its favor, however, is that such a requirement for funding would discourage employers from beginning new pension plans. But it seems to the present writer that, despite this possible discouraging effect, the statute ought to require sufficient funding to meet the employer's promises as set forth in the pension plan documents and that employers should be required to make absolutely clear to their employees the contingencies upon which pension rights depend.

Massachusetts

The Massachusetts law enacted in 1956 and amended in 1958 provides for a health, welfare and retirement trust funds board, consisting of the Commissioner of Banks, the Commissioner of Insurance, the Commissioner of Labor in Industries. The legislation applies to all health, welfare and retirement funds derived in whole or in part from contributions from employers or employees or both.

Funds providing benefits for 25 or more employees must register in the form prescribed by the board including certified copies of the trust, contracts, corporate by-laws and all other documents creating or relating to the trust funds. A penalty of $5.00 a day may be imposed for neglecting to file a registration on time.

The trustees are required to file an annual report with the board within five months after the end of the calendar or fiscal year. The report must be signed and certified under oath and contain the following information: the value of the fund as of the end of the fiscal year; the amount contributed by the employer or employees; the amount of benefits paid for each class of benefits; the number of employees covered; the salaries and fees paid for or charged to the fund, to whom paid, in what amount, and for what purposes.

If some or all of the benefits under the fund are provided by an insurance carrier or by a hospital, surgical or medical service or by any other similar type of plan, such reports shall also include for the year the premium rate or subscription charge; the number of persons covered by each class of benefits; the total claims incurred and the total claims paid by such insurance carrier or service plan; dividends, commissions, and administrative, service or other fees paid by such insurance carrier or service plan, and other information.

The board may, with the approval of a judge of a probate court, examine the books and records and investigate the administration of any trust, and the board may require the attendance and sworn testimony of witnesses. No trustee or employer, or labor organization representing any employees eligible for benefits under a trust required to register by law, and no officer, agent or employee of any such trustee, employer or labor organization shall receive any payment or any other thing of value from any insurance company, insurance agent, insurance broker, or any hospital, surgical or medical service plan, in connection with the solicitation, sale, service or administration of a contract providing benefits for such trust or receive any payment, commission, loan, service or any other thing of value from such trust, except that they may receive any benefits under a trust to which they are otherwise entitled. They may also receive from such trust reasonable compensation for necessary services and expenses incurred in connection with the official duties of the trust. This regulation, however, does not affect the payment of any dividend or rate credit due to the policy holder or contract holder under the terms of an insurance or annuity contract.

Furthermore, no insurance company, insurance agent or insurance broker, and no hospital, surgical or medical service plan, may make any payment to any employee welfare fund or to any employer or labor organization representing any employee eligible for employee benefits or employee of any such fund, employer or labor organization, in connection with the solicitation, sale, service or administration of a contract providing employee benefits for the fund.

Trustees who are subject to this law having their principal office located outside of Massachusetts must appoint an agent for the service of process and register the name and address of the agent with the board. In the case of failure to comply with this provision the commissioner of corporations will be deemed to be the attorney for the trustee for service of process.

If the board finds that any trust has been depleted by wrongful or negligent actions, it may bring an action for the benefit of the beneficiaries or intervene in an action brought against a person whose act or omission has caused the depletion.

The law directs that a summary of the annual report must be filed along with the report itself and be made available for public inspection.

The board in its discretion may also direct the trustees to distribute or otherwise publish copies of the summary to all employers, employees and labor organizations participating in the trust. All other reports and information in the possession of the board shall be confidential communications, neither subject to subpoena nor made public unless the ends of justice and the public advantage will be served by publication.

Section 5 of the Massachusetts Act provides that anyone who is convicted of embezzling or misappropriating trust funds, or of falsifying or destroying records with intent to defraud or wilfully and knowingly filing false statements or of violating the provisions relating to payments for service shall be punished by a fine of not more than $10,000 or by imprisonment for not more than five years, or by both.

The law exempts certain specialized types of plans, such as charitable or educational funds.

Section 7 provides that the board may waive requirements of this act with respect to trusts which have complied with the laws of other states or of the United States. But where a waiver has been granted the board shall require the filing with it copies of documents submitted to other states or to the United States. A waiver may be withdrawn at any time and action by the board in this matter is subject to judicial review. The statute also requires that in addition to other penalties prescribed by law, any person or employer or officers of employer corporations who refuse or wilfully fail or grossly neglect to pay contributions they have contracted for within thirty days after such payments are due shall be punished by a fine of not less than $10 nor more than $50 or by imprisonment for not more than two months, or by both.

The amendments to the Massachusetts law became effective January 1, 1959.[76]

We have quoted the Massachusetts statute at length because it is the most comprehensive and carefully elaborated of all the state laws. Like the Connecticut law, it covers all funds. An especially good feature of this legislation is the requirement that all fund documents must be submitted for the approval of the supervisory board. This enables the state authorities to ensure that false or misleading information is not put into the hands of fund beneficiaries. This kind of supervision, in the light of the recent findings of the New York State Insurance Department, is a "must" for pension plan legislation. There may be some support for the

[76] Ch. 778, Par. 2, Laws 1957, as amended by Ch. 665 Laws 1958; Ann. Laws of Mass. Ch. 151D.

argument that it will hamper the pension movement to require full funding or to force these plans into a prematurely conceived mold, but no valid objection can be raised against requiring information about the kind of performance that the fund is able to maintain. We might add that even this statute could be improved by an explicit requirement of information for employees.

The power given to the supervisory board to sue on behalf of fund beneficiaries and the provision making it a crime to embezzle or otherwise deplete these funds are a means of cutting through the problems which would face an employee trying to get into court to protect his interest in a trust. This may be the most desirable way of handling this problem. We should recognize, however, that here, as well as in the other states having such legislation, the state enters strongly into the new structure of property control now being created by pension trusts. It is at least a step toward making the control of large amounts of property a public matter.

New York

The New York law, passed and amended in 1956–1957, regulates any trust fund established or maintained jointly by the employer and a labor organization, whether directly or through trustees. Employee funds managed by corporate trustees are under the supervision of the superintendent of banking; those managed by noncorporate trustees are regulated by the superintendent of insurance. However, if the principal office of the employer is located outside of New York State and the plan does not benefit more than twenty employees within the state, it is not subject to this control.

Trustees are required to submit such information as the respective superintendent requests. The superintendent may examine the fund whenever he deems it necessary, but he must make an examination every five years.

Persons having custody of documents, etc., may be examined under oath; a report must be made of every examination and it may contain conclusions and recommendations. In any legal action such a report is presumptive evidence.

Annual reports are required.

Out-of-state employers whose trustees are subject to, and comply with, regulatory laws of any other state or the United States government may be excused from these requirements.

Only those payments permitted by the superintendent of insurance may be made between an insurance company, agent, broker, hospital or medical service and the trustees. With the exception of this authority, the provision is much like the Massachusetts statute in prohibiting such payments.

Premiums to insurance companies must be paid by check, and dividends and retrospective rate credits must be paid by check or credit memoranda.

The superintendent may impose pecuniary penalties and remove trustees who wilfully fail to comply with the statute. Where a fund is depleted by wrongful or negligent action, a superintendent may notify the Attorney General, who may then bring an action for the benefit of persons interested in the fund.

Violation of the statute is a misdemeanor.[77]

In New York the banking and insurance superintendents have broad powers and the law pertaining to pension funds certainly has teeth. The California-type requirement for funding is absent, but the superintendents may make recommendations. While the New York type of legislation is, perhaps, a compromise on this point, it is probably best suited to the yet evolving state of the pension funds.

The New York law, however, is subject to a serious limitation in being restricted only to jointly managed funds. It leaves the largest groups of pension funds, the strictly union or employer-managed funds, free from supervision. This law and its provisions are extremely important because a significant portion of all pension funds are in New York. The New York Banking Department has found that the $7.5 billion in pension and other welfare funds in New York banks in 1955 amounted to almost 60 per cent of all such funds in the United States.[78] Of course, the application of the New York law is limited to those plans having twenty or more employees within the state, but the effect of New York legislation is still great, covering as it does more than 2.6 million employees (as of 1955).[79]

This law has been a bone of contention between the state administration and the legislature since its adoption in 1956 and it will probably be made more extensive in its coverage. Certainly, if the legislators admit that these plans need regulation, as they have by going as far as they did,

[77] New York Banking Law § 61 and New York Insurance Law § 37a.
[78] George A. Mooney, *Pension and Other Employee Welfare Plans*, New York State Banking Department, 1955, p. i.
[79] *Ibid.*, p. 47.

it is not consistent to exempt the most significant segment of them from supervision.

Washington

Legislation passed by the state of Washington in 1955 requires that the commissioner of insurance examine employee welfare funds at least every five years, and oftener if he wishes. A copy of the instruments and amendments establishing the fund must be filed with the commissioner and he may also require regular and special reports concerning the fund's transactions.

Those who contract for insurance and health care service with a welfare fund must file a copy of the contracts and a statement of the commissions or compensations paid in this connection. All reports and statements are open to inspection by the public.[80] Wilfull failure to comply with the law is punishable by a fine of not more than $1,000, or by imprisonment up to one year, or by both.

Wisconsin

The Wisconsin Act of 1957 is applicable to funds which receive contributions at an annual rate of more than $2,000 from employers located in the state or which pay benefits to twenty-five or more persons employed within the state. It is left to the insurance commissioner to define which funds are required to register.

Books and records must be kept according to accurate accounting methods.

The commissioner may examine a fund as often as he wishes, but must do so every five years. He may also call for special statements in addition to the required annual statement which must be made available to any contributing employer, the union and any employee covered by the fund.

All employers having their business in Wisconsin and contributing to such funds must file a statement of contributions.

The statute contains stiff penalties for false statements and for embezzlement of funds. The attorney general may sue on behalf of beneficiaries and intervene in suits brought by them, and the commissioner may seek court injunctions to carry out his order.

The statute contains the usual waiver provision for funds not located in the state and subject to examination by another state or the federal

80 Washington Laws, Extraordinary Session, 1955, Ch. 8, April 4, 1955; Rev. Code of Wash. Title 48, Insurance, Ch. 48.52.

government, if the commissioner is provided with a copy of such an examination.[81]

REGULATION OF INVESTMENTS UNDER
BANKING LAWS

Corporate trustees, who do the lion's share of investing of pension trust funds, are of course subject to state banking laws. These institutions are thus under the surveillance and inspection of the state banking departments, which attempt to enforce a high degree of fiduciary responsibility. The portion of state laws pertaining to the activities of fiduciaries is most significant for our study.

By 1950 the so-called "prudent-man rule" for investment of funds had been adopted through legislation or court decision in thirty-seven states, the District of Columbia and Hawaii.[82] The older type of regulation, followed by states that do not have the prudent-man rule, sets out a specific enumeration of the kinds of investment that may be made by a trustee. These securities are what is called the "legal list" of the state. Where the prudent-man rule is in operation, there is no "legal list," except in a modified form as in New York. The New York statute, which became effective July 1, 1950, provides an excellent example for our examination because New York trust institutions handle about one-third of the personal trust property of the nation.[83] As we have already noted, the New York State Banking Department estimated that as of September 1955, the banks in its jurisdiction held $7.5 billion of trusteed pension and welfare funds, or almost 60 per cent of all such funds in the United States.[84] The modified prudent-man rule of that state is contained in Section 21 of the New York Personal Property Law, which begins as follows:

A fiduciary holding funds for investment may invest the same in the kinds and classes of securities described in the succeeding paragraphs of this subdivision provided that investment is made in such securities as would be acquired by prudent men of discretion and intelligence in such matters who are seeking a reasonable income and the preservation of their capital.[85]

The New York law permits investment by fiduciaries in "bonds, de-

---

[81] Ch. 552 (appr. Aug. 7, 1957, eff. Aug. 22, 1957), creating Ch. 211 of Wisconsin Laws.

[82] Erwin W. Boehmler, *Financial Institutions,* Irwin, Homewood, Illinois, 1951, p. 431.

[83] *Ibid.*

[84] New York State Banking Department, *op. cit.,* p. i.

[85] New York Personal Property Law § 21(1).

bentures, notes, equipment trust obligations or other evidences of indebtedness and shares of common and preferred stocks"[86] but further limits investment in common stocks to 35 per cent of the total trust fund and prescribes that these stocks must be "registered on a national securities exchange" approved by the Securities and Exchange Commission. Eligible stocks must also have a ten-year record of earnings.[87]

The law also provides that under certain conditions fiduciaries shall not be liable for losses resulting from ineligible investments. Where such investments are turned over to the fiduciary by a trust agreement, it is not held responsible provided that due care and prudence has been used in the disposition or retention of the ineligible investment.[88]

Effect of Banking Regulations

The net effect of these New York State regulations is to make possible the unlimited discretion contained in the following provision from a standard trust agreement:

> ... to purchase or subscribe for any securities or other property and to retain in trust such securities or other property, to sell for cash or on credit, to grant options, to convert ... or otherwise to dispose of any securities or other property at any time held by it.[89]

Investment activities carried out under such broad powers would be subject to the standard of the prudent-man rule, but, other than that, the trustee would be freed from any liability by the terms of the enabling instrument. Even in cases where the trustee is restricted by the limits of the New York law, he would still be able to invest up to 35 per cent of the trust funds in common stocks. This latitude becomes very significant when we are dealing with assets as sizable as those in a pension trust.

In summary, the purpose of state banking laws and the activities of banking superintendents is to see that corporate trustees conform to the terms of the trust indenture. Further influence on the pension trusts re-

[86] *Ibid.*, § 21(m).

[87] New York Banking Law § 235(26)(c). The prudent-man rule was interpreted in *In re* City Farmers Trust Co., 189 Misc. 942, 68 N. Y. S. 2d 43 (1947); *In re* Loose's Will, 167 Misc. 764, 4 N. Y. S. 2d 611 (1938); Guarantee Trust Co. of N. Y. v. Fisk, 244 App. Div. 200, 278 N. Y. S. 809, *aff'd*, 270 N. Y. 550, 200 N. E. 312 (1935). "Prudence" is dealt with in *In re* Wick's Estate, 1 Misc. 2d 360, 45 N. Y. S. 2d 188 (1955); *In re* Patchogue Citizens Bank & Trust Co., 89 N. Y. S. 2d 208 (1949).

[88] New York Personal Property Law § 21(6); *In re* City Bank Farmer & Trust Co., 270 App. Div. 572, 61 N. Y. S. 2d 484, *aff'd*, 296 N. Y. 662, 69 N. E. 2d 818 (1946).

[89] See sample form of Trust Indenture, Article Fourth, Appendix B; Prentice Hall, *Pension and Profit Sharing Service*, ¶ 8181.8.

sults from provisions in the banking laws requiring competence and conservatism in investment. The administration of the banking laws and the traditions that have been built up in trustee institutions provide an excellent guarantee that large pension funds will be conserved and invested efficiently and prudently. And since the large banks are the major channel for financial control of pension fund assets, we can expect a high degree of responsibility in their management. The state banking departments, and the laws they administer, do not, however, touch the substantive provisions of pension plans. The only effective supervision of these plans is in the area of strictly financial management.

INSURANCE DEPARTMENT CONTROLS

Since pension trusts are in some respects similar to life insurance the suggestion has often been heard that they be made subject to similar controls. All states carefully regulate the activities of insurance companies and the pension and welfare funds they administer in many ways. Legislation and regulation are specific and detailed on the subjects of investment, minimum actuarial valuation standards, the form and content of annuity contracts and certificates of insurance, and equitable treatment of claimants. Although the large number of pension plans financed through insurance companies are not the subject of this study, we should take note of the regulatory activities of state insurance departments because in many states supervision of pension trust activities, which is surely in the making, will be given over to the insurance authorities. Already in New York State the Insurance Department has been given investigatory powers in pension trust matters even though the Department's activities are seriously hampered by an opinion of the Attorney General that the enabling statute is limited to the jointly managed Taft-Hartley type of pension program. The insurance departments are, of course, peculiarly well adapted to review and supervise the actuarial aspects of pension programs.

Statutory limitations on the investments of insurance company funds are much stricter than those which apply to other fiduciaries. Investment is permitted only in the safest classes of securities. An excellent example of this conservatism is to be found in the provisions of the New York State Insurance Law concerning investment in stocks.[90]

Investment in preferred stocks of solvent corporations is permitted to

[90] New York Insurance Law § 81.

the extent of 20 per cent of the issuer's preferred stock and 2 per cent of the insurance company's admitted assets. Common stocks may be purchased if they have a long record of earnings and are registered on a national securities exchange. Stock investment is, however, subject to two limitations: first, an investment in any one institution may not exceed 2 per cent of the issuer's common stock and one-tenth of 1 per cent of the insurance company's admitted assets; and, secondly, the aggregate holdings of the insurance company in common stock may not exceed 3 per cent of its admitted assets or one-third of the sum of its capital stock and surplus, whichever is less.[91]

Such limitations result in a very conservative stock investment policy and stand in striking contrast to the more liberal regulations of fiduciaries. Recent studies by New York State authorities found that very few pension plans limit themselves to the type of securities eligible for savings banks and life insurance companies. The New York State Insurance Department investigation of private employee benefit plans revealed that among the noninsured pension programs studied, 37 per cent authorized investment of the type permissible for fiduciaries while 40 per cent of the funds were not subject to restrictions of any kind.[92] Similarly, the State Banking Department found that 61 per cent of the corporate-trusteed pension plans it studied in 1955 contained no restrictions at all on investment. Many commentators have noted the distinct advantage this wide investment latitude gives to the trusteed plan as opposed to the insured type of plan, since it enables the corporate trustee to turn in a better record of earnings than is possible under the conservative limitations of insurance investment. If, as seems likely, noninsured pension funds are ultimately brought under the regulation of state insurance departments, the result may be a more conservative investment policy.

TAXATION OF INSURED PENSION PLANS

While this study is concerned primarily with noninsured pension plans, the subject of the tax treatment of insured pension plans is pertinent since, to a degree, the prevalence of noninsured plans is a result of preferential tax policy. The life insurance companies maintain that they suffer a serious competitive disadvantage owing to the fact that their group life policies, group annuity contracts, deposit administration contracts, etc.,

[91] *Private Employee Benefit Plans*, p. 115.
[92] *Ibid.*, p. 117.

are subject to federal and state taxation, while corporate trustees pay no tax at all on their pension trust business.

Federal Taxation

Insurance company spokesmen point out that, for a typical pension plan, a variation of one-fourth of one per cent in the rate of interest will produce a differential of 6 or 7 per cent in the long-run cost of the plan. Ray Peterson, vice president and associate actuary of the Equitable Life Insurance Society, has stated that "The effect of the federal income tax, compared with a tax-exempt trust enjoying the same rate of earnings before tax [3.50 to 4.00 per cent] is to increase the cost of insured plans by 6.7 to 7.7 per cent."[93] Mr. Peterson also pointed out that for group annuity contracts covering 200 to 500 lives — typical insured plans — expenses may range from 5 to 2 per cent of contributions. There is no question that federal taxation of earnings derived from pension fund investments represents a serious discrimination against the insurance companies in their efforts to compete for this type of business.

Attempts have been made to remedy this situation through federal legislation. The latest of these attempts, H.R. 4245, was introduced into the 86th Congress by Representative Wilbur D. Mills. This bill would grant to the insurance companies a deduction on their investment income. The amount of the deduction would be computed by multiplying the reserves held for qualified pension plans by the company's actual earnings rate. The companies would not be permitted to treat any of their pension reserves in this manner in computing 1958 taxes but one-third of the pension fund earnings could be so treated in 1959, two-thirds in 1960, and 100 per cent beginning in 1961.

State Taxation

It is the practice in many states to consider sums paid for annuities as taxable premiums, and in some states the premium tax is as high as 2 per cent. Study of the expenses of seven large insurance companies in 1949 revealed that the average expenses of the companies in administering group annuity business was 1.89 per cent of the cost of the group annuity contract. As a result of the state taxation of annuity business the average expenses of these companies were increased 40 per cent. In those states

[93] Statement of Ray Peterson, October 30, 1957, Life Insurance Association of America.

where the premium tax was 2 per cent, the tax amounted to more than all other group annuity expenses combined.[94]

Albert Pike, actuary of the Life Insurance Association of America, summed up the state and federal tax burden this way:

> For group annuities the interest loss is a burden approximately equivalent to the burden of a 5 per cent to 7 per cent premium tax, on top of actual state premium taxes which in the annuity field average slightly less than 1 per cent. It is at least 10 times the average commission rate on our group annuity business and two or three times the average total expense rate including commissions.[95]

To say the very least, the taxation of qualified pension plans financed through the medium of insurance is inconsistent with the federal and state exemptions granted to plans financed through a corporate trustee. If there is any reason for discrimination between the two types of financing it has not been brought forward. In any case, we may conclude that increased expense to insurance companies as a result of taxation has been a factor in the preference for the trusteed as against the insured type of financing. It is questionable whether the insurance companies will be able to offset the competitive advantage already gained by the banker-trustees even after the tax inequality is abolished.

SUMMARY

From our analysis of the impact of government upon the pension movement the federal tax laws emerge as the largest single influence on the structure of pension funds. In order to reap the advantages of favored tax treatment, employers have had to formalize their plans, dedicate pension reserves irrevocably to the use of their employees and provide for equality of treatment among beneficiaries.

Federal and state banking laws have not greatly influenced the form or administration of pension plans except insofar as they may have encouraged the trusteed form of plan by permitting liberal investment policies. The banking laws have had their effect more in regulating to some degree the extent and the use of the economic power that has gravitated into the hands of the corporate trustees.

[94] Statement of Henry S. Beers for the American Life Convention and Life Insurance Association of America to the Life Insurance Committee of the National Association of Insurance Commissioners, April 26, 1950.

[95] *Proceedings* of the American Bar Association Section of Insurance, Negligence, and Compensation Law, 1957, p. 122.

The insurance laws, with their traditional emphasis on conservative investment, together with the tax disadvantages which the insurance companies suffer, have had the effect of making the insured forms of retirement benefits more costly. These two governmental policies have contributed to the decisions which have placed the majority of pension fund beneficiaries under the trusteed form of plan financing.

The state and federal laws have done little or nothing, thus far, to protect the pension funds from the depredations of unscrupulous trustees, labor leaders and racketeers. This is partly the result of lack of information and apathy on the part of the beneficiaries themselves, but it must be admitted that there has been very little legal machinery available for them to use in their own defense.

Aroused public interest has resulted in legislation in six states assigning the duty of protecting pension funds to state officials. This is undoubtedly the pattern we can look for in the future. The common law of trusts may contain in its concepts the necessary means to enable pension beneficiaries to protect themselves, but the courts have not yet made the applications needed to protect employee rights. Indeed, judicial doctrine and precedent has not yet had time to form. As in so many other areas in our present social structure, the swiftly evolving needs of the present have outstripped the capacities of the existent social machinery.

One suspects, however, that we are witnessing more than just the supplementing of cumbersome and tardy methods of dealing with the problems of protecting private rights. What is happening is that the rights themselves are passing over into the public domain. The aggrieved beneficiary of a trust will no longer stand before the courts to plead his own interest. In his place will stand a commissioner or the state's attorney pleading the cause of the public weal. The pensioner will be represented, but only as a member of a class. He is even now a very representative member of the "Paraproprietal Society," which we shall discuss in the concluding chapter.

BENEFICIARIES

IN COURT

The Collective Bargaining Agreement

The Pension Plan

The Trust Indenture

Even in the simplest type of pension program there are a number of inherent relationships which may become the basis of legal action. An examination of the judicial determination of property rights in pension funds should properly include consideration of what has happened to the basic pension plan documents, the union contract, the trust indenture and the plan itself in the courts.

THE COLLECTIVE BARGAINING AGREEMENT

The charter of union power in pension matters may be said to be contained in Section 8(a)(5) of the Taft-Hartley Act, which makes it an unfair labor practice to refuse to bargain collectively on matters (as described in Section 8(d)) respecting rates of pay, wages, hours of employment or other conditions of employment.[1] One of the most significant developments in the history of the private pension movement occurred in 1948 when the National Labor Relations Board and the Court of Appeals for the Seventh Circuit held in *Inland Steel* v. *NLRB*[2] that pension and

---

[1] 49 Stat. 453 (1935), as amended, 29 U. S. C. § 159(a) (1952).

[2] 77 N.L.R.B. 1 (1948), *enforcement granted,* 170 F. 2d 247 (7th Cir. 1948), *cert. denied,* 336 U. S. 960 (1949).

retirement plans are subject matter for compulsory collective bargaining within the meaning of the Taft-Hartley Act. The court upheld and quoted with approval the NLRB contention that

realistically viewed, this type of wage enhancement or increase, no less than any other, becomes an integral part of the entire wage structure, and the character of the employee representative's interest in it, and the terms of its grant, is no different than any other case where a change in the wage structure is effected.[3]

The court disagreed with the company's argument that pension benefits were not wages, saying that the better and more logical argument was on the other side. As proof of its contention that pension benefits are included in the term "wages," the court cited cases in which the NLRB was upheld when ordering that pension and other beneficial insurance rights be restored to employees in accordance with its authority to order reinstatement of employees with back pay.[4] For example, it was held in *NLRB* v. *Stackpole Carbon Co.* that "the insurance rights in substance were part of the employee's wages."[5] The court also cited a similar construction of the term "wages" in the Social Security Act[6] and in the Internal Revenue Code.[7]

The court somewhat weakened its conclusion with regard to wages by stating that whatever could be said about including pensions under that term, no argument could be made exempting pensions from the phrase "other conditions of employment."[8] However, in the case of *W. W. Cross & Co.* v. *NLRB* the Court of Appeals in enforcing an order of the NLRB held:

. . . believing a group insurance program to fall within the scope of the word "wages" as used in the act [National Labor Relations Act of 1947], we see no need to consider, and therefore explicitly pass, the question whether such a program could also be included within the scope of the phrase "other conditions of employment."[9]

---

[3] 170 F. 2d at 251.

[4] This authority is contained in Section 10(c) of the act, 29 U. S. C. 160(c) (1952). See Butler Bros. v. NLRB, 134 F. 2d 981, 985 (7th Cir. 1943).

[5] 128 F. 2d 188, 191 (3d Cir. 1942).

[6] 49 Stat. 642, 52 U. S. C. 409 (1952). Social Security Board v. Nierotko, 327 U. S. 358, 365 (1945).

[7] Internal Revenue Code of 1954, § 3121. Hooker v. Hoey, 27 F. Supp. 489 (1939), aff'd, 107 F. 2d 1016 (2d Cir. 1939).

[8] 170 F. 2d at 251.

[9] 174 F. 2d 875, 878 (1st Cir. 1949).

While these decisions are not finally conclusive of the issue in all circumstances where it may arise, they should go far in settling the question whether or not the funds contributed to a pension trust are wages. The next logical step will be for the courts to say that these funds actually belong to the employees.

ENFORCEMENT OF PENSION RIGHTS
BY THE UNION

If a collective bargaining agreement is to be the basis of a suit for pension rights in a federal court, the suit must be brought by a union in cases where the Taft-Hartley Act is relied on to establish jurisdiction. That act under Section 301 authorizes suits by employers and unions but gives no standing to individual employees to enforce collective bargaining agreements in the federal courts.[10] However, it appears from recent court decisions that the union may not sue the employer for pension rights of its members on the basis of the jurisdiction granted by the Taft-Hartley Act.

Jay-Ann Case

The case of *International Ladies' Garment Workers' Union* v. *Jay-Ann Co.*, decided in 1956, is directly in point.[11] In this case the court held that federal courts have no jurisdiction in an action by a union to compel an employer to pay sums into a health and welfare fund according to a collective bargaining agreement, despite the fact that the operations of the employer and the union were interstate. In arriving at this conclusion, the Court of Appeals for the Fifth Circuit said, "Our decision of the jurisdictional point on this appeal is controlled by the ruling of the Supreme Court in *Association of Westinghouse Salaried Employees* v. *Westinghouse Corp.* . . ."[12] The court took the *Westinghouse* decision to mean that "neither the language nor legislative history of Section 301 was sufficient to indicate that Congress intended to authorize a union to enforce the personal rights of employees for whom it had bargained to receive compensation for services rendered their employer."[13]

Although he agreed with the conclusion reached by the majority in the

[10] 61 Stat. 156 (1947), 29 U. S. C. 185 (1952); Zaleski v. Local 401 of United Electrical Workers, 91 F. Supp. 552 (D. N. J. 1950); Schatte v. International Alliance of Theatrical Stage Employees, 84 F. Supp. 669 (S. D. Cal. 1949), *aff'd on other grounds*, 182 F. 2d 158 (9th Cir. 1949), *cert. denied*, 340 U. S. 827 (1950).
[11] 228 F. 2d 632 (5th Cir. 1956).
[12] 228 F. 2d at 633.
[13] *Ibid.*

Jay-Ann case, Judge Rives argued that this was an improper interpretation of Section 301 of the Taft-Hartley Act and the *Westinghouse* decision.[14] His argument was that Section 301 conferred federal jurisdiction of the subject matter of the violation of a contract between an employer and a union. Its purpose, he said, was to promote industrial peace in matters affecting interstate commerce by providing express statutory recognition of the binding effect of the collective agreement on both union and employer. As proof of this he quoted from the legislative history. Nor, to his mind, was the union seeking to enforce merely personal rights since he said:

> It seems to me that in the *Westinghouse* case . . . Chief Justice Warren and Justices Black, Reed, Douglas and Clark, left the door open for federal jurisdiction of an action to enforce a right under the contract claimed by the union as an entity, and that there is nothing in the Court's decision in that case to the contrary.[15]

An examination of the *Westinghouse* case and the subsequent case of *Textile Workers Union* v. *Lincoln Mills*[16] will bear out Judge Rives' contention.

Westinghouse Case

The *Westinghouse* case, decided in 1955, involved a collective bargaining agreement which required full salary for a year unless the employees were absent on furlough or leave of absence. About 4,000 employees were absent on a certain day, but for neither of these reasons. The union sought to have the court interpret the contracts and enter judgment in favor of the individual employees for unpaid salaries. Four separate opinions were written by the Court, resulting in a good deal of discussion as to the real holding of the case.[17]

Justice Frankfurter, with whom Justices Minton and Burton joined, wrote the opinion for the Court holding that Section 301 does not imply the existence of a body of federal substantive law for application to suits brought under it. He further felt that since in this suit neither diversity

[14] Association of Westinghouse Employees v. Westinghouse Corp., 348 U. S. 437 (1955). For other applications of this decision, see: Ferguson-Steere Motor Co. v. Int'l Brotherhood of Teamsters, 223 F. 2d 842 (5th Cir. 1955); Int'l Longshoremen's Union v. Libbey, McNeill and Libbey, 221 F. 2d 225 (9th Cir. 1955).

[15] 228 F. 2d at 636.

[16] 353 U. S. 448 (1957).

[17] Mendelsohn, *Enforceability of Arbitration Agreements Under Taft-Hartley Section 301*, 66 Yale L. J. 167 (1956); Notes, 50 Nw. U. L. Rev. 289 (1955); 1955 U. Ill. L. F. 336.

of citizenship nor a federal question provided a basis for jurisdiction, a serious Constitutional problem presented itself: i.e., can Congress empower the federal courts to take jurisdiction in cases not "arising under" any federal law except the jurisdictional grant? Justice Frankfurter felt it better to avoid this question on the grounds that neither the statute nor its legislative history indicated that suits of this nature were ever contemplated. Finally, he said, "The employees have always been able to enforce their individual rights in state courts . . . To this extent, the collective bargaining contract has always been enforceable."[18]

The substance of the concurring opinion of Justices Warren and Clark has been given above as quoted in the majority opinion in the *Jay-Ann* case. They felt the union was seeking to enforce personal rights. Justice Reed concurred for the same reason, though he felt that some federal law might be applicable in suits under Section 301.

Justice Douglas, joined by Justice Black, dissented, arguing that the union should be allowed to bring this suit. He felt that "What the union obtains in the collective bargaining agreement it [the union] should be entitled to enforce or defend in the forums which have been provided."[19]

From an analysis of the *Westinghouse* decision it appears that five of the justices do leave the door open for a union to sue as an entity on a collectively bargained contract.

Lincoln Mills Case

Further support of this position is provided in the *Lincoln Mills* case where the Supreme Court again took up the question of Section 301.[20] This time the majority opinion was written by Justice Douglas, with Justices Burton and Harlan writing a concurring opinion and Justice Frankfurter dissenting.

In the *Lincoln Mills* case a union sought specific performance of an agreement to arbitrate in a collectively bargained contract. The Court held that there is a federal substantive law which is to be applied in suits under Section 301 and that the Taft-Hartley Act requires a federal court

[18] 348 U. S. at 460–461.

[19] 348 U. S. at 467.

[20] For discussion of arbitration and other related aspects of the problem of the Lincoln Mills case, see: Cox, *Grievance Arbitration in the Federal Courts,* 67 Harv. L. Rev. 591 (1954); Mendelsohn, *Enforceability of Arbitration Agreements Under Taft-Hartley Section 301,* 66 Yale L. J. 167 (1956); Murphy, *The Enforcement of Grievance Arbitration Provisions,* 23 Tenn. L. Rev. 959 (1955); Shulman, *Reason, Contract, and Law in Labor Relations,* 68 Harv. L. Rev. 999 (1955).

to grant specific performance of a promise in a collective bargaining agreement. The Court declared that the substantive federal law is to be fashioned by the courts from the policy of our national labor laws.

Justice Douglas drew support for his opinion from the legislative history of the Taft-Hartley Act and read that history much as Judge Rives read it in the *Jay-Ann* case:

Viewed in this light, the legislation does more than confer jurisdiction in the federal courts over labor organizations. It expresses a federal policy that federal courts should enforce these agreements on behalf of or against labor organizations and that industrial peace can be best obtained only in that way.[21]

In support of their opinions both Judge Rives and Justice Douglas quoted this section of the Senate report on the Taft-Hartley Act concerning Section 301:

Consequently, to encourage the making of agreements and to promote industrial peace through faithful performance by the parties, collective bargaining agreements affecting interstate commerce should be enforceable in the Federal courts. Our amendment would provide for suits by unions as legal entities and against unions as legal entities in the Federal courts in suits affecting commerce.[22]

It seems clear enough from these statements that the union can sue on its collective bargaining contract, and it further appears that the Supreme Court ruling is not limited to arbitration provisions. But does its holding cover the situation of a union suing to enforce pension rights? In his majority opinion Justice Douglas distinguished the *Lincoln Mills* situation from that of the *Westinghouse* case. He said that in the *Westinghouse* case the union was suing for unpaid wages on behalf of 4,000 employees and that the basic question concerned the standing of the union to sue and recover on those individual employment contracts.[23] He was of the opinion that the union had no standing to sue in this case. The *Lincoln Mills* case, however, concerned the right of a union to enforce an agreement which it made with an employer, and its action could properly be brought under Section 301. Justice Douglas also said, in a footnote, that the *Lincoln Mills* case did not deal with situations in which individual employee rights were in issue. He cited the *Westinghouse*

21 353 U. S. at 455.
22 Senate Report No. 105, 80th Cong., 1st sess., 1947, p. 15. For discussion see Bickel and Wellington, *Legislative Purpose and the Judicial Process: The Lincoln Mills Case,* 71 Harv. L. Rev. 1 (1957); also Note, 57 Colum. L. Rev. 1123 (1957).
23 353 U. S. at 456.

decision, implying that the problem of suits involving the rights of individuals was dealt with there.[24] From this reference and from the nature of the other cases he cites, the inference is plain that Section 301 does not grant jurisdiction in matters of individual rights even though they arise out of a collective bargaining agreement.[25]

Justice Burton, with whom Justice Harlan joined in a concurring opinion, made the point very clear: "The District Court had jurisdiction over the action since it involved an obligation running to a union — a union controversy — and not uniquely personal rights of employees sought to be enforced by a union. (Citing *Westinghouse.*)"[26] From this it would appear that a union cannot sue for pension rights in a federal court when such a suit will amount to an attempt on the part of the union to enforce personal rights. However, there seems to be room here for the distinction that Judge Rives sought to make in the *Jay-Ann* case.[27] His argument was that the union was seeking to enforce payments to a health and welfare fund, and that the medical care and retirement benefits to which each employee might be entitled under the contract could not be foretold. This, in his mind, constituted a suit by the union as an entity which would not be ruled out by the *Westinghouse* decision.

In the light of the statements of the Supreme Court in the *Lincoln Mills* case, this would seem to be a good argument. If it is a correct interpretation of the *Lincoln Mills* and *Westinghouse* distinctions, then it may be possible for a union to sue an employer for not living up to his contract to make periodic contributions to a pension fund, but it could not sue to enforce the pension rights of individual employees in any situation where the basis of the suit would be the individual contracts of employment. For enforcement of personal rights, employees would have to have recourse to state courts or be prepared to establish diversity of citizenship between themselves and the defendant in order to enter the federal courts, something that is often very difficult.

The importance of closing the doors of the federal courts to unions seeking to sue on pension agreements is highlighted when we recall that Section 301 of the Taft-Hartley Act was enacted precisely in order to provide a forum in which collective bargaining agreements could be en-

[24] 353 U. S. at 459.
[25] These cases, besides Westinghouse, are: Moore v. Ill. Central R. Co., 312 U. S. 630 (1941); Slocum v. Delaware L. & W. R. Co., 339 U. S. 239 (1950); Transcontinental Air v. Koppal, 345 U. S. 653 (1953).
[26] 353 U. S. at 460.
[27] 228 F. 2d at 636.

forced. It has always been true in state jurisdictions that a labor union cannot sue to vindicate the personal rights of its members.[28] The reason is of course that such a suit is based on the personal contract for hire between the employee and the employer and that a union is not a real party in interest.

The most appropriate remedies that federal law provides a group of aggrieved pensioners are the class suit and the spurious class action permitted by the Federal Rules of Civil Procedure.[29] In the latter type of suit it is possible, if other conditions are fulfilled, to establish diversity of citizenship between certain members of a class of employees and the employer and to join those employees who cannot establish diversity of citizenship by having them intervene as interested parties. Many of the states do not provide for such a spurious class action,[30] but then there is not the same need for this jurisdictional remedy. We may conclude, however, that, as the law now stands, enforcement of pension rights against an employer must be undertaken by the employee himself.

ENFORCEMENT OF RIGHTS BY THE EMPLOYEE

The next question to consider is: How can an individual employee protected by a union agreement enforce his pension rights in court? Unless he establishes diversity of citizenship, the federal courts would seem to be closed to him.[31] The state courts have permitted the individual employee to sue as a third-party beneficiary[32] or on the grounds that the hiring contract incorporates the collective agreement[33] or as a principal for whom the union is agent.[34]

At best, however, these remedies are uncertain and are nearly always open to the objection that the employee has no proprietary right in the fund even though this is not explicitly stated in the plan document — as

---

[28] See, for example, Communications Workers of America v. Brown, 252 S. W. 2d 103 (1952); Quinn v. Buchanan, 298 S. W. 2d 413 (1957).

[29] Federal Rules of Civil Procedure, Rule 23; Shiply v. Pittsburgh L.E.R. Co., 70 F. Supp. 870 (W. D. Pa. 1947).

[30] Simeon, *Class Suits under the Codes*, W. Res. L. Rev. 1 (1955).

[31] Schatte v. Theatrical Employees, see note 10.

[32] Ryan v. Ryan, 156 Kan. 348, 133 P. 2d 119 (1943); Gulla v. Barton, 164 App. Div. 293, 149 N. Y. Supp. 952 (3d Dept. 1924); Held v. Britten-Fenton Co., 180 Misc. 1077, 44 N. Y. S. 2d 58 (Sup. Ct. 1943). A suit by a non-union member was also allowed, Leahy v. Smith, 137 Cal. App. R. 884, 290 P. 2d 679 (Cal. 1955).

[33] Hudson v. Cincinnati Ry., 152 Ky. 711, 154 S. W. 47 (1913); Aulich v. Craigmyle, 248 Ky. 678, 59 S. W. 2d 560 (1933).

[34] Christiansen v. Local 680, Milk Drivers, 126 N. J. Eq. 508, 10 A. 2d 168 (Ch. 1940); Mueller v. Chi. & N. Ry., 194 Minn. 83, 259 N. W. 798 (1935).

it frequently is. The employee always has the option of proceeding against the trustees themselves in the case of union plans and we shall see a number of instances where this has been done. But this remedy is ineffective to coerce employers who cannot in turn be sued by the union officials. A more effective way of enforcing employee rights is available where there is a joint board of trustees with employer representatives, but only a small minority of pension funds are of this type.

We shall discuss this matter later in more detail and merely observe here that the employee's woes are serious even at the outset of his suit when he is seeking standing to sue.

THE PENSION PLAN

For one who is seeking to sort out the basic legal relationships that prevail among the parties involved in a pension trust, the cases on the subject present a bewildering maze. As the Senate Subcommittee on Welfare and Pension Funds commented in its report: "The application of well-established doctrines of trust law to the field of employee benefit trust funds is a most difficult task"; these funds are ". . . posing an entirely new concept for dealing with property that has no parallel elsewhere in the law."[35]

In *Hurd* v. *Illinois Bell Telephone Co.* the federal District Court for the Northern District of Illinois presented one of the most thorough analyses of the pertinent cases yet made, but it was forced to conclude that the rules of law on the subject cannot be reconciled in all cases.[36] One of the greatest difficulties in reconciling the cases arises from the kind of confusion the court discovered in the *Hurd* case when it said that the plaintiff was trying to turn the creator of the trust into a trustee.[37] The issue here was whether or not the company, which was also the administrator of the fund, was within its rights in reducing its monthly payment to a pensioner by an amount equal to half of his social security benefits. The court determined that as between employer and employee the relationship was not one of trusteeship but of contract. Since the company was the creator of the trust, it could not be the trustee. In such diverse situations as now exist, it is necessary to consider the cases according to

[35] Senate Report No. 1734, 84th Cong., 2d sess., 1956, p. 67.
[36] 136 F. Supp. 125, 133 (N. D. Ill. 1955), *aff'd*, 234 F. 2d 942 (7th Cir. 1956); *cert. denied*, Seybold v. Western Electric Co., 352 U. S. 918 (1957), *rehearing denied*, 352 U. S. 977 (1957).
[37] 136 F. Supp. at 135.

the varying types of pension administration. This treatment will at least have the merit of locating and narrowing the areas of disagreement, if not of reconciling the cases.

Perhaps the most fundamental question that can be asked with regard to the property rights in pension trusts is: Are they true trusts? But this is precisely where the division of opinion arises, for pension plans have been called both trusts and contracts. In the following discussion of cases bearing on this issue we shall consider first the relationships of employers, unions and employees. The legal status of the financial trustee will then be analyzed as a separate subject.

THE PENSION PLAN AS A TRUST

Throughout this study we have recognized the division of pension trusts into three types of administration: Taft-Hartley or joint funds, union funds and employer-managed funds. We shall consider the legal status of each of these in turn.

Taft-Hartley Funds

Whatever the confusion that may exist on the point of contract versus trust in other areas, it seems quite clear that the Taft-Hartley type of pension fund — managed jointly by representatives of management and of the union and by a third or neutral representative — is a trust. The significant case on this point is *Van Horn* v. *Lewis*.[38] Here the fund was made up of contributions from the employers and was administered by three trustees, one representing the union, another the management and the third chosen by both sides. The court said: "It is a beneficial Fund, and the rules applicable to charitable trusts undoubtedly apply, and the majority of the Trustees have a right to act..."[39]

Similarly, in *Upholsterers International Union* v. *Leathercraft Furniture Co.* the court said, "... we cannot say that the fund in question is not a trust fund."[40] In other words, the fund is a trust. The court in the *Van Horn* case thought the question unworthy of debate, but in the *Upholsterers* suit the court gave the following reason for its decision: "There can be no dispute that the fund, which is actually money earned by the employee members, must be used for their sole and exclusive benefit."[41]

[38] 79 F. Supp. 541 (D. C. 1948).
[39] 79 F. Supp. at 544.
[40] 82 F. Supp. 570, 575 (E. D. Pa. 1949).
[41] 82 F. Supp. at 574.

Indeed, in all of these cases this would seem to be the operative question: Whose money is it? If the funds in question actually do belong to the employees, then it is reasonable to declare the arrangement a true trust.

The number of pertinent cases is not large, but whenever the issue has been considered the so-called Taft-Hartley funds have been declared to be trusts.[42] These funds do not present the problem of confusion about the identity of the trustee arising in the *Hurd* case since they have a body of trustees clearly separate from the donor or settlor of the trust. We find less agreement, however, in determining that these funds are charitable trusts.

Union Funds

It is fairly well established that a union fund which is set up as a pension trust in form is also one in fact. In the case of *Guilford* v. *Arthur*[43] an Illinois court held that in a situation where real estate was conveyed in trust for widows and orphans of locomotive engineers, with power conferred on the Brotherhood to dispose of the property for the uses and purposes specified, a charitable trust was established. The court adopted as its own a rule taken from *Perry on Trusts.* "It is immaterial how uncertain, indefinite and vague the cestui qui trust or final beneficiaries of a charitable use [may be], provided there is a legal mode of rendering them certain by means of trustees appointed or to be appointed."[44]

Two recent New York cases applied the *Van Horn* doctrine to union funds. The first, *Application of Townsend,* was a case in which the labor union tried to prevent the state superintendent of insurance from examining the welfare fund records on the ground that he had no jurisdiction since the pension fund assets belonged to the union.[45] The court rejected this contention, saying: "The trustees are holding the assets of the funds for the individuals who are the beneficiaries. They are not holding them for the employers' association, the individual employees, or the union. The trust records are their records."[46]

In *People* v. *Cilento,* a New York criminal case, the court followed the rulings in the *Van Horn, United Garment* and *Upholsterers* cases, saying

[42] In addition to the two cases cited above the same conclusion was reached in United Garment Workers of America v. Jacob Reed's Sons, 83 F. Supp. 49 (E. D. Pa. 1949) and United Marine Division v. Essex Transportation Co., 216 F. 2d 410 (3d Cir. 1954).

[43] 158 Ill. 600, 41 N. E. 1009 (1895).

[44] *Loc. cit.*

[45] 206 Misc. 619, 130 N. Y. S. 2d 322 (1954).

[46] 206 Misc. at 623.

that "The Federal Courts have held that union welfare funds are trust funds and are governed by the laws relating to trustees."[47]

The case of *Booth* v. *Security Mutual Life Insurance Co.*[48] is another situation in which a court found a union trust fund to be a true trust. As this action illustrates the legal possibilities for employee protection in the trust form of pension fund, it merits a full discussion. In this case three individual employees, members of a local union, alleged conspiracy to divert trust fund assets against certain officers of the international union, an insurance agency and an insurance company. In answer to a motion that local members had no right to sue because they were not proper representatives of the union members, the court declared that they were proper representatives since the other members were so numerous and scattered that it would be impractical to bring them all into court. Furthermore, the interest of the plaintiffs was held to be coextensive with that of the class as a whole.

The defendants also claimed that the suit was barred by the trust indenture, which provided that, upon failure of the trust, the union and the then members would be entitled to the proceeds. But the court held that there was no failure of the trust and so the union members had a right to bring suit against the trustees for not protecting the trust. The defendants further relied upon the following wording of the indenture: "No employee . . . shall have any individual or representative right . . . upon any assets or funds held by or under the control of 'The Social Security Department,' except such rights as are otherwise in this agreement provided for."[49] But the court held that the individual union members had a contingent beneficial interest in the trust assets which they had a right to protect. Furthermore, the court said, any provision preventing the individual members from protecting their beneficial interests would be illegal under Section 302(c) of the Taft-Hartley Act.[50]

Finally, the court held that it did not matter that the beneficiaries' interests were contingent, citing *Scott on Trusts* as its authority.[51] The normal duty to request the trustees to bring suit was not required of the plaintiffs here, said the court, since the trustees themselves participated

---

[47] 207 Misc. 914, 917, 143 N. Y. S. 2d 14, *aff'd*, 1 App. Div. 2d 206, 149 N. Y. S. 2d 14, *rev'd on other grounds*, 2 N. Y. 2d 55 (1956).
[48] 155 F. Supp. 755 (D. C. N. J. 1957).
[49] 155 F. Supp. at 760.
[50] *Ibid.*, citing Upholsterers International Union v. Leathercraft Furniture Co.
[51] 2 Scott, *Trusts*, § 200, 1501 (2d ed. 1956).

in the breach of trust. In such a case, the right in equity to sue inheres in the beneficiary of the trust.

This case answers some of the difficulties facing employees in securing their rights which we noted earlier in the analysis of pension trusts. Three individuals were allowed to represent all other employees covered by a pension trust. The escape clauses were not allowed to protect the trustees, although it is somewhat doubtful if this would have been the case if the Taft-Hartley Act could not have been invoked. Pension rights had not vested, but the contingent interest was recognized. Finally, the plaintiffs were excused from the useless obligation of requesting the trustees to sue. This case is proof that much could be accomplished to protect the rights of employees if pension funds in general could be found to be true trusts.

Another case in which a pension plan was held to be a trust was *George v. The Trustees of the Kaiser-Frazer UAW–CIO Retirement Fund*,[52] which concerned a trust fund established for the employees of the Kaiser-Frazer Corporation. The fund was created by the company, which paid in six cents for each hour an employee worked for the company. At the time of the suit, August 1954, the trust fund assets were approximately $6 million. The purpose of the fund was to provide retirement benefits for the employees and some pensions were being paid at the time of the suit. In November 1953, the company disposed of its plants at Willow Run, Michigan, leaving some 11,000 employees without work. A group of these employees brought suit, claiming that in these circumstances the trust fund should be terminated. The employees sought to have the court order payment of benefits to employees already retired and to have the balance of the fund divided among the remaining employees in proportion to the number of hours they had been employed.

While the plan and the collective bargaining agreement contained explicit provisions for the termination of the pension trust, the plaintiffs maintained that these provisions were not applicable. The terms of the agreement providing for the pension fund declared that the title to all sums paid into the fund should be vested exclusively in the trustees. It was further provided that "The moneys to be paid by the Company into the said Retirement Fund shall not constitute or be deemed wages, salary or compensation due to any individual employee. . . . Neither shall

[52] George v. Haber, 343 Mich. 218, 72 N. W. 2d 121 (1955).

any such employees have any vested rights hereunder to any of the moneys of the Retirement Fund."[53]

The agreement also declared that the fund should qualify for exemption as an irrevocable pension trust according to the terms of the Internal Revenue Code. The term of the agreement was to be five years from November 1949. On June 1, 1950, a further contract had been made concerning the fund, providing in part as follows:

ARTICLE X — NO VESTED INTEREST: Neither the Company nor any Employee of the Company, nor the Union nor any member of the Union, nor any person claiming by, through or under any of them, shall have any right, title, or interest in or to the Retirement Fund, or any part thereof, excepting the right of the Employee to retirement benefits or retirement disability benefits as provided hereunder. *No Employee shall receive any part of the Company payments instead of such retirement benefits or retirement disability benefits, nor receive a cash consideration in lieu of such benefits either upon the termination of this Retirement Trust Agreement or his withdrawal through severance of employment or otherwise.* (Emphasis supplied.)[54]

In its decision, the court declared that the original intention of the parties to the contract was to limit benefits strictly to the terms of the plan and the supplemental agreements. The decision relied heavily on a provision stating that in the event of termination, the funds, after providing for necessary expenses, should be used to assure the continued payment of benefits to employees who were either retired at the time of termination or were 65 years of age or over, and who had five or more years of credited service at the time of termination.

The plaintiffs argued that the agreement did not contemplate termination of operations at the Willow Run plant. They said that the termination created a situation justifying the court to take equitable jurisdiction to terminate the trust and dispose of the fund in a manner other than that contemplated by the parties. But the court said that it was clear from the terms of the agreement how the parties intended the remaining moneys in the fund to be used. The court further held that there was no reason why the intent of the creators of the fund could not be carried out and that what the plaintiffs were really asking the court to do was to modify the agreement according to a new scheme.

The court held further that it was unable to order benefit payments to the plaintiffs because the express terms creating the trust fund gave them no right or interest in the fund. The principle governing the court's deci-

[53] 72 N. W. 2d at 123.
[54] 72 N. W. 2d at 124.

sion was the well-established rule that a trust may not be terminated before it has accomplished the purposes for which it was established, so long as those purposes can be accomplished.

The Pension Fund as a Charitable Trust

In cases already cited, it has been asserted that the pension trusts are charitable trusts. But we submit that the essential requirements of a charitable trust are lacking in the case of the pension trust. In the first place, these trusts are not charitable or eleemosynary in nature. There may have been a day when giving a pension to an employee could be regarded as an act of generosity on the part of the employer and in isolated instances this is so even today. Characteristically, however, the pension has come to be looked upon as an earned right, due the employee in justice, not charity. Yesterday's largess has become today's legitimate demand.

Neither is there any merit to the argument that since the beneficiaries of a pension fund are "indefinite," pension trusts are like public charitable trusts. The primary purpose of a public charitable trust is to protect a trust whose beneficiaries, usually some group of the public at large like the "poor white orphans of Philadelphia," are either unable or unwilling to require from the trustees an accounting of their stewardship. In the case of the pension trusts the only indefiniteness about the beneficiaries arises from the uncertainties surrounding their continuous employment with the company. The beneficiaries, potential or actual, are always known. Furthermore, they have more than the remote interest that, for example, the ordinary citizen with two good eyes might have in a public charitable trust for the blind. The stake of pension trust beneficiaries is much more immediate and can often be measured in terms of dollars and cents that would, in the absence of a fund, appear in their pay envelopes.

A legal ruling that these trusts are public charitable trusts would place them in the care of the state, with the duty of enforcement devolving on the Attorney General.[55] Some states, such as Wisconsin, allow a suit by an "interested party" on behalf of the state.[56] We would favor a policy by which courts would grant to the beneficiaries of pension trusts the traditional rights of beneficiaries so that they could sue on their own behalf.

[55] For a discussion of this, see Bogert, *State Supervision of Charities,* 52 Mich. L. Rev. 633 (1954).
[56] Wis. Laws, 1945, Ch. 459, 822.

The most recent tendency, however, is to supplement private remedies by legislation authorizing state officials to bring suit on behalf of pension and welfare plan beneficiaries. For example, New York has made the following provision in its banking and insurance laws:

> In any case where, after notice and a hearing, the superintendent [of Banking or Insurance] finds that any employee welfare fund has been depleted by reason of any wrongful or negligent act or omission of a trustee or of any other person, he may transmit a copy of his findings to the Attorney General, who may bring an action in the name of the people of the State, or intervene in an action brought by or on behalf of an employee, for the recovery of such fund for the benefit of the employees and such other persons as may have an interest in the fund.[57]

We may expect other states to follow the lead of New York with the result that trustees of pension plans will be held accountable by the state rather than by the beneficiaries. This development will, of course, do nothing to enhance the proprietary interest of pension fund beneficiaries.

Employer Funds

Where the employer-managed type of fund is in question we find a serious difference of opinion in the courts as to whether a plan is to be called a trust or not. The ambiguity arises over the fact that the legal document defining the rights of the parties is usually a pension plan of the single-employer–administered type described earlier. If there is a formal trust indenture involved at all, it is usually executed by the employer-manager of the plan and a corporate trustee. The question that will come before the courts is, therefore: Is this "plan," in which the employee or his representatives are called beneficiaries, a trust or not? In the typical case the plan will be noncontributory and the donor or settlor of the trust will be the employer.

Such was the case of *Hurd* v. *Illinois Bell Telephone Company*, referred to earlier.[58] The Court of Appeals affirmed the decision of the lower court that the plaintiffs, retired employees, could not urge that the pension plan was a trust. The lower court had held that the plaintiffs were trying to turn the creator of a trust (The Bell Telephone Company) into a trustee;[59] and that the trust element of the case was irrelevant. "If misconduct were charged against Bankers Trust (trustee of the fund), the law of trusts would be relevant. But the plaintiff's rights in

---

[57] New York Insurance Law § 37(d) 5; New York Banking Law § 71, 5.
[58] 136 F. Supp. 125 (N. D. Ill. 1955), *aff'd*, 234 F. 2d 942 (7th Cir. 1956).
[59] 136 F. Supp. at 135.

relation to the Bell System are contractual."[60] On this point the Court of Appeals said: "A pension plan is a unilateral contract which creates a vested right in those employees who accept the offer it contains by continuing in employment for the requisite number of years."[61]

This case, therefore, establishes two propositions: (1) in the typical employer-managed trust, the employer is not the trustee, and (2) the banker-trustee stands in a trustee relationship to the employees covered by the plan.

But the *Hurd* case does not represent the only view. In the case of *Union Pacific Co.* v. *Artist* it was held that a medical fund for employees was in fact a trust.[62] The facts were that Union Pacific required its employees to contribute to the support of a medical department. The company paid the additional fees needed for maintaining this service. The plaintiff, Artist, brought suit for malpractice in one of the hospitals supported by the fund and claimed that his contribution was compulsory. The defense of the Union Pacific was that since this was an eleemosynary institution, the company should not be held liable for malpractice. The court decided that:

> These contributions of twenty-five cents per month from each employee, and from $2,000 to $4,000 per month from the Company, constituted a trust fund devoted to the purpose of furnishing hospital accommodations . . . There is no doubt that any one of these employees could compel the application of this fund to the purpose for which it was collected, in any Court of equity having jurisdiction.[63]

For this and other reasons, the court concluded that the Union Pacific Company was conducting a charitable enterprise and that appropriations for this purpose were a gift or a charity. The fact that the company may have had a selfish motive in its charity did not affect the issue. The intent to handle the funds for a charitable purpose was held to be controlling.

Still another view of the relationship of the parties to a pension fund was held in *Whitely* v. *Mammoth Life and Accident Insurance Co.*[64] In this case, the pension fund was set up in the form of a trust for employees. For some time the trustee recognized the trust but later repudiated it. A complaint was filed by the stockholders seeking either the appoint-

[60] *Loc. cit.*
[61] 234 F. 2d at 946.
[62] 60 Fed. 365 (8th Cir. 1894).
[63] 60 Fed. at 369.
[64] 273 S. W. 2d 42 (Ky. Ct. App. 1954).

ment of a new trustee or cancellation of the trust and return of the stock. The court held that the company "was the donor of the trust, and therefore would be entitled to assert failure of the trust or to demand its enforcement."[65] It went on to say that even if the arrangement were not so construed the company would be a third-party beneficiary of the trust.

Other cases reveal some consequences of this issue of whether or not the typical pension plan is a true trust, but they shed little additional light on the central problem.[66]

Unquestionably, employer-managed pension funds have some features of a trust other than the name they bear. Still, the ambiguous situation in which the pension fund is *called* a trust and has many of its characteristics and yet is *not* a trust is unhappy at best. The principal objection to this situation is, of course, that the so-called trustee has all the powers and prerogatives of property management with none of the obligations to account to the beneficiary for his stewardship.

Accountability of the Trustee to the Beneficiary

It is possible to exclude a union from the right to demand an account, but a question may be raised as to whether the trust instrument may provide that the trustees need not account to beneficiaries. In this connection Bogert has observed:

> The settlor ought not to be able to oust the court of its constitutional or statutory jurisdiction, or to override the acts of the legislature concerning information to be furnished by trustees to their beneficiaries. Provisions of this sort . . . would seem against public policy and void . . .[67]

The cases on this point are by no means decisive, but it seems that the balance of opinion is that the settlor cannot relieve trustees of their duty to account to beneficiaries in a court of equity.[68] The cases opposed to this proposition generally state that the beneficiaries are merely objects of the settlor's generosity and thus may be given rights as limited as the settlor may determine.[69] But even these cases are in agreement that if fraud or breach of trust is alleged, the limitations may be ignored,

[65] 273 S. W. 2d at 43.

[66] For example, alienation of an employee's interest may depend on whether the pension fund is a true trust. 70 Harv. L. Rev. 490, 499 (1957); Seventy-first Street & Broadway Corp. v. Thorne, 10 N. J. Misc. 99, 157 A. 851 (Sup. Ct. 1932); Note, "Insulating Pension Benefits from Creditors," 2 Stan. L. Rev. 270 (1951).

[67] Bogert, *Trusts and Trustees*, Sec. 972 (2d ed. 1952).

[68] Kent v. Universal Film Mfg. Co., 200 App. Div. 539, 193 N. Y. Supp. 838 (1st Dept. 1922).

[69] *In re* Tarby's Estate, 25 N. J. Misc. 236, 95 A. 2d 774 (1953); Keller's Estate, 224 Pa. 523, 73 A. 926 (1909).

since the exemption from the duty to account is intended to apply only to faithful trustees.

The validity of decisions approving limitations seems open to doubt when viewed in an industrial setting where many pension plans are established by collective bargaining. Today pensions are no longer in the exclusive domain of the employer,[70] and indeed for tax purposes pension funds must be permanently dedicated to the exclusive benefit of the employees. In that light, limitations on the duty of the trustees to account fully to the employees seem a denial of one of the essential premises of the modern employee pension system. Furthermore, as a matter of general trust principles, it would appear that:

A settlor who attempts to create a trust without court accountability in the trustee is contradicting himself. A trust necessarily means rights in the cestui (beneficiary), enforceable in equity. If the trustee cannot be called to account, the cestui cannot force the trustee to any particular line of conduct with regard to the trust property or sue for breach of trust. The trustee may do as he likes with the property, and the cestui is without remedy. If the settlor really intends a trust, it would seem that accountability in chancery or other court must inevitably follow as an incident. Without an account the cestui must be in the dark as to whether there has been a breach of trust and so is prevented as a practical matter from holding the trustee liable for a breach.[71]

The refusal of a court of equity to be bound by the settlor's direction in the trust instrument does not condemn the entire trust to invalidity. Rather the offending clause can be ignored and the rights of the beneficiaries determined as if it did not exist.

THE PENSION PLAN AS A CONTRACT

We have seen from the preceding discussion that certain pension plans have been held by the courts to give rise to a contractual relation between the trust or fund and the employee. We shall now discuss in some detail the contractual nature of employer-managed pension funds.

Contract versus Gratuity

As we have already noted in the *Hurd* case, involving the typical pension trust, the court declared that the relationship of the employee to the fund was contractual. The court arrived at this conclusion with some difficulty since it had first to dispose of the argument that the pension promised the employee was, in fact, a gratuity and gave rise to no legally enforceable rights. Indeed, the court cited an imposing array of opinions

[70] Inland Steel Co. v. NLRB (see p. 164).
[71] Bogert, *Trusts and Trustees*, Sec. 972.

to the effect that a "noncontributory pension plan did not give rise to an enforceable unilateral contract."[72]

This is, in fact, the traditional view and historically the courts have upheld clauses in pension plans which stated that the pensions in question were gratuities. Thus in the case of *Pennie v. Reis* in 1889, the first decision of this question, the court ruled that a policeman's pension was a gratuity even though the sums going to create the fund, two dollars a month, were stated to be part of his compensation.[73] Similarly in *Mc-Nevin v. Solvay Process Co.* (1898) and *Dolge v. Dolge* (1902), it was held that pensions voluntarily created by the employer were gifts and that it was within the complete discretion of the pension committee to give or withhold the promised pension.[74]

The reasoning behind these decisions is well set forth in the case of *Umshler v. Umshler*. Here the court stated that the pension was a gratuity because (1) the granting of a pension was wholly voluntary on the part of the company, (2) benefits were paid from the treasury of the company, (3) the pensioner had made no contribution to the fund, and (4) the application for a pension stated that the pension was a gratuity and might be discontinued.[75]

Nevertheless, some courts have gone to great lengths to disallow these gratuity clauses,[76] though, as yet, these decisions are in the minority. To return to the *Hurd* case, the court claimed that in reviewing previous cases it had found a distinction justifying its own conclusion that the employee does have a contractual right with regard to the fund. It said: "A careful reading of the decisions indicates, however, that even the states following a strict view of pension plans would enforce employees rights in a separately established trust fund."[77]

[72] 136 F. Supp. at 133, citing Hughes v. Encyclopaedia Britannica, Inc., 1 Ill. App. 2d 514, 117 N. E. 2d 880, 42 A. L. R. 2d 456 (1954); Umshler v. Umshler, 332 Ill. App. 494, 76 N. E. 2d 231 (1947); Dolan v. Heller, 30 N. J. Super. 440, 104 A. 2d 860 (Ch. 1954); Menke v. Thompson, 140 F. 2d 786 (8th Cir. 1944); McCabe v. Consol. Ed. Co. of N. Y., 30 N. Y. S. 2d 445 (City Ct. N. Y. 1941); Webster v. Southwestern Bell Telephone Co., 153 S. W. 498 (T. Civ. App. 1941).

[73] 132 U. S. 464 (1889).

[74] McNevin v. Solvay Process Co., 32 App. Div., N. Y. 610 (1898); Dolge v. Dolge, 70 App. Div. 517, 75 N. Y. Supp. 386 (4th Dept. 1902); Menke v. Thompson (see note 72).

[75] 332 Ill. App. 494, 76 N. E. 2d 231, 233 (1947).

[76] The clearest are: Schofield v. Zion's Co-op Mercantile Institution, 85 Utah 281, 39 P. 2d 342 (1934); Psutka v. Michigan Alkali Co., 274 Mich. 318, 264 N. W. 385 (1936); see also Mabley & Carew Co. v. Borden, 129 Ohio St. 375, 195 N. E. 697 (1935); Note, 99 U. Pa. L. Rev. 701 (1951).

[77] 136 F. Supp. at 133.

Since there is a growing tendency in pension literature to regard the pension as a deferred wage, it is to be hoped that the courts will begin to follow this view. As the *Hurd* case demonstrates, some are already doing so, at least in cases where an employer has set up an independent fund for pensions. There is really no reason for denying that pensions are wages even when the pension is paid out of the corporate treasury. This is particularly true in the case of an established plan with a definite and clear promise of pension payments.

The problem presented in court actions involving the gratuity clause might be solved by application of the principle of promissory estoppel.[78] The theory grounding such an action would be that the employee had relied on his employer's promise and had suffered some detriment as a result. Two factors which will or should influence courts in arriving at such a conclusion are: (1) if the employer had been in the practice of paying pension benefits an employee might reasonably rely upon a pension promise or offer; and (2) the employee did not have access to pension literature giving him full information about the employer's disclaimers. Under such circumstances an employee could argue that his reliance upon the employer's promise was reasonable. These arguments would not apply with equal force in collectively bargained pension plans since it may be presumed that the bargaining agent has had the benefit of expert advice on the provisions of the plan.[79]

Bilateral versus Unilateral Contract

In the absence of a trust, the employee must look to his contractual rights in order to enforce his pension payments. When there is a question of termination of employment it becomes important to determine whether the contract concerning the pension is bilateral or unilateral. It would seem from the nature of the usual conditions of employment that most pension arrangements would be construed as unilateral contracts. Since the right to a payment out of a pension fund usually does not vest in the employee until certain service requirements have been fulfilled,

[78] Recovery has been allowed in the following pension cases, which, however, did not involve gratuity clauses: Hunter v. Sparling, 87 Cal. App. 2d 711, 197 P. 2d 807 (1948) (alternative holding); Langer v. Superior Steel Corp., 105 Pa. Super. 579, 161 Atl. 571 (1932) (alternative holding).

[79] For discussion of the contractual nature of pensions, see Somers & Schwartz, *Pension and Welfare Plans; Gratuities or Compensation?* 4 Ind. & Lab. Rel. Rev. 77 (1950); Note, *Consideration for the Employer's Promise of a Voluntary Pension Plan,* 23 U. Chi. L. Rev. 96 (1955).

the employer's offer is often construed to be a continuing one. The employee's acceptance, then, can be accomplished only by putting in the required years of service. A bilateral contract, however, would be in effect only if the employee agrees at the beginning to work for a specific length of time and the employer agrees to compensate that service with a pension.

Thus the usual pension contract would be unilateral. If, then, an employee voluntarily leaves his employment before fulfilling the terms of the offer, he has no rights. The same would be true if he were discharged for cause. If, however, the employer discharges him in bad faith, for example to avoid paying the pension, the employee can recover what is due him.[80] But even when the employer is acting in good faith, it has been held that an employee may recover unless he has been discharged for a cause which would justify dismissal under a bilateral contract.[81] The operative principle here is that a promisor cannot rely on a condition the fulfillment of which he has prevented.

The courts have taken continuous employment as sufficient consideration for these contracts, without requiring proof that the pension was the reason why the employee stayed on the job.[82]

Reservation of Rights

As we have already noted in earlier discussions of the pension plan document, pension offers frequently reserve to the employer the right to amend, revise or terminate a pension plan at will. These clauses are similar in effect to the gratuity clause, and one court has suggested that such provisions might make the offer illusory.[83]

In some instances, although they are in the minority where the problem has arisen, courts have looked with disfavor on these clauses. The case of *Schofield* v. *Zion's Co-op. Mercantile Institution* concerned a noncontributory pension plan containing a provision that nothing in the plan should be so construed as to give the employee a pension claim or a right

[80] Bos v. United States Rubber Co., 100 Cal. App. 2d 565, 224 P. 2d 386; Montgomery Ward & Co. v. Guignet, 112 Ind. App. 661, 45 N. E. 2d 337 (1942).

[81] American Security Life Insurance Co. v. Moore, 37 Ala. App. 552, 72 So. 2d 132 (1954); Roberts v. Mays Mills, 184 N. C. 406, 114 S. E. 530 (1922).

[82] Wilson v. Rudolph Wurlitzer Co., 48 Ohio App. 450, 194 N. E. 441 (1934); Gilbert v. Norfolk & W. Ry., 114 W. Va. 344, 171 S. E. 814 (1933).

[83] Bromberg v. United Cigar–Whelan Stores Corp., 19 CCH Lab. Cas. ¶ 66203 and 79061 (N. Y. S. Ct. 1951) (dictum).

to continued employment.[84] The court subjected the clauses in question to the narrowest interpretation in order to conclude that the plan contained an offer which became binding on the employer upon satisfaction of the conditions laid down. But the courts have also honored these clauses to the point of allowing an employer to amend a plan in such a way that the employee was deprived of his pension.[85] It may be argued that in the present early days of pension experience such clauses ought to be upheld in order to permit an employer to embark on a pension program without jeopardizing his whole future. But this is the only excuse, and such clauses ought to be scrutinized most carefully by the courts to see if the employee was unfairly induced by the employer to rely on the promise of a pension.

Scope of Administrative Authority

The *Hurd* case, to which frequent reference has been made because it embodies the pension trust arrangement most typical of modern pension programs, arose out of a determination that the employee pension should be reduced by one-half of the social security benefits. The principal affirmative argument by the Illinois Bell Telephone Company was made in reliance on a clause in the plan giving the benefit committees authority to "determine conclusively for all parties all questions arising in the administration of the plan."[86] The determination by these committees was, therefore, to be final and, according to the defense, as long as there was no showing of bad faith the employee had no grievance.

After citing an imposing array of cases in which this type of clause was upheld,[87] the court undercut these authorities by saying that all the decisions dealt with cases concerning only routine matters of administration and not with a "legal interpretation of an important provision of the plan." The court would not accept this defense because, as it said, the judicial mind is strongly against the propriety of allowing one of the parties to be, in effect, the judge in its own case.[88]

[84] 85 Utah 281, 39 P. 2d 342 (1934); see Note, *Legal Status of Private Industrial Pension Plans,* 53 Harv. L. Rev. 1375, 1379 (1940).

[85] Fickling v. Pollard, 51 Ga. App. 54, 179 S. E. 582 (1935); Umshler v. Umshler, 332 Ill. App. 494, 76 N. E. 2d 231 (1947).

[86] 136 F. Supp. at 154.

[87] Menke v. Thompson, 140 F. 2d 786 (8th Cir. 1944); W. U. Tel. Co. v. Robertson, 146 Ark. 406, 225 S. W. 649 (1920) and others. See 136 F. Supp. at 154.

[88] Citing R'way Passenger & Freight Conductor's Mutual Aid and Benefit Ass'n v. Robinson, 147 Ill. 138, 159–160, 35 N. E. 168, 176 (1893); Patton v. Babson Statisti-

This makes consoling reading although the authorities which the court cites for its opinion are relatively old. Support for the view that courts may upset the determinations of a pension administrative body can also be drawn from two more recent decisions. In the case of *Bednar* v. *United Mine Workers Fund*[89] the court upheld a miner who challenged the decision of a union pension committee that he could not obtain his pension because he had not fulfilled the requirements for continuous employment. (He had failed through no fault of his own to work the last two days before retirement.) In the case of *Forrish* v. *Kennedy*[90] it was held that the union trustees of a pension fund could not deny a pension to a coal miner who fulfilled all of the eligibility requirements except for a violation of the union's constitution prohibiting union members from selling intoxicating liquors.

It must be remembered, however, that the *Forrish* and the *Bednar* cases concerned labor union plans subject to the law of trusts and that these were not decided on the basis of contract law. In the *Forrish* case the court said that the purposes of a trust could not be frustrated by the whim or caprice of the trustees and that courts of equity can always intervene. The *Schofield* case, previously cited, also upset the determination of a pension board despite an exclusive-determination clause.[91] When a court is faced with one of these clauses, however, the presumption will be in favor of the employer and, while it may be possible to overturn a pension committee's decision, it will be uphill work for any plaintiff. The weight of opinion, at least numerically speaking, is against him.[92]

THE TRUST INDENTURE

A surface reading of the typical trust indenture empowering a corporate trustee to manage the funds of a pension plan would lead one to conclude that it is, in fact, a true trust. In some cases the duties of the corporate trustee may be merely ministerial so that it is nothing more than a

cal Organization, Inc., 259 Mass. 424, 156 N. E. 534 (1927). In these cases the court invalidated a provision to the effect that the decision of the president was final in plan matters.

[89] 25 CCH Lab. Cas. ¶ 68352.

[90] 105 A. 2d 67 (Pa. S. Ct. 1954).

[91] See note 84.

[92] Such provisions have been held to impose a discretionary duty like that of an architect in construction contracts. Clark v. New England Tel. & Tel. Co., 229 Mass. 1, 118 N. E. 348 (1918). Thus a decision in good faith is required. On the same point see George A. Fuller Co. v. Brown, 15 F. 2d 672 (4th Cir. 1926) (bonus); Montgomery Ward and Co. v. Reich, 131 Colo. 407, 282 P. 2d 1091 (1955) (bonus).

depository.[93] But the usual arrangement is for the corporate trustee to have enough investment power to make it more than a custodian.

In view of the large number of pension funds and the many employees covered, it is surprising how few cases there are defining the position of the corporate trustee. The *Hurd* case is one of the few that does this and, to date, it is the most authoritative. The fact is, however, that the case contains only an implication, not even a full-fledged dictum, to the effect that the employee has any rights against the Bankers Trust Company, the corporate trustee of the fund.[94] It is clear enough that the Trust Company is a true trustee and, from another statement, it appears that the court regards the Telephone Company as the creator of the trust.[95] But what if the employee *had* sued the financial trustee? Presumably, the employee could bring suit against the trustee if he had completed the necessary service and age requirements to qualify for a pension. But clauses in the trust agreements with the corporate trustee state, in effect, that only the employer corporation and the corporate trustee may be parties to any suit involving the trust. This is a peculiar type of trust in which beneficiaries have no way of enforcing their rights, if, indeed, a trust is contemplated at all.

This situation has been met in court actions concerning union funds. For example, in the *Upholsterers* case[96] the following statement from *United Garment Workers of America* v. *Jacob Reed's Sons* was quoted with approval: "A provision in the by-laws or regulations denying the employee members the right to resort to the courts to protect their beneficial interest in the fund is of no legal effect."[97] This rule is now applied in cases involving union funds. Why should it not also be applicable to employer funds? The only valid objection might be that the pension in question is a gratuity and not due to the pensioner by right. However, it is submitted here that this way of considering pensions is outmoded and that the presence of clauses in the pension trust indentures excluding suits by pensioners represents an anachronism.

It is doubtful, however, that an employee who had not yet become eligible for his pension by completing age and service requirements would be able to sue the corporate trustee for an accounting. A court

[93] Dick Bros., Inc. v. Comm. of Int. Rev., 205 F. 2d 467 (3d Cir. 1953).

[94] 136 F. Supp. at 135.

[95] *Loc. cit.*

[96] Upholsterers International Union v. Leathercraft Furniture Co., 82 F. Supp. 570 (E. D. Pa. 1949).

[97] 83 F. Supp. 49, 52 (E. D. Pa. 1949).

would probably inform such a plaintiff that he had no standing to sue if he could not allege substantial or complete performance of the conditions of eligibility.

But if we ask who is the beneficiary, the only real candidate we have is the pensioner. He ought to be able to protect his own rights in a pension trust. If he cannot, the state will have to appoint someone to see that he is protected, as has been done in New York and five other states.

Liquidation of a Pension Fund

The question of the distribution of assets when a pension fund has to be terminated sheds considerable light on the problem of rights in a fund during its lifetime. The trust instrument ordinarily provides for a specific type of distribution upon termination of the fund. This is one of the requirements of the Internal Revenue Code.[98]

In cases where there is no such provision a court of equity may take the problem under its cognizance.[99] In such a distribution the court will normally set aside funds in a way that will continue full pensions for those who have qualified and impose a resulting trust upon the remainder of the funds.[100] In the *Coe* and *Walters* cases and in the *Crescent Athletic Club* case the employer was allowed to participate in the distribution of the remaining funds.[101] However, on the theory that pension contributions are really wages, any excess in the trust fund ought to be turned over to the employees. It may be argued that, as contributors, the employees should be the beneficiaries of a resulting trust.

It has been suggested that the doctrines of *bona vacantia* or *cy pres* might be applied.[102] But the justification for the application of the doctrine of *bona vacantia* would be that the funds cannot revert to the contributors because it is too difficult to determine who they might be. In the case of any well-managed pension plan such a situation would scarcely arise. On the other hand, the fact that some pension trusts have been de-

[98] Internal Revenue Code of 1954, § 401.

[99] 4 Scott, *Trusts*, § 400, 430 (2d ed. 1956).

[100] Coe v. Washington Mills, 149 Mass. 543, 21 N. E. 966 (1889); Walters v. Pittsburgh & Lake Angeline Iron Co., 201 Mich. 379, 167 N. W. 834 (1918). In these cases it was declared inequitable to limit the scope of the resulting trust only to those employees working at the time the employer went out of business. But in *In re* Printers Soc'y (1899) 2 ch. 184, the beneficiaries of the trust were limited to those working for the employer at the time he went out of business. Coe v. Washington Mills does not touch this point.

[101] *In re* Crescent Athletic Club, 33 F. Supp. 132, 134 (E. D. N. Y. 1940) (dictum).

[102] Note, 70 Harv. L. Rev. 496, 501 (1957).

clared to be charitable trusts would leave the way open for the application of *cy pres,* and the employees as the intended beneficiaries of the fund would be the objects of the benefits intended.

On the whole, it would be more consistent to establish a resulting trust to cover the excess funds, since in nearly all cases it would be possible to identify the beneficiaries. This problem could readily be anticipated and settled by an employer if he would take the trouble to insert in the trust indenture a provision that any surplus will be returned to him as the settlor of the trust and that it is not intended to provide the pensioners with more than the benefits stipulated in the plan. This seems an equitable way of foreseeing the problem in ordinary cases, for in creating and maintaining the fund the employer intends to provide for a certain level of benefits for the employees. The present tax law allows the employer to recover such surplus as may result from inaccurate actuarial computation of the amounts required to provide future benefits.

In cases where the employer goes into bankruptcy and the pension program is in the form of a trust, the courts do not agree on whether money owed by the employer to the trust should be regarded as wages. If the money owed to the trust is considered as wages, it is owed to the trustee as a wage assignee and has a priority up to $600 per employee covering a three-month period.[103]

The court held in *In the Matter of Schmidt* that no formal assignment of wages to the trustee is necessary since the court may determine that there is an equitable assignment from the very nature of the trust. Although creditors cannot reach pension funds in the case of bankruptcy even though the employer himself is the trustee, a difficulty may arise when the employer does not segregate funds or pay them over to a trust even though the pension plan may contain this requirement. It was held in *McKee* v. *Paradise* that in such a case the employer is to be considered a debtor to the trust and that there is no constructive or implied trust in the unsegregated assets of the employer.[104] The difficulty is that no *res* can be identified. It has been held, therefore, in an interpretation of the Federal Bankruptcy Act, that even a statute that tried to circumvent this rule would not create a trust.[105]

---

[103] In the Matter of Schmidt, 24 CCH Lab. Cas. ¶ 68012 (S. D. Cal. 1953) (welfare fund); *In re* Ross, 117 F. Supp. 346 (N. D. Cal. 1953) (vacation pay). *Contra,* in the Matter of Brassel, 135 F. Supp. 827 (N. D. N. Y. 1955).

[104] 299 U. S. 119 (1936).

[105] *In re* Frank, 25 F. Supp. 1005 (S. D. N. Y. 1939); Jennings v. United States Fidelity & Guarantee Co., 294 U. S. 216 (1935). The statute in question was N. Y. Debt. & Cred. Law Par. 21–a.

Conclusion

Our quest throughout this study has been to determine the property rights created by the pension trusts. In this chapter we have been seeking to define the rights of the pensioner in the expectation that any genuine property rights in the pension trusts would surely appear when the pensioner went to court. Yet we have found that, for an institution the size of the pension system, there is very little case law defining property rights. From the law that does exist it appears that, except for a small class of these funds, a pension beneficiary acquires almost no rights at all until he has completed a lifetime of work for an employer. Even at that time his rights are limited to his monthly allowance and are conditioned by certain provisions in the pension plan that are subject to the discretion of his employer. He has no clearly defined rights to enforce against a trustee with regard to the management of the trust as a whole, either before or after he begins to draw his pension.

It is true that the legal machinery is extant whereby firmer legal rights could be guaranteed to the pensioner, but as yet the courts have not erected a system of property rights upon which the pensioner can rely. At this point in the evolution of the private pension system, whatever rights prospective or actual pensioners may have are contractual rights, not property rights.

The unusual nature of this state of affairs becomes evident when we reflect that the pension trusts represent great aggregations of wealth, but that it is also wealth without ownership. Perhaps, then, it is a contradiction to call this wealth "property." "Capital" might be a better term to apply to these trusts since it is a word that does not so clearly imply ownership. The functions of ownership are replaced by managerial control — the subject of the next chapter.

THE ANATOMY

OF CONTROL

Size of the Pension Trusts

Investment of Pension Funds

The Parties in Interest

Concentration of Control

Summary and Conclusions

The control of the wealth of the pension trusts is a question of deep concern to a nation that has always been sensitive to the alignment of its money power. Public concern over the vast size of pension assets has been mounting because these funds are undoubtedly forming a new nucleus of power which is bound to have far-reaching effects upon our society and economy.

Thus far we have examined the organization of the pension trusts and the rights of the various parties connected with them. These are the factors which will determine who exercises control over them. We now attempt a quantitative analysis of the economic power of the pension trusts to find out how great it is, who exercises the power and who is affected by it. This inquiry will involve a survey of the entire range of relationships in which the pension trusts are engaged. While we have already discussed many of these relationships, we shall now be seeking to give specific dimensions to the economic power generated by these institutions and to describe how it is distributed. This amounts to a dissection of the structure of one of our major financial institutions. The articulation of its structure will also serve to illumine the anatomy of economic control in our modern society.

SIZE OF THE PENSION TRUSTS

The growth of total assets of the pension trusts will, to a large extent, determine their economic power. These holdings, when compared with those of other owner groups, will also serve as an index of their possible influence upon corporate control and the capital market.

The latest of the series of annual reports on noninsured corporate pension funds begun by the Securities and Exchange Commission in 1954 shows that at the end of 1957 the book value of their total assets amounted to $19.3 billion.[1] At market value they were close to $20 billion. Since the assets of these funds have been increasing by a larger absolute figure each year, growing at the rate of $1.9 billion in 1954, $2.1 billion in 1955, $2.4 billion in 1956 and $2.7 billion in 1957,[2] it is fair to estimate that by the end of 1958 the market value of corporate pension fund assets will exceed $23 billion.

But in its first comprehensive report of pension fund holdings in 1954, the SEC indicates that its estimates of total assets omit funds of considerable magnitude, such as funds of religious, educational and nonprofit organizations. Thus, its series of estimates do not include funds of Protestant churches and other groups holding assets of $500 million at the end of 1954 or of the Teachers Insurance and Annuity Association of America with assets of over $400 million. Pension and welfare funds of unions operated on a nationwide basis are also omitted.[3] As of the end of 1958, then, it would be reasonable to estimate the total amount of noninsured pension fund holdings to be in the neighborhood of $27 billion.[4]

---

[1] SEC Statistical Series, Release No. 1533, June 8, 1958, p. 1.

[2] Unless otherwise indicated, assets of corporate pension funds are given at book value.

[3] SEC, *Survey of Corporate Pension Funds, 1951–1954*, 1956, p. 2.

[4] The SEC series of studies of pension funds, which are of particular importance because as yet they provide the most comprehensive and reliable information in the field, are based on sample data obtained from companies selected to provide the best possible representation of American corporations. The SEC data do not include insured pension plans or that part of the railroad pension funds falling under the Railroad Retirement Act. Other types of employee benefit plans are also excluded. See *Survey of Corporate Pension Funds, 1951–1954*, p. 22.

Private versus Public Funds

The next step in pinpointing the pension trusts on a map of our economy is to compare them in size and growth with the other retirement systems. As yet the total assets in private pensions are smaller than the total assets in public systems.

As Table 11 shows, the total assets in all public and private pension and retirement funds amounted to about $80.6 billion in 1957. Of this amount, 59 per cent was held in federal, state and local government retirement systems. Old-age and survivors insurance, with assets of $22.4 billion, alone accounted for about 28 per cent of *all* pension funds. Assets of state and local retirement plans made up nearly 17 per cent of the total, and those of the civil service and railroad retirement systems amounted to about 9 per cent and 5 per cent, respectively. Private funds accounted for 41 per cent of pension reserves, with self-administered corporate pension funds holding 24 per cent of the total and insurance companies holding 17 per cent.

Table 11

ASSETS OF PUBLIC AND PRIVATE PENSION AND RETIREMENT
FUNDS, END OF YEAR, 1950, 1954–1957[a]

(*Billions*)

Type of Fund	1950	1954	1955	1956	1957	Increase in 1957
All types	$36.5	$61.4	$67.7	$74.1	$80.6	+$6.5
Private	11.1	22.1	25.5	29.1	33.3	+ 4.3
Corporate noninsured funds	5.5	12.2	14.2	16.6	19.3	+ 2.7
Insured pension funds	5.6	10.0	11.2	12.4	14.0	+ 1.6
Public	25.4	39.3	42.3	45.0	47.2	+ 2.2
Railroad retirement	2.3	3.5	3.6	3.7	3.7	b
Civil service retirement	4.3	6.0	6.5	7.0	7.7	+ .7
State and local retirement	5.3	9.2	10.6	11.9	13.4	+ 1.6
Old-age and survivors insurance	13.7	20.6	21.7	22.5	22.4	− .1

Source: Based on statistics developed by the SEC to update *Survey of Corporate Pension Funds, 1951–1954,* November 1958.

[a] Except for insured plans, excludes funds of religious, educational, nonprofit, unincorporated business and union organizations.
[b] Less than $50 million.

Between 1950 and 1957 private reserves nearly tripled while public funds did not even double. Furthermore, corporate pension funds showed the largest annual increases and in 1957 accounted for more than 40 per cent of the growth of all retirement funds during that year.

Pension Funds as a Form of Individual Savings

A comparison of the ways in which individuals invest their savings provides further help in placing noninsured corporate pension funds in their proper perspective.[5] Savings of individuals in financial assets, such as insurance, stocks and bonds, and bank deposits, totaled $27.4 billion in 1957. Of this amount, saving in the form of insurance and pensions, both private and public, represented $10.9 billion, or close to 40 per cent. All forms of private insurance and pension reserves accounted for about one-fourth of the savings.

For the first time in the five-year period shown in Table 12, the flow of savings into private pension funds was greater in 1957 than the amounts going into insurance company reserves. Contributions to pension funds accounted for well over one half of the savings represented by private insurance of all types in 1957 as compared with about 42 per cent in 1953.

Contributions to noninsured corporate pension funds alone, which increased by $2.7 billion in 1957, represented one-third of savings in the form of private insurance and close to 10 per cent of all financial savings in that year. Table 12 also shows the growing importance of this type of pension fund as compared with insured pension programs. For the past two years payments flowing into noninsured pension funds have been close to two-thirds of the amounts added to all private pension reserves. If the comparison were made on the basis of market value, the proportion of assets held by noninsured pension funds would be still greater since the insured funds hold a smaller portion of their reserves in the form of common stocks.

INVESTMENT OF PENSION FUNDS

The assets of $19.3 billion accumulated by corporate pension funds at the end of 1957 were in large part invested in corporate bonds and stocks. An SEC analysis of the portfolios of these funds shows that more than four-fifths of the total value of the portfolio was represented by corporate securities. Investment in U. S. government obligations accounted

[5] SEC Statistical Series, Release No. 1543, July 15, 1958, p. 3.

Table 12

FINANCIAL SAVINGS OF INDIVIDUALS IN
THE UNITED STATES, 1953–1957[a]
(*Billions*)

Type of Saving	1953	1954	1955	1956	1957
Total financial savings	$22.0	$19.9	$25.6	$26.4	$27.4
Insurance	10.1	9.9	10.7	11.5	10.9
Private insurance and pension reserves	6.9	7.3	7.6	8.0	7.8
Insurance reserves	3.9	4.2	4.2	4.4	3.6
Insured pension reserves	1.1	1.2	1.3	1.2	1.6
Noninsured pension reserves	1.8	1.9	2.1	2.4	2.7
Government insurance and pension reserves	3.2	2.6	3.1	3.5	3.1
Securities	3.4	.2	6.3	5.2	6.0
U. S. savings bonds	.2	.6	.3	− .1	−1.9
Other U. S. government	b	−1.6	1.6	1.5	2.0
State and local	1.8	.7	1.7	1.4	2.0
Corporate and other	1.3	.6	2.7	2.3	4.0
Bonds and notes	.4	− .1	1.6	.8	2.7
Investment company shares	.4	.5	.8	.9	1.0
Other preferred and common stock	.5	.2	.3	.4	.3
Currency and deposits	4.9	5.4	3.8	4.9	5.7
Savings and loan association shares	3.6	4.4	4.8	4.8	4.8

Source: SEC Statistical Series, Release No. 1543, July 15, 1958, p. 3.

[a] Savings of individuals, in addition to personal holdings, cover savings of unincorporated business, trust funds and nonprofit institutions in the forms shown in the table.

[b] Less than $50 million.

Note: Net financial savings were only $16.6 billion in 1957 since total savings were offset by $10.8 billion in individuals' debts.

for about 10 per cent of the holdings and mortgages for about 2 per cent, while the rest of the holdings were in cash, bank deposits and other assets. (See Table 13.)

Among the various types of corporate holdings, debt issues were far in the lead and accounted for more than half of the $19.3 billion held by the pension trusts. Investment in common stocks was next in line, accounting for a quarter of the book value of the total assets.

Comparison of these proportions with the ratios of holdings for 1951

Table 13

CORPORATE PENSION FUND ASSETS, END OF 1957

Type of Asset	BOOK VALUE		MARKET VALUE	
	In Millions	Per Cent	In Millions	Per Cent
Total assets	$19,319	100.0	$19,857	100.0
Cash and deposits	368	1.9	368	1.8
U. S. government securities	2,032	10.5	1,987	10.0
Corporate bonds	10,392	53.8	9,784	49.3
Own company	641	3.3	596	3.0
Other companies	9,751	50.5	9,188	46.3
Preferred stock	611	3.2	550	2.8
Common stock	4,770	24.7	6,024	30.3
Own company	584	3.0	860	4.3
Other companies	4,187	21.7	5,164	26.0
Mortgages	313	1.6	312	1.6
Other assets	833	4.3	830	4.2

Source: Based on statistics developed by the SEC to update *Survey of Corporate Pension Funds, 1951–1954,* July 1, 1958.

reveals a marked trend toward greater investment in corporate securities. During the seven-year period, investment in corporate bonds increased from 45 per cent to 54 per cent of the aggregate holdings while the proportion invested in common stocks more than doubled.

The SEC's findings are reinforced by the New York State Banking Department's analysis of all investments held by New York banks for pension, profit-sharing, thrift and other employee welfare plans.[6] These totaled $6.5 billion on September 30, 1954. Since 90 per cent of these assets were owned by pension trusts, their portfolio distribution serves as a good check upon the SEC figures, which were based on sample data for corporate pension trusts.

The New York study showed that $6.3 billion, or 97 per cent of the total assets of the welfare funds, was invested in corporate and government securities. This proportion closely parallels the investment of pen-

[6] George A. Mooney, *Pension and Other Employee Welfare Plans,* A Survey of Funds Held by State and National Banks in New York State, New York State Banking Department, 1955, p. xi. (Hereafter referred to as New York State Banking Department, *op. cit.*)

sion fund holdings found by the SEC. The distribution of the combined securities portfolio itself also follows a closely similar pattern:

18.4 per cent invested in U. S. government obligations
57.0 per cent in corporate and other bonds
3.1 per cent in preferred stock
21.5 per cent in common stock

The Banking Department graded the security portfolios of the welfare funds for credit quality and found that 99 per cent of all the securities were considered to be of investment grade, i.e., of a quality satisfactory for investment by banking institutions under standards regarded as conservative by the Department. Most of the securities noted as substandard were only a single rating below investment grade.

We have already noted in Chapter 3 that, as institutional investors go, the pension trusts tend to purchase stocks of the highest price. This ties in with the Banking Department's finding that the security portfolios of pension and welfare funds are of a uniformly high grade of investment quality.

Favored Equities

The study of the New York banks also supported the findings of the Senate Committee on Banking and Currency that the pension trusts concentrated their common stock purchases within a rather short list of favored securities. The Senate study found that the pension funds made one-fourth of their purchases from a list of 25 stocks.[7] The New York Banking study found evidence of even higher concentration. Over 90 per cent of all the stocks held by the New York banks for all employee welfare funds were in 206 stock issues. Moreover, over half of all the welfare fund assets in common stocks were invested in the 35 stocks listed in Table 14, and two-thirds of all stock investments were in 60 stocks.

Since the stocks favored by the New York banks are those of the largest corporations, the combined holdings of the banks never amount to a very impressive percentage of all the shares of any given issue. Still, in 50 of the full list of 206 stocks the banks owned more than 2 per cent of all the shares outstanding (not including corporations formed by the trustee for the purpose of owning real estate). These are combined holdings of all the banks, so we do not know what concentration might have existed

[7] *Institutional Investors and the Stock Market, 1953–1955,* Staff Report to the Senate Committee on Banking and Currency, 84th Cong., 2d sess., 1956, p. 25.

Table 14

COMMON STOCKS FAVORED BY NEW YORK BANKS FOR
EMPLOYEE BENEFIT PORTFOLIOS, 1954

Corporations	Aggregate Market Value of Common Stock Holdings in Employee Benefit Portfolios (*Millions*)	Per Cent of the Stock Issue Held by Bank Trustees
Value of all stockholdings in New York trusteed pension funds	$1,354.7	
Holdings in 35 leading stocks	700.3 (*51.7%*)	
Socony Mobil Oil	50.3	2.64
J. C. Penney	49.4	6.95
General Electric[a]	39.6	.98
International Business Machines	38.3	2.58
Standard Oil Company of New Jersey[a]	35.6	.48
Texas Company[a]	35.3	1.49
American Telephone & Telegraph[a]	33.4	.39
Westinghouse Electric	29.0	2.22
General Motors[a]	27.6	.30
International Paper	25.6	2.80
Union Carbide & Carbon[a]	23.0	.92
E. I. du Pont de Nemours[a]	21.9	.29
Gulf Oil	17.3	1.03
Standard Oil of California[a]	16.5	.71
B. F. Goodrich	16.0	1.43
Christiana Securities	15.5	.91
National Lead	15.3	2.19
Dow Chemical	15.0	1.41
Sears, Roebuck[a]	13.9	.74
American Can[a]	13.3	2.73
Kennecott Copper	12.4	1.09
United States Steel[a]	12.2	.63
Aluminum Company of America	12.1	1.34
Shell Oil	12.0	.71

Table 14 (continued)

Corporations	Aggregate Market Value of Common Stock Holdings in Employee Benefit Portfolios (*Millions*)	Per Cent of the Stock Issue Held by Bank Trustees
National City Bank of New York	11.9	2.67
Phillips Petroleum	11.7	1.07
Continental Oil Company of Delaware	11.5	1.57
Monsanto Chemical	11.4	2.08
Commonwealth Edison	11.0	1.45
Johns-Manville	10.9	3.89
Crown Zellerbach	10.8	2.33
Minneapolis-Honeywell Regulator	10.4	3.10
National Cash Register	10.3	4.67
Allied Chemical & Dye	10.1	1.09
American Gas & Electric	9.6	1.75

Source: George A. Mooney, *Pension and Other Employee Welfare Funds,* New York State Banking Department, 1955, pp. 3 and 4.

[a] Stocks also included for study in *Institutional Investors and the Stock Market, 1953–1955,* Staff Report to the Senate Committee on Banking and Currency, 84th Cong., 2d sess., 1956, p. 3.

in individual banks. However, given the rapid rate of increase of pension fund stockholdings and the fact that fewer than thirteen large banks hold nearly all of these assets, we must conclude that corporate control is one possible result of the increase in pension trust capital.

Portfolio Composition by Industry

Thus far in our investigation of the financial power of the pension trusts we have examined the investment of their assets as a whole. Now our inquiry narrows to the distribution of assets within the ranks of the pension trusts themselves.

Table 15 shows how the pension trust portfolios are invested by different industry groups. Total assets, given in the first column, indicate that pension investments are highly concentrated in the manufacturing, communications and trade industries, with manufacturing accounting for almost two-thirds of all the assets.

The national average of asset distribution will be largely the result of the policies of these three leading groups since in 1957, for example, the SEC found that the manufacturing industry held 72 per cent of all the stocks, 56 per cent of all the bonds and 70 per cent of all government securities owned by the pension trusts. Corporate bonds are the specialty of the communications industry, which owns 24 per cent of all pension trust holdings of this type. The trade group prefers stocks, holding 13 per cent of the total.

It should be added that the manufacturing group includes a large number of funds, many of them of considerable size, while communications consists mainly of the American Telephone & Telegraph pension system with over $2.8 billion in assets in 1958.[8] The trade group includes the Sears, Roebuck fund with assets of $704 million at the end of 1957, or

[8] *Business Week,* January 31, 1959, p. 96.

Table 15

DISTRIBUTION AND RATE OF RETURN OF PENSION FUND ASSETS, BY INDUSTRY, 1957

Industry	Total Assets (*Millions*)	PERCENTAGE DISTRIBUTION BY TYPE OF INVESTMENT					Rate of Return[a]
		Total	U. S. Government Bonds	Corporate Bonds	Corporate Stocks	Other	
All industries	$19,319	100.0	10.5	53.8	27.9	7.8	3.84
Manufacturing	12,224	100.0	11.5	48.6	31.4	8.5	3.83
Communications	2,769	100.0	3.9	93.1	1.1	1.8	3.24
Trade	1,528	100.0	10.7	25.1	46.4	17.8	4.57
Electric, gas and water	928	100.0	5.5	60.8	28.5	5.3	3.94
Transportation	873	100.0	15.5	45.5	34.3	4.7	4.03
Financial and real estate	734	100.0	17.6	54.1	21.4	6.9	4.41
Extractive, construction and service	263	100.0	13.7	48.7	30.4	7.2	3.86

Sources: Based on statistics developed by the SEC to update *Survey of Corporate Pension Funds, 1951–1954,* July 31, 1958. Figures on rate of return are from SEC Statistical Series, Release No. 1533, June 8, 1958.

[a] Income from dividends, interest and rent divided by average of assets at beginning and end of year (at book value) less one-half the investment income.

nearly half the assets of the whole group.[9] Together, these three groups hold about 85 per cent of all pension trust assets.

Perhaps the most outstanding fact that emerges from a comparison of investment practices, such as that shown in Table 15, is the wide variation in policy from industry to industry. Investment in U. S. government bonds ranges from 3.9 per cent to 17.6 per cent of the portfolio, corporate bonds make up from 25.1 per cent up to 93.1 per cent, and stocks show a similar range. This variation in policy becomes especially interesting when we reflect that these funds have the same basic objectives, buy securities in the same markets and must, in many cases, be administered by the same trustees.

The nearest thing to a pattern of investment practice that emerges results from combining stocks and bonds to see how much of a given industry portfolio is composed of corporate securities. Taken this way, the range is narrower, but there is still considerable variation. The following tabulation illustrates this point:

Industry	Per Cent of Assets in Corporate Securities	Rank According to Earnings
Communications	94.2	7
Electric, gas and water	89.3	4
Manufacturing	80.0	6
Transportation	79.8	3
Extractive, construction, service	79.1	5
Financial and real estate	75.5	2
Trade	71.5	1

The figures in the right-hand column rank the groups according to the earnings of their investments. However, it is very difficult to gauge the success of their investment policies merely by the rate of earnings indicated here since this rate does not include capital gains.[10] An earnings-price ratio would be more informative. We can conclude, however, that the heavy concentration in bonds of the communications group, as shown in Table 15, has very little to recommend it. Theirs is the lowest rate of return and their bonds, unlike stocks, will not appreciate in value.

[9] *The Savings and Profit-Sharing Fund of Sears, Roebuck and Co. Employees,* Prospectus, June 30, 1958.

[10] For example, the Sears, Roebuck fund, admittedly an outstanding example, showed a gain of 55 per cent on its Sears stock, having paid $322.9 million for shares worth $492 million at the end of 1957. Financial Statement, March 31, 1958.

Common Stock Investment

The foregoing analysis of investment practices does not give us a clear picture of policy, but it is about all we have to go on. The following information on the distribution of stock purchases in selected industries, though still sketchy, suggests that a more detailed analysis of investment policies would indicate a more consistent pattern.

Table 16, based on the SEC survey of 1954 — the most recent information available — indicates that the largest number of industrial funds were grouped around the national average of 19 per cent investment in common stocks. While 83 per cent of the funds had some holdings of common stock, 53 per cent had from 1 to 25 per cent of their assets in common stock and 28 per cent had from 25 to 50 per cent of their assets so invested. These proportions did not vary widely among representative funds in different industries.

Portfolio Composition by Size of Fund

A more clearly defined pattern emerges when we compare the asset distribution of the pension funds grouped according to size. As Table 17 shows, the smaller pension funds tend to invest relatively more of their assets in U. S. government bonds than do the larger funds. And, as pension funds increase in size, we see that they invest a larger proportion of their portfolio in corporate bonds. These tendencies can doubtless be ex-

Table 16

INVESTMENT OF PENSION FUND ASSETS IN COMMON STOCK
OTHER THAN OWN COMPANY, BY SELECTED INDUSTRIES, 1954

Per Cent of All Assets in Common Stocks	PER CENT OF TOTAL NUMBER OF FUNDS IN:			
	All Indus- tries	Manufac- turing	Trade	Electric and gas
Total	100	100	100	100
None	17	14	31	13
1–25	53	55	37	57
25–50	28	29	26	25
50–75	1	1	4	1
More than 75	1	1	2	4

Source: Based on sample data in SEC, *Survey of Corporate Pension Funds, 1951–1954,* 1956, p. 12.

plained by the need for greater conservatism in the investment policies of the smaller funds, which, because of their limited resources, are less able to absorb a fall in the price of securities.

This pattern and its explanation does not seem to apply in the case of common stocks, however, since the smaller funds appear to invest a larger portion of their assets in common stocks than do the funds of greater size. One possible explanation for this variation is that the larger funds, having so much more to invest in common stocks, may be experiencing difficulty in finding enough issues of high quality at a reasonable price. We should note also that the portfolio distribution in the largest size group is probably thrown off by the very large American Telephone & Telegraph fund, which had no investments at all in common stocks at the time these averages were computed.

These trends in portfolio distribution have been evident since 1954 and are particularly significant as an indication of what pension funds will do with their assets as they increase in size with the passage of time.

Comparison with Holdings of Other Investors

A breakdown of the distribution of ownership of all corporate securities in 1957 will help to define the influence of the pension trusts in the

Table 17

PERCENTAGE DISTRIBUTION OF CORPORATE PENSION FUND ASSETS,
BY SIZE OF FUND, END OF 1957

Size of Fund (*Thousands*)	Total Assets	U. S. Government Bonds	Corporate Bonds	Preferred Stock	Common Stock	Other
Total[a]	100.0	10.5	53.8	3.2	24.7	7.8
$0–$499	100.0	10.5	40.1	3.5	34.7	11.2
$500–$999	100.0	16.6	40.0	5.2	26.4	11.8
$1,000–$2,499	100.0	12.9	44.5	4.0	27.9	10.7
$2,500–$4,999	100.0	13.9	47.9	3.6	24.8	9.8
$5,000–$9,999	100.0	11.9	50.0	4.5	27.2	6.4
$10,000–$19,999	100.0	10.4	52.7	3.6	24.6	8.7
$20,000–$99,999	100.0	8.4	53.1	4.4	26.5	7.6
$100,000 and over	100.0	7.7	59.7	1.7	23.3	7.6

Source: Statistics compiled by the SEC, October 1958 (based on sample data).

[a] Distribution based on universe estimates.

capital market. The estimated market value of corporate stocks and bonds outstanding at the end of that year was $375 billion, according to the SEC. (See Table 18.) Individuals held somewhat less than three-quarters of this amount and institutions owned almost all of the remainder — close to 26 per cent. In contrast with investment by individuals, which was largely in stocks, the bulk of the assets of institutional investors — nearly 74 per cent — was held in the form of corporate bonds.

Among all the owners of corporate securities, the pension trusts now hold third place, although as yet their total investment represents somewhat less than 5 per cent of the total value of the holdings, as compared with 72 per cent for individuals and 12 per cent for life insurance companies. Their relative position in the market is, however, highly significant in view of the distribution of their investments. The pension trusts already own close to 11 per cent of the total value of the corporate debt issues and 2.3 per cent of the stocks. Even this relatively small proportion of stock ownership places the pension trusts third in the ranks of in-

Table 18

ESTIMATED OWNERSHIP OF CORPORATE SECURITIES BY
CLASS OF INVESTOR, DECEMBER 31, 1957

	IN BILLIONS AT MARKET VALUE			PER CENT		
Class of Owner	Total	Stocks	Bonds and Notes	Total	Stocks	Bonds and Notes
All classes	$375.0	$283.0	$92.0[a]	100.0	100.0	100.0[a]
Institutional investors	97.1	29.4	67.7	25.9	10.4	73.6
Corporate pension funds	16.4	6.6	9.8	4.4	2.3	10.7
Life insurance companies	44.9	3.7	41.2	12.0	1.3	44.8
Investment companies	13.4	12.5	.9	3.6	4.4	1.0
Banks	8.0	.9	7.1	2.1	0.3	7.7
State and local government trust funds	4.8	.4	4.4	1.3	0.1	4.8
Other institutions	9.6	5.3	4.2	2.5	1.9	4.6
Domestic individuals[b]	271.4	247.4	24.0	72.4	87.4	26.1
Foreign investors	6.4	6.1	.3	1.7	2.2	0.3

Source: Statistics compiled by the SEC, October 8, 1958.

[a] Includes quasi-government debt issues for which separate data were not available.
[b] Includes personal trust funds and nonprofit organizations.

vestors in stocks, and, as we have seen, their holdings are highly concentrated in a relatively small number of stock market leaders.

The estimates in Table 18 also indicate the growing importance of pension trusts among institutional investors as a group. The value of their security holdings in 1957 was greater than that of any other group of institutions, with the exception of the insurance companies. As investors in corporate stocks, the pension trusts have indeed outstripped the insurance companies and are second only to the investment companies.

Further light is thrown on the increasing stature of the pension trusts among institutional investors by the report of the Senate Committee on Banking and Currency on common stock holdings at the end of 1954. At that time pension trusts ranked sixth among institutional investors (or financial intermediaries) on the basis of total assets, and fourth on the basis of common stock holdings. (See Table 19.) The table also gives

Table 19

ESTIMATED HOLDINGS OF COMMON STOCK BY PRINCIPAL

FINANCIAL INTERMEDIARIES, DECEMBER 31, 1954

| | ASSETS, IN BILLIONS | | |
Investing Group	Total	Holdings of Common Stock	Common Stocks as Per Cent of Total Assets
All groups	$430.1	$52.2	12.1
Trust departments of banks (personal trust funds, including common trusts)	70.0[a]	33.0[a]	47.0[a]
Investment companies[b]	10.0	8.7	87.0
Non-life insurance companies	20.4	5.2	25.0
Pension funds (trusteed corporate funds)	13.5	3.2	24.0
Life insurance companies	84.5	1.3	1.5
Mutual savings banks	29.3	0.6	2.0
Commercial banks	202.4	0.2	0.1

Source: Institutional Investors and the Stock Market, 1953–1955, Staff Report to the Senate Committee on Banking and Currency, 84th Cong., 2d sess., 1956, p. 53.

[a] Very rough estimates based on scattered data. Estimates exclude agency or custodian accounts. See note 35 for later figures.

[b] Includes holding companies whose principal function may be to hold securities of a single affiliated company.

striking evidence of the advantage that pension trusts enjoy over life insurance companies in being able to place a higher percentage of their assets in common stocks.

In view of the increase in their security holdings in both amount and relative significance in the market by 1957, there is no doubt that pension trusts are becoming extremely important in the field of investment in corporate securities. This trend will become more evident later in this chapter when we examine the increasing volume of pension trust funds flowing into the market for common stock.

Investment in Securities of Employer

Much has been said in the course of the various hearings by governmental agencies on the subject of pension fund investment in the common stocks of the employing company. As of the end of 1954, investments in the stock of the employer amounted to $321 million (book value), or 2.7 per cent of the total assets of all funds.[11] But if the Sears, Roebuck fund is excepted, the proportion of total assets in stock of the employing company drops to one-half of one per cent.

In its study of 1,024 pension funds with assets of nearly $5 billion, the New York State Banking Department learned that these funds held a total of $315 million, or only .06 per cent, in the stock, obligations and other property of the employers, their affiliates and subsidiaries.[12] Ninety-five per cent of these investments were, moreover, of investment grade.

THE PARTIES IN INTEREST

To speak of the "ownership" of the assets of pension trusts involves some ambiguity because of their peculiar nature. At least three groups have some form of interest in these funds: (1) the beneficiaries or the employees, (2) the contributors to the trust, and (3) the trustees. The trustees are in turn divided into two groups: the "plan" trustees and the financial or corporate trustees.

Ownership therefore involves a complexus of relationships reflecting the various controls over pension trust assets and the claims upon them. Whatever the property rights in pension trusts may be, the actual practice at present confines the beneficiaries' rights to claims upon these

---

[11] SEC, *Survey of Corporate Pension Funds, 1951–1954*, 1956, p. 13.
[12] New York State Banking Department, *op. cit.*, p. xvi.

funds and places control in the hands of the contributors (usually the employers) and the trustees of the funds. We shall first discuss the beneficiaries — who they are and the limits of their rights.

THE BENEFICIARIES

The SEC has estimated that at the close of 1956 there were 14.3 million persons covered by private employee pension plans, including insured, funded and pay-as-you-go plans. Of these employees, 9.2 million were covered by funded trusteed plans and 4.1 million were under insured plans, with the remainder in pay-as-you-go programs.[13] In its *Survey of Corporate Pension Funds, 1951–1954,* the SEC reported that the number of covered employees was about one-fourth of all business employees. Since that time the proportion has remained about the same.

Size of Covered Employee Groups

Since information on the size of employee groups in all pension plans is not available, we shall turn again to the New York State Banking Department study of 643 pension plans covering more than 2.6 million employees. This study provides a helpful analysis of the distribution of plans according to the size of employee groups in 1953. A glance at Table 20 shows that the great majority of employees covered by the New York plans are in pension systems of very large size. It shows, in fact, that a relatively small percentage of the plans (37 per cent) cover nearly 96 per cent of the employees and have almost 93 per cent of the assets.

These findings are consistent with analyses of pension plans according to the degree of unionization and the industry of the employer, which support the conclusion that private pensions are farther advanced in the larger and more concentrated industries.

Union Members of Pension Plans

The reader will recall from the discussion of the rights of pensioners in Chapters 3 and 4 that the employers commonly reserve to themselves the right to modify pension plans, reduce payments and so forth. Most pension plans also provide that the administrators appointed by the employer shall have the power of final determination over interpretation

[13] Based on statistics developed by the SEC to update *Survey of Corporate Pension Funds, 1951–1954* and presented by Vito Natrella, Chief Statistician, SEC, in 1957 Proceedings of the Business and Economic Section of the American Statistical Association.

of the plan and other disputes over pensions. Thus in most cases the power of his labor union will be the only recourse for an employee who feels that his employer is denying his rights. Furthermore, the collective bargaining agreement will often determine the substance of a pension plan or modify it from time to time. For these reasons it is important to know how many employees enjoy union representation.

The Senate Subcommittee on Welfare and Pension Funds reported that of the 12.5 million employees under pension plans in 1954, 7.2 million, or 58 per cent, were under collectively bargained programs.[14] The findings of the study of 643 New York plans closely parallel those of the Senate subcommittee. Of the 2.6 million employees covered by these plans in 1954, more than 1.6 million, or almost 63 per cent, were members of unions. Table 21 indicates the distribution of the plans according to the extent of union membership among the employees covered by the plans. It shows that while a large number of the plans cover situations in which there is not a high degree of unionization, a majority of the em-

[14] Senate Report No. 1734, 84th Cong., 2d sess., 1956, p. 83. Based on U. S. Department of Labor data for mid-1954 with allowance for increase to end of 1954.

Table 20

COVERED EMPLOYEES AND ASSETS HELD BY CORPORATE TRUSTEES
IN NEW YORK PLANS,[a] BY SIZE OF EMPLOYEE GROUP,
FISCAL YEAR ENDING IN 1953

Size of Employee Group	PLANS		COVERED EMPLOYEES		BOOK VALUE OF ASSETS	
	Number	Per Cent	Number	Per Cent	In Millions	Per Cent
Total	643	100.0	2,620,143	100.0	$3,163.3	100.0
1–199	211	32.8	15,936	0.6	47.3	1.5
200–499	119	18.5	39,610	1.5	87.1	2.7
500–999	74	11.5	52,569	2.0	96.5	3.1
1,000–4,999	149	23.2 ⎫	357,485	13.7 ⎫	444.5	14.1 ⎫
5,000–14,999	54	8.4 ⎬ 37.2	430,350	16.4 ⎬ 95.9	813.2	25.7 ⎬ 92.7
15,000 and over	36	5.6 ⎭	1,724,193	65.8 ⎭	1,674.7	52.9 ⎭

Source: George A. Mooney, *Pension and Other Employee Welfare Plans,* New York State Banking Department, 1955, p. xvii.

[a] Includes only "New York" plans, i.e., those of companies employing 20 or more employees in New York State. The statistics for the most part reflect conditions as of the last fiscal year ending in 1953, since 624 of the plans holding 83 per cent of the total assets reported figures for that period.

Table 21

DEGREE OF UNION MEMBERSHIP IN NEW YORK PLANS, 1954

Per Cent of Union Membership	PLANS		COVERED EMPLOYEES	
	Number	Per Cent	Number	Per Cent
Total	643	100.0	2,620,143	100.0
None	325	50.5	251,798	9.6
1–19	48	7.5	274,845	10.5
20–39	25	3.9	93,837	3.6
40–59	51	7.9	415,255	15.8
60–79	60	9.3	348,497	13.3
80–99	56	8.7	767,999	29.3
100	78	12.1	467,912	17.9

Source: George A. Mooney, *Pension and Other Employee Welfare Plans,* New York State Banking Department, 1955, p. xviii.

ployees are in the smaller group of large-sized plans which do have a sizable union membership.

Some rather significant findings came to light in both of the studies with regard to the pension plans *wholly* administered by unions. Such plans cover a very small proportion of all the participants in pension programs. The Senate subcommittee estimated that they comprised only 0.5 per cent of *all* workers under pension plans.[15] Similarly, the New York authorities found that only 22 of the 643 New York plans they investigated were union-sponsored and covered not much more than 4 per cent of the total number of employees in these plans.[16]

Industrial Groupings

As yet there are no figures showing the distribution of pension beneficiaries by industry. We shall present, instead, the most recent information on the distribution of pension assets by industry on the assumption that the pensioners themselves will be distributed among the industries in roughly similar proportions.

An SEC analysis of assets of pension funds classified by the industry of the employer reveals that as of the end of 1957 the manufacturing industry was the outstanding leader in the pension trust field, with assets

[15] *Ibid.,* p. 14.
[16] New York State Banking Department, *op. cit.,* p. xviii.

of $12.2 billion or more than 63 per cent of the total. The next largest industry was communications, with pension fund assets of $2.8 billion. In considering the communications industry, it must be remembered that the pension fund of the American Telephone & Telegraph Company is the largest pension trust, and one of the oldest, with assets in 1956 amounting to $2.4 billion. The third largest industry group, trade, had assets aggregating over $1.5 billion in 1957. (See Table 22.)

Table 22

DISTRIBUTION OF PENSION FUND ASSETS, BY INDUSTRY, 1953–1957

Industry	BOOK VALUE (MILLIONS), END OF YEAR				
	1953	1954	1955	1956	1957
All industries	$10,222	$12,153	$14,230	$16,639	$19,319
Manufacturing	6,036	7,329	8,731	10,391	12,224
Communications	1,852	2,074	2,294	2,530	2,769
Trade	912	1,050	1,205	1,355	1,528
Electric, gas and water	495	582	685	798	928
Transportation	339	438	549	695	873
Financial and real estate	450	516	577	648	734
Extractive, construction and service	138	165	190	221	263

Source: SEC Statistical Series, Release No. 1533, June 8, 1958.

Within the manufacturing group, pension funds in the primary iron and steel industry held the largest share of the assets, followed fairly closely by those in the petroleum and coal products industry and in motor vehicles. By 1957 each of six manufacturing groups had topped the billion-dollar mark in pension fund assets. Their shares of the $12.2 billion assets held by all manufacturing groups were as follows (per cent):[17]

Iron and steel products	14.5
Petroleum and coal products	12.3
Motor vehicles	12.1
Electrical machinery and equipment	11.2
Chemicals and allied products	8.5
Machinery, except electrical	8.2

[17] Based on SEC statistics to update *Survey of Corporate Pension Funds, 1951–1954,* July 31, 1958.

In an analysis of the types of securities favored in the investment policies of the various manufacturing industries, the SEC found that in general these funds were invested in corporate bonds, common stocks and U. S. government bonds, in that order.

WHAT ARE THE BENEFICIARIES' RIGHTS?

The employee members of the pension plans have been described in the preceding sections as "beneficiaries" and "beneficial owners." We may now ask, to what extent are they beneficiaries? In other words, how much security do pension trusts really offer? In this section we shall discuss monetary benefits and the conditions and limitations to which they are subject. At the end of the discussion one fact should emerge clearly: aside from a conditioned and limited right to a monthly stipend, the pension trusts in no sense create proprietary rights for their beneficiaries.

Methods of Determining Benefits

Benefit formulas differ widely from plan to plan and could in themselves be the subject of a lengthy study. For our purpose it is sufficient to determine generally what types of benefit formulas are most frequently used. The most popular methods are (1) computation of benefits by multiplying a rate based on career salary or final average salary, and (2) flat monthly benefits for each year of credited service. The second type of formula is intended mainly for wage employees and is preferred by the largest funds such as those in the automobile industry. Table 23 summarizes the type of formulas for future service found in the plans studied by the New York State Banking Department. We may add in passing that more than half of the 643 plans studied in New York provided for a benefit rate for prior service equal to that for current service.[18]

Disability and Death Benefits

The largest New York plans normally include provisions for disability benefits while only half of the employees in the smallest plans have this benefit. The fact that 90 per cent of the employees in large plans covering 15,000 or more workers are provided with disability benefits is undoubtedly the result of union influence. Under plans covering workers

[18] The New York State Banking Department made a detailed breakdown of each of the types of formula shown in Table 23 according to industry, size of employee group and degree of unionization. See New York State Banking Department, *op. cit.*, p. 110.

who are 100 per cent unionized, for example, 9 out of every 10 employees have this protection. To sum up the New York plans as a whole, 52 per cent of them, covering 79 per cent of the employees, included some provision for disability.

Relatively few of the New York plans provide death benefits. Only one-fifth of the plans and about the same percentage of the employees have this coverage. The contrast here with the more general interest in

Table 23

PLANS IN NEW YORK STATE, BY BENEFIT FORMULA, 1954[a]

Type of Formula	Number of Plans	Covered Employees (*Thousands*)	AVERAGE MONTHLY BENEFITS[b] ASSUMING CONSTANT EARNINGS OF:			
			$2,400	$3,600	$6,000	$18,000
All plans	643	2,620.1	$52	$58	$130	$492
Unit benefit for each year of credited service:						
At rate based on actual or career average salary	287	665.0	53	81	166	610
At rate based on final or final average salary	106	692.7	53	52	96	388
Flat monthly benefits:						
For specified number of years of service	61	255.4	—	30	—	—
For each year of credited service	33	693.2	—	52	—	—
Miscellaneous formulas	146	240.7	47	60	133	515
No future service formula	10	73.2	—	—	—	—

Source: George A. Mooney, *Pension and Other Employee Welfare Plans,* New York State Banking Department, 1955, p. 97.

[a] Includes only "New York" plans, i.e., those covering 20 or more employees in New York State.

[b] Average monthly pension benefit (exclusive of the social security benefit) payable at normal retirement based on 30 years of future service and assuming constant annual earnings in the amounts shown. The average is arrived at by multiplying the 30-year future benefit payable under each plan in the relevant group by the number of employees covered by the plan, adding together all products and dividing the total by the aggregate number of covered employees in the group. In considering these averages, note that: (1) the original computation of the 30-year benefit was furnished by the employer; in cases of obvious error, or where no figures were supplied, either appropriate adjustments were made or the averages were computed without them; (2) minimums and maximums sometimes resulted in wide variations in the amount of benefits payable under plans which otherwise provide the same basic benefits.

disability benefits indicates that the unions apparently have not pressed for death benefits since this provision is rare in wholly unionized plans.[19]

Total Payments to Beneficiaries

The SEC reported that in 1957 corporate pension funds paid out benefits totaling $628 million, or about 15 per cent more than they distributed in 1956. The rate of increase was somewhat lower than for several previous years, for example, a 25 per cent rise between 1954 and 1955 and 17 per cent between 1955 and 1956.[20]

Within the manufacturing industry, which paid out well over half of the total benefits in 1957, the leading industries were motor vehicles, primary iron and steel, and electrical machinery and equipment, each of which distributed more than $40 million in pension benefits. Other business and industrial groups paying out large amounts were trade, $81 million; communications, $65 million; and financial and real estate funds, $38 million.[21] The relatively large pension outlays now being distributed by these nonmanufacturing industries can be explained, to a considerable extent, by the fact that these industries have some pension programs of rather long standing, such as the Sears, Roebuck fund, the American Telephone & Telegraph fund and the plans of financial institutions including the large banks.

Claims on Funds Compared to Assets

From the evidence available, we may judge that the pension funds are keeping abreast of their current obligations as they accrue. A large number of the plans studied by the New York State Banking Department submitted actuarial estimates of liabilities. Reports from 582 plans showed total liabilities of over $5.2 billion on account of retired and active members. The book value of the assets in these same funds was somewhat over $3.1 billion. However, nearly all of the unfunded obligations related to funding for services performed *before* the pension plans were set up. This unfunded "past service liability" amounted to about $2.1 billion. A breakdown of assets and liabilities reveals, as may be expected, that as the size of the employee groups in the pension plans increases, the disparity between liabilities and assets also increases. Thus, for the largest-

[19] *Ibid.*, pp. xxiv, xxv.
[20] SEC Statistical Report No. 1426, 1956, p. 4; No. 1533, 1958, p. 5.
[21] Based on SEC statistics to update *Survey of Corporate Pension Funds, 1951–1954,* July 31, 1958.

sized plans — those covering 15,000 employees or more — the current claims were nearly $3.1 billion while the assets amounted to $1.7 billion.[22]

This disparity between assets and obligations is not necessarily alarming because most of these pension funds are of fairly recent origin, and assets to cover past services cannot be expected to be brought into balance with liabilities immediately. Figures relating to years prior to 1954, which would indicate the rate at which the gap was being closed, are not available.

Vesting of Benefits

In the survey made by the New York State Banking Department in 1955, the investigators found that 279 of the 643 plans studied, or 43 per cent, provided for vesting of all or part of the benefits accruing from the employer's contributions before early or normal retirement. They found that such provisions were included in two out of three of the contributory plans as compared with 43 per cent of all plans. The plans including vesting provisions covered only 21 per cent of the total number of employees represented, while those with no provision for vesting covered 79 per cent of the participating employees. Further examination of the statistics reveals that as the size of the employee group in a pension plan increases, the percentage of employees covered by vesting decreases. For example, in the pension plans covering employee groups of less than 200 participants, almost half of the employees were covered by plans containing vesting provisions. In the plans affecting 5,000 to 14,999 employees, less than 36 per cent of the employees were covered by vesting provisions. This decline continued until in the plans in which 15,000 or more employees participated, only 13 per cent of the employees were covered by some kind of vesting arrangement.[23]

As the degree of unionization of employees covered by pension plans goes up, the percentage of employees covered by vesting provisions goes down. Thus, under plans in companies in which all of the workers were unionized, only 1.2 per cent of the employees were covered by vesting. In the case of employee groups 80 to 90 per cent unionized, the coverage was found to be somewhat more than 7 per cent.[24] This phenomenon is probably explained by the fact that the most highly unionized groups of

---

[22] New York State Banking Department, *op. cit.*, pp. xxv, xxvi and 136.
[23] *Ibid.*, pp. xx, 77.
[24] *Ibid.*, p. 76.

employees are in the largest pension plans, such as those covering telephone and auto workers.

This picture becomes even clearer when we add the further information that close to 72 per cent of all the employees covered by these "New York" pension plans are in participating groups of 15,000 or more and that this size group is 84 per cent unionized.[25] As noted earlier, the lack of vesting in plans covering large groups of employees may be compensated for, to a relatively small extent, by the fact that some of these plans are industry-wide and managed by many employers jointly with the union so that there is a degree of labor mobility at least within the industry.

Age of Retirement

In 600 of the 643 New York plans the normal retirement age for males is 65; in 12 plans, 60 or under; and in 31 plans, between 67 and 70. In most of the plans the normal retirement age for females is the same as for males; when they differ, the retirement age for females is lower.

More than half (58 per cent) of the plans contain a requirement for compulsory retirement either at the usual retirement age of 65 or in some cases at a more advanced age. Four out of five of the plans designating a compulsory retirement age do, however, reserve to the employer the right to permit employees to work beyond the normal retirement age and the trend seems to be toward allowing some leeway in the matter. More than 40 per cent of the plans contain no provision for compulsory retirement.[26]

Limitations of Beneficiaries' Rights

The first of the serious restrictions upon the employee's right to his expected benefit under a pension plan is the employer's *power to amend a pension plan* at his sole discretion. In 86 per cent of the plans studied by the New York authorities the employers have this prerogative.

The *power to reduce or suspend contributions* to the pension fund is a limitation of employees' rights as serious as the power to amend. In most of the New York plans, the employer has this right. But, as we observed earlier in the study, it may be argued that the incorporation of this provision in a pension plan is a practical necessity. Actually, in only eighteen of the New York plans studied has such a right of suspension or reduc-

[25] *Ibid.,* p. 45.
[26] *Ibid.,* p. xxi.

tion ever been exercised, and in five of those cases it was done because the fund was considered inadequate to meet liabilities.[27]

The most drastic limitation of employees' rights lies in the employer's *power to terminate the pension plan* altogether. This ultimate power the employers have reserved to themselves in 89 per cent of the New York plans studied by the Banking Department. Table 24 describes the provisions for distribution of the funds in the event of termination.

Table 24

ANALYSIS OF PROVISIONS FOR TERMINATION OF PLANS

| | | NUMBER OF PLANS | | |
Description of Provision	Total	With Pro- vision	Without Pro- vision	No Answer Given
Plan may be terminated at any time at the option of the employer	643	577	64	2
That in the event of termination: Retired members shall be given a preference in that part of the fund contributed by the employer	643	413	216	14
Certain active members shall be given a preference over other active members in that part of the fund contributed by the employer	643	239	383	21
Any part of the fund remaining after satisfaction of all liabilities under the plan may be returned to the employer	643	272	345	26

Source: George A. Mooney, *Pension and Other Employee Welfare Plans,* New York State Banking Department, 1955, p. 81. Includes only "New York" plans, i.e., those of companies employing 20 or more employees in New York State.

Pension Rights after Retirement

The three preceding limitations on employees' rights have to do with modification of the entire plan, possible changes that will affect all plan members. But in many plans even the individual employee who has begun to enjoy his benefits may have them suspended, modified or revoked if his case falls under certain conditions of the plan. As many as 34 per

[27] *Ibid.,* pp. 58, 59, 61.

cent, or 221, of the 643 New York plans contained one or more such provisions. Table 25 summarizes the conditions under which the individual employee's benefits may be reduced or suspended.

Rights to Information

In nearly all of the 643 New York plans the beneficiary receives either the text of the plan or a booklet describing it, or, if this is not done, he is told that the plan is available on request. Periodic statements of financial condition were given to each participant in less than 15 per cent of the

Table 25

SUSPENSION, MODIFICATION OR REVOCATION
OF PENSIONS AFTER RETIREMENT

Grounds for Suspension, Modification or Revocation Permitted under Plan[a]	Number of Plans Containing Provisions
Payment may be suspended upon:	
Re-employment by the same company, or, in the case of industry-wide plans, in the same industry	61
Taking employment with a competitor or engaging in other activities detrimental to the interests of the company	146
Taking other employment or employment at a salary exceeding a fixed amount	8
Misconduct by the employee	27
Pension may be reduced to the extent of:	
All or part of salary received in other employment	10
Disability or other benefits received under the plan	5
Any increase in social security benefits	17
Workmen's compensation and/or other benefits received under public plans	4

Source: George A. Mooney, *Pension and Other Employee Welfare Plans,* New York State Banking Department, 1955, p. 113. Includes only "New York" plans, i.e., those with employers who employ 20 or more employees in New York State. Non-"New York" plans were not asked to supply information covered by this table.

[a] These grounds for suspension, modification or revocation are contained in 221 separate plans. The other 422 "New York" plans contain no provisions. Not tabulated are the following grounds for suspension of benefits: termination of plan or of contributions by the employer and failure to furnish required information or to comply with other procedural requirements — not tabulated because applicable to all plans; assignment or attempt to assign benefits or bankruptcy of employee — not tabulated because benefits, although withheld from pensioner, are generally applied for his benefit. Also not tabulated, because not within scope of this table, are grounds for suspension, modification or revocation of disability benefits.

plans although twice that many provided for inspection of the financial reports on request.[28]

THE CONTRIBUTORS TO THE TRUST

In our treatment of beneficiaries' rights we have disposed of the question of claims on pension funds. The question of their control remains. The traditional logic of property would have it that "he who pays the piper calls the tune." We might expect the employers, then, to direct pension policy since their current contribution to these funds is seven times greater than that of their employees. The employers actually do exercise a large measure of control although it is in many cases limited by union influences. How control is exercised through trustees will be the subject of the next section. Our present concern is the amount and distribution of the contributions on which the power to determine policy is based.

For information on the sources of contributions to pension funds, we turn to the annual analyses made by the Securities and Exchange Commission. The SEC reported that employers' contributions to pension trusts amounted to $2.3 billion in 1957 compared with contributions from employees of $316 million. Income was also received in the form of interest, dividends, profits on the sale of assets, and from other earnings. (See Table 26.)

[28] *Ibid.*, p. 43.

Table 26

CORPORATE PENSION FUND RECEIPTS, BY INDUSTRY, 1957

(*Millions*)

Industry	Employer Contributions	Employee Contributions	Income from Interest, Dividends and Rent
All industries	$2,303	$316	$677
Manufacturing	1,583	180	425
Electric, gas and water	119	10	33
Transportation	120	59	31
Communications	223	—	85
Trade	144	45	64
Financial and real estate	76	20	30
Extractive, construction and service	37	3	9

Source: Based on statistics developed by the SEC to update *Survey of Corporate Pension Funds, 1951–1954,* October 1958.

Percentagewise, employers contributed about 69 per cent of the total receipts in 1957, or about the same proportion as in 1955 and 1956. Since most of the plans are noncontributory, the employees' share is relatively small, amounting to 9.5 per cent in 1957, or a slightly higher percentage than in 1956.

Further analysis of the receipts shows that the proportion of employer and employee contributions varies widely in different industries. In the manufacturing and communications industries, for example, employers paid in a much larger proportion than they did in trade and transportation (Table 26).

Contributory Plans

The New York State Banking Department study of 643 pension funds in that state found that the number of contributory plans tends to decrease as the size of the employee group covered increases. As Table 27 shows, 41 per cent of all the contributory plans were in companies employing less than two hundred workers while less than 3 per cent of the plans covering 15,000 or more employees were of the contributory type.

Similarly, as the degree of unionization increases, the percentage of contributory plans decreases. Thus, well over half (59 per cent) of the contributory plans in New York State covered employees with no union membership, while only 3.4 per cent covered wholly unionized employees. The average pension payable under contributory plans was found

Table 27

DISTRIBUTION OF CONTRIBUTORY PLANS IN NEW YORK STATE
BY SIZE OF COVERED EMPLOYEE GROUP, 1954

Size of Covered Employee Group	CONTRIBUTORY PLANS		ALL PLANS	
	Number	Per Cent	Number	Per Cent
Total	230	100.0	643	100.0
1–199	95	41.3	211	32.8
200–499	38	16.5	119	18.5
500–999	27	11.7	74	11.5
1,000–4,999	40	17.4	149	23.2
5,000–14,999	24	10.5	54	8.4
15,000 and over	6	2.6	36	5.6

Source: George A. Mooney, *Pension and Other Employee Welfare Funds,* New York State Banking Department, 1955, p. 66.

to be substantially the same as under noncontributory plans.[29] In a significant number of instances, however, a collective bargaining agreement stipulated the amount of the periodic contribution to be paid into the fund by the employer or left it to the impartial determination of an actuary.

THE TRUSTEES

In most cases the authority over a pension trust ultimately rests with the employer, though his authority is often circumscribed by a union contract (as in the cases of pension plans covering 60 per cent of all the employees in private plans) or shared with a union or other employers in joint administrations.

Furthermore, the administrative authority over pension plan operations is usually divided from the strictly financial problems of managing the fund assets. This results in a division of authority over pension trusts between two groups, "the plan trustees" or administrators, and the financial trustees. We shall first attempt to determine who appoints the administrators in order to show who controls the policies of the pension trusts. The scope of the administrators' authority is not in question here since their function is merely to execute the general policy laid down in the pension plan itself.

Administrators

In our attempt to discover where the authority over pension trusts actually resides, it will not suffice merely to classify all plans according to types of administration since the majority of employers and assets are joined in a relatively small number of plans of large size. Thus, the New York study shows that 93 per cent of the employers participate in multi-employer plans which make up only 37 per cent of all the New York plans. (See Table 28.) About two-thirds of all the New York employers participate in area or industry-wide plans sponsored by unions. The inference is clear that there is great concentration in these plans since this type represents only about 3 per cent of all the plans. To say that these plans are union-sponsored does not mean that the union shares in their administration, but only that the provisions of the plan were arrived at through collective bargaining.

The actual division of authority in the New York plans is analyzed in

[29] *Ibid.*, p. 67.

Table 28

NEW YORK STATE PLANS, BY TYPE OF ADMINISTRATION, 1954

| | PLANS | | EMPLOYERS | |
Type of Administration	Number	Per Cent	Number	Per Cent
Total number of plans	643	100.0	6,144	100.0
Single-employer plans	406	63.1	406	6.6
Multi-employer plans	237	36.9	5,738	93.4
Administered by employers with affiliated or subsidiary employers	213	33.1	1,630	26.5
Union-sponsored plans covering employers in the same industry or area	22	3.4	4,098	66.7
Other multi-employer plans	2	0.3	10	0.2

Source: George A. Mooney, *Pension and Other Employee Welfare Funds,* New York State Banking Department, 1955, p. 38.

Table 29. The majority of employees covered by these plans, 67 per cent, are subject to an administrative body consisting of the employer or his appointees. All but a few of the remaining employees are in plans in which the union and employer are equally represented in the administrative body. But even in many of these plans the general power of administration is retained in the employer. It is therefore possible that in New York the pattern of employer control is the same as that found by the Senate subcommittee (in 1954 an estimated 86 per cent of all employees covered by pension plans were subject to administrations controlled by the employers). There is not enough data in the New York study for comparison, but the high percentage of employers in joint administrations seems out of line with the conclusions of the Senate subcommittee indicating that the great majority of employees were covered by plans controlled by single employers.

By way of summary we estimate that probably about four-fifths of all employees are under pension plans in which the employers have ultimate control. In pension plans which include nearly two-thirds of all employees, however, the provisions of the plan itself have been arrived at jointly with a union. Since the bulk of pension assets will be subject to the same administrative authority as are the employees, we estimate that employers have the ultimate power of administration of about four-fifths

Table 29

NEW YORK PLANS ACCORDING TO COMPOSITION OF
ADMINISTRATIVE BODY, 1954

Administrative Body	Number of Plans	COVERED EMPLOYEES	
		Number	Per Cent
Total	643[a]	2,620,143	100.0
The employer or an appointed pension board or committee	556[b]	1,758,211	67.1
A pension board or committee with equal representation of the employer and the employees or their union	69[c]	847,328	32.3
A pension board or committee with: A majority appointed by the employer and a minority by the employees or their union	15	13,975	0.5
A majority appointed by the employees and a minority by the employer	3	629	—

Source: George A. Mooney, *Pension and Other Employee Welfare Funds,* New York State Banking Department, 1955, p. 123.

[a] Includes only "New York" plans, i.e., those of companies employing 20 or more employees in New York State.

[b] Appeals of individual benefit are provided for in 77 of these plans.

[c] In many of these plans, the general power of administration is retained by the employer. However, certain broad administrative powers are delegated to a joint board of administration and, for purposes of this table, the latter are treated as the administrator of the plan. In 65 of these plans (in all of which employee representatives are selected by the union), provision is made for the resolution of disputes by the appointment of an arbitrator, mediator or the equivalent. In 3 of the 4 remaining plans, other provision is made for appeals of individual benefit and/or other decisions of the administrator.

of all pension assets — subject only to such restrictions as a union may have put into the pension plan at the bargaining table.

Financial Trustees

The purpose of employing a financial trustee to handle the investment policies and management of the pension funds is twofold. First, it is desirable to place the funds in the hands of an independent agent to protect them from any possible exploitation by an employer or a union. Second, a corporate trustee, such as the trust department of a bank, is able to provide expert financial management of the pension fund assets.

But to accomplish both of these ends it is usually necessary to grant the financial trustee somewhat wider discretion than the pension plan administrators enjoy. How much authority does the financial organization managing the investment of the pension assets actually have? This question will be discussed in the next section of this chapter under the heading "Concentration of Control." Here we shall point out only that the employer usually appoints the financial trustees and pays them directly. Under the provisions of many of the plans, the corporate trustee must also render an account to the employer or the plan administrator, although, as we shall see, the direction and control of investment policy and management is placed, to a large extent, in its hands.

CONCENTRATION OF CONTROL

Much has been said publicly about the economic power that becomes available to those who control the investment policies of pension funds. We should now take a look at the amount of concentration of control represented by some of the largest pension funds and the form that it takes. In this section, also, we shall attempt to analyze the degree of control exercised by financial trustees and, finally, the effect of concentrated ownership of pension fund assets on the securities market.

CONCENTRATION OF ASSETS
IN INDIVIDUAL FUNDS

In their analysis of privately funded plans, the SEC found a high degree of concentration of pension fund assets in a relatively small number of the largest funds. The distribution of the assets of these funds is shown in Table 30, which clearly indicates the high degree of control held by the largest funds. We see that in 1957, 55.3 per cent of the assets were owned by less than 2 per cent of all the funds. In contrast, only 2.3 per cent of the assets were distributed among the large number of funds of the smallest size.

A similar picture emerges when we look at the distribution of the assets among the various types of securities. We find that less than 2 per cent of the funds — those of the largest size — held 57 per cent of the investments in corporate bonds in 1957, and that somewhat less than 14 per cent of the funds held as much as 85 per cent. The dominating position of the largest funds is less marked in the case of holdings of U. S. government bonds, but even here the relatively few funds in the $100 million-

and-over class held nearly half of the total investments in this type of security.

Table 30 also shows how much of the investment in common stocks is controlled by a relatively small number of funds. Less than 14 per cent of all the funds — those with total assets of $10 million or more — held more than 80 per cent of the investment by pension funds in common stocks of companies other than their own.

The New York State Banking Department study of 1,024 funds implements and reinforces the findings of the SEC with regard to the powerful influence of the largest pension funds in the investment picture. Section A of Table 31, showing the distribution of assets by size of fund, reveals that slightly more than a third of the funds, those with holdings of $1 million or more, owned almost 97 per cent of all the assets. Funds in the largest size category alone held 61 per cent of the assets although they represent only a small proportion of the total number of funds.

The Banking Department's analysis of the smaller group of 643 "New

Table 30

PERCENTAGE DISTRIBUTION OF PRINCIPAL ASSETS OF CORPORATE PENSION PLANS, BY SIZE OF FUND, END OF 1957

Size of Fund (*Thousands*)	Plans	DISTRIBUTION OF ASSETS			
		Total	U. S. Government Bonds	Corporate Bonds[a]	Common Stocks[b]
Totals	100.0	100.0	100.0	100.0	100.0
$0–$499	38.6	2.3	2.7	1.8	3.3
$500–$999	13.0	1.2	2.3	0.9	1.3
$1,000–$2,499	15.2	3.0	4.3	2.6	3.6
$2,500–$4,999	10.3	3.9	6.0	3.6	4.3
$5,000–$9,999	9.1	6.0	7.9	5.7	7.4
$10,000–$19,999	7.3 ⎫	10.2 ⎫	11.8 ⎫	9.8 ⎫	10.2 ⎫
$20,000–$99,999	5.0 ⎬ 13.8	18.1 ⎬ 83.6	16.9 ⎬ 76.8	18.7 ⎬ 85.4	19.7 ⎬ 80.1
$100,000 and over	1.5 ⎭	55.3 ⎭	48.1 ⎭	56.9 ⎭	50.2 ⎭

Source: Based on statistics developed by the SEC to update *Survey of Corporate Pension Funds, 1951–1954*, October 1958.

[a] Does not include "own company" bonds, which amounted to only 3.3 per cent of all pension fund assets.

[b] Does not include "own company" stocks, which amounted to only 3.0 per cent of all pension fund assets.

Table 31

DISTRIBUTION OF ASSETS OF NEW YORK PENSION FUNDS, BY SIZE OF FUND
AND ACCORDING TO CORPORATE TRUSTEE CONTROL,

FISCAL YEAR ENDING IN 1953[a]

(*Dollar Figures in Thousands*)

| | PLANS | | TOTAL | | BOOK VALUE OF ASSETS | | | | |
Distribution of Funds	No.	Per Cent	Amt.	Per Cent	Cash	Bonds	Pref. Stocks	Com. Stocks	Other Assets
A. By Size of Fund (*Thousands*)									
Total	1,024	100.0	$4,894.5	100.0	$93.6	$3,983.2	$138.6	$613.3	$65.5
Under $99	279	27.2	12.0	0.2	2.4	7.3	.4	1.6	.3
$100–$499	252	24.6	61.8	1.3	4.8	42.4	3.2	10.3	1.0
$500–$999	124	12.1	90.7	1.9	5.2	64.9	3.6	15.0	2.0
$1,000–$4,999	221	21.6	504.2	10.3	18.9	361.3	26.7	86.3	10.9
$5,000–$9,999	58	5.7	392.3	8.0	11.5	283.0	22.0	63.0	12.8
$10,000–$24,999	50	4.9	843.5	17.2	15.5	626.7	34.8	156.3	10.1
$25,000 and over	40	3.9	2,989.9	61.1	35.3	2,597.6	47.9	280.7	28.4
B. According to Corporate Trustees									
Total	1,024[b]	100.0	$4,894.5	100.0	$93.6	$3,983.2	$138.6	$613.3	$65.5
13 largest banks	882	86.1	4,818.5	98.5	91.5	3,931.0	132.9	601.4	61.5
38 other banks	142	13.9	76.0	1.5	2.1	52.2	5.7	11.9	4.0

Source: George A. Mooney, *Pension and Other Employee Welfare Plans*, New York State Banking Department, 1955, p. 31.

[a] Includes both "New York" plans in companies employing 20 or more employees in New York State and non-"New York" plans in companies employing less than 20 persons in New York State. The statistics for the most part reflect conditions as of the fiscal year ending in 1953, since 624 of the plans holding 83 per cent of the total assets reported figures for that period.

[b] Eighteen plans have individual trustees who hold part of the assets (believed to be relatively small) and 7 plans have other corporate trustees located outside of the state (Mich., Mo., Mass., Ill., Pa., Va., Md., Ohio and Ga.) that hold part of the assets of the plans. None of these assets are included in this table.

York" plans shows a similar concentration of assets. Since these figures have already been presented in Table 20, we need only to recall that slightly more than a third of these New York plans owned 93 per cent of the total assets and included 96 per cent of the covered employees.

CONCENTRATION OF CONTROL IN
FINANCIAL TRUSTEES

The financial power centered in the largest pension funds is impressive, but the handling of the pension fund investments produces an even greater concentration of control than is indicated by the figures on the distribution of assets among the funds. The practice of turning investment authority over to corporate trustees has brought about a situation in which a single trustee — usually a large bank — may have financial control over many pension funds.

We shall find in the following discussion that investment powers over pension funds have been largely placed in their hands. This was indicated during the Senate hearings in 1955 in testimony which revealed that 65 large banks had investment control over nearly three-quarters of the assets of the 5,269 pension and other employee benefit trust accounts they administered.[30]

Further evidence of a large measure of control entrusted to the corporate trustee is provided by the New York study of 1,024 pension funds which showed that in approximately 90 per cent of the plans the trustee has general investment responsibility either alone or subject to the veto, direction or approval of the employer or the plan administrator. In fact, in more than 60 per cent of the pension funds with assets of over $2 million there are no general restrictions on investments. The rest of the funds restrict investment to "legals" and some of them are specifically restricted to the types of investment permitted to insurance companies in New York State.[31]

The New York Banking Department found also that as the size of the funds grows larger, the employers or administrators tend to cede more responsibility to the financial trustees. Thus all but seven of the forty funds having assets of $25 million or more have placed investment powers completely in the hands of the trustees, without requiring approval or direction or providing for the right of veto. Similarly in more than

---

[30] Hearings on S. Res. 40, 84th Cong., 1st sess., 1955, Part 3, p. 890.
[31] New York State Banking Department, *op. cit.*, p. xv.

three-fourths of the fifty funds in the $10–$25 million class, the financial trustee has full responsibility for investing the assets.[32]

We must remember, however, that in the standard type of trust instrument, the right is reserved to the employer to change the trustee at any time. Thus, whether or not a veto power is part of the investment provisions of the indenture, the employer invariably has the last word. We should keep in mind, also, that the employer usually appoints the financial or corporate trustee. This was the case in all but 3 per cent of the 1,024 pension plans studied by the New York banking authorities. In only two of the plans was the trustee appointed by the union and in eight others by the joint action of the employer and the union.

In the same group of pension funds the financial trustee customarily accounts to the employer alone or to the employer and the plan administrator jointly. This was the case in seven out of every ten of the New York plans. The remaining plans provide that the accounting be made to a person or group other than the employer who administers the plan.[33]

Reference to the part of the New York study covering the distribution of pension fund assets among the banks points up the marked degree of trustee concentration in a relatively few banks. Out of total assets of $4.9 billion in 1953, more than 98 per cent was held by the thirteen largest banks. Less than 2 per cent was controlled by thirty-eight other banks. (See Section B of Table 31.)

More recent figures in the New York study show that stockholdings of the thirteen largest banks amounted to 99 per cent of *all benefit funds* held in the New York banks in September 1954.[34] Since pension funds represent more than 90 per cent of these funds, the stock investments of pension funds, which we have discussed earlier in this chapter, are actually the investments controlled by these thirteen banks.

The significance of the concentration resulting from pension trust accumulations is heightened when we consider other funds which the same banks administer. Perhaps the most reliable estimate of the total holdings of the trust departments of banks representing personal trust funds, including common trusts, is contained in the Senate subcommittee report to which we have already referred. The estimate, which is admittedly

[32] *Ibid.*, p. 30.
[33] *Ibid.*, p. 24.
[34] *Ibid.*, p. 31.

rough, sets the total at $70 billion in 1954.[35] Although we have little data to go on, undoubtedly the degree of concentration for personal trusts is not as high as that for pension trusts. Still, it seems likely that a fairly large portion of the private trusts are concentrated in the same banks as the pension trusts.

Turning again to the list of common stocks in which trusteed pension funds are invested, we must conclude that if the New York experience is taken into account, stocks held in trust for pension funds are actually controlled by a small number of banks acting as financial trustees.

IMPACT ON THE SECURITIES MARKETS

To perform their functions properly, pension trusts must rapidly convert the contributions they receive into profitable and secure investments. The pension trusts have found the answer to their needs in the corporate securities markets where they had invested as much as 82 per cent of their assets by the end of 1957. Rates of return on their investments show that corporate securities have served the pension trusts well. We shall now attempt to determine what effect these larger purchasers have had upon the operations of the securities markets.

For some time now, the pension trusts have been making most of their investments in the corporate securities markets. In 1957, for example, the net increase in the total assets of these pension funds was $2.7 billion, of which $1.7 billion was invested in corporate bond and note holdings and approximately $1.0 billion in stocks.[36] Since percentagewise their investment distribution remained about the same in 1957 as in 1956,[37] we may conclude that nearly all pension trust contributions and earnings were being funneled directly into the corporate securities markets.

Furthermore, the pension funds have been pouring greater amounts every year into these investment channels. Not only have they had more to invest, but a greater proportion of their portfolios have been given

---

[35] Table 19, p. 205. Since this book went to press a study made for the American Bankers Association (*Report of National Survey of Personal Trust Accounts,* July 10, 1959) has revealed that personal trust holdings amounted to $49.7 billion in 1958. The projections of the Bankers' study were based on a sample of 4,229 representative accounts in 412 banks. It is estimated that $30.7 billion, or nearly 62 per cent of the total assets, was invested in common stocks.

[36] SEC Release No. 1533, June 8, 1958, pp. 1, 2.

[37] The percentage of stocks held by pension funds increased by 1.1 and the percentage of bonds by 1.5 over the 1956 averages. These were the largest shifts except for the government securities component, which made up 3.3 per cent less of total assets in 1957 than in 1956. (Based on statistical tables developed by the SEC, July 31, 1958.)

over to stocks and bonds. The ratio of corporate bonds to total assets was 45 per cent in 1951 and 54 per cent in 1957, rising each year with but one exception. The rise in common stocks was even sharper, from 12 per cent in 1951 to 25 per cent in 1957. The American Telephone & Telegraph fund, the largest of all pension funds, has long avoided equity investments, but in 1958 its trustees were instructed that up to 10 per cent of the assets could be invested in common stocks. This one fund alone, with over $2.8 billion in assets, will be a powerful new presence in the stock market.

It will not be surprising, in the light of these facts, to find that the pension trusts occupy a commanding position in the securities markets. During the 1950s, as Table 32 shows, the pension trusts have been the largest purchasers of stock among institutions and fall only a little behind net purchases of individual investors, with whom they are rapidly catching up. In bond purchases the pension trusts were outstripped only by the life insurance companies and by individuals in certain years.

Comparison of net purchases of corporate securities by pension trusts with the amount of new securities offered for sale annually will help us estimate the importance of pension trust capital flowing into the securities markets. As we see in Table 33, a total of $52.3 billion in new corporate securities was offered for sale in the period from 1953 through 1957. Over the same period, net purchases by corporate pension trusts amounted to $9.9 billion, or about one-fifth of the value of new securities added to the market. These figures do not indicate what proportion of the new securities the pension trusts purchased, but they do serve as an indicator of how much of the expansion of the market was due to the influx of capital from pension funds. In fact, the pension funds have been investing in higher-grade securities so that we may say they have been responsible for freeing new investment funds "representing one-fifth of the equity capital requirements of all corporations."[38]

If we confine the comparison to common stocks alone, we find that net purchases of stocks by the pension trusts equaled close to 30 per cent of the value of all new issues offered for sale in the five-year period.

The record of net purchases of corporate securities, as shown in Table 32, also indicates less variation in the pattern of buying for pension trusts than for any other group of purchasers. This suggests that these funds are less subject to market influence than any other group or, to put it

[38] Vito Natrella, *op. cit.*, p. 8.

Table 32

NET PURCHASES OF CORPORATE SECURITIES,
BY CLASS OF INVESTOR, 1953–1957
(*Billions*)

	NET PURCHASES					
Class of Investor	Cumulative Totals 1953–1957	1953	1954	1955	1956	1957
PREFERRED AND COMMON STOCKS						
All classes	$15.0	$2.4	$2.5	$2.9	$3.5	$3.7
Institutions	8.8	1.4	1.7	1.6	1.8	2.3
Corporate pension funds	3.6	.5	.6	.7	.8	1.0
Life insurance companies	.5	.2	.3	.1	−.1	c
Investment companies	2.6	.3	.4	.5	.6	.8
Banks	.6	.1	.2	.1	.1	.1
Other institutions	1.6	.3	.3	.3	.4	.3
Domestic individuals[a]	5.5	1.0	.7	1.1	1.4	1.3
Foreign investors	.7	.1	.1	.1	.3	.1
BONDS AND NOTES[b]						
All classes	$30.0	$4.8	$3.8	$5.4	$5.6	$10.4
Institutions	24.8	4.5	4.0	3.9	4.8	7.6
Corporate pension funds	6.3	1.0	1.2	.9	1.5	1.7
Life insurance companies	11.1	2.7	2.1	1.6	2.2	2.5
Investment companies	.3	c	c	c	.2	.1
Banks	1.3	.2	−.2	.1	−.3	1.5
State and local government trust funds	2.9	.3	.6	.6	.6	.8
Other institutions	2.6	.1	.2	.7	.6	1.0
Domestic individuals[a]	5.4	.4	−.1	1.6	.8	2.7
Foreign investors	.1	c	c	c	c	.1

Source: Securities and Exchange Commission, Section of Economic Research, July 22, 1958.

a Includes personal trust funds and nonprofit organizations. Net purchases of securities by individuals do not reflect borrowing on securities.

b Includes quasi-government debt issues for which separate data on holdings are not available.

c Less than $50 million.

Note: Figures are rounded and will not necessarily add to the totals.

Table 33

NEW CORPORATE SECURITIES OFFERED FOR CASH SALE, 1953–1957

(*Billions*)

Type of Security	Cumulative Totals 1953–1957	1953	1954	1955	1956	1957
All types	$52.3	$8.8	$9.5	$10.2	$10.9	$12.9
Common stocks	9.5	1.3	1.2	2.2	2.3	2.5
Preferred stocks	2.9	.5	.8	.6	.6	.4
Bonds, debentures and notes	39.9	7.0	7.5	7.4	8.0	10.0

Source: U. S. Department of Commerce, *Statistical Abstract of the United States, 1956*, p. 468; *1958*, p. 471 (based on SEC annual reports).

positively, that the pension trusts have a greater stabilizing influence on the market than any other group of buyers.

Comparison of total purchases and sales of common stocks made by the pension trusts will indicate the volume of their market activity. In the following tabulation their annual purchases and sales are set forth along with total stock sales on all U. S. registered exchanges for the years 1953 through 1957. If we add purchases and sales to get the total value of pension trust activities in the market for common stocks and compare the result with total sales on all exchanges, we find that the activities of the pension funds do not account for a very impressive amount of all sales. For example, their share by value of all sales of common and preferred stocks amounted to 3.5 per cent in 1953 and to about 4.3 per cent in 1957:[39]

Year	*Pension Trust Transactions (millions)* Purchases	Sales	Total	*Stock Sales on All Registered Exchanges (millions)*
1953	$ 513	$ 74	$ 587	$16,660
1954	738	148	886	28,075
1955	858	249	1,107	37,868
1956	1,000	229	1,229	35,018
1957	1,186	208	1,394	32,059

[39] SEC Release No. 1533, June 8, 1958, p. 2; U. S. Department of Commerce, *Statistical Abstract of the United States, 1958*, p. 468.

The pension trust portion of annual sales may be small, but this does not rule out the possibility that the pension trusts might have a strong impact on the market on a given day or during a certain period of time.

At the same time, the annual record of purchases and sales clearly indicates that the market activities of the pension trusts result in a steady withdrawal of stocks from active trading. The pension trusts have been purchasing larger amounts of stocks annually, with sales amounting to a decreasing proportion of total purchases. Sales by pension trusts mounted annually until 1956, when they dropped about $20 million below the previous year's total. In 1957 they decreased again by the same amount. This kind of market behavior cannot be ignored in an attempt to explain the stability of the market in the face of a business recession such as that of early 1958 or a steady rise in stock prices without significant setbacks such as occurred in the third quarter of 1958.

Finally, the impact of pension trust buying is greatest in the blue chip list of stocks. Over one-fourth of the net purchases of the thirty large pension funds investigated by the Senate Committee on Banking and Currency was from a list of 25 stocks. Pension trusts also paid the highest prices for stocks among all the institutional buyers examined.[40]

An exact, quantitative estimate of the impact of the pension trusts upon the securities markets may be impossible, but some fairly definite conclusions may be drawn from the data in hand.

1.   The pension trusts, which now own more than 2 per cent of all the corporate stocks outstanding along with 11 per cent of the bonds, are, through their market activity, rapidly increasing their proportions of ownership of these securities. (See Table 18.) In 1957 they made 27 per cent of the net purchases of stocks and 16 per cent of the net purchases of corporate bonds. (See Table 32.)

2.   Their purchasing record as compared with total sales of common stocks suggests that, while they purchase in sufficient volume to affect stock prices at a given point of time, their impact on the market is not made through a large volume of purchases and sales. They account for only a relatively small proportion of total sales — in the neighborhood of 4 per cent.

3.   The impact of the pension trusts on the market is effected by their steady withdrawal of the highest-priced stocks from active trading, amounting in 1957 to more than a fourth of the value of all new issues in that year.

40 *Institutional Investors and the Stock Market, 1953–1955*, p. 47.

4. Their purchases of stocks do not, therefore, result in an expansion of the active market, but in a contraction of it — to the extent of approximately 30 per cent of all the new securities sold over a five-year period.

5. The buying policies of the pension trusts will probably act as a stabilizing influence on the securities markets in times of recession whereas in prosperous times they will tend to make the prices of securities rise. This conclusion is less evident and, perhaps, less certain than the first four, yet it follows logically from the data we have presented. Whether or not the impact of the pension trusts is good or bad is difficult to say. It seems we pay for the stability we need at certain times at the price of an inflationary force at other times. The pension funds can reduce their buying during inflationary periods, but only within limits which are imposed by their constant need to invest current contributions.

6. The final point to be considered in connection with market impact is that the buying power of the pension trusts is subject to the control of a relatively small number of banks. The extent of this concentration is difficult to determine, as we have seen earlier, but it is safe to say that the pension trusts represent greater concentration of control of buying power than any of the other investor groups with which we have been comparing them.

But when we reflect that a very large portion of individual stockholdings and purchases is in the hands of banks administering personal trust funds, we raise a very intriguing question. To what extent are private trust funds concentrated in the hands of those banks which administer the pension funds? The stockholdings for personal trusts in the hands of banks were estimated to be between $33 and $38 billion at the end of 1954.[41] There is very little information as to the actual amount of these funds and still less about their location. Still, the sheer size of these holdings leads us to suspect that it is the large banks which, through the activities of their trust departments, are in fact the group of investors that have the greatest potential for exercising corporate control through stock ownership.

SUMMARY AND CONCLUSIONS

The estimated market value of the assets of private noninsured pension funds in 1958 was about $23 billion. At the end of 1957 these funds held

---

[41] See Table 19 and Chapter 2.

about a quarter of all public and private pension and retirement funds. Contributions to the pension trusts in that year amounted to more than one-third of individuals' savings in the form of private insurance of all types. The pension trusts accounted for about 10 per cent of all the financial savings of individuals.

The favorite investment medium for the noninsured private funds is corporate securities. Assets in this form amount to more than four-fifths of the total value of their reserves. About a quarter of the book value of their assets is invested in common stocks which are chosen from a rather narrow range of high-priced issues. Although the pension trusts do not lead the other institutions either in total assets or stockholdings, they are purchasing common stocks at a more rapid rate than any other institutional type of investor. Indeed, corporate pension trusts probably outrank even individuals as purchasers of common stocks.[42]

The presence of the pension trusts in the stock market results in a steady withdrawal of the highest-priced stocks from active trading as they are seldom sellers of stock. The pension trusts are, however, heavy purchasers, accounting for as much as 27 per cent of net purchases of stocks in 1957. During the five-year period 1953–1957, they purchased equities equal in amount to close to 30 per cent of all new issues offered for sale. These funds pour money into the market, but since they keep what they buy, the over-all effect is to contract rather than to expand the market. No doubt the pension trusts represent a stabilizing influence, but we cannot escape the conclusion that their activity must also be driving the prices of blue-chip securities upward.

Perhaps the most critical question posed by large accumulations of stocks in the hands of pension trustees concerns corporate control. At present, the most pertinent statistics on this point tend to allay this concern. The New York Banking Department report shows that, as of 1954, all the New York banks combined seldom held alarming amounts of the stock in any one corporation (in fifty instances more than 2 per cent, but very little more). But these figures actually applied to not more than 13 banks and, one suspects, to probably not more than 6 or 7 banks. Stock acquisitions have been made in considerable amounts since 1954 and they are going to be greater in the future. National statistics indicate that the New York pattern is not unique; there is a growing concentration of

[42] Figures for stock purchases by individuals include purchases made for personal trust funds. If we were to subtract these purchases from the annual totals for individuals, the pension trusts would be the leading group of buyers.

pension funds in the banks. Furthermore, we have seen that in a majority of the plans the financial trustees are given discretion in the matter of investment and that this practice becomes more common as the funds increase in size. There is also a high degree of concentration among the funds themselves. We must conclude, therefore, that corporate control is a real possibility.

The question of economic power in the pension funds becomes more urgent when we consider that their activities are not subject to the same degree of governmental regulation as are those of other financial institutions of comparable size. We find a greater concentration of control in the pension trusts than among the mutual funds, the insurance companies, and, probably, the banks holding personal trusts. And yet, unlike the pension trusts, the mutual funds are subject to the regulation of the SEC, the insurance companies are rigidly governed by state agencies and the trustees of personal trusts have to account to beneficiaries (though this accounting may not amount to much as a preventive check). The bank trustees are therefore in a position to wield considerable economic power through their control of the pension trusts, a power which is further extended through their stockholdings for personal trusts.

But the economic power of the bank trustee is not without its check, which may come from the employer who appoints the financial trustee for the pension funds. The designation of the trustee is almost universally reserved to the employer, even where the administration of the plan is in the hands of a committee which has employee representation. In 97 per cent of the 1,024 pension plans studied by the New York Banking Department the financial trustee was appointed by the employer. In current practice the financial trustee is given the power to invest the assets of a pension fund as he chooses, but as pension plans are now set up the employer can, in nearly all instances, revoke the arrangement and assume direction of the investment program, either by taking it over himself or by directing the financial trustee to follow a specified policy. Thus the managers of the corporation, who already wield great economic power, have a power potential which they do not exercise in the investment programs of the pension trusts of their companies.

The employer in his turn faces a check which may be imposed by the labor union since pension plans now including close to two-thirds of all covered employees are the result of collective bargaining agreements. So far the unions have, for the most part, been content to bargain about benefits, vesting, conditions for entrance into the plan, etc., leaving the financing of the plan to the employer. But they could interest themselves in the financing of pensions, as some unions have already done.

While their influence in the operation of pension plans usually stops at the collective bargaining table, the unions do have representation in the administration of pension plans covering something less than a third of the employees. Even within this group of plans, however, the employer often retains ultimate control. Union participation through collective bargaining is most common in the largest plans, those of the multi-employer, area- or industry-wide type.

Aside from the influence that his union can bring to bear in his behalf, the employee has little to say about how a pension plan is set up or operated. The great majority of plans give the employer the right to amend or terminate the plan at will or to reduce payments. In a third of the New York plans the employer reserved the right to suspend pension payments even after pensions had begun. Financial statements are rarely made available, although most plans provide for the distribution of a copy of the plan.

The cumulative effect of all these reservations of rights is to make the expectation of actual pension payments, in the absence of a protective union contract, very much dependent upon the willingness and ability of the employer to continue funding a plan and to pay out benefits when the time for retirement arrives. Pension expectations are not independent of business cycles and the actual realization of benefits may, in fact, vary with economic conditions.

In the end, the anatomy of control of the pension trusts may be described quite simply. In general, financial control has been delegated by the employers to the banker-trustees, which exercise considerable power in the capital markets as a result. The employer controls the day-to-day operation of the plan itself, in many cases in accordance with a basic agreement arrived at with a union. It is the employer who, either unilaterally or in conjunction with a union, fixes the amount of pensions and usually alone determines how a plan is to be financed. The employee himself, without his union, has little or nothing to say about the pension plan which, ultimately, is financed out of his earnings. The income of the retired work force in 1980 is, to an important degree, in the control of the employers.

PENSION TRUSTS
IN 1970

Earlier Projections of Size

A Projection Based on Performance

Future Pension Trust Investments

Private pension funds have shown such phenomenal growth in recent years that the future size of their asset accumulations has become a matter of earnest speculation. Speculation it is, because their future size will be determined by many incalculable factors. Some of these incalculables are as broad as the levels of national prosperity, growth in population, social security legislation, and policy decisions by unions as to what improvements to press for in the coming years. Once all these factors have been established by hypothesis, there remain the questions more directly pertinent to pension funds themselves, such as their rate of earnings, extent of funding, amount of vesting, and so forth.

A thorough study of this problem, although it would be of great interest and value, is impossible within the scope of this work. Yet, since the impact of the pension trusts on property ownership is our major concern, something must be said of the potential growth of these funds and the channelling of their investments.

If the past contains any hint of the future, the impact of the pension trusts on the economy will be far-reaching because their growth will be great. The pension trusts, as Table 34 indicates, began the decade of the twenties with assets of approximately $50 million. Between 1920 and

Table 34

GROWTH OF NONINSURED PRIVATE PENSION FUNDS, 1920–1957
(*Millions*)

Year	Total Assets	Increase in 5-Year Period	Year	Total Assets	Increase During Year
1920	$ 50	—	1950	$ 5,526	—
1925	150	$ 100	1951	6,876	$1,350
1930	550	400	1952	8,505	1,629
1935	800	250	1953	10,222	1,717
1940	1,100	300	1954	12,153	1,931
1945	2,700	1,600	1955	14,230	2,077
1950	5,200	2,500	1956	16,639	2,410
			1957	19,319	2,680

Sources: 1920–1940 — Raymond W. Goldsmith, *Study of Savings in the United States,* Princeton University Press, Princeton, 1955.

1945–1950 — R. F. Murray, "A Fresh Look at Pension Funds," *Trusts and Estates,* November 1955.

1950–1956 — Securities and Exchange Commission, as reported in Vito Natrella, "Implications of Pension Fund Accumulations," *Proceedings, American Statistical Association,* September 1957, Table 2.

1930 their assets increased tenfold; during the thirties they doubled and during the forties considerably more than quadrupled in size. The rate of growth in the 1950s promises to continue or perhaps outstrip the record of the 1940s since, according to the SEC, the funds increased in amount more than two and a half times in the first five years of the decade. To quadruple their 1950 total of $5.5 billion by 1960, the pension funds would have to add to their assets at the rate of about $2 billion a year, which was about the rate of growth in 1955. But the increases for 1956 and 1957 were greater than this amount, $2.4 and $2.7 billion respectively. Therefore, we may expect that the book value of noninsured pension trust assets by the beginning of 1960 will be in the neighborhood of $25 billion, or more than four times their value in 1950.

EARLIER PROJECTIONS OF SIZE

Adolf Berle's Estimate

In the course of the New York State Insurance Department hearings on pension funds in 1956, Adolf A. Berle, Jr., noted that estimates of the figure at which pension funds would level off ran from an optimistic $214 billion to a conservative $60 billion.[1] Mr. Berle's own estimate was that employees' pension funds will rise by 1975 to somewhere in the neighborhood of $80 billion. He did not enumerate all the factors that went into his estimate but pointed out that in twenty years we would see both a larger working population and a larger proportion of it protected by pension plans. An estimate that 30 million employees would be covered by employees' funds in twenty years he regarded as rather low. Since the labor force reached 68 million at the end of 1958, and at least 14.3 million employees were covered in 1956, there seems to be considerable merit to Mr. Berle's contention concerning the labor force. In his testimony Mr. Berle indicated that this sum might be equally divided between the noninsured pension trusts and insured plans. However, statistics which have since become available seem to indicate that the noninsured funds are increasing more rapidly than the insured funds.[2]

If the gradual trend toward trusteed types of plans continues, and if we consider that the accumulation of trusteed funds is already in excess of insured funds, it is quite probable that at least by 1975 the noninsured funds will comprise two-thirds of all funds invested for pension plans.

Brookings Estimate

Perhaps the most elaborate attempt at projection of the future of pension funds was made by Charles L. Dearing in a study of industrial pensions published by the Brookings Institution in 1954.[3] Mr. Dearing made a comprehensive analysis of the large number of relevant factors which will influence the size of pension funds and based his predictions upon the evidence of questionnaires to a significant cross section of corporations maintaining pension funds. In addition to general economic factors, an attempt was made to include the effects of increased price levels, wider coverage of vesting provisions and liberalization of benefits. The final estimate, which the author considered to be conservative, was that the annual rate of payments to meet pension obligations would reach about $6.6 billion by 1960, and that $6 billion of this would represent

[1] Public Hearing, Welfare and Pension Funds, N. Y. State Insurance Department, 1956, Statement of A. A. Berle, Jr., Exhibit 1, p. 7. (Mimeographed.)

[2] Note figures contained in Table 11 (p. 193) showing that the noninsured funds made up about 58 per cent of all private funds in 1957. The 1956 edition of *A Study of Industrial Retirement Plans* by the Bankers Trust Company also indicates a trend away from the insured type of plan to the trusteed type. Cf. p. 23 of that study.

[3] Charles L. Dearing, *Industrial Pensions,* Brookings Institution, Washington, 1954, Chapters 6 and 7.

net additions to the supply of individual money savings.[4] This figure was based on an annual contribution of $200 in 1960 for each of an estimated 22 billion workers covered by pension plans at that time.[5] In the light of recent developments in many industries this estimate does not seem so very conservative now although it included adjustments for increased benefits offset by a number of cost-reducing factors.

A More Recent Estimate

By 1957 considerably more data on the size and coverage of pension funds had become available and the Chief Statistician of the Securities and Exchange Commission, Vito Natrella, was able to make predictions that are probably nearer the mark. Employing methods similar to Dearing's, but using over-all aggregates rather than data for separate industries, Natrella predicted that contributions to noninsured private pension funds would amount to $3.2 billion in 1960 and $4.4 billion in 1965.[6] He estimated that contributions to all private plans would amount to $6.2 billion in 1965. On this basis he further estimated that the assets of the noninsured funds would amount to $29.2 billion at the end of 1960 and $51.7 billion at the end of 1965. Finally, according to Natrella's projections, the insured funds, which amounted to $16.6 billion in 1956, would more than double by 1965.

These estimates were made in terms of 1956 dollars and were based on the rather important assumptions that benefit payments would more than double and that interest rates would remain at current levels. Other factors in Natrella's estimates differed considerably from those that figured in Dearing's projections. For example, Natrella's estimates of probable employee coverage were lower. He thought that pension fund coverage in 1960 would include approximately 17 million persons and would reach 20 million in 1965.

These estimates are conservative enough, especially as they do not take into account the new spurt of growth that will result from tax deduction and exemption of pension funds for the self-employed.

A PROJECTION BASED ON PERFORMANCE

Our method of predicting the future growth of pension funds will be based upon certain conclusions which can be drawn from the recent his-

[4] *Ibid.*, pp. 167 and 175.
[5] *Ibid.*, p. 130.
[6] Vito Natrella, "Implications of Pension Fund Accumulations," *Proceedings, American Statistical Association*, September 1957, p. 14.

tory of asset accumulations. The annual rate of growth of pension fund assets will be taken as a norm of what they will amount to in future years. In the face of other more complicated methods of prediction this approach may seem all too simple. At the same time this method has built into it, as it were, all of the factors that would go into a more complex estimate, i.e., increase in the labor force and the number of plans, progressive inflation, liberalization of benefits, etc. In the early years of the pension fund movement projection on the basis of annual increases in assets would have been quite unreliable, but since 1950 their growth has begun to assume a fairly steady pattern.

The reliability of this method can be demonstrated by an examination of the growth of the assets of the life insurance companies, institutions very similar to the pension trusts. In each decade of the present century, the life insurance companies have doubled their assets in geometric progression and they have shown such a steady rate of annual increase for the past decade that prediction of their size in the near future is a simple matter.

Recent Pattern of Pension Fund Growth

Examination of the growth in corporate pension fund assets for the five years 1953 to 1957, as reported in Table 35, shows that these funds increased their assets each year by 22, 19, 17, 17 and 16 per cent of their previous year's total. If we assume that this rate of growth continues to drop by one percentage point a year, then by the end of 1960, noninsured pension fund assets would reach a total of $28.6 billion and by 1962 they would total $35.6 billion.

These estimates are somewhat lower than those made by Natrella. His figures apparently led him to believe that pension fund contributions would continue to increase by greater amounts each year at least until 1965 because he estimated the annual contribution to noninsured funds in 1960 at $3.2 billion and in 1965 at $4.4 billion. According to the method of projection we have employed, the annual increase (from all sources) for 1960 will amount to $3.4 billion and will continue to rise until 1962 when contributions will amount to $3.5 billion, an increase of about 10 per cent of the total assets of the previous year. If we continued our assumption of a one per cent annual drop in the rate of increase beyond this point, then the annual increases would become smaller and smaller. Yet it is logical to conclude that the annual increases in total assets of pension funds will continue to grow until the time when a large number of the pension funds begin to level off and are able to reduce their annual con-

Table 35

DISTRIBUTION OF CORPORATE PENSION FUND ASSETS
BY TYPE, 1953–1957

Type of Asset	1953	1954	1955	1956	1957
	BOOK VALUE (MILLIONS), END OF YEAR				
Total assets	$10,222	$12,153	$14,230	$16,639	$19,319
Cash and deposits	313	296	343	332	368
U. S. government securities	2,297	2,284	2,536	2,293	2,032
Corporate bonds	5,181	6,359	7,225	8,704	10,392
Own company	n.a.	n.a.	n.a.	598	641
Other companies	n.a.	n.a.	n.a.	8,106	9,751
Preferred stock	397	454	510	570	611
Common stock	1,649	2,286	2,958	3,774	4,771
Own company	342	382	434	505	584
Other companies	1,307	1,904	2,524	3,269	4,187
Mortgages	n.a.	n.a.	146	230	313
Other assets	384	473	511	736	833
	PERCENTAGE INCREASE IN EACH COMPONENT				
Total assets	22.0	18.9	17.1	16.9	16.1
Cash and deposits	18.1	−5.4	15.9	−3.2	10.8
U. S. government securities	6.2	−0.6	11.0	−9.6	−11.4
Corporate bonds	25.1	22.7	13.6	20.5	19.4
Preferred stock	19.9	14.4	12.3	11.8	7.2
Common stock	36.8	38.6	29.4	27.6	26.4
Mortgages	—	—	—	57.5	36.1
Other assets	38.6	23.2	8.0	44.0	13.2

Source: SEC Statistical Series, Release No. 1533, June 8, 1958, p. 4.
n.a.: not available.

tributions. As we shall see below, this levelling off cannot possibly occur before 1970.

Our conclusion that the annual increases in pension fund assets cannot decrease in amount before full maturity of the pension plans is based on the mechanics of pension plan funding. Funding is done on an actuarial basis, which means that annual payments into the fund are calculated so that the cost of the benefits is spread equally over the service lives of covered employees. We have seen in Chapter 5 that in order to qualify for tax deduction an employer must limit his contributions to current liabilities. There can, therefore, be no question of larger contributions for current service in the early years of pension plans. The same reasoning does not apply to payments for past service liabilities. But before carrying our efforts at projection any further, we should try to determine when the majority of pension plans may be expected to mature.

When Pension Funds Will Level Off

Since annual contributions to pension funds are calculated to spread equally over the service lives of the employees covered by the plan, we may expect these payments to continue at a steady rate until a large number of the employees originally covered by the plan begin to retire. At this time the cost of their benefits should have been paid in and they will be supported by the earnings of the fund. But contributions will have to be made for those who subsequently came into the plan and be continued until there is enough money in the fund to support all pensioners and the reserves for the pensioners who die off are sufficient to meet liabilities for incoming members of the plan. At this point the pension plan will theoretically level off and the annual contributions will diminish considerably. When all pension plans have reached this stage, however, any growth that takes place will represent only the additional reserves accumulated to provide for increases in benefits and expansion of the labor force. This means that after the levelling-off period total asset growth will proceed at a much slower pace. The question now is: When will this drop in the rate of growth begin?

The New York State Banking Department has tabulated the 643 plans it studied according to the percentage beginning in each of the years 1940 to 1954. The following tabulation, based on the Banking Department's figures, gives a rough idea of the time when the 643 plans in operation in 1954 will begin to mature.[7]

Per Cent of 643 New York Plans	Beginning in:	Will Not Mature before:
96.1*	1940–1954	1970–1984
43.5	1940–1949	1970–1979
52.6	1950–1954	1980–1984
77.9	1945–1954	1975–1984

* Less than 4 per cent were set up *before* 1940.

[7] Compiled by the author from annual percentages given by the New York State Banking Department, *Pension and Other Employee Welfare Plans*, 1955, Table 40. In drawing up the table a thirty-year service requirement has been assumed.

We can readily see from this calculation that there cannot be any great slowing in the rate of pension fund accumulation before 1970. In all likelihood significant decreases will not occur before 1975 since 78 per cent of the plans did not begin operations until 1945 or after. This conclusion is reinforced when we note that half the plans were not set up until 1950 or later. The Banking Department also reported that 45 per cent of the employees covered by the 643 plans were under plans beginning in 1950, the year of greatest increase. It is probable, therefore, that the rate of asset accumulation will decrease only slowly until 1980.

We can reasonably assume that these New York plans are fairly representative of all private pension plans in the United States and that, if there are differences in timing, developments in other areas of the country would have lagged behind New York's. In any case, it is conservative enough to conclude that a significant decrease in the rate of pension fund accumulation will not occur before 1970.

Projections for 1965 and 1970

The farther we extend our projections, of course, the more we have to rely on guesswork. Still, we have seen valid reasons for assuming that the rate of increase in accumulation, while it will be slow, will not actually turn downward before 1970. We shall assume, then, that after 1962 the rate of combined pension fund increases will remain steady at about 10 per cent. It is quite possible that this rate of increase will fall slightly before the decade ends, but if the drops of only 0.2 and 0.8 per cent in the rates of increase for 1956 and 1957 are any index, our assumption for increases up to 1962 may be too conservative. We are therefore striking an average with the assumption of a 10 per cent rate of accumulation until 1970.

An objection may be raised that since the funding of past service liability is usually carried out on a ten-year basis, this type of funding will be completed before the end of the period we are considering. But the statistics quoted from the New York study indicate that the impact of this factor is already being felt and there has not been any sharp downturn in the rate of increase.

On the basis of the above assumptions, then, we conclude that the assets of private noninsured pension funds will reach a total of $47.3 billion at the end of 1965 — an increase of about $19 billion over our estimate for 1960. At this time noninsured funds will represent about 60 per cent of the accumulated assets of all private pension funds, which will then total about $79 billion. These totals are lower than those projected by Natrella: his estimates would give all private pension funds assets of more than $85 billion in 1965.[8] He apparently assumed that asset accumulation would proceed at a higher rate since he estimated the 1965 contributions to noninsured plans at $4.4 billion. If we add interest at 3.5 per cent and other income and deduct the benefit payments, his estimates would indicate an annual increase in noninsured pension fund assets in excess of $5.2 billion. The projection we advance for this figure in 1965 is $4.7 billion.

If we carry out the assumption of a 10 per cent annual increase through the end of the decade we arrive at an estimate of about $84 billion total assets for all private noninsured pension funds by the end of 1970. On the further assumption that the growing preference for noninsured funding will continue, these funds will amount to about two-thirds of the $126 billion aggregate which we estimate for all privately financed pension reserves at that time.

Although Natrella did not carry his projections beyond 1965, the conclusions he reached indicate a considerably larger rate of increase in pension fund assets than we have assumed. Compared with his projections our assumptions are conservative. They appear even more conservative in the light of the following projections of the U. S. labor force for the period in which we are interested:

> Between 1955 and 1960, it will be the workers past 35 years of age who will dominate labor force growth; those 35 to 64 years of age will increase by over 800,000 a year, on the average. But in the following 5-year period the influx of over half a million young workers a year (aged 14 to 24 years) will tax training, placement, and managerial skills. . . . When 1965 is reached, a new era in manpower will begin. On the average, almost 1 million workers a year between the ages of 20 and 35 will be added to the current labor supply until 1975.[9]

Furthermore, the assumption of a drop of as much as one percentage point each year in the rate of asset accumulation seems too high in light of the fact that the drop was considerably less than one per cent in 1956 and 1957 — 0.2 per cent and 0.8 per cent — as we have already pointed out. If we assume, then, a drop in the rate of increase of only 0.6 per cent a year until 1965, total assets for the noninsured funds at the end of that year would be $52.7 billion. Assuming further that the rate of increase

8 Natrella, *op. cit.*, p. 14.
9 U. S. Department of Commerce, Bureau of the Census, *Current Population Reports,* Labor Force (Series P–50, No. 69), October 1956, p. 8.

levels off at about 11 per cent instead of at 10 per cent, these funds would reach a total of about $89 billion in 1970, which would bring the estimate for all private pension assets up to around $134 billion.

When we consider all of the circumstances that may affect the rate of pension fund accumulation and give special weight to the estimates of population growth, even our second projection is well within the limits of probability. While the projections seem to involve tremendous sums of money, we must remember that by their very nature the pension trusts must follow a course of steady accumulation. Barring any major financial calamity they will do just that. Still, these projections indicate a slowing rate of growth. In the 1940s and again in the 1950s the noninsured funds quadrupled in size, while according to our second and larger estimate their assets will increase 3.8 times from 1955 to 1965 and only triple from 1960 to 1970.

The figures we offer here are, of course, in no sense predictions of the actual amounts the funds may accumulate by 1970; they are merely projections based on certain assumptions. For the purposes of this study these projections are of value mainly to give some dimensions to the impact the pension trusts will have on the future of our economy.

FUTURE PENSION TRUST INVESTMENTS

When we come to estimate the future size and forms of pension trust investments we are faced with a host of new variables. To avoid making mere conjectures we shall limit our consideration to present trends and their probable consequences without attempting to arrive at definite predictions.

Distribution of Pension Trust Assets

Reference to Table 36 shows that the direction in pension trust investments is definitely toward corporate securities at the expense of U. S. government securities. The strongest trend in the five-year period 1953–1957 has been this movement away from U. S. securities, which comprised about a fifth of the pension fund assets at the beginning of the period and only a tenth at the end. At the same time the percentage of assets invested in stocks rose appreciably to about one-fourth of the total. The gains made by corporate bonds were much less.

The growing preference for common stocks is the investment trend

Table 36

PERCENTAGE DISTRIBUTION OF CORPORATE PENSION FUND
ASSETS BY TYPE, 1953–1957

Type of Asset	PER CENT OF BOOK VALUE, END OF YEAR				
	1953	1954	1955	1956	1957
Total assets	100.0	100.0	100.0	100.0	100.0
Cash and deposits	3.1	2.4	2.4	2.0	1.9
U. S. government securities	22.5	18.8	17.8	13.8	10.5
Corporate bonds	50.7	52.3	50.8	52.3	53.8
Own company	—	—	—	3.6	3.3
Other companies	—	—	—	48.7	50.5
Preferred stock	3.9	3.7	3.6	3.4	3.2
Common stock	16.1	18.8	20.8	22.7	24.7
Own company	3.3	3.1	3.0	3.0	3.0
Other companies	12.8	15.7	17.7	19.6	21.7
Mortgages	—	—	1.0	1.4	1.6
Other assets	3.8	3.9	3.6	4.4	4.3

Source: Statistics developed by SEC to update *Survey of Corporate Pension Funds, 1951–1954,* July 31, 1958.

most likely to persist. The past record of stock earnings, discussed in Chapter 4, along with the continuing threat of inflation, are powerful arguments supporting this conclusion. Furthermore, the risk of stock purchases lessens as funds increase in size, and some of the larger funds are investing a much higher proportion of their assets in common stocks than the average of 25 per cent for all funds combined. For example, as of 1957, General Motors had 40 per cent of its pension trust invested in stocks.[10] General Electric is reported to have 32 per cent of its pension fund assets in common stock, Sears, Roebuck 76 per cent, Bethlehem Steel 66 per cent and du Pont 35 per cent.[11] Apparently the pension funds have not yet reached a limit in the proportion of stocks they want to acquire.

It seems reasonable, then, to anticipate that by 1965 the pension trusts will have 35–40 per cent of their total assets invested in common stocks.

[10] *U. S. News and World Report,* March 22, 1957, p. 133.
[11] *Business Week,* January 31, 1959, p. 98.

This conclusion is strongly indicated by the gain of two percentage points a year in the relative position of their stockholdings shown in Table 36. In line with the projections made above for total assets of all noninsured funds, these holdings would represent an investment of $17–$21 billion.[12] This would imply that the present proportion of corporate bonds will decrease somewhat, although they will still make up the largest segment of the portfolios, and that the proportion of U. S. securities will decline still further. Indeed, in 1957 they represented only 7.7 per cent of the portfolios of the largest funds.[13]

The Problem of Control

We recall from Chapter 2 that all types of financial institutions now own close to one-third of the shares outstanding on the stock market. Furthermore, these holdings, which are in the so-called blue-chip equities, give the financial institutions a share in the largest corporations. If the private pension funds keep up their present rate of stock purchases, they will continue to add materially to the upward squeeze on the prices of blue-chip securities now operative in the stock market.

It is quite likely, too, that certain large New York banks will soon approach a point where their combined holdings of stocks for pension funds could give their opinions considerable weight in the councils of the larger corporations. While it is the policy of many large corporations to include provisions in their pension plans to prevent their funds from gaining control of other corporations, no such restrictive policy has yet been announced by the banks. Unquestionably, they will seek to spread their stock investments widely to stave off acquiring the responsibility of corporate direction as long as possible. But as the stock purchases of the pension funds continue to grow, we can anticipate that at some time in the not-too-distant future the banker-trustees are going to be faced with an uncomfortable choice. They will have to buy into a position of authority in the larger corporations or reject profitable investments in order to avoid the responsibilities that accompany large shareholdings.

It may be that market influences along with the antitrust laws provide sufficient checks on the banks to prevent them from acquiring significant control of the larger corporations. As more pension fund money is invested in blue-chip equities the prices of these securities will continue

[12] In 1955 the New York Stock Exchange estimated that equity holdings for all types of pension funds in 1965 would amount to $17 billion. (See p. 32, n. 44.)

[13] See Table 17, p. 203.

to rise and at some point this form of investment may be pegged at a price high enough to slow the rate of institutional acquisitions. At the same time the Antitrust Department could not ignore the domination of corporate policy by Wall Street. It is possible that the larger pension funds are already deciding against too rapid acquisition of blue-chip stocks. As we have noted in Chapter 7, as a group they have tended to invest a smaller portion of their portfolios in common stocks than do the smaller funds.

Countering these checks, however, are the tremendous advantages of equity investments. Considerable influence over corporate policy might be wielded by the institutional investors without sufficient concentration of control to enable the Antitrust Department to make a case of Sherman Act violation against the financial institutions. But one thing should be clearly recognized. The power now exists in the financial trustees of pension funds to purchase enough stock to control or at least to influence our corporations. Similarly, with their large equity holdings the bankers could make a plaything of stock prices. It is most unlikely, of course, that the financial institutions will make any major moves seriously detrimental to the common good, but it is healthy to recognize that the power to do so is there if strategically placed financiers wish to exercise it.

Beyond any doubt serious and anxious questions put to corporate management with regard to their operating policy and future plans will have reverberations in the councils of corporate managers. Indeed, in many cases the institutional investors will be obliged to ask these questions. But even though an institutional investor may be seeking to avoid control, a large sell-off of the securities of any one company would have a weighty impact upon its corporate policy. This is true now. We have shown in this chapter that it will be increasingly true in the foreseeable future.

It may not be too much to say that the center of influence in our economy, having left the Wall Street of the 1920s and migrated in the 1930s and 1940s to the provincial centers of corporate power, has now returned to New York financial circles. What is more, the financial strength now building up in the New York banks is of a different character. The power position that was consolidated in the 1920s was deliberately sought by the financiers and had no stable institutional character. But, as we have already noted, the present concentration of financial power is not so much the result of a drive for power as it is of (1) social demands which require the aggregation of great wealth to provide security, and (2) the fortunate presence of the financial institutions as apt media for administering this wealth. The alignment of forces now taking shape is of an institutional and permanent character which will be part of our economic and social structure for some time to come. What we are witnessing is a genuine evolutionary development rather than a temporary consolidation of power resulting from personal acquisitiveness.

A POLICY FOR

PENSION TRUSTS

The Test of Security

The Test of Freedom

The Problem of Ownership

We are now ready to look further into the question posed at the beginning of this study: What will be the impact of the private noninsured pension trust funds upon the ownership and control of productive property in the United States? In the face of the evidence presented in the previous chapters, it is clear that the pension trusts do have an impact which is a subject of growing public concern and that we should now be able to draw some conclusions as to its nature and extent. We shall first discuss the influence of pension trusts upon those who feel it most, the employees. The broader impact of the pension trust system upon our society will be the subject of the final chapter.

Any appraisal of pension trusts should begin with a discussion of the ends they are to serve. Since they are a form of property organization, they ought, in some way, to promote the same ends that property itself serves. Certainly their operation should not be contrary to those ends. Property, as we conceive it in the United States, is traditionally a source of independence. This means, at the very least, freedom from want. But for us independence means more. It also includes the self-determination which derives from the free choice of how a man is to provide for his present livelihood and his future security. In the context of our discussion of the pension system this means that freedom from want must not be purchased at the cost of economic independence, so that the worker in our society becomes the ward of the corporation.

The rise of the pension trust is not an isolated phenomenon and, in judging its worth, the social context in which it appears should be kept in view. To a great extent a man's freedom during his working life is already severely circumscribed, at least in the very significant respect that he has no proprietary interest in the enterprise in which he is employed. This proprietary interest and its attendant freedoms have ceased to be characteristic prerogatives in the average man's life for so long now that their loss is no longer felt and the want of them is not pressing. But now, with the advent of the pension system, a significant portion of the worker's compensation is withheld from him and channeled into compulsory savings. This simply means that the area of proprietorship for the average worker is that much more circumscribed.

For the future beneficiary, then, the problem posed by pension trusts is: How may freedom from want in the future be secured without loss of economic independence? When tested by this question the pension trusts have two serious defects: (1) they are as yet an imperfect instrument for securing the employee's future, and (2), as presently constituted, the proprietary right of the employee in a pension trust is so slight that his economic freedom is seriously limited. The following summary of the present status of pension trusts will attempt to show to what extent these two criticisms are valid. Suggestions will also be offered for making pension trusts better instruments for fulfilling the two requirements of security and economic freedom.

THE TEST OF SECURITY

How well then do the plans and the ways in which their assets are handled and safeguarded protect the security of the beneficiaries and insure them from want in the future? As we have seen in Chapters 3 to 6, certain defects in the typical plans, combined with lack of public knowledge and legislative control of the whole pension movement, still leave much to be resolved and corrected if the beneficiary's rights under his pension plan are to be clearly understood and, in fact, if his expectation of retirement benefits is to be fully realized.

THE PLANS THEMSELVES

When we ask how effectively the pension trusts provide security for their beneficiaries we pose the most practical question possible since pension programs are designed for just this purpose: to insulate the pensioner from want after his working life. Yet in a very large number of pension plans the expected benefits of the covered employee are subject to conditions which make his freedom from want in the future far from certain.

Termination

In the first place, termination of the fund is very often left to the discretion of the employer. This means that, entirely apart from anything the employee might be able to do effectively, he might find that after some twenty or twenty-five years of service his employer has decided to terminate the entire pension plan and leave him with no pension at all. Furthermore, pension plans often contain no provision for sharing whatever assets are in the fund at termination. How the various pensioners and prospective pensioners might share the pooled capital is often vague or wholly unprovided for. In most plans, too, the employer's liabilities are limited to the amount of contributions in the fund.

Amendment

Similarly, amendment of the pension plan is frequently left wholly within the power of the employer. He may elect to reduce pension payments at any time at his discretion, as has already happened in the case of at least one very large pension fund. Since the determination of the amount of the periodic contributions is usually reserved to the employer, the employee will have no legitimate complaint if at some future date the fund should prove inadequate to serve the needs of all its pensioners. Very often the employer reserves the right to suspend contributions altogether.

Other Restrictions

Certain other types of restrictions upon the right to receive a pension seem grossly unfair to the employees. These include provisions in the plan aimed at preventing an employee from working for a competitor or being re-employed in the same industry. In some instances such clauses may be justified but for the average worker they are to be deplored. Restrictions such as reduction of pension because of other income earned during retirement or making pensions contingent upon "fluctuation of income" or upon continued good conduct can make the pension promise almost illusory.

Inadequate Information

Defects such as these are aggravated in many cases by a serious lack of sufficient information about the conditional nature of pension promises. A study of 188 New York pension plans showed that less than half of the plans told the whole truth and that 70 of them were definitely misleading and 34 were silent as to the conditional nature of promises.

Whatever excuse there might be for other defects in pension programs, there seems no excuse for failing to give an employee sufficient information to enable him to plan for his future. Misleading information about the nature and amount of the pension benefit is little short of criminal, and an employer responsible for such statements about a company plan ought to be held to his misleading promises in court. The expectancy of a pension may influence a worker's economic conduct over a period of twenty or thirty years, and misinformation about his benefits can result in his being stranded without resources at the end of his working life.

Another important area of information is the financial statement of the condition of the fund. Financial reports are made available in only a minority of pension funds and are supplied to beneficiaries in still fewer cases. Adequate information about both the conditional nature of the promises and the resources of the fund is a *sine qua non* for any proposed legislation concerning pension trusts.

Need for Vesting

Many of the defects in pension plans mentioned above would be cured by vesting the accumulated assets in the beneficiaries. We have seen the prediction that, as pension plans are now constituted, no more than 50 per cent of the employees presently covered will ever receive a cash benefit from the plan. The New York State study reveals that approximately 4 out of 5 of the employees covered by the large number of plans in that state were not protected by vesting.

Vesting of pension benefits as they accrue would make the broad powers of termination, amendment and restriction more equitable because at any given time an employee would be able to claim the funds that had been set aside for his future, or at least he would have a guarantee of receiving them at retirement.

Inadequate Legal Protection

The acid test of the substantiality of a pensioner's property right comes when he attempts to enforce that right in a court of law. Regardless of which party to the trust he may wish to sue, the employee or pensioner finds serious obstacles in his way.

If the employee should try to sue the employer on the promises contained in the pension plan, he will first have to overcome the traditional theory that a pension is a gratuity. Thus far, a majority of courts have upheld provisions in pension plans to the effect that they are gratuities. Since there have been some holdings and dicta to the contrary, however, it is to be hoped that at least in the absence of the gratuity clause the courts will construe pensions as deferred wages. Moreover, as the pension movement reaches maturity, the courts should scrutinize gratuity clauses more carefully. The entire plan should be examined to see if enough consideration does not accrue to the employer to justify construing the plan as a contract.

At present the most solid judicial view would seem to be that the pension plan constitutes a unilateral contract. Such a view — and it is difficult to make a case for a bilateral contract in the usual pension plan — leaves the employee subject to the contingency of dismissal and so militates against security unless, of course, there is a collective bargaining agreement. But this is another difficulty which could be solved by the introduction of vesting.

Another obstacle to an employee's suit against his employer is the tendency of the courts to uphold clauses giving the right of amendment and exclusive interpretation to the employer.

If the employee attempts to sue his employer on the basis of a collective bargaining agreement his success in a federal court would depend on being able to show diversity of citizenship because the Taft-Hartley Act gives the right of the federal forum only to the union. Nor can the union sue for an employee's pension since this right has been held to be personal. Pension legislation by Congress could solve this problem.

Furthermore, if an employee should seek to bring his suit for pension rights on an equitable basis his claim would be heard only if he were suing a union-managed or jointly managed fund. Such funds have been declared to be true trusts. In an employer-managed fund it has been held that the only trustee-beneficiary relationship existing lies between the employee and the bank which holds the funds in accordance with a trust agreement executed by the employer and the bank. But if an employee were to sue the banker-trustee for an accounting, for example, he would be met with the defense of escape clauses in the trust indenture stating that only the employer may bring an action against the trustee bank and that the bank is responsible only to the employer.

In such a case if the courts wished to hold that the bank is the only trustee, they would be placed in a dilemma. They would either have to uphold the escape clauses, thus denying the employee the time-honored rights of a beneficiary, or they would have to strike down the escape clauses. It is safe to say that any court would be reluctant to choose either of these alternatives.

The Remedy: The Bank-Trustee as Agent

Many of the legal problems discussed above arise out of the theory that the bank is a trustee. At this point the alternative proposition may be advanced that the bank is in fact an agent.

The way the typical trust agreement is drawn establishes an exclusive relationship between the employer and the bank-trustee: the beneficiary has no right to intervene. The employer may change the trust agreement or the financial trustee at any time and meanwhile the bank is accountable only to him. The employer also directs disbursements to the pensioners and he may, and in many cases does, exercise a degree of investment control. Such an arrangement sounds like the type of contract in which the employer is the principal and the bank is his agent.

It may be asked of the banks whether they wish to retain the immunity of their escape clauses and be agents or be, in fact, true trustees. The concept of agency is quite broad enough to cover the present activities of banks in handling pension funds. But it is doubtful whether the trust concept can be stretched that far. The source of the difficulty lies in the effort of the banks to have the freedom of a trustee without the concomitant accountability to the beneficiary.

As yet this issue has not been squarely met in any court although it is almost inevitable that it will be. It would be more conformable to the facts of the typical pension situation to call the employer the trustee and the bank his agent. The objection may be raised, as the court did in the *Hurd* case, that this interpretation would assign to the employer the double role of trustee and settlor or contributor. (See p. 178.) But the employer himself has elected to play two parts, and such double identity presents no obstacle in other areas of the law. Not to go far afield for an example, the trustee of a pension fund is very often also the president or other officer of the corporation. This is the case in the Sears profit-sharing fund. The same person may be an executor and a legatee or a trustee and a beneficiary. Similarly, a bank serving as the financial trustee of a pension fund may have dealings with itself in another capacity.

Finally, if pensions are regarded as deferred wages — and this theory is gaining ground in the courts — then the assets of a pension fund belong to the employee, and the employer, insofar as he directs their administration, is in fact executing a trust. And even if the deferred-wage theory is not accepted, in the vast majority of pension funds the assets are placed irrevocably beyond ownership by the employers.

The last and perhaps most serious obstacle to suit by an employee arises from the fact that, typically, he has no vested interest in the pension fund until he reaches retirement age. Any claim he may make up to the time when pension payments are actually due will be met with the objection that his rights are contractual and as yet give him no financial interest in the fund. But if, as we have been arguing, the fund is a true trust and the employer is the trustee, there would be a measure of protection available to the prospective pensioner. The basis for a suit by him to protect his interests before retirement would lie in the contention that the fund is really held in trust for the employees although their rights to payments have not fully matured. The further merits of the argument that pension funds belong to the employees will be examined later in this chapter.

DEFECTS IN MANAGEMENT OF FUNDS

Thus far we have been examining the structure of pension plans to show how well or poorly they provide for the security of the worker. Of equal importance is the actual day-to-day functioning of the pension system under the direction of its managers.

Dishonest management has, in the case of some union funds, actually looted the fund under its control. Among other irregularities in management that have been uncovered are payment of excessive premiums to insurance representatives, abdication of responsibility for administration of the fund by employers in favor of unions, and, as disclosed in the course of the recent Senate investigation, some very dubious self-serving investments of pension funds by employers. These examples of doubtful or dishonest practice, when compared with the total picture, are relatively few in number and, though in individual instances the sums involved are large, they do not affect the pension movement as a whole. Still, for the defrauded workers they are tremendously significant and the cases of fraud that have been brought to light have generated so much publicity that legislation has recently been enacted by Congress to protect pension reserves from exploitation.

More pertinent to the subject of this study, however, are other defects in the management of pension funds which are not the result of dishonest practices but are much more widespread and difficult to cure. These defects stem from a lack of application of what is required to set up a stable and equitable pension system.

One of these inadequacies has to do with funding. About 6 per cent of all pension plans are unfunded and it is safe to say that a good many more are not yet adequately funded. This is a serious defect because as a pension plan matures, the expenses involved begin to rise very sharply and there is great danger that an unfunded or pay-as-you-go plan will not be able to meet its obligations. It is probably too much to require that no pension plan may be set up without funding, but once a plan is funded its reserves ought to be permanently out of the reach of the employer. If a plan is not funded, the law should rigidly require that the employees be told of the extremely contingent nature of their pension expectation.

The lack of information available to employees can be laid at the door of fund managers. This should be remedied. The management of a fund which takes the welfare of the beneficiaries seriously to heart cannot, in fairness, leave them in ignorance of the true nature of their pension rights.

Another serious defect of the system is that the employee seldom has representation in the management of the fund. The basic thinking of employers about pension funds has not yet grown up to the idea that these assets in fact belong to the employees and that they are therefore entitled to some voice in the management of the funds. This defect should not be laid wholly at the door of management, however, since the unions may be criticized for not pressing hard enough for such representation. True, in many statements of union policy employee representation has been declared an objective, but as yet no concerted effort has been made in this direction.

LEGISLATIVE REMEDIES

These, then, are the principal defects from the point of view of the security provided by pension funds. Our next step will be to analyze recent legislation designed to remedy some of these defects.

The present federal law governing welfare and pension plans was enacted on August 28, 1958.[1] This law had a respectable history in Congress beginning in 1954 with the formation of a subcommittee of the Senate Committee on Labor and Public Welfare which undertook studies and investigations under the chairmanship of Senator Irving M. Ives of New York.[2] Though this subcommittee on welfare and pension funds studied the over-all characteristics of private employee benefit plans, it restricted its field investigations to collectively bargained, jointly administered welfare funds, uncovering such abuses as mismanagement and waste in the administration of a number of plans. In its report of January 10, 1955 the committee recommended a federal disclosure act embracing all types of plans to insure protection of beneficiaries' rights and interests. The committee further recommended continuation and extension of the investigation.

In the 84th Congress the study was continued under the chairmanship of Senator Paul H. Douglas.[3] After hearings in March and April of 1955 a second interim report was issued in July of that year, dealing primarily with abuses in the Laundry Workers Union. It disclosed embezzlement, exorbitant commissions, improper service fees, and other irregular insurance practices, and collusion and complicity among insurance, union, and employer representatives. The committee also cited abuses in the painters, cleaners and caulkers fund as examples of the ease with which an employee benefit fund can be plundered where there is no public information available concerning the conduct and administration of the plan.

The scope of the inquiry was then enlarged to include pension plans, unilaterally administered welfare plans, insurance company practices, industry-wide plans, and other types of employee security programs. During the latter part of 1955 state laws were examined and state and federal agency authorities were interviewed to determine how much protection was given to employee benefit plans. The final report of this

---

[1] 72 Stat. 997 (1958), 29 U. S. C. 301–309 (1952).
[2] S. Res. 225, as amended, 83d Cong., 2d sess., May 1954.
[3] S. Res. 40, 84th Cong., 1st sess., February 5, 1955.

committee recommended a federal disclosure act covering all types of employee welfare plans.[4]

During the 85th Congress no less than twenty-seven bills were introduced for the purpose of providing federal legislation to protect employee benefit plans. A subcommittee of the Senate Committee on Labor and Public Welfare examined the various bills and heard testimony from executive agencies, management, insurance and banking representatives, trade union representatives, actuaries and others, after which it reported a bill, S. 2888, to the full committee.

In the meantime the House of Representatives had been busy with its own investigation. The Committee on Education and Labor established a special subcommittee to study pending proposals for legislation on employee benefit plans, which at that time numbered no less than twenty-one in the House alone. The full committee finally recommended passage of H.R. 13507 on July 28, 1958.[5]

A joint conference on the two bills resulted in the recommendation that the amended S. 2888 be passed by both houses. The resulting Welfare and Pension Plans Disclosure Act is the present law with which we have to deal.

Welfare and Pension Plans Disclosure Act

The purpose and scope of this act is announced in Section 2 to be:

to protect interstate commerce in the interests of participants in employee welfare and pension benefit plans and their beneficiaries, by requiring the disclosure and reporting to participants and beneficiaries of financial and other information with respect thereto.

The definitions of terms in Section 3 of the act make it clear that every type of plan is to be included whether established by an employer or employee organization, or by both. After dealing with welfare benefit plans the act defines an "employee pension benefit plan" as "any plan, fund, or program which is *communicated* or its benefits described *in writing* to the employees" and which is established "for the purpose of providing for its participants or their beneficiaries, . . . retirement benefits, and includes any profit sharing plan which provides benefits at or after retirement."

[4] Senate Report No. 1734, 84th Cong., 2d sess., 1956.
[5] House Report No. 2283, 85th Cong., 2d sess., 1958.

Coverage

The act applies to any employee welfare or pension benefit plan if it is established or maintained by any employee organization or by employers engaging in commerce or in any industry or activity affecting commerce, or by both. This section also exempts (1) plans administered by the federal or state governments or by a political subdivision of either, (2) plans which were established only for the purpose of complying with workmen's compensation or unemployment compensation laws, and (3) plans which are exempt from taxation under Section 501(a) of the Internal Revenue Code of 1954 and are administered as a corollary to membership in a fraternal benefit society described in Section 501 (c)(8) of the Code or by organizations described in Section 501(c)(3) and 501(c)(4) of the code, or (4) plans covering not more than twenty-five employees.

Disclosure and Reporting

The duty of disclosure falls upon the administrators of the employee welfare benefit plans and pension plans, and they are required to publish, sign and swear to a description of the plan. They must also submit an annual financial report.

Sections 6 and 7 of the act prescribe what information is to be published, as follows:

(1) The names and addresses of the administrators, their official position with respect to the plan and their relationship to the employer or to any employee organizations and any other offices or employment held by them.

(2) The name, address and description of the plan and the type of administration.

(3) The schedule of benefits.

(4) The names, titles and addresses of any trustee or trustees.

(5) Whether the plan is mentioned in a collective bargaining agreement.

(6) Copies of the plan or of the bargaining agreement, trust agreement, contract or other instrument under which the plan was established and is operated.

(7) The source of the financing of the plan and the identity of any organizations through which benefits are provided.

(8) Whether the records of the plan are kept on a calendar-year basis or on a policy or other fiscal-year basis and if on the latter basis the date of the end of such policy or fiscal year.

(9) The procedures to be followed in presenting claims for benefits under

the plan and the remedies available under the plan for the redress of claims which are denied in whole or in part.

(10) Amendments to the plan reflecting changes in the data and information included in the original plan, other than data and information also required to be included in annual reports.

Section 7 of the act requires the administrator to publish an annual report with respect to his plan within 120 days after the end of the calendar year or within the same period after the end of the fiscal year. The prescriptions for this report are very comprehensive. They include the amounts contributed by employer and employees, benefits paid, number of employees covered, a summary statement of assets, liabilities, receipts and disbursements of the plan, and a detailed statement of the salaries and fees and commissions charged to the plan, to whom paid and for what purposes. The information required by this section must be sworn to by the administrator or certified by an independent certified or licensed public accountant. There are special requirements for information if the plan provides benefits through the services of an insurance carrier.

If the plan is funded through the medium of a trust, the report must include:

(1) The type and basis of funding, actuarial assumptions used, the amount of current and past service liabilities, and the number of employees, both retired and nonretired, covered by the plan.

(2) A summary statement showing the assets of the fund broken down by type.

(3) A detailed list, including information as to cost, present value, and percentage of total fund, of all investments in securities or properties of the employer or employee organizations, or of any other party in interest such as officers, trustees or employees of the fund. With respect to securities listed on an exchange subject to regulation by the Securities and Exchange Commission or securities registered under the Investment Company Act of 1940 or those registered under the Public Utility Holding Company Act of 1935, the identity of securities, brokerage fees and commissions need not be revealed, but the totals of the respective investments in common stock, preferred stock, bonds and debentures must be listed at their aggregate cost or present value, whichever is lower.

(4) Further, the administrator must give a detailed list of all loans made to the employer, employee organization, or other party in interest by reason of being an officer, trustee or employee of the fund, including the terms and conditions of the loan and the name and address of the borrower.

(5) In cases where the plan is funded through a trust invested in whole or in part in one or more insurance annuity contracts with an insurance carrier, the report need only include the type and basis of funding, actuarial assumptions used in determining contract payments, the number of employees, both retired and nonretired, covered by the contract and, except for benefits completely guaranteed by the carrier, the amount of current and past service liabilities based on those assumptions, and the amount of all reserves accumulated under the plan. The same information is required for plans funded through a contract with an insurance carrier.

(6) In the case of unfunded plans, the report must include total benefits paid to retired employees for the last five years, broken down by year.

Publication

Section 8 of the act provides that the above information (including all amendments or modifications thereto upon their effective date) and the latest annual report shall be made available to any fund participant or beneficiary at the principal office of the plan. Copies of the description of the plan, its amendments and modifications, and a summary of the latest annual report must be mailed to any participant or beneficiary of a plan upon written request. Two copies of the description of the plan and the annual report must be filed with the Secretary of Labor and he is to make these documents available in the Public Document Room of the Department of Labor.

Enforcement

Section 9 of the act contains the provisions for its enforcement and imposes a penalty of $1,000, or imprisonment for not more than six months, for failure to comply with the law. Furthermore, any administrator who fails to supply a beneficiary or participant with the information required under the act within thirty days may in the discretion of a court become liable for damages in the amount of $50 a day from the date of such failure or refusal. The district courts of the United States are given jurisdiction, and falsification of the reports is subject to the usual penalties (five years imprisonment or a $5,000 fine, or both) under federal law.[6]

Section 10 exempts administrators from any requirement to supply information required under the act to any agency of a state other than the agency of the state in which such plan has its principal office, if copies

---

[6] 18 U. S. C. A. § 1001 (1952).

of the plan and annual report are on file with the agency of the home state. However, any state may obtain such *additional* information as it may desire relating to any plan or may regulate the plan in any other way. Finally, the provisions of this act cannot be construed to exempt or relieve any person from liability resulting from other laws of the United States or any state affecting the administration or operation of employee welfare or pension benefit plans.

Evaluation of the Legislation

The merits and defects of this legislation may be considered under two heads: first, does it provide machinery to accomplish what it sets out to do? and, second, does it go far enough in dealing with the problems presented by the pension funds?

With regard to the first point, that is, the adequacy of disclosure requirements, one great merit of the legislation is that it embraces all types of plans. In this feature it is superior to the bill introduced by Senator Gordon Allott, which excluded coverage of pension plans established on the basis of a fixed level of benefits, and to the bill introduced by Senator Barry Goldwater, which would have included only the Taft-Hartley type of plan.[7] There appears to be no valid reason why any type of pension or welfare plan should be excluded from disclosure requirements, since all of them present similar opportunities for unscrupulous exploitation.

While the present legislation will provide information as to the total amounts of stock which the pension funds have purchased, there is nothing in the required information which will indicate to what degree a pension trust may be buying control of a corporation other than that of the employer. The bill proposed by Senator Allott in the 85th Congress contained a provision that would be useful here. It required a detailed listing of all securities (except those of the United States) the cost of which exceeded 5 per cent of the fund or 10 per cent of the outstanding securities or obligations of any one issue.

The new law has also been criticized for not requiring a uniform system of reporting. The requirements of the act with regard to the manner of reporting are so broad that participants and beneficiaries of benefit plans could easily be kept in ignorance of the true nature of their pension program. This could be done simply by overwhelming them with a mass of

---

[7] S. 2137, 85th Cong., 1st sess., May 22, 1957 (Allott bill); S. 1813, 85th Cong., 1st sess., April 8, 1957 (Goldwater bill).

complicated and technical information which would hamper them in determining their rights. A uniform and simple form of reporting may be too much to ask at the moment, but such a system of reporting should be the first objective of the studies that can now be made with the information to be supplied to the Secretary of Labor.

A uniform and simple system of reporting would be of great advantage from an administrative point of view as well. Secretary of Labor Mitchell gave the Senate Subcommittee on Welfare and Pension Fund Legislation what he said was a conservative estimate of 250,000 plans which would be required to register if no exemption for smaller plans was made. On this basis the Secretary estimated that his Department would have to employ one person for every 600 plans and in succeeding years one person for every 850 plans.[8] However, the statute does contain an exemption for plans covering less than 25 employees. Data gathered from the 1954 experience of four of the largest life insurance companies indicated that 42.5 per cent of their group insurance policies included only 2.5 per cent of all the employees covered. These were small-sized plans covering less than 50 employees.[9] While such limited information makes it very difficult to estimate how many plans will register, it is quite possible that the Secretary of Labor, who is to get two copies of each plan and annual report, may receive anywhere from 800,000 to a million documents to file and examine.

Other criticisms leveled against the law are: that the penalty for failure to comply with the act is too small; that an employee who might sue an administrator for failure to supply him with requested information could be fired and so lose his right to recover; that state prosecutions for perjury under the act will be blocked by diversity of citizenship; that the language saying that the administrator *may* swear to the annual report provides an easy method of escape from responsibility; that there is vagueness in requirements like "a summary statement of assets, liabilities, receipts, and disbursements"; that the law does not require an independent audit; that the lack of a uniform method of reporting elaborated in cooperation with the states leaves administrators with an undue burden of providing different kinds of information.

In addition to these weaknesses in the new law in view of its announced purpose, there is reason to think that this legislation does not

[8] Senate Report No. 1440, 85th Cong., 2d sess. (Minority View of Senator Allott), U. S. *Code Congressional and Administrative News,* No. 15, p. 4850 (1958).
[9] *Ibid.* (Majority), p. 4832.

attempt enough. For example, it should include a provision to the effect that embezzlement of employee welfare or pension funds is a federal offense. One of the outstanding facts developed in the investigations of the congressional committees was the shocking amount of pension and welfare fund embezzlement which has gone unpunished. Furthermore, federal legislation on this point is needed: with so many of these funds operating in more than one state, it is difficult for state courts to establish jurisdiction.

Another feature that should be considered seriously for inclusion in legislation at this time is a provision similar to the regulations contained in the Federal Trust Indenture Act of 1939.[10] It would require that a pension or welfare trustee be free from conflicting interests and would guarantee the pensioner's right to sue individually. If the pensioner is a real party in interest in a pension program, there is no reason why he should not be able to reach the banker-trustee.

In conclusion we may say that while the present federal legislation is a step in the right direction, it is still a small advance in the face of the public outcry and demonstrable need for effective legislation. At the same time the federal legislators may be commended for their restraint in not pre-empting the entire field of state regulation of employee benefit funds.

THE TEST OF FREEDOM

Historically, the people of the United States have committed themselves to an economic system based on the private ownership of property. The reasons for this commitment lie in the belief that private ownership promotes individual freedom. Recently, enthusiastic proponents of pension and profit-sharing funds have been hailing them as instruments for creating a people's capitalism. By this they probably mean that the worker is given enough property to make him economically independent, that he is somehow a proprietor or an owner.

But it should be obvious from our discussion of the limitations in the security aspects of pension plans that the typical beneficiary is, in his present situation, neither a proprietor nor an owner. As pension plans are typically constituted, the worker during the period of his employment has no vested interest in the property being reserved for his future support. Further, it is highly doubtful that he could go to court to pro-

---

[10] 53 Stat. 1149, 15 U. S. C. § 77aaa-77ooo (1952).

tect his expectancy. And, moreover, he enjoys none of the prerogatives of management and direction that usually pertain to ownership or proprietorship.

Restrictions on Freedom of Action

There are still other ways in which the pension system limits the employee's independence. During his working life he may enjoy his hope for a pension only so long as he keeps his job. He may be dismissed or he may be forced to seek other employment. His freedom to change employers is usually curtailed by the loss of pension rights which such a change entails. With regard to the management of his own affairs, the employee is not asked whether he wants to save or not, or how much he wishes to save. Neither is he free to choose the form his savings will take. He cannot invest the capital that is reserved for him in a home, in a business of his own, or even in life insurance.

As the employee grows older, another sanction is placed upon leaving his job. Owing to the fact that an employee cannot take his pension credits with him when he leaves his job, the pension system is creating a class of unemployables. Workers 45 and over are finding it more difficult to get new jobs because it is, of course, more expensive to initiate a program of full pension benefits for them. All the evidence available tends to show that where pension plans exist labor turnover has decreased. Certainly a lowered rate of labor turnover has its good aspects, but when these are the result of coercion felt over the prospect of losing one's pension, it may be argued that stability is purchased at too high a price.

Thus pension funds operate to reduce an employee's freedom during his working life. Can the same be said of his years of retirement? Certainly a measure of freedom is gained from the monthly benefit check, but it is still freedom of a limited order.

In the first place, the pension reserves accumulated to support the retiree are not like savings. The pensioner has no control over the principal, no share in its management, and he can draw upon it only to the extent of his monthly check. Furthermore, his pension is still subject to the power of the employer, or the employer and the union, to amend or terminate the plan. How free, then, can he be in the use of such other savings as he has accumulated if he knows his pension may be reduced?

Also, when we consider such restrictions commonly placed upon the continuous receipt of pension payments as the prohibition against reemployment, we must conclude that these are an unfair extension of the right of an employer to control the activities of his former employees.

Finally, the pattern of pension fund investment (about 82 per cent in corporate securities), together with the almost universal limitation of fund liabilities to the sums actually in the fund, makes the pensioner dependent upon the current level of economic prosperity. An adequately funded pension plan is well insulated against ordinary business fluctuations, but in the event of a major and prolonged depression these funds might fall into serious difficulties.

These are criticisms, to be sure, but they are not intended as a condemnation of the entire pension movement. Indeed, the means are available to remedy many of the present defects. It is probably true that security cannot be purchased without some payment in the coin of freedom, but this does not justify the practices we have criticized. The introduction of full vesting would, at a stroke, remove many of the objectionable features of pension funds.

THE PROBLEM OF OWNERSHIP

A further analysis of the criticisms we have outlined will point up certain basic conceptions about the nature of pension trusts which are the source of their present defects. The early concept that pensions are gratuities explains why we do not find in the pension system more guarantees of the beneficiary's rights. Obviously, if the pension *is* a gratuity, there is no reason why an employer should not surround his gift with any conditions he chooses.

But the pension system has undergone such radical changes since the turn of the century that employee benefits can no longer be called gifts. As a result of these changes, there are powerful arguments for saying that the assets of pension funds rightfully belong to the employees.

The Plan as a Contract

A good case can be made that the employee provides valid consideration in return for the promise of a pension. The advantages accruing to an employer from a long and continuous service are considerable. This point becomes important when the pension changes from an occasional act of largess into a permanent policy. When an employer institutionalizes his pension "gifts" he really holds out an offer of reward; and when an employee relies on that offer and remains in the service of a company for a long period of years because of a consistent pension policy, this constitutes a contract which cannot be changed by labeling the pension a "gratuity which creates no rights." To say otherwise would be to allow an employer all the advantages of a firm contract offer with none of the responsibilities that result from its acceptance. This argument has force even when applied to one employer. It has much more force when pensions cover up to one-fourth of the working population.

Pensions as Deferred Wages

A second argument favoring the employees' right to ownership of pension funds is that the courts have declared that pensions are wages for purposes of collective bargaining. True, what may be wages in one context may not be in another: for example, disputes have arisen over whether a pension is a wage for purposes of bankruptcy proceedings.[11] But pensions have been declared by the courts to be wages in the context of discriminatory discharge, social security and taxation.[12] The Supreme Court in the case of *U. S.* v. *Carter* has recently declared pension contributions to be "part of the compensation for the work to be done by . . . employees."[13] This suit was brought on the basis of the Miller Act, which requires a bond for the protection of persons supplying labor for the construction of federal public buildings.[14] The trustees of a pension fund successfully sued the surety on a contractor's bond because the contractor had not paid contributions to a pension fund before going into bankruptcy.

To say that pension fund assets belong to the employees is a step the courts have not yet taken. It is, however, a logical step to take on the premise that pensions are actually wages. Further proof of this may be adduced from what often occurs in the negotiation of a collective bargaining agreement. A group of employees will take a pension plan or an increase in pension benefits in lieu of immediate wage increases. There can be no question in such cases that pensions are actually a deferred wage or a kind of compulsory savings system. There can be no question either that both employers and employees regard pensions as a form of compensation for service.

---

[11] "Union Retirement and Welfare Plans: Employer Contributions as 'Wages' under Section 64a(2) of the Bankruptcy Act," Note, 66 Yale L. J. 449.

[12] See Chapter 6.

[13] U. S. for the Benefit and on Behalf of Harry Sherman v. D. G. Carter, 353 U. S. 210, 217 (1957).

[14] 49 Stat. 793, 40 U. S. C. A. 270a(1, 2), 270(b) (1952).

The Trust Indenture

A third argument may be drawn from the form pension funds have taken. The typical pension trust indenture states that the funds in trust are irrevocably dedicated to the benefit of the members of the pension plan. Thus the funds have left the ownership of the employer as effectively as if they had been put into the pay envelopes of the employees. The trust form has been adopted for these funds precisely for the purpose of reserving them solely for the employees. If the pension funds do not belong to the employees, to whom can they belong?

Implications of the Federal Tax Policy

Still another argument may be drawn from the tax policy of the federal government. The pension movement gained its greatest impetus from the privileges of deduction and exemption granted to pension funds. But the purpose of this legislation is clearly to benefit the employees, not the employers. A very large amount of the assets that make up pension funds are there because the federal government by its tax policy intends them to be put to the service of employees. Indeed, placing the funds beyond the recall of the employer is one of the primary requisites for tax privileges. We can argue, then, that if the employers accept the privileges, they ought to align themselves with the policy underlying them.

Social Advantages of Employee Ownership

Finally, great social advantages may be derived from treating pension funds as the property of the pensioners. A property interest in the pension fund would return to the worker some of the economic independence which the pension system has taken from him. As acknowledged owners, employees would be given some share in the direction and control of the pension funds. This would mean that they should have some voice in the investment of these assets and an effective say in such matters as amendment and termination of the plan. A voice in investment policy would allow the employees to help direct fund investment into channels beneficial to them, such as housing and savings and loan activities. Furthermore, if the employees are considered the owners there is no justification for restricting a pensioner's activities after retirement.

A policy such as we have outlined will offset the tendency to limit economic freedom of action inherent in the very nature of the pension system.

The basic policy behind pension funds is now in a state of transition. The movement is too large and too various in its manifestations to enable anyone to say as yet what the underlying policy actually is. This much, however, may be said for certain: pensions are no longer gratuities, although they are not yet considered the property of the employees. The vital question at the moment is, therefore: To whom do they belong? They cannot be said in any proper sense to be "owned" by either the employer or the employee. In fact no one actually "owns" them, although at the present time many of the prerogatives of ownership are being exercised by pension fund managers and financial institutions. The impact of managerial control of the property of the pension trust is the subject of the next chapter.

THE PARAPROPRIETAL SOCIETY

The Great Domains

Modern Parallels

The Transition

Beyond Property: The Paraproprietal Society

The peculiar nature of the pension trusts and the existence of similar financial institutions suggest that the twentieth century man is subject to the impact of newly emerging social forces. The nucleus of rights which we call property has undergone a process of fission resulting in new forms of power over men. If we are to understand what is occurring, we shall have to formulate new or enlarged concepts to explain the relationships that are coming to be. It will be difficult to come by a conceptual framework that is sufficiently original to match a radically changing social order, closely enmeshed as we are in the working schemes of our day. Still, ours is not the only age which has had to meet the problems of property and it may be that by turning our search for a concept back to a remote age with a well-defined system of rights and powers we will gain the perspective we need. There are striking parallels between the kind of structure we are evolving and the development of medieval society. Since the feudal system began with a separation of control from the ownership of productive property, one of the salient features of our own society, the parallels between its institutions and ours cannot fail to be instructive.

THE GREAT DOMAINS

In the early part of the eighth century Charles Martel was faced with the problem of creating a force sufficient to withstand the waves of Moslems invading southern France. The Frankish soldier was a redoubtable adversary, but he fought on foot encumbered with heavy armor, sword and shield, and could easily be outmaneuvered in battle by the lightly garbed Moslem on his swift Arabian steed. The problem was to meet the darting cavalry of the invader with a force that could match the Moslems in mobility and preserve the Frankish superiority in armor. The solution achieved by Charles was to affect the economic and social organization of Europe for centuries to come.

The device that military shrewdness dictated was to mount the Frankish yeomen on armored horses. But horse and armor and absence from his glebe during the planting season were things far beyond the means of the Frankish soldier. Martel met this problem by conscripting the lands of the churches and apportioning them among his fighting men in parcels large enough to support armored troops of horse in the field whenever they should be needed. Thus the church lands passed into the hands of a newly created military class, who undertook to defend the church's title to the land against all comers, to appear ready for battle when the lord should call and to protect the serfs attached to the land.

In time the owners of the great estates perceived the value of this use of landed wealth which was entirely in the interest of the grantor who turned over control of his lands to others "on condition that the concessionaire served him, not only with his own person, but with a number of vassals in proportion to the importance of the benefice conceded."[1] Thus did the system become so universal that these domains became the centers of the economic and political life of the times. The society was agricultural and for those who resided within the domain there was no advantage in going outside the lands of their lords. In the absence of trade, the cities as centers of manufacturing died out and the domains of the rising nobility became sufficient unto themselves. There was no such thing as profit since a man could not sell his product if he produced more

[1] Henri Pirenne, *Mohammed and Charlemagne,* Meridian, New York, 1957, p. 272, quoting P. Guilhiermoz, *Essai sur l'origine de la noblesse en France au Moyen Age,* 1902, p. 123.

than he required to feed and clothe himself. In a nonmercantile society the domain was a social institution, not an enterprise, and men were bound to the land as hereditary tenants. Of the great domains Henri Pirenne says:

It must not be supposed that those who were subject to this servitude felt it as a burden . . . it was so completely adapted to their condition of hereditary tenants under the protection of a powerful lord that they regarded it as their natural state and submitted to it of their own free will. It was a necessary result of the domainal organization: the inevitable juridical consequence. How could liberty be valued by men whose very existence was guaranteed only by the place they occupied on the land, and under the jurisdiction of their seigneur, and whose security therefore was all the greater in proportion as they were more intimately incorporated in the domain?[2]

MODERN PARALLELS

At first sight it would appear that no social system could be more diametrically opposed to the one in which we are now living than the system of the great domains. But if we consider certain aspects of this system of property organization we discover some intriguing parallels to the modern relationship of men to property.

Profits

Let us consider first the aspect in which the domainal system appears to be most opposed to twentieth century capitalism. In the great domains there was no such thing as production for profit. The profit motive has traditionally been thought of as the mainspring of the capitalist system. It may have been so during the period of the early growth of capitalism and to some extent it is today, but the typical modern American is a salaried employee or a wage earner. At most ten million Americans, as stockowners, are interested or moved by the profit motive, and even for them profits are only a supplement to their primary source of income. To these we may add the small businessmen, steadily diminishing until they now make up only about 13 per cent of our working population. For most stockowners, profits are much more like rent.

The situation could hardly be otherwise when the corporation is populated, directed and managed by people who, by reason of their participation in the enterprise, do not therefore share in its profits. Even those

[2] Henri Pirenne, *A History of Europe*, Norton, New York, 1939, p. 101.

executives who hold substantial amounts of stock in their corporations regard themselves as managers, not proprietors. The interests of the managerial class are tied to the corporation itself, not to its profits. It is true that their tenure is dependent upon the successful production of profit, but profit is not the primary reward for which they work.

Independence

What is more, the corporation's first concern is with itself. The modern corporation has developed to a point where the annual profit record is not its principal goal: rather are the profits necessary means to something far more important, the continued healthy existence of the corporation.

Indeed the modern corporations are like the great domains in that they are the social institutions which give the dominant character to our society. The great names of American business fit this description to a surprising degree. General Motors, du Pont, U. S. Steel, Alcoa and General Electric employ our sons, fathers or brothers. Their research and innovations transform our lives, quietly with home appliances or dramatically with atomics and space flight, brashly with TV advertising or culturally with subsidies for education. A corporation can invest a billion dollars in "America's future" and create a climate of confidence or spread an air of pessimism by laying off thousands of workers. Corporations have built towns and destroyed them. Their decisions in these matters are perhaps never taken without regard to other social pressures, but then neither was the domain entirely independent of the crown, the church or popular feeling.

This brings us to perhaps the most critical consideration in our comparison between the domain and the corporation. A man's place in medieval society was determined by his place in the domain. Today men are bound to their corporations. A man's security is now all the greater in proportion as he is more intimately associated with the corporation. The role he plays in his corporation to a large extent determines his financial condition, his social status and, often enough, his politics.

Power over Property

Consideration of the legal structure which assigned the lord, the vassal and the tenant to their places in the great domain is very suggestive of the kind of relationship that may be growing up between men as the result of control of the wealth in the corporations. The vassal to whom Charles Martel gave land so that he could go to war did not own the land that served the needs of himself and his lord. The land still belonged to the church, which had only been deprived of control of the land. Similarly, the owners of the estates kept their titles, giving up only control of the use of their land. The tenure of the vassals under their lords was a kind of contract granting the use of productive wealth on condition of service. Thus, as long as the property could be handed down to male successors it would remain in the family of the vassal, because one of the conditions for holding the land was the ability to present oneself as a soldier for battle in the interests of the lord of the domain.

Perhaps the most suggestive feature of the domainal system is this fundamental concept of property tenure that lay behind it. Throughout feudal times the concept prevailed that property tenure in the noble class was conditioned upon the performance of a service. When the service terminated, the right of tenure terminated.

The parallel suggested here is that the present-day corporate managers are like the vassals of the great domains. They have control, but not ownership, of great wealth, yet their tenure in power is in fact limited by their continuing ability to perform a service. The service on which their tenure is dependent is not clearly defined by written contract (nor was it in feudal times). But there is, nevertheless, a certain standard of performance below which they cannot fall without incurring the wrath of the public and the displeasure of consumers.

Insofar as there are existing regulatory statutes governing the corporation and agencies with some supervisory powers over them, the conditions of tenure in power are, to an extent, spelled out. But insofar as they are the result of economic pressures, for example a buyers' boycott, the threat of antitrust action, the possibility of new legislation, the standards are rather vague and formless. As time goes on the standards will doubtless become more and more crystallized. The rulers of the modern domains will know better what are the conditions of their tenure in power. At present there is great difficulty in determining whether or not they are in fact meeting a standard which justifies their continuance in power, and probably the rulers themselves are the ones who suffer the most from uncertainty about what is expected of them.

Power Follows Property

The vassals of the great domains were not property owners, but control over the land made them the rulers of the society in which they lived. In the course of years the seigneur on the continent and the lord of the manor in England exercised a true juridical power over the vassals who held land under him and the serfs who worked the soil.[3]

Observation of the function of property in society leads us to the conclusion that power does follow property, as has often been said, but the power really attaches to him who controls the use of property. The man who controls property is the man who gains power in the social sphere. He employs others; he creates wealth; upon him depends the functioning of the economic system. Rights of ownership are a source of power only so long as they are joined with the right to control the use of property. Therefore, if the right to use property be separated from ownership, as happened in the modern corporate system and the domainal system, power separates from ownership and goes to him who holds control.

A second conclusion follows immediately. The power which follows control of property gravitates to those who can use property. This is true because property has in it the capabilities of producing wealth and thereby of attracting men who will put themselves under the direction of one who can unite their energies and skills to material things in such a way as to produce something society values. Thus power follows the control of property by one who is able to make use of the property in order to perform a function. But this ability to perform a function is conditioned by the nature of the society which seeks the fruits of property.

The power that came to the rulers of the great domains resulted from their peculiar position with relation to the conditions of the times. The society was agricultural, therefore land was wealth. They controlled the land, therefore theirs was the power. When a mercantile society sprang up, the power ebbed from the lords of the domains and flowed into the coffers of the merchants. With the industrial revolution manufacturing dominated the interests of men and the corporations became the means for employing the wealth necessary for production. Again control of property created powers which now flowed into the domains of the corporate managers.

More careful scrutiny of the ebb and flow of the power that results from property control is instructive. We discover that where property holding is more widespread — divided up among many — there is less external limitation of the use which can be made of the power that follows property. But where property is concentrated and great power results,

[3] Marc Bloch, "The Rise of Dependent Cultivation of Seigniorial Institutions," Chapter 6 in J. H. Clapham and Eileen Power, *The Cambridge Economic History of Europe,* Cambridge University Press, Cambridge, 1941, p. 225.

a compensatory reaction occurs and property tenure is conditioned on the performing of a service.

This proposition is illustrated by a comparison of the Roman concept of property tenure with the feudal concept that prevailed in the domainal system. The ruling principle in Roman property organization was the concept of *dominium.* This concept

denotes full legal power over a corporeal thing, the right of the owner to use it, to take proceeds therefrom and to dispose of it freely. The owner's *plena potestas in re* (full power over a thing) is manifested by his faculty to do with it what he pleases and to exclude anyone from the use thereof unless the latter has acquired a specific right on it (a servitude, an usufruct) which he might obtain only with the owner's consent.[4]

The Roman public authority might impose limits to private ownership for the sake of public order, but the essence of property ownership in the Roman system consisted of this freedom to use property. The Roman estates were great and the land owners wealthy, but compared to the domainal system property ownership was fairly widespread in Roman times. As we have seen, the rights of property in feudal times coalesced into the great domains, but here property control was conditioned by a standard of service which had to be met in order to continue the property tenure.

The contrast between widespread and concentrated property holding and the concomitant rights over property is similar when we compare the property system of the nineteenth century with that of the modern corporate system. In England and America before the rise of the corporations property holding was fairly widespread and the essential notion behind property rights was that a man should be free to do with his property as he pleased. But when control of property coalesced in the corporation there evolved a set of limitations upon the use of power resulting from property control. The tendency of power to require its own limitation was remarked by Adolf Berle in *The 20th Century Capitalist Revolution* when he noted that respect for the rights of those who are subject to power is a necessary condition for the survival of authority.[5]

The "Laws" of Property

What has been said about property can now be summed up in a series

[4] Adolf Berger, *Encyclopedic Dictionary of Roman Law,* Transactions of the American Philosophical Society, New Series, Volume 43, Part II for 1953, p. 441.

[5] Adolf A. Berle, Jr., *The 20th Century Capitalist Revolution,* Harcourt, Brace, New York, 1954, p. 68.

of four propositions which will aid in our understanding of the new society that is evolving as a result of changing property tenure.

I. Power follows the control of property.

II. Control of property gravitates to those who can, by the use of property, perform a function valuable to society.

III. Where property holding (control) is more widely diffused there is less limitation of the use which can be made of the power that follows property.

IV. Where the control of property is concentrated and great power results, a compensatory reaction occurs and property tenure is conditioned on the performing of a service.

To these four relationships a corollary or fifth law may be added which follows from laws II and IV.

V. The limitation of the powers that emerge from control of property concentrations originates from the same causes that created the concentration of power.

The explanation of this lies in law II, namely, that control gravitates to those who can perform a function. The functions which the possessors of power perform are themselves limited. Any use of the powers beyond the scope of the function results in a loss of power because society will not support the use of power in areas where it is not justified by a legitimate function.[6] The meaning of these laws will become clearer as we apply them in our analysis of the impact of the new power upon society.

THE TRANSITION

We have shown earlier that the financial institutions and, most notably, the pension trusts are becoming new centers of power in our society. We are now prepared to explain why.

Control over property has gravitated to the managers of the financial institutions because they perform a function which is valuable to society. This function is to distribute among the generality of the people the wealth which the corporations are creating. What is wanted by society

---

[6] These "laws" of property are advanced as valid in the historical context discussed above. Whether they would be operative in a society like Soviet Russia, where economic and political forces cannot be juxtaposed, remains to be determined. Two possibilities remain to be explored: first, that even the monolithic state will have to bow to the laws of property or, second, that the propositions here enunciated are but limited applications of more general laws which define the limits of power whatever its form.

at the moment is economic security through widespread diffusion of the fruits of productive property among the many.

As gross inequality of income tends to disappear, the wealth of corporations could conceivably be parcelled out through greater diffusion of share ownership in the corporations, but this method has not found favor since it involves a risk which the person of small means is unprepared to take. But the financial institutions — the mutual funds, the insurance companies, the pension trusts and the trust departments of banks — stand ready to take the capital produced by individuals for reinvestment in the capitalistic system. These institutions operate on such a broad scale that the advantages of capital investment are realized with a minimum of risk. The rewards originally assigned to risk capital are now made available to the man who has little or no capital to risk. It is intriguing to realize that capitalism's children, the banks, the insurance companies and the mutual funds, are now rapidly socializing the wealth in the great domains of capitalism, the corporations.

Is It Capitalism?

The system of property tenure that is thus evolving is not socialism. Neither title nor control is lodged in the government. But even the few characteristics we have already noted make us wonder if the emerging system may be called capitalism. Certainly, much of the paraphernalia of capitalism remain. Corporate earnings are still called profits; stock investments, even the safest "blue chips" that have never missed a dividend, are still considered risk capital and rewarded accordingly.

Let us take the case for capitalism as stated with great authority by the very knowledgeable Committee for Economic Development. They say of our system: "Its outstanding economic characteristic is that risk and enterprise by the individual is encouraged, with 'profit' as the main incentive; and with 'loss' as a quick destroyer of any enterprise that society will not support."[7] After further discussion of our economy the Committee concludes: "As a generality this state of affairs might be described as decentralized economic initiative."[8]

Set in contrast to the picture of concentration among corporations roughly sketched in Chapter 2 and against recent figures on the sources of capital (about 22 per cent of the long-term capital requirements from

[7] Committee for Economic Development, *Economic Growth in the United States,* New York, 1958, p. 20.
[8] *Ibid.,* p. 21.

1947 to 1957 inclusive came from sources outside the corporations them-selves)[9] these statements are somewhat surprising. Whose capital is really being "risked"? Who is doing the risking, and how much risk is there? Corporate managers risk the capital of the corporations and finan-cial institutions risk the capital of their beneficiaries. But the institutions would be the first to deny that there is much risk involved. The important point is that true capitalists, that is, owners who actually risk their own money, are a very small minority in the present system.

There is no need to overstate the case; the figures are available and they speak for themselves. It would be untrue to say that capitalism has passed from the modern scene. Many of its elements are still present and operative, nearly all of its forms are giving good service; but genuine capitalism flourishes only in the area of small business, which is not the dominant characteristic of our system. It is much nearer the truth to say that our economic system is in a stage of transition. The mechanics of the transition and even the motive force have been provided by capital-ism itself.

The Motive

Capitalism, through the device of the corporation, produced great aggregations of wealth and as time went on a demand built up to dis-tribute this wealth more widely. Before the rise of the financial institu-tions the corporations did distribute the fruits of their industry in the form of the products and services they offered and the wages they paid; but more was wanted. People, impelled by a desire for greater security, wanted to share in the capital wealth itself. It is important to realize that the drive was to share in capital wealth, that is, *income-producing wealth,* and that the effect of financial institutions is to distribute this kind of wealth. The institutions purchase either shares in the corpora-tions or claims upon their assets. Thus, by participating in the activities of the financial institutions, the people are now becoming sharers in the income-producing powers of capital wealth.

Motivation is a strange thing; no doubt the desire for a share in capital wealth was sparked and fed by the rising wages that capitalism paid.

The Mechanics of Transition

Capitalism and its corporations must also be given the credit for creat-

---

[9] *U. S. Income and Output,* A Supplement to the *Survey of Current Business,* U. S. Department of Commerce, 1958, p. 12. Only about 6.6 per cent of the long-term capital requirements was derived from the sale of stocks.

ing enough wealth so that people generally could become sharers in the system. The build-up of sufficient wealth to make individuals sharers in the fruits of capital is accomplished in two ways. First, individuals themselves may accumulate enough wealth to contribute to insurance companies, mutual funds and trust funds. The second way is engineered by the corporations. They initiate pension funds or profit-sharing systems to which they themselves make the contributions for their employees.

What is done with this wealth when it is gathered is what causes the relocation of control over property and the power that goes with control. With the rise of the corporations, control of productive property was severed from ownership by the corporate device. Henceforth control was free to migrate since it was attached to shares of stock and, to some extent, to bonds,[10] which could be bought and sold. What made stocks and bonds desirable was that they represent shares in income-producing property. When the desire to share capital wealth grew great enough, bonds and stocks were a ready-made medium, and the financial institutions began to carry out the transaction. This they did by buying stocks and bonds to hold in trust for persons even of moderate means, but in doing so they could not help acquiring the control that goes with these shares of capital wealth.

This transition, then, makes the people sharers in capital wealth, but it also lodges control and power in financial institutions like the pension trusts. An analysis of the effects of this shift of property interests will demonstrate the new relationships that are growing up between the individual and the major institutions of our society.

The Migration of Power

The pension trust system results in making the worker's hope for the future a matter of contractual rights, a labor agreement, a pension plan, and an agreement between the plan administrators and the trustees of the funds. Employers, sometimes with and sometimes without the union, determine the conditions and terms of the employee's pension rights. The employer along with a corporate trustee manages the pension fund, controls investments, determines contributions and acts as property

[10] Bonds are evidences of debt secured by claims on capital assets. Bondholders share in capital wealth because the income that bonds produce is created by the employment of the capital investment they represent. Some measure of control attaches to bondholdings because corporate policy must be shaped in such a way as to keep its lines of credit open. It is more through the operation of the capitalistic system than by direct right to share in management that bondholders influence the direction of corporate policy.

owner, although he has forever divested himself of any right to the funds. The employee is thus very much dependent upon the continued solvency and good will of the employer and the ability of his union to continue negotiating a contract that will prevent the employer from diminishing pension rights.

Property rights of the pensioner in one of these funds are thus reduced to an absolute minimum. A thorough examination of the legal documents and court decisions controlling rights in pension funds reveals that while there are many persons who have a claim of interest upon them, there is no one who can properly be said to be an "owner" of these large accumulations of wealth.

Analysis of the arrangements surrounding the pension trusts shows that individual employers exercise great authority over the actual day-to-day determination of pension payments to their employees while financial authority is almost wholly turned over to a relatively small group of banks. It is a point of pride made by many managements that they in no sense control the investment of pension funds, the voting of stock or the placement of debt capital which the trustees manage. The net result is a large gain in economic power for the financial community.

Through its tax laws the federal government has had a strong influence on the present structure of the pension trusts. Other than this, the role of the government so far has been to stand by and let the pension funds grow in size and form as they would. But since the private pensioner is unable to look after his own interests in a pension trust, recent legislation has given the state and federal governments the role of protecting his interests. This has become necessary because the courts have not had time to match their thinking with the rapid growth of a new legal device. The result is that whatever private rights a pensioner may have in a trust fund, he has very little power or authority to bring influence to bear upon the managers of these trust funds. The rights of a pensioner will now be divided between union and government officials who will vindicate the pensioner's rights for him.

Every indication is that pension trusts will continue their accelerating rate of growth at least until 1970, at which time their capital accumulations will represent a greater proportion of the national wealth than they do at present. Since it is in the very nature of pension trusts to concentrate control of capital, the new alignments of power they have brought about are likely to be permanent features of our society.

Pension trusts are thus the product of the formative activity of corporations, bank-trustees, labor unions and the federal government. Control by the employees for whom these funds were created is nonexistent. The employee does not become independent by reason of a body of capital wealth gathered for his benefit, but through his dependence upon this wealth he has become subject to decisions which are made by others concerning his welfare. Capital reserves dedicated to an employee's future may work to free him from want, but they do not make him more independent. The employee gains economic security without corresponding economic power.

This is a situation which ought to interest anyone who is concerned with the economic freedom of the working man, but the build-up of property in the pension funds has a far wider impact on our society. The preceding analysis reveals that while there is no gain in economic power for the employee there is a considerable increase of power in the corporate employers, in the labor unions and in the financial trustees on the economic side, and in government on the political side. Power follows property and it does so inevitably. Thus power has come to those who control the concentrations of property that have been created to serve our workers.

For other classes of people similar concentrations of property are being created in the insurance companies, personal trust funds (often with the same trustees as the pension funds), mutual funds, etc. Power is following property into all of the financial institutions which purchase shares of capital wealth for their clients. The economic power that is growing in the institutions is being drawn, or shunted away, from the generality of the people. The growth of these new powers along with the powers already in the hands of the corporations is producing a society whose economic life is based on a structure of the powers that result from control of property. It is not a society organized by individual property ownership and diffused power. Property ownership is not the organizing principle; power is. This is the direction of the transition, to the paraproprietal society.

BEYOND PROPERTY:
THE PARAPROPRIETAL SOCIETY

If we look back at the self-employed enterpriser of an earlier era — the farmer, the cobbler, the baker, the tailor — at least as he has been ideally characterized, we see in him a man whose advantages in ownership might be described as independence. He could look to his fields or shop, his tools and his custom for the things that made up what he considered the good life. These tangible things, under a lock to which he held the key, were the source of his continued sustenance and determined his status in the community. He derived pleasure from their control and increase. They purchased his leisure and entertainment. They were his insurance in old age and the inheritance of his children. For all of these he looked to a unitary thing, his shop or fields combined with his skill, and of this one thing he was the master. Barring any public calamity they would provide him with all he needed and wanted in life.

Today's man has neither shop nor field, nor the satisfaction of work that puts his personal stamp on a product. He depends upon others to fix the time of his labor and his leisure. Protection for his old age comes from the government, the insurance company or the pension fund, and the inheritance he will leave his children is largely dependent upon the same institutions. As a result of his ties to these external sources of the good life he finds himself no longer independent. Where he was once master of a domain — small, perhaps, but his own and tangible — he now looks to a complex of contracts, equities and expectancies over which he has very little control. Though he enjoys comforts of which his forebears did not even dream, by their standards he would be considered poor. His tangible wealth is small, though his security may be great.

But nostalgic recall of bygone days is of service only because it shows us how differently our economic life is organized now. It is questionable how many men in an entire nation really knew the independence that property ownership could bring. Certainly the standard of living is higher in our country today than it has ever been for the generality of men. There is greater wealth and its fruits are more widely shared. It is even true, probably, that we have more possessory property holding now than ever before, but the kind of property that is so held, that is, nonproductive property, is not the kind of property that gives power and influence in society.

It is evident that the type of property interest that gives a man status and influence in the present society derives from the power to control productive wealth. But this power comes to a man through his position in a corporation or similar organization. Productive wealth has been made the property of institutions and so it is by gaining a position in relation to one of these institutions that a man gains the power and influence over others that control of productive wealth generates.

It cannot be denied that some power and influence still attaches to the man of great possessory wealth, but unless his wealth is turned to productive uses, he is rather respected than obeyed. Our society is not structured around this kind of authority.

Institutions that determine a man's relationship to productive property and to other men are the structuring elements of today's society insofar as it is given form by economic relationships. Thus we conclude that *a man's relationship to things — material wealth — no longer determines his place in society* (as it did in a strong proprietary system) *but his place in society now determines his relationship to things.* This is the consequence of the separation of control over property from individual ownership.

The name given to this new type of society, paraproprietal, is an attempt to express in a word the nature of its structure. Our society is called paraproprietal, or beyond property, because in it the connection between man and things, which is another way of saying property, is so attenuated that the fundamental function of property is not dominant, though it still serves a purpose. Certain things began to be called property in Western society because they "belonged" to a man, pertained to him in a special way, were "proper" to him. They were, in a sense, the extension of his personality. Thus the fundamental notion of property is intimately connected with the ideas of "own" and "ownership." But there is nothing personal about General Motors or the Metropolitan Life Insurance Company in this sense. "Mine" and "thine" have very little meaning when applied to them. Something that is owned by everyone is truly owned by no one. Ownership in connection with the modern institutional organization of wealth has very little of its former meaning.

Yet the concepts of the property system still have functions, and we have seen them at work as devices for transferring control over property when we examined the transition of control earlier in this chapter. We might describe the change that has taken place in just these terms. Where once the concepts of property served the function of attaching things to men, they now serve the function of assigning powers over things. The thing itself is not given to a man, power over it is. The objects exchanged in such a system are not the things themselves but powers over things. This is why we can say that our society has passed from a property system to a power system.

The Limits of Power

It is important to realize that though property concepts are now serving new functions, the basic laws of property we have derived from studying the ebb and flow of power that results from property will still be operative. The power system that is now emerging will still be controlled by these laws and the new vassals of the great domains would do well to take heed of them. If great power resides in these users of property, great things will be expected of them. Failure to use their powers in a way that meets the inevitable standard which conditions their tenure will result in a migration of property and power elsewhere. The paraproprietal society is a stage of transition, not yet completed.

Our great domains differ from those of the feudal age in that the grantors of power are the people themselves. These people may appear to be impotent beneath the powers of the rulers of the domains, but they have powers, economic and political, which can be brought to bear upon their vassals. Another great difference between our society and that of the feudal domains is that our domains exist alongside a well-organized political power centered in a strong government. Juridical power does not lie with the economic rulers. Thus the reserved powers of the new lords, the people, are considerably stronger. Their problem will be to keep the powers of their two vassals, the economic and political, separate and in balance.

Property and Men

One problem remains to be considered: the effect of the paraproprietal society on the men who live in it. In the present system of property tenure we have to look elsewhere for the benefits that once derived from the ownership of private property. These benefits stemmed from the fact that the property system challenged a man to acquire and manage property so that he could provide for himself and his family. The challenge was a great one, for he could acquire as much wealth as it lay in his power to create. In doing this a man was forced to develop his own person and to realize his native potentialities as fully as he could under the spur to bend the goods of this world to his service. Ideally, this system would produce a man of initiative and personal responsibility. But it had this limitation: of itself, the system would only produce a man who was concerned with the getting and making of material things.

Today, the resources to meet man's material needs, at least in the United States, are in much more abundant supply. What is more, these needs are being met without the exercise of the traditional freedom and responsibility that made the private property system so desirable. Is it possible that we have evolved a system that no longer requires the extension of personality formerly achieved by the individual employment of possessory property?

The problem that arises in the area of personality would seem to be connected with the notion of responsibility. Already we see demands upon our economic system which it may not be able to meet. In the past, when a man was a responsible proprietor, he was well acquainted with the limitations of the system and was unlikely to make demands which he could not wrest from the economy himself. Now that the great majority of individuals are, in a sense, the beneficiaries of the system but in no sense its operators, they may make demands which they do not and, indeed, cannot have any responsibility to provide for. Thus, popular pressure for wages, profits, security benefits and the like may grow far beyond the capacities of our economic system. It is very possible that the irresponsible claims that presently cause our inflationary spiral result from excluding the great majority of our people from any real participation in the control of productive property. It may well be that in meeting these challenges, in learning to live with a new system of social organization, we will recapture the initiative for creation of self that was the chief merit of the private property system.

There is a measure of control over the vassals of the corporate domains now; let us keep this and strengthen it, continuing to press for a system in which corporate management and the private individual will behave responsibly with regard to the common good. Along with this effort we should begin a new quest for possible areas of human fulfillment. Care and concern over material wealth will always be the task of every man to a greater or lesser degree and we cannot be indifferent to the alignment of powers over property. But it has become possible also to plan for an age when men stand on the accomplishments of the past, the conquest over feeding and clothing themselves, and look to a frontier to win in the world of the spirit. There is no reason why personality realization must be accomplished only in purely economic realms, even for the so-called common man. The spirit of every man is capable of indefinite development.

APPENDIX A

This pension plan and the supplemental agreement which follows are reproduced here by permission of the General Motors Corporation.

THE GENERAL MOTORS
HOURLY-RATE EMPLOYES
PENSION PLAN

ARTICLE I

ESTABLISHMENT OF THE PLAN

General Motors Corporation on behalf of itself and its Divisions and as agent for its directly or indirectly wholly-owned and substantially wholly-owned domestic subsidiaries will establish subject to the approval of its Board of Directors and its Stockholders, a pension fund either by a trust agreement with a trustee or trustees or by contract with an insurance company or insurance companies, or both, and with respect thereto shall make such payments or contributions as will be sufficient to maintain the fund on a sound actuarial basis as well as to pay expenses incident to the operation and management of the Plan.

ARTICLE II

ELIGIBILITY FOR RETIREMENT AND AMOUNT OF PENSIONS

Section 1. Normal Retirement

(a) (1) Any employe who on or after October 1, 1950 shall have attained the age of 65, shall have completed 10 or more years of credited service as provided in Article III and shall cease active service, shall be entitled to receive a pension.

(2) An employe separated from the Corporation's active employment because of quit, discharge or release on or after January 1, 1950 and prior to October 1, 1950, and who at the time of such separation had attained age 65 and had completed 10 or more years' credited service, shall be eligible on October 1, 1950 for a pension commencing October 1, 1950, in accordance with the provisions of this section.

(3) An employe on lay-off or approved Corporation leave of absence on October 1, 1950 and who on that date has 10 or more years of credited service and who has neither broken seniority nor returned to work at the date the employe reaches age 65, or October 1, 1950, whichever is later, shall be entitled to receive a pension as hereinafter provided in this section.

(b) The monthly pension payable to a pensioner who was retired pursuant to the provisions of Section 1(a) of this Article II with benefits payable commencing prior to September 1, 1958 shall be $2.35 for each year of credited service (without 30-year limitation), for any pension falling due for months commencing on or after September 1, 1958, provided that the minimum monthly pension payable to any such pensioner, including the Primary Insurance Benefit payable under the Federal Social Security Act as determined in Article IV, shall be $4 for each year of credited service to a maximum of 25 years.

The monthly pension payable to an employe who is retired pursuant to the provisions of Section 1(a) of this Article II with benefits payable commencing on or after September 1, 1958 shall be:

(1) $2.40 for each year of credited service accrued prior to January 1, 1958;

(2) $2.43 multiplied by credited service accrued in the year 1958; and

(3) $2.50 for each year of credited service accrued subsequent to December 31, 1958.

Section 2. Early Retirement

(a) On or after October 1, 1950, any employe who has attained age 60 but not age 65 and who has 10 or more years of credited service may retire at the option of the employe, or may be retired at the option of the Corporation or under mutually satisfactory conditions.

(b) (1) An employe retired at the option of the employe may at the election of such employe receive either

(i) a monthly pension commencing at age 65 determined in accordance with Section 1(b) of this Article II and based upon the credited service of the employe at the time of early retirement (without 30-year limitation) for any pension falling due for months commencing on or after June 1, 1955 or

(ii) a monthly pension commencing at time of early retirement in accordance with Section 1(b) of this Article II and based upon the credited service of the employe at the time of early retirement (without 30-year limitation) for any pension falling due for months commencing on or after June 1, 1955, such pension being reduced by 6/10 of 1 per cent for each complete calendar month by which such employe is under the age of 65 at the time of early retirement and assuming the continuation of the Social Security Act as in effect at that time.

(2) An employe retired at the option of the Corporation or under mutually satisfactory conditions pursuant to Section 2(a) above with benefits payable commencing prior to September 1, 1958 shall receive a monthly pension commencing at early retirement of $4.70 for each year of credited service (without

30-year limitation) for any pension falling due for months commencing on or after September 1, 1958.

The monthly pension payable to an employe retired at the option of the Corporation or under mutually satisfactory conditions pursuant to Section 2(a) above with benefits payable commencing on or after September 1, 1958 shall be:

(1) $4.80 for each year of credited service accrued prior to January 1, 1958;

(2) $4.86 multiplied by credited service accrued in the year 1958; and

(3) $5.00 for each year of credited service accrued subsequent to December 31, 1958.

(3) The monthly pension determined in (b) (1) (ii) above shall not be redetermined thereafter. The monthly pension determined in (b) (2) above shall be payable until age 65, or, if earlier, until the age at which the employe becomes eligible for a Primary Insurance Benefit. At such age a redetermination shall be made and the monthly pension thereafter paid shall be in accordance with Section 1(b) of this Article II. Such redetermined monthly pension shall not be reduced by the amount of the applicable Primary Insurance Benefit.

(c) An employe discharged for cause on or after October 1, 1950, after such employe has attained age 60 but before age 65 and has at least 10 years of credited service shall be entitled only to the benefits provided under Section 2(b)(1) of this Article II.

Section 3. Automatic Retirement

(a) An employe age 68 or older on January 1, 1952 shall be automatically retired on that date, and thereafter an employe will be automatically retired on the first day of the month following the 68th birthday of the employe.

(b) An employe who has not broken seniority on May 31, 1950 and who after October 1, 1950 reaches the automatic retirement date of subsection (a) above prior to September 1, 1958 with more than 5 but less than 10 years of credited service and retires, shall, notwithstanding the provisions of Article II, Section 1(a)(1), receive a monthly pension of $23.50 for any pension falling due for months commencing on or after September 1, 1958. If such employe reaches the automatic retirement date of subsection (a) above on or after September 1, 1958, he shall receive a monthly pension of $24.00 for any pension falling due for months commencing on or after September 1, 1958.

(c) An employe may remain actively employed after the automatic retirement age or date of subsection (a) above only with the approval and at the option of the Corporation. No service beyond age 68 shall be credited.

Section 4. Total and Permanent Disability Retirement

(a) An employe who subsequent to October 1, 1950 becomes totally and permanently disabled after the 50th birthday of the employe and prior to attaining age 65, and has at least 15 years of credited service, shall be eligible for a disability pension as hereinafter provided; except that the 50th birthday limitation shall not apply to any employe who is actively at work for the Corporation on or after June 1, 1955.

(b) An employe shall be deemed to be totally and permanently disabled when on the basis of medical evidence satisfactory to the Corporation the employe is found to be wholly and permanently prevented from engaging in any occupation or employment for wage or profit as a result of bodily injury or disease, either occupational or non-occupational in cause, but excluding disabilities resulting from service in the armed forces of any country.

(c) The monthly pension payable to such a disabled employe who was retired pursuant to the provisions of Section 4(a) of this Article II with benefits payable commencing prior to September 1, 1958 shall be $4.70 per month for each year of credited service to the date such disability commenced (without 30-year limitation) for any pension falling due for months commencing on or after September 1, 1958.

The monthly pension payable to such a disabled employe who is retired pursuant to the provisions of Section 4(a) of this Article II with benefits payable commencing on or after September 1, 1958 shall be:

(1) $4.80 for each year of credited service accrued prior to January 1, 1958;

(2) $4.86 multiplied by credited service accrued in the year 1958; and

(3) $5.00 for each year of credited service accrued subsequent to December 31, 1958.

Such pension shall be payable to the disability pensioner during the continuance of total and permanent disability in accordance with Article VII, Section 1, until the disability pensioner attains age 65, or, if earlier, until the age at which the disability pensioner becomes eligible for a Primary Insurance Benefit. At such age a redetermination shall be made and the monthly pension thereafter paid shall be in accordance with Section 1(b) of this Article II, based on service at the date of disability. Such redetermined monthly pension shall not be reduced by the amount of the applicable Primary Insurance Benefit. Any disability pension prior to such redetermination shall be subject to deductions as provided in Article IV.

(d) Any disability pensioner may be required to submit to medical examination at any time during retirement prior to age 65, but not more often than semi-annually, to determine whether the pensioner is eligible for continuance of the disability pension. If on the basis of such examination it is found that the pensioner is no longer disabled or if the pensioner engages in gainful employment, except for purposes of rehabilitation as determined by the Corporation, the pensioner's disability pension will cease. In the event the disability pensioner refuses to submit to medical examination the pension will be discontinued until the pensioner submits to examination.

Section 5. Employes Not Actively at Work

The absence of an employe from active work at the time such employe would be eligible to retire under the Plan shall not preclude the employe's retirement without return to active work, provided that such absence is due to lay-off, sick leave or other Corporation approved leave of absence commencing subsequent to October 1, 1950 and provided that there has been no loss of credited service.

ARTICLE III

CREDITED SERVICE

Section 1. Credited Service Prior to October 1, 1950

Credited service prior to October 1, 1950 shall be computed to the nearest 1/10 year and shall be the sum of:

(a) the number of years following the employe's plant seniority date on October 1, 1950 but preceding October 1, 1950, plus

(b) (1) any period or periods of active service as an hourly or salaried employe to any plant or Division of the Corporation preceding the employe's seniority date on October 1, 1950, provided that if there was an absence interval equal to two years or more between periods of active service with the Corporation beginning with the last day of active service in the period immediately preceding such interval, no service prior to such interval shall be counted, except this proviso shall not apply to any such interval commencing on or after January 1, 1930 and ending on or before June 1, 1934, plus

(2) any period of absence prior to October 1, 1950 under a lay-off or approved leave of absence immediately following any period of active service credited under Section 1(b)(1) of this Article provided

(i) the absence to be credited was less than one year, and

(ii) employe was on the roll in the plant for a period of at least six months prior to the first day of absence to be credited, and

(iii) employe returned to active service in the same plant immediately following the period of absence to be credited, and

(iv) it can be definitely established on the basis of records of the Corporation that the period of absence was not the result of a quit or discharge, plus

(c) any additional period or periods of service with a company acquired by the Corporation prior to October 1, 1950 in which company the Corporation had a stock interest at the time of acquisition of such company, computed on the same basis as set forth in 1(b) above, provided, however, that the period of service for which the employe may receive credit for service with such company shall not extend prior to the date on which the employe was hired by the acquired company or the date at which the Corporation acquired an interest in such company, whichever is later.

Section 2. Credited Service Subsequent to October 1, 1950

(a) (1) Credited service commencing with October 1, 1950, and thereafter, shall be computed for each calendar year for each employe on the basis of total hours compensated by any plant or Division of the Corporation during such calendar year while the employe has unbroken seniority and prior to the employe attaining age 68. Any calendar year in which the employe has 1700 or more compensated hours shall be counted a full calendar year. Where the employe's total hours compensated during a calendar year are less than 1700 hours, a proportionate credit shall be given to the nearest 1/10 of a year. For the calendar year 1950 no more than a year's credit will be given including credit for service prior to October 1, 1950.

(2) For the purpose of computing credited service, hours of pay at premium rate shall be computed as straight time hours.

(b) For the purpose of computing compensated hours under subsection (a) of this Section 2, an employe who after October 1, 1950 shall be absent from work because of occupational injury or disease incurred in the course of such employe's employment with the Corporation, and on account of such absence receives Workmen's Compensation while on Corporation approved leave of absence shall be credited with the number of hours that the employe would have been scheduled to work during such absence, provided that no employe shall be credited with service under this subsection after retirement.

(c) Any salaried employe transferred to an hourly-rate job subsequent to October 1, 1950, who thereby becomes an employe covered by the Plan shall have credited to the nearest 1/10 year any credited service the employe had as of the date of such transfer under any Corporation retirement plan for salaried employes, provided that there shall be no duplication of credited service, nor credited service of more than one year in respect of any calendar year by virtue of this subsection.

(d) If an employe who retired or was retired under the Plan for reasons other than total and permanent disability is rehired, such employe shall not accumulate any additional credited service by reason of such reemployment.

(e) For the purpose of computing compensated hours under subsection (a) of this Section 2:

(1) An employe who after October 1, 1950 and prior to June 1, 1955 was absent from work because he entered into active service in the armed forces of the United States and who was given a Corporation approved leave of absence for such period shall be credited with the number of hours that the employe would have been scheduled to work during such absence.

(2) An employe, who on or after June 1, 1955 left or leaves work to enter into active service in the armed forces of the United States and for that reason was or is given a Corporation approved leave of absence, shall be credited with the number of hours while in service that he would have been scheduled to work during such leave; provided, however, that credited service based on such hours shall not exceed four years, or such longer period during which he has reemployment rights pursuant to any federal law, and provided, further, that the employe is reemployed in accordance with the terms of such leave of absence.

Section 3. Loss of Credited Service

(a) After October 1, 1950 an employe will lose all credited service for purposes of this Plan and, if reemployed, shall be considered a new employe for purposes of this Plan:

(1) if the employe quits,

(2) if the employe is discharged or released,

(3) if the employe's seniority is broken for any other reason; except that there shall be no loss of credited service for purposes of this Plan if seniority is lost as a result of transfer or reassignment of employment by the Corporation or where there is a change of employment within the Corporation resulting from acceptance of employment with a plant or Division of the Corporation while on lay-off from another and recall is refused and the plants or Divisions involved approve such change of employment.

(b) Any employe who breaks or has broken seniority on or after October 1, 1950 and thereby loses or has lost credited service under subsection (a) above and then is or was later reemployed by any plant or Division of the Corporation shall, upon making proper application, have such credited service reinstated provided the employe acquires or acquired seniority within 36 consecutive months following the last day the employe worked for the Corporation prior to the loss of credited service.

(c) Any employe retired under the total and permanent disability provisions of this Plan and who is subsequently reemployed by the Corporation and has seniority reinstated, will have credited service at the time of disability retirement reinstated.

ARTICLE IV

DEDUCTIONS ON ACCOUNT OF SOCIAL LEGISLATION

Section 1. Determination of Deductions for Federal Social Security Primary Insurance Benefits

(a) The Primary Insurance Benefits payable under the Federal Social Security Act, as amended, as now in effect, or as hereafter amended, which are referred to in the determination of pensions under Article II shall be included in such determination even though the employe either does not apply for, or loses part or all of such payments through delay in applying for them, by entering into covered employment, or otherwise.

(b) Old age benefit payments or disability benefit payments, other than those payable on a basis of "need" or because of military service, under any future federal legislation, amending, superseding, supplementing, or incorporating the Federal Social Security Act, as amended, or benefits provided therein, shall be considered as Primary Insurance Benefits under the Federal Social Security Act for the purposes of the Plan.

(c) If an employe is eligible for Primary Insurance Benefits at the time of retirement or thereafter, such employe shall provide the Corporation with evidence of the amount of the Primary Insurance Benefit which such employe would be eligible to receive. If the employe is not eligible to receive a Primary Insurance Benefit at the time of retirement the employe shall unless waived by the Corporation request the Social Security Administration (at least 30 days prior to retirement) to provide such data as may be necessary to estimate the Primary Insurance Benefit to which the employe might become entitled.

(d) In the event the Primary Insurance Benefit under the Federal Social Security Act, as amended, is changed by amendment, the Primary Insurance Benefit as changed by such amendment shall be used in redetermining the minimum benefit provided in Section 1 of Article II hereof.

(e) If the pension of a retired employe has commenced under the Plan, any change in the pensioner's Primary Insurance Benefit under the Federal Social Security Act, as amended, shall not be construed to cause a change in the amount of such pension except to the extent that such changes may be caused by a subsequent amendment to the Act.

Section 2. Deductions for Workmen's Compensation and Disability Benefits

(a) In determining the monthly pension benefits payable to any pensioner, a deduction shall be made unless waived by the Corporation or prohibited by law, equivalent to all or any part of any of the following benefits payable to such pensioner by reason of any law of the United States, or any political subdivision thereof, which has been or shall be enacted, provided that such deductions shall be to the extent that such benefits have been provided by premiums, taxes or other payments paid by or at the expense of the Corporation:

(1) Workmen's Compensation (except payments specifically allocated for hospitalization or medical expense, fixed statutory payments for the loss, or 100% loss of use, of any bodily member, payments for loss of industrial vision, or redemption awards payable prior to the date monthly pension benefits first become payable).

(2) Disability benefits.

(b) If the benefits deductible under subsection (a) are stated as a specified amount per week for a designated calendar period, then the monthly amount shall, for purposes of this Section 2, be 4 1/3 times such weekly amount. For any calendar month during which the amount of benefits deductible under subsection (a) when thus computed on a monthly basis exceeds the amount of the monthly pension benefit otherwise payable for that month, no monthly pension benefit shall be payable. For any calendar month in which the amount of benefits deductible under subsection (a) when computed on a monthly basis is less than the monthly pension benefit payable for that month, such lesser amount shall be deducted from the monthly pension payable for that month.

(c) Lump sum awards providing for the payment in advance of Workmen's Compensation benefits which are definitely allocable to specific weeks in a calendar period will be deducted on the same basis as if the award had been payable on a weekly basis.

(d) If the Workmen's Compensation is not allocable to any specific calendar period, including redemption awards payable subsequent to the date monthly pension benefits first become payable, then an equivalent monthly amount of such award shall be computed, for purposes of this Section 2, as 4 1/3 times the amount of the weekly Workmen's Compensation benefit provided by the applicable statute for the pensioner and the pensioner's dependents. The total Workmen's Compensation award shall be divided by such computed equivalent monthly amount to determine the number of months and fractions of months during which monthly pension benefits shall not be payable.

A R T I C L E   V

FINANCING

Section 1. Trust Fund

The Corporation shall execute a trust agreement with a trustee or trustees selected by the Corporation to manage and operate the pension fund and to receive, hold and disburse such contributions, interest and other income as may be necessary to pay such of the pensions or portions thereof under this Plan as are not provided for by an insured fund. The Corporation may establish an insured fund with such insurance company or companies as it may select for the payment of such of the pension or portions thereof under this Plan as are not provided for in a trusteed fund.

The Corporation will determine the form and terms of any such trust agreement which may authorize the inclusion of obligations and stock (common and preferred) of the Corporation and its wholly-owned subsidiaries among the investments of the pension fund provided for by such trust agreement; may modify any such trust agreement from time to time to accomplish the purposes of this Plan; may remove any trustee, and select any successor trustee; and select and change insurance companies.

Section 2. Contributions

(a) The Corporation, subject to Article IX, Section 1, shall make such contributions to the trustee or pay such premiums under any insured contract for the purposes of providing pensions under the Plan as shall be required under accepted actuarial principles to maintain the Plan and pension or insured fund in a sound condition and shall pay for expenses incident to the operation and management of the Plan.

(b) No employe shall be required to make any contributions to the Plan.

Section 3. Irrevocability

(a) The Corporation shall have no right, title or interest in the contributions made by it to the trustee and no part of the pension or insured fund shall revert to the Corporation, except that after satisfaction of all liabilities of the Plan as set forth in Article IX, such contributions as may have been made by the Corporation as the result of overpayments may revert to the Corporation.

(b) The pension benefits of the Plan shall be only such as can be provided by the assets of the pension fund or by any insured fund and there shall be no liability or obligation on the part of the Corporation to make any further contributions to the trustee or insurance company in event of termination of the Plan. No liability for the payment of pension benefits under the Plan shall be imposed upon the Corporation, the Officers, Directors or Stockholders of the Corporation.

A R T I C L E   V I

ADMINISTRATION

Section 1.

The Corporation shall be responsible for the general administration of the Plan and for carrying out the provisions thereof.

Section 2.

(a) The Corporation shall have all such powers as may be necessary to carry out the provisions of the Plan except as the powers and duties of the Corporation may be modified by any collective bargaining agreement.

(b) Subject to the limitations of (a) above, the Corporation may from time to time establish rules for the administration of the Plan and the transaction of the Plan's business.

(c) In making any such determination or rule, the Corporation shall pursue uniform policies and shall not discriminate in favor of, or against any employe or group of employes.

A R T I C L E   V I I

PENSION BENEFITS

Section 1. Pension Payments

(a) (1) Pensions shall be paid monthly.

(2) Until the Plan is approved by the Stockholders, the benefits payable shall be only those determined by the Plan as constituted prior to September 1, 1958 and upon approval by the Stockholders any excess of the amounts of pension, payable under the terms of this Plan, falling due for months commencing on or after September 1, 1958 over the amounts of pension actually paid or payable for such months shall become payable on or as of the first of the month following the date upon which the Plan is approved by the Stockholders.

(3) The first monthly payment of an employe's pension other than for total and permanent disability shall be on the first day of the month following the month in which the employe actually retires, and the pension shall be payable monthly thereafter.

(4) Total and permanent disability pensions shall be payable monthly during the continuance of such total and permanent disability and while the pensioner otherwise remains eligible for such benefits. Such payments shall begin the later of:

(i) the first day of the month following the date the required proof of such disability is received by the Corporation, or

(ii) the first day of the month which includes the date the employe has been continuously and totally disabled for a period of 6 months.

Successive periods of absence due to the same disability as that upon which claim for total and permanent disability pension is based and aggregating at least six months will be considered the same as one continuous absence provided that the aggregate will not include any period of such absences which precedes the last day at work by more than one year.

(5) Pension payments shall not commence until the cessation of any weekly sickness or accident benefits payable to the employe under any plan to which the Corporation has contributed. If such sickness and accident benefits during any month are payable for a period of less than 4 1/3 weeks the monthly pension benefit payable for that month shall be reduced by the percentage which such period of sickness and accident benefits is of 4 1/3 weeks.

(b) A pensioner who is reemployed by the Corporation shall continue to receive, during such reemployment, any monthly pension benefits to which the pensioner might otherwise be entitled. The pensioner shall not accrue any additional credited service as a result of such employment and the monthly pension benefits of such pensioner shall not be adjusted in any way with regard to such employment upon subsequent cessation of active service. The foregoing is not applicable to a disability pensioner who recovers and returns to work, provision for whom is made in Article II, Section 4(d) and Article III, Section 3(c).

(c) In the event that it shall be found that any pensioner to whom a pension is payable is unable to care for the affairs of such pensioner because of illness or accident any payment due (unless prior claim therefor shall have been made by a duly qualified guardian or other legal representative) may be paid to the spouse, parent, brother or sister or other person deemed by the Corporation to have incurred expense for such pensioner otherwise entitled to payment. Any such payment shall be a payment for the account of the pensioner and shall be a complete discharge of any liability of the Plan therefor.

Section 2. Retention of Deferred Pension if Separated

(a) Any employe who loses accumulated credited service under the provisions of Article III, Section 3 by breaking seniority on or after June 1, 1955 shall, if such employe then has attained age 40 but not age 60, be eligible for a pension commencing at age 65 provided the credited service of such employe at separation is at least 10 years.

(b) The monthly amount of such deferred pension for an employe separated prior to September 1, 1958 shall be $2.25 multiplied by the employe's credited service in effect at the time of such loss of credited service less any such service credited for any period prior to January 1 of the year in which the employe attains or attained age 30. The monthly amount of such deferred pension for an employe separated on or after September 1, 1958 shall be:

(1) $2.40 for each year of credited service accrued prior to January 1, 1958;

(2) $2.43 multiplied by credited service accrued in the year 1958; and

(3) $2.50 for each year of credited service accrued subsequent to December 31, 1958; provided, however, that no credited service shall be used in the above

calculation for any period prior to January 1 of the year in which the employe attains or attained age 30. The pension shall be payable the later of the first day of the month following the month (i) in which such employe attains age 65, or (ii) during which the plant from which such employe last separated from the Corporation receives a written request from such former employe. This written request must be filed with such plant not earlier than 60 days prior to his 65th birthday and not later than his 70th birthday, otherwise no deferred vested pension benefit shall be payable at any time.

(c) If an employe is reemployed by the Corporation after having qualified for a deferred pension in accordance with this Section 2, such employe shall, in lieu thereof, have reinstated the credited service in effect when such deferred pension was granted provided such employe qualified for such reinstatement under Section 3(b) of Article III; otherwise, such employe shall have reinstated only the credited service on which the deferred pension of such employe was based.

Section 3. Non-Alienation of Benefits

The pension fund shall not in any manner be liable for or subject to the debts or liability of any employe, separated employe, retired employe or pensioner. No right, benefit or pension at any time under the Plan shall be subject in any manner to alienation, sale, transfer, assignment, pledge or encumbrances of any kind. If any person shall attempt to, or shall, alienate, sell, transfer, assign, pledge or otherwise encumber accrued rights, benefits or pensions under the Plan or any part thereof, or if by reason of bankruptcy or other event happening at any time such benefits would otherwise be received or enjoyed by anyone else, the Corporation in its discretion may terminate the interest of such employe or pensioner in any such benefit and instruct the trustee to hold or apply it to or for the benefit of such employe or pensioner, his or her spouse, children or other dependents, or any of them as the Corporation may instruct; provided, however, that any pensioner who elects Blue Cross, Blue Shield, or equivalent coverage, made available under the General Motors Insurance Program for Hourly-Rate Employes (Exhibit B–1) may, insofar as it is consistent with the regulations governing the plans providing such coverage, participate in such coverage and have deducted from the monthly pension of such pensioner, pursuant to the pensioner's written authorization and direction acceptable to the Corporation, the required contribution for such coverage.

ARTICLE VIII

MISCELLANEOUS PROVISIONS

Section 1. No Enlargement of Employment Rights

The Corporation's rights to discipline or discharge employes shall not be affected by reason of any of the provisions of the Plan.

Section 2. Internal Revenue Service Approval

This Plan as amended is contingent upon and subject to obtaining and retaining such approval of the Commissioner of Internal Revenue as may be necessary to establish the deductibility for income tax purposes of any and all contributions made by the Corporation under this Plan as being qualified for tax exemption under the provisions of Sections 401, 404, and 501(a) or other applicable provisions of the Internal Revenue Code. Any modification or amendment of the Plan may be made retroactively, if necessary or appropriate, to qualify or maintain the Plan as a plan and trust meeting the requirements of Sections 401, 404, and 501(a) of the Internal Revenue Code, as now in effect or hereafter amended, or any other applicable provisions of the federal tax laws, as now in effect or hereafter amended or adopted, and the regulations issued thereunder.

Section 3. Corporation Board of Directors and Stockholders Approval

Continuation of the Plan as amended in 1958 is contingent upon obtaining the approval of the Corporation's Board of Directors and Stockholders not later than June 1, 1959.

ARTICLE IX

AMENDMENT AND TERMINATION

Section 1. Amendment

The Corporation reserves the right to amend, modify, suspend or terminate the Plan by action of its Board of Directors, provided, however, that no such action shall alter the Plan or its operation, except as may be required by the Internal Revenue Service for the purpose of meeting the conditions for qualification and tax deduction under Sections 401, 404, and 501(a) of the Internal Revenue Code, in respect of employes who are represented under a collective bargaining agreement in contravention of the provisions of any such agreement pertaining to pension benefits as long as any such agreement is in effect. Except as provided in Article V, Section 3, no such action shall operate to recapture for the Corporation any contributions previously made to the trustee or insurance company under the Plan, nor, except to the extent necessary to meet the requirements of the Internal Revenue Service or any other governmental authority, to affect adversely the pensions of employes already retired or the trust fund or insured fund then securing such pensions.

Section 2. Termination of Plan

If the Corporation terminates the Plan in accordance with Section 1 above any Corporation contributions made after such termination for the duration of any collective bargaining agreement shall be segregated by the trustee as a separate fund or funds for disposition as hereinafter provided. The amount of the trust fund assets otherwise held by the trustee shall be allocated, subject to provision for expenses of administration or liquidation, for the following pension purposes and in the following manner and order to the extent of the sufficiency of such assets:

(a) First, to provide the pensions for life to the persons who are pensioners under the Plan on its date of termination. The allocation of the amount for this purpose shall be based on immediate life annuity values without death benefit, as determined by the actuary of the Plan. Any reductions in such pensions revealed as necessary by the insufficiency of the trust fund assets at or after the date of termination of Plan shall be determined by the actuary in a uniform manner on the basis of similar annuity values.

(b) Second, if any such assets remain after complete allocation for the purposes of (a) above, to provide the pensions for life, to the extent possible, to the employes who (i) have reached their normal retirement date, or (ii) have been approved for disability pensions, but have not commenced to receive their pensions by the date of termination of the Plan. The allocation of the amounts, if any, for full or reduced pensions for such employes shall be on the basis of immediate life annuity values without death benefit in the same manner, with application for reduction of pensions, as in (a) above.

(c) Third, if any such assets remain, after complete allocation for the purposes of (a) and (b) above, they shall be allocated to the employes who were eligible to retire under the early retirement provisions of Article II, Section 2, on the date of termination of the Plan. The allocation of the amount for this purpose shall be computed on the early retirement pension to which they would have been entitled on such date if retired under Article II, Section 2(b)(1)(ii), and shall be based on immediate life annuity values without death benefit in the same manner, with application for reduction of pensions, as in (a) above.

(d) Fourth, if any such assets remain after the complete allocation for the purposes of (a), (b), and (c) above, they shall be allocated to employes who remain who have a pension interest because of credited service on the date of termination of the Plan, but not beyond the value of such interest, on a basis proportionate to the actuarial value of such interests of such employes. Within this group shall be included such separated employes with eligibility for deferred pensions under the provisions of Article VII, Section 2 as (i) make written inquiry regarding their interests within one year subsequent to the date of termination of the Plan, or (ii) respond within one year after the date of mailing of a registered letter which the Corporation or trustee shall direct to the last known address, on the records of the Corporation, of each such separated employe.

In addition to the allocation as of the date of the termination of the Plan, of the trust fund as set forth in the foregoing subparagraphs (a), (b), (c), and (d), any separate fund or funds held by the trustee in accordance with the first sentence of this Section 2, shall be allocated under the same basis, procedure and order as in such subparagraphs, for the purpose of providing any employes or pensioners who are represented by any such collective bargaining agreement and whose pensions are reduced or are not reached by the main allocation under (a), (b), (c), and (d) above, with their pensions or the balances thereof, as the case may be, to the extent possible through the complete allocation of such separate fund or funds.

The allocation referred to in this Section 2 when determined by the actuary and trustee, may be implemented through the continuance of the existing trust fund or through a new trust instrument for that purpose or through the purchase by the trustee of insurance company annuity contracts or by a combination of these media.

If the allocations produce a pension of less than $40 a year for any person, the trustee may pay in lieu of a pension a lump sum of equivalent actuarial value.

A R T I C L E X

DEFINITIONS

1. Employe

(a) Any person regularly employed in the United States by the Corporation or by a wholly-owned or substantially wholly-owned domestic subsidiary thereof, on an hourly-rate basis, including:

(1) hourly-rate persons employed on a full time basis;

(2) hourly-rate persons on incentive pay plans;

(3) General Motors Institute students and students from other educational institutions who are enrolled in cooperative training courses on hourly rate;

(4) part time hourly-rate employes who, on a regular and continuing basis, perform jobs having definitely established working hours, but the complete performance of which requires fewer hours of work than the regular work week, provided the services of such employes are normally available, for at least half of the employing unit's regular work week.

(b) The term "employe" shall not include:

(1) temporary employes,

(2) employes represented by a labor organization which has not signed an agreement making this Plan applicable to such employes.

2. Effective Date of Plan and Amendments

(Plan) October 1, 1950
(1st Amendments) June 1, 1953
(2nd Amendments) June 1, 1955
(3rd Amendments) Not later than June 1, 1959

3. Trustee or Insurance Company

The bank or banks, trust or insurance company or companies or any combination thereof designated by a trust agreement or contract as the medium for financing the Plan.

4. Seniority

Seniority means the period following the most recent date of hire by the Corporation and subsequent to which there has been no loss of credited service (as loss of credited service is defined in the Plan), or if the employe is represented under a collective bargaining agreement, seniority will be as defined in such agreement.

5. Primary Insurance Benefit

Primary Insurance Benefit means the amount payable to a pensioner excluding the benefit, if any, in respect of dependents, as, or corresponding to, the "Primary Insurance Benefit" defined in Title II of the Federal Social Security Act as amended, as now in effect or as hereafter amended.

6. *Trust Fund; Pension Fund; Insured Fund*

The General Motors Hourly-Rate Employes Pension Plan fund established by payments made by the Corporation in accordance with Article V herein. Such fund therein called the trust fund shall be comprised of either a pension fund or insured fund, or a combination thereof.

SUPPLEMENTAL AGREEMENT

BETWEEN

GENERAL MOTORS CORPORATION

AND THE

UAW—AFL—CIO

(Pension Plan)

dated October 2, 1958

On this 2nd day of October, 1958, General Motors Corporation, hereinafter referred to as the Corporation, and the International Union, United Automobile, Aircraft and Agricultural Implement Workers of America, affiliated with the American Federation of Labor and Congress of Industrial Organizations, hereinafter referred to as the Union, on behalf of the employes covered by the collective bargaining agreement of which this Supplemental Agreement becomes a part, agree as follows:

Section 1. *Establishment of Plan*

Subject to the approval of its Board of Directors and Stockholders, the Corporation will establish an amended pension plan, hereinafter referred to as the "Plan," a copy of which is attached hereto as Exhibit A–1 and made a part of this agreement to the extent applicable to the employes represented by the Union and covered by this agreement as if fully set out herein, modified and supplemented, however, by the provisions hereinafter. In the event of any conflict between the provisions of the Plan and the provisions of this agreement, the provisions of this agreement will supersede the provisions of the Plan to the extent necessary to eliminate such conflict.

The Plan, as set forth in Exhibit A–1, and the Plan as it may be modified and supplemented by superseding provisions of this agreement, as above provided, are both contingent upon and subject to obtaining and retaining such approval of the Commissioner of Internal Revenue as the Corporation may find necessary to establish the deductibility for income tax purposes of any and all payments made by the Corporation under both plans as being tax exempt under Sections 401, 404 and 501(a) or other applicable provisions of the Internal Revenue Code. Any modification or amendment of either the Plan, or the Plan as modified and supplemented by this agreement, may be made retroactively by the Corporation with the consent of the Union, if necessary or appropriate, to qualify or maintain the Plan as a plan and trust meeting the requirements of Sections 401, 404 and 501(a) of the Internal Revenue Code, as now in effect or hereafter amended, or any other applicable provisions of the federal tax laws, as now in effect or hereafter amended or adopted, and the regulations issued thereunder, provided that pension benefits under the Plan are not diminished.

Until the Plan is approved by the Corporation's Board of Directors and Stockholders, and by the Commissioner of Internal Revenue, all as hereinbefore provided, the benefits payable shall be only those determined under the Plan as constituted prior to September 1, 1958; provided, however, that prior to the receipt of such stockholder approval but following approval by its Board of Directors and its receipt of the favorable ruling from the Commissioner of Internal Revenue as set forth above, the Corporation will pay to retired employes for the months commencing on or after September 1, 1958 and prior to June 1, 1959 any excess amounts equal to the difference between the monthly pension calculated in accordance with the terms of the Plan, attached hereto as Exhibit A–1, and the monthly pension paid or payable in accordance with the terms of the Pension Plan which was attached as Exhibit A–1 to the Supplemental Agreement (Pension Plan) between the parties dated June 12, 1955 (which agreement was terminated on May 29, 1958). Any such excess amounts payable for months prior to the receipt of the aforementioned Board of Directors and the Commissioner of Internal Revenue approvals, shall be payable the first of the month following the date upon which the last of these two approvals is received by the Corporation, and any such amounts payable thereafter shall be paid on the first of the month at the same time as the related pension is paid.

In the event that the Plan is disapproved by either the Board of Directors or the Stockholders of the Corporation, the Corporation within thirty days after any such disapproval will give written notice thereof to the Union and this agreement shall thereupon have no force or effect. In that event the matters covered by this agreement shall be the subject of further negotiation between the Corporation and the Union.

Section 2. Financing

(a) A trustee or an insurance company, or both, shall be designated by the Corporation, and a trust agreement or contract, or both, executed between the Corporation and such trustee or insurance company, or both, under the terms of which a pension fund or insured fund, shall be established to receive and hold contributions payable by the Corporation, interest, and other income, and to pay the pensions provided by the Plan.

(b) The Corporation agrees to pay over irrevocably to the trustee or insurance company as of each anniversary of the effective date of the Plan during the period of this agreement, contributions or payments for the pension plan in the amount of the sum of (i) and (ii) below as determined and certified as of each such anniversary date by one or more actuaries chosen by, but independent of, the Corporation, and qualified through Fellowship in the Society of Actuaries (hereinafter referred to as the actuary):

(i) the annual "current service" or "normal cost" contribution attributable to a year's cost accruals in respect of assumed continuous service after each such anniversary date,

(ii) the "prior service contribution" computed as that part of the present value, at each such anniversary date, of the prospective pensions payable under the Plan for employes, pensioners and former employes who are entitled to a deferred pension then covered by the Plan which is in excess of:

   (aa) the value of the trust fund, as then comprised of any contracts and total other assets, invested and uninvested, such total assets being valued on a basis at least equal to the total cost thereof, plus

   (bb) the then present value of the prospective "current service" or "normal cost" determined by the actuary in accordance with (i) above.

such excess part being amortized according to the following schedule:

(1) in respect of the portion of such excess part attributable to the level of benefits established by the Corporation's pension plan as constituted prior to June 1, 1953 — the thirtieth anniversary of the Corporation's pension plan (October 1, 1980),

(2) in respect of the portion of such excess part attributable to the increase in the level of benefits established by amendments to the Corporation's pension plan effective as of June, 1953 — the thirty-third anniversary of the Corporation's pension plan (October 1, 1983),

(3) in respect of the portion of such excess part attributable to or arising from the further increase in the level of benefits and the granting of additional benefits by reason of amendments to the Corporation's pension plan effective as of June 1, 1955, the thirty-fifth anniversary of the Corporation's pension plan (October 1, 1985),

(4) in respect of the portion of such excess part attributable to or arising from the granting of additional benefits by reason of amendments to the Corporation's pension plan effective as of September 1, 1958, under this Supplemental Agreement — the thirty-eighth anniversary of the Corporation's pension plan (October 1, 1988).

(c) The Corporation may contribute or pay additional amounts to the trustee or insurance company, or both, under (b) above in any year without such additional amounts being construed to reduce any thirty-year period for the completion of the "prior service contributions" of subsection (b)(ii) above. If the Corporation has contributed any such additional amounts prior to any anniversary date of the Corporation's pension plan or shall contribute any such additional amounts prior to any anniversary date of the Plan falling within the duration of this agreement, the Corporation may as of such anniversary, contribute a lesser amount than otherwise determined by (b) above for such anniversary, provided that the value of any contracts and total other assets as valued in accordance with (b)(ii)(aa) above at such anniversary, shall not be less than the amount estimated by the actuary to be the value as if contributions and payments up to and including, such anniversary date had been made as provided in (b) above and no additional amounts had been contributed or paid prior to such anniversary.

(d) The Corporation by payment of the contributions or amounts as hereinbefore provided in this section shall be relieved of any further liability, and pensions shall be payable only from the trust fund or the insured fund or both.

(e) The Corporation will cause the Board of Administration as established under the provisions of Section 3(a) hereinafter to be furnished annually with a statement certified by the actuary, that the amount of the trust fund is or is not less than the amount then required by this Section 2 to be in such fund.

(f) The Corporation will cause the aforesaid Board of Administration to be furnished annually with a report, prepared by the actuary, in respect of each year's actuarial valuation of the Plan, setting out the amount of the annual contributions under the Plan required in accordance with this Section 2, and a statement of the interest rate, mortality rates, withdrawal rates and retirement age assumptions adopted for the valuation.

Section 3. Administration

(a) Board of Administration

(1) There shall be established a central Board of Administration hereinafter referred to as the Board, composed of six members, three appointed by the Corporation and three by the Union. Each member of the Board shall have an alternate. In the event a member is absent from a meeting of the Board, his alternate may attend and when in attendance shall exercise the duties of the member. Either the Corporation or the Union at any time may remove a member or alternate appointed by it and may appoint a member or alternate to fill any vacancy among members or alternates appointed by it.

No person shall act as a member of the Board of Administration or as an alternate for such member unless notice of his appointment has been given in writing by the party making the appointment to the other party.

(2) The Board shall meet at such times and for such periods for the transaction of necessary business as may be mutually agreed upon by its members.

(3) To constitute a quorum for the transaction of business, the presence of four members of the Board shall be required. At all meetings of the Board the member or members present appointed by the Corporation shall have in the aggregate a total of one vote to be cast on behalf of the Corporation, and the member or members present appointed by the Union shall have in the aggregate a total of one vote to be cast on behalf of the Union.

(4) The compensation and expenses of the Corporation members will be paid by the Corporation and the compensation and expenses of the Union members will be paid by the Union and no part of such compensation or expenses will be paid from the trust fund.

(5) The Corporation shall cause to be furnished to the Board of Administration annually, as of each anniversary date of the Plan, (i) a statement showing in summary form the value of the assets which comprise such fund by general categories of investment, such value being determined on a basis at least equal to the total cost thereof for each such category, and in addition, (ii) such information as to age, sex and service of hourly-rate employes of the Corporation as a whole in the United States and as to the number of pensioners and

amount of pensions by age groups, as the Board may reasonably require, but in no event shall the Corporation be required to furnish the Board with any data not furnished by the Corporation to the actuary.

(6) The Corporation would cause to be furnished to the Board of Administration annually a statement setting forth:

(a) The value of the trust fund computed in accordance with subsection (b)(ii)(aa) of Section 2 hereof as of the previous anniversary date of the Plan.

(b) Additions during year:

(i) payment by General Motors into the fund

(ii) interest and dividends received by the fund

(iii) net profits realized on sales of securities by the fund, and

(iv) total additions.

(c) Pension payments to retired employes during year.

(d) The value of the trust fund computed in accordance with subsection (b)(ii)(aa) of Section 2 hereof as of the anniversary date of the Plan for the year for which the statement is being submitted.

(7) The Board of Administration shall have no power to add to or subtract from or modify any of the terms of this agreement or the pension plan, nor to change or add to any benefit provided by said agreement or pension plan, nor to waive or fail to apply any requirement of eligibility for a benefit under said agreement or pension plan.

(8) Any case referred to the Board of Administration on which it has no power to rule shall be referred back to the parties without ruling.

(9) No ruling or decision of the Board of Administration in one case shall create a basis for retroactive adjustment in any other case prior to the date of written filing of each such specific claim.

(10) There shall be no appeal from any ruling by the Board which is within its authority. Each such ruling shall be final and binding on the Union and its members, the employe or employes involved, and on the Corporation.

The Union will discourage any attempt of its members and will not encourage or cooperate with any of its members, in any appeal to any Court or Administrative Board or Agency from a ruling of the Board of Administration.

(b) Impartial Chairman

(1) The Corporation and the Union shall mutually agree upon and select an Impartial Chairman, who shall serve until requested in writing to resign by three Board members.

(2) The Impartial Chairman will not be counted for the purpose of a quorum, and will vote only in case of a failure of the Corporation and Union by vote through their representatives on the Board to agree upon a matter which is properly before the Board and within the Board's authority to determine; provided that the Impartial Chairman may vote only on matters involving the processing of individual cases, not on the development of procedures.

(3) The fees and expenses of the Impartial Chairman will be paid one-half by the Corporation and one-half by the Union.

(c) As soon as possible after the effective date of this agreement, the Union and Corporation members of the Board of Administration shall work out matters such as but not limited to: (1) procedures for establishing Local Pension Committees at the Divisions or plants involved; (2) the authority and duties of such Local Pension Committees; (3) the procedures for reviewing applications for pensions; (4) the handling of complaints regarding the determination of age, service credits, and computation of benefits; (5) procedures for making appeals to the Board; (6) means of verifying service credits to which employes are entitled under the Plan; (7) methods of furnishing information to employes regarding past and future service credits; (8) the amount of time the Union members of the local committees may be permitted to leave their work to attend meetings of the Local Pension Committees; (9) how disputes over total and permanent disability claims will be handled; (10) the review of pertinent information about the Plan for dissemination to employes; (11) how pension payments will be authorized by the Board. All such matters shall be consistent with all other provisions of the Plan and this agreement. The working out of the procedures outlined in this section shall be the responsibility of the Corporation and Union members of the Board, and the Impartial Chairman shall have no power to decide any question with respect thereto.

The provisions of Agreement Implementing Sections 3(c) of the Supplemental Agreement, Pension Plan, dated May 29, 1950 which were agreed to by the Board pursuant to the foregoing are incorporated herein by reference and are a part hereof and effective with respect to the administration of the Plan as fully as if set out herein at length.

(d) Except as provided otherwise in this agreement, the general administration of the provisions of the pension plan shall be the responsibility of the Corporation.

(e) The Board and any member of the Board, or the Local Pension Committees or any member of Local Pension Committees, shall be entitled to rely upon the correctness of any information furnished by the Union or the Corporation. Neither the Board nor any of its members, nor the Local Pension Committees nor any of its members, nor the Union nor any officer or other representative of the Union, nor the Corporation nor any officer or other representative of the Corporation shall be liable because of any act, or failure to act, on the part of the Board or any of its members, or the Local Pension Committees or any of its members or any person, except that nothing herein shall be deemed to relieve any such individual from any liability for his own fraud or bad faith.

(f) No matter respecting the Plan as modified and supplemented by this agreement or any difference arising thereunder shall be subject to the grievance procedure established in the collective bargaining agreement between the Corporation and the Union.

(g) Credited service shall be granted an employe who is absent from his work pursuant to Paragraph 24 of the National Agreement, or on a leave of absence under Paragraph 109 of the National Agreement if the leave was granted for the purpose of permitting the employe to serve as an elected officer of the Local Union at his plant, or if the leave was granted under Paragraph 109(a) of the National

Agreement for the purpose of permitting the employe to hold a position on the Staff of the International Union while on such leave.

An employe granted a leave under this section shall be credited with 40 hours for each complete calendar week since October 1, 1950 while he is on such leave, if he would otherwise have been scheduled to work, and provided he meets the requirements of the leave; but in no event shall the employe be credited with more than 1700 hours, including compensated hours, in any calendar year.

Section 4. Automatic Retirement

There shall be automatic retirement at the ages and on the basis specified in the Plan but such automatic retirement dates shall not affect the Corporation's right to discharge or otherwise discipline employes, subject to any pension rights under the Plan, prior to the automatic retirement date, provided, however, that any employe so discharged or disciplined shall have the right to file a grievance in accordance with the grievance procedure established in the collective bargaining agreement.

Section 5. Effect of Retirement on Employment Status and Seniority

(a) An employe who retires or is retired under the terms of the pension plan shall cease to be an employe and shall have his seniority canceled.

(b) An employe who has been retired on a total and permanent disability pension and who thereby has broken his seniority in accordance with subsection (a) above, but who recovers and is subsequently reemployed shall have his seniority reinstated as though he had been continued on a sick leave of absence during the period of his disability retirement.

(c) If an employe retired for reasons other than total and permanent disability, who has lost seniority in accordance with subsection (a) above, is rehired, such employe will have the status of a new employe and without seniority, and he shall not acquire or accumulate any seniority thereafter, for any purpose under this agreement.

Section 6. Suspension of Benefits at Option of Employee

Notwithstanding any other provisions of this Plan, an employe entitled to receive a pension may, for personal reasons and without disclosure thereof, request the Local Pension Committee in writing to suspend for any period payment of all or any part of such pension otherwise payable to him hereunder. The Local Pension Committee, on receipt of such request, shall authorize such suspension, in which event the employe shall be deemed to have forfeited all rights to the amount of pension so suspended, but shall retain the right to have the full pension otherwise payable to him hereunder reinstated as to future monthly payments upon written notice to the Local Pension Committee of his desire to revoke his prior request for a suspension under this section.

Section 7. Duration of Agreement

This agreement and Plan shall continue in effect until the termination of the collective bargaining agreement of which this is a part.

APPENDIX B

The following is the specimen form of trust agreement of the Chase Manhattan Bank.

SPECIMEN FORM

OF

TRUST AGREEMENT

(The Plan should include an express provision that the Trust Agreement is a part of the Plan and an executed copy of the Trust Agreement should be physically attached to the original of the plan.)

This Agreement made as of the_____day of_____, 19___, by and between_____, a corporation organized under the laws of the State of_____(hereinafter referred to as the "Company") and THE CHASE MANHATTAN BANK, a banking corporation organized and existing under the laws of the State of New York (hereinafter referred to as the "Trustee"),

WITNESSETH:

WHEREAS, the Company has adopted the "_____ Plan" for its eligible employees (hereinafter referred to as the "Plan"); and

WHEREAS, an Administrative Committee (hereinafter referred to as the "Committee") has been created to administer the Plan; and

WHEREAS, under the Plan, funds will from time to time be contributed to the Trustee, which funds, as and when received by the Trustee, will constitute a trust fund to be held for the benefit of the members under the Plan or their beneficiaries; and

WHEREAS, the Company desires the Trustee to hold and administer such funds and the Trustee is willing to hold and administer such funds pursuant to the terms of this Agreement:

NOW, THEREFORE, in consideration of the premises and of the mutual covenants herein contained, the Company and the Trustee do hereby covenant and agree as follows:

FIRST: The Trustee shall receive any contributions paid to it in cash or in other property acceptable to it. All contributions so received together with the income therefrom and any other increment thereon (hereinafter referred to as the "Trust Fund") shall be held, managed and administered by the Trustee pursuant to the terms of this Agreement without distinction between principal and income and without liability for the payment of interest thereon. The Trustee shall not be responsible for the collection of any contributions to the Plan.

SECOND: Subject to the provisions of Article THIRD hereof, the Trustee shall from time to time on the directions of the Committee make distributions out of the Trust Fund to such persons, including the Committee or any member thereof, in such manner, in such amounts and for such purposes (including the purchase of life insurance and/or annuity contracts) as may be specified in the directions of the Committee.

The Trustee shall be under no liability for any distribution made by it pursuant to a direction of the Committee and shall be under no duty to make inquiries as to whether any distribution directed by the Committee is made pursuant to the provisions of the Plan.

THIRD: A. Notwithstanding anything to the contrary contained in this Agreement, or in any amendment thereto,

It shall be impossible, at any time prior to the satisfaction of all liabilities with respect to the members under the Plan or their beneficiaries, for any part of the Trust Fund (other than such part as is required to pay taxes and administration expenses) to be used for, or diverted to, purposes other than for the exclusive benefit of the members under the Plan or their beneficiaries.

B. In making a distribution upon a direction as authorized herein, the Trustee may accept such direction as a certification that such payment complies with the provisions of this Article and need make no further investigation.

FOURTH: The Trustee shall have the following powers and authority in the administration of the Trust Fund, to be exercised as provided in Article FIFTH hereof:

A. To purchase or subscribe for any securities or other property and to retain in trust such securities or other property.

B. To sell for cash or on credit, to grant options, convert, redeem, exchange for other securities or other property, or otherwise to dispose of any securities or other property at any time held by it.

C. To settle, compromise or submit to arbitration, any claims, debts or damages, due or owing to or from the Trust, to commence or defend suits or legal proceedings and to represent the Trust in all suits or legal proceedings.

D. To exercise any conversion privilege and/or subscription right available in connection with any securities or other property at any time held by it; to oppose or to consent to the reorganization, consolidation merger, or readjustment of the finances of any corporation, company or association or to the sale, mortgage, pledge or lease of the property of any corporation, company or association any of the securities of which may at any time be held by it and to do any act with reference thereto, including the exercise of options, the making of agreements or subscriptions and the payment of expenses, assessments or subscriptions, which may be deemed necessary or advisable in connection therewith, and to hold and retain any securities or other property which it may so acquire.

E. To exercise, personally or by general or by limited power of attorney, any right, including the right to vote, appurtenant to any securities or other property held by it at any time.

F. To borrow money from any lender including the Trustee in its individual capacity in such amounts and upon such terms and conditions as shall be deemed advisable or proper to carry out the purposes of the Trust and to pledge any securities or other property for the repayment of any such loan.

G. To manage, administer, operate, lease for any number of years, regardless of any restrictions on leases made by fiduciaries, develop, improve, repair, alter, demolish, mortgage, pledge, grant options with respect to, or otherwise deal with any real property or interest therein at any time held by it, and to hold any such real property in its own name or in the name of a nominee, with or without the addition of words indicating that such property is held in a fiduciary capacity, all upon such terms and conditions as may be deemed advisable.

To renew or extend or participate in the renewal or extension of any mortgage, upon such terms as may be deemed advisable, and to agree to a reduction in the rate of interest on any mortgage or to any other modification or change in the terms of any mortgage or of any guarantee pertaining thereto, in any manner and to any extent that may be deemed advisable for the protection of the Trust Fund or the preservation of the value of the investment; to waive any default whether in the performance of any covenant or condition of any mortgage or in the performance of any guarantee, or to enforce any such default in such manner and to such extent as may be deemed advisable; to exercise and enforce any and all rights of foreclosure, to bid in property on foreclosure, to take a deed in lieu of foreclosure with or without paying a consideration therefor and in connection therewith to release the obligation on the bond secured by such mortgage, and to exercise and enforce in any action, suit or proceeding at law or in equity any rights or remedies in respect to any such mortgage or guarantee.

H. To hold part or all of the Trust Fund uninvested.

I. To employ suitable agents and counsel and to pay their reasonable expenses and compensation.

J. To register any securities held by it hereunder in its own name or in the name of a nominee with or without the addition of words indicating that such securities are held in a fiduciary capacity and to hold any securities in bearer form.

K. To form corporations and to create trusts to hold title to any securities or other property, all upon such terms and conditions as may be deemed advisable.

L. To make, execute and deliver, as Trustee, any and all deeds, leases, mortgages, conveyances, contracts, waivers, releases or other instruments in writing necessary or proper for the accomplishment of any of the foregoing powers.

> (The following form of subdivision may be used where it is contemplated that the trust fund may participate in any pooled trust fund maintained by the Bank for employee benefit trusts. If so, the letter "M" should be added

to the letters set forth in the second alternative (consent power) and third alternative (directed power) of Article FIFTH.)

M. To transfer, at any time and from time to time, such part or all of the Trust Fund as it shall deem advisable to THE CHASE MANHATTAN BANK as Trustee of any trust maintained by it as a medium for the collective investment of funds of pension, profit-sharing or other employee benefit trusts of which it may from time to time be acting as Trustee, and may withdraw any part or all of the Trust Fund so transferred. The provisions of any such trust shall be deemed a part of this agreement.

THE THREE FOLLOWING ALTERNATIVE FORMS OF ARTICLE "FIFTH" MAY BE CONSIDERED IN SETTING FORTH INVESTMENT CONTROL AND RESPONSIBILITY

(1. The following form of Article Fifth may be used when the Trustee is to have sole investment control without prior approval or direction of the Committee.)

FIFTH: The powers listed in Article FOURTH of this Agreement shall be exercised by the Trustee in its uncontrolled discretion.

(Note 1: If desired, the words "by the Trustee in its uncontrolled discretion" may be substituted for the words "as provided in Article FIFTH hereof" at the beginning of Article FOURTH. Subsequent articles will then have to be remembered.)

(Note 2: If a veto power is desired, the following paragraph may be added to the above.)

At any time irrespective of any prior action with respect to any securities or other property, the Committee may veto and disapprove the further retention of any particular asset by the Trustee, in which event the Trustee shall immediately dispose of such disapproved asset in accordance with any written directions of the Committee. The Trustee shall not be liable for any loss sustained in connection with any such disapproved asset.

(Note 3: If subdivision M of Article FOURTH is included in the agreement the following sentence should be added to the foregoing paragraph.)

The Committee may also at any time direct the Trustee to withdraw any part of the interest of the Trust Fund held in any pooled trust fund pursuant to subdivision M of Article FOURTH.

(2. The following form of Article FIFTH may be used when investment control is to be subject to the approval of the Committee.)

FIFTH: The powers listed in the subdivisions lettered A, B, C, D, E, F, G and H of Article FOURTH of this Agreement shall be exercised by the Trustee only with the written approval of the Committee. The other powers listed in Article FOURTH shall be exercised by the Trustee in its uncontrolled discretion.

The Trustee shall not be liable for any loss sustained by the Trust Fund by reason of the failure of the Committee to approve any action proposed by the Trustee under any of the powers listed in the said subdivisions, lettered "A" to "H" inclusive.

(3. The following form of Article FIFTH may be used when the administration of the Trust is to be directed by the Committee and must be used when securities of the Company are purchased.)

FIFTH: The powers listed in the subdivisions lettered A, B, C, D, E, F, G and H of Article FOURTH of this Agreement shall be exercised by the Trustee only if, when and in the manner directed in writing by the Committee. It shall be the duty of the Trustee to act strictly in accordance with each such direction. The Trustee shall be under no duty to question any direction of the Committee, to review any securities or other property held in the Trust Fund, or to make suggestions to the Committee with respect to the exercise or non-exercise of the said powers. The other powers listed in Article FOURTH shall be exercised by the Trustee in its uncontrolled discretion.

The Trustee shall be under no liability for any loss of any kind which may result by reason of any action taken by it in accordance with any direction of the Committee or by reason of its failure to exercise any of the said powers because of the failure of the Committee to give such direction.

THE TWO FOLLOWING ALTERNATIVE FORMS OF ARTICLE "SIXTH" MAY BE CONSIDERED IN DEFINING AUTHORIZED INVESTMENTS.

(1. The following form of Article SIXTH may be used if investments are to be restricted to "trustee legals.")

SIXTH: The words "securities or other property" as used in this Agreement shall be deemed to refer to such stocks, bonds, notes or other evidences of indebtedness or ownership, in which trustees are authorized to invest under the laws of the State of New York as such laws exist from time to time.

(2. The following form of Article SIXTH may be used if investments are not to be restricted to "legals.")

SIXTH: The words "securities or other property" as used in this Agreement shall be deemed to refer to any property, real or personal or part interest therein, wherever situate, including but without being limited to governmental, corporate or personal obligations, trust and participation certificates, leaseholds, fee titles, mortgages and other interests in realty, preferred and common stocks, and any other evidences of indebtedness or ownership, even though the same may not be legal investments for trustees under the laws applicable hereto.

(Note: If securities of the employer are to be acquired by the Trustee, the words "including securities or other property of the Company" should be inserted after the word "ownership.")

SEVENTH: The Trustee shall pay out of the Trust Fund all real and personal property taxes, income taxes and other taxes of any and all kinds levied or assessed under existing or future laws against the Trustee or the Trust Fund.

The Trustee shall be paid such reasonable compensation as shall from time to time be agreed upon by the Company and the Trustee. Such compensation and all expenses of administration of the Trust including counsel fees shall be withdrawn by the Trustee out of the Trust Fund unless paid by the Company.

Notwithstanding the provisions of Article SECOND hereof all payments under this Article SEVENTH may be made without the approval or direction of the Committee.

EIGHTH: The Trustee shall render from time to time accounts of its transactions to the Committee and the Committee may approve such accounts by an instrument in writing delivered to the Trustee. In the absence of the filing in writing with the Trustee by the Committee of exceptions or objections to any such account within sixty (60) days, the Committee shall be deemed to have approved such account; and in such case, or upon the written approval of the Committee of any such account, the Trustee shall be released, relieved and discharged with respect to all matters and things set forth in such account as though such account had been settled by the decree of a court of competent jurisdiction. No person other than the Company or the Committee may require an accounting or bring any action against the Trustee with respect to the Trust or its actions as Trustee.

NINTH: The Trustee shall be fully protected in relying upon a certification of a member of the Committee with respect to any instruction, direction or approval of the Committee, and protected also in relying upon a certification of the Company as to the membership of the Committee as it then exists, and in continuing to rely upon such certification until a subsequent certification is filed with the Trustee.

The Trustee shall be fully protected in acting upon any instrument, certificate, or paper believed by it to be genuine and to be signed or presented by the proper person or persons, and the Trustee shall be under no duty to make any investigation or inquiry as to any statement contained in any such writing but may accept the same as conclusive evidence of the truth and accuracy of the statements therein contained.

The Trustee shall not be liable for the proper application of any part of the Trust Fund if distributions are made in accordance with the written directions of the Committee as herein provided, nor shall the Trustee be responsible for the adequacy of the Trust Fund to meet and discharge any and all distributions and liabilities under the Plan. All persons dealing with the Trustee are released from inquiry into the decision or authority of the Trustee and from seeing to the application of any moneys, securities or other property paid or delivered to the Trustee.

Neither the Trustee nor any member of the Committee shall be liable hereunder except for its or his own negligence or willful misconduct.

TENTH: Any Trustee acting hereunder may resign at any time by giving written notice to the Company. The Company may remove any Trustee at any time and in the case of the resignation or removal of any Trustee the Company shall appoint a successor Trustee. Any successor Trustee shall have the same powers and duties as those conferred upon the Trustee named in this Agreement. The removal of a Trustee and the appointment of a new Trustee shall be by a written instrument delivered to the Trustee.

ELEVENTH: This Agreement, other than paragraph A of article THIRD, may be amended by the Company at any time or from time to time and in any manner, and the provisions of any such amendment may be made applicable to the Trust Fund as constituted at the time of the amendment as well as to the part of the Trust Fund subsequently acquired; provided, however, that no such amendment shall increase the duties or change the compensation of the Trustee without its consent. Any such amendment shall be by a written instrument delivered to the Trustee.

TWELFTH: This Agreement and the trust created hereby may be terminated at any time by the Company, and upon such termination or upon the dissolution or liquidation of the Company in the event that a successor to the Company by operation of law or by the acquisition of its business interests shall not elect to continue the Plan and this Trust, the Trust Fund shall be paid out by the Trustee as and when directed by the Committee in accordance with the provisions of Article SECOND hereof.

THIRTEENTH: This Agreement and the Trust created hereby shall be construed, regulated and administered under the laws of the State of New York, and the Trustee shall be liable to account only in the courts of that state. All contributions of the Trustee shall be deemed to take place in the State of New York. The Trustee may at any time initiate an action or proceedings for the settlement of its accounts or for the determination of any question of construction which may arise or for instructions, and the only necessary parties defendant to such action shall be the Company and the Committee, except that the Trustee may, if it so elects, bring in as parties defendant any other person or persons.

FOURTEENTH: Any Company which is a subsidiary of the Company or which may be affiliated with the Company in any way and which is now or may hereafter be organized under the laws of the United States of America, or of any State or Territory thereof, may, with the approval of the Board of Directors of the Company by resolution of its own Board of Directors adopt the Trust if such subsidiary or affiliate shall have adopted the Plan.

Any such subsidiary or affiliate may at any time segregate from further participation in the trust under this Trust Agreement. Such subsidiary or affiliate shall file with the Trustee a document evidencing its segregation from the Trust Fund and its continuance of a trust in accordance with the provisions of this Trust Agreement as though such subsidiary or affiliate were the sole creator thereof. In such event, the Trustee shall deliver to itself as Trustee of such trust such part of the Trust Fund as may be determined by the Committee to constitute the appropriate share of the Trust Fund then held in respect of the participating members of such subsidiary or affiliate. Such former subsidiary or affiliate may thereafter exercise in respect of such Trust Agreement all the rights and powers reserved to the Company and to the Committee under the provisions of this Trust Agreement.

In a similar manner, the proportionate share of the assets then held in respect of employees in any division, plant, location or other identifiable group or unit of the Company or of any subsidiary or affiliate may be segregated, and the Trustee shall hold such segregated assets in the same manner and for the same purposes as provided above in the event of segregation of a subsidiary or affiliate and the Company or any successor owner of the segregated unit shall have the rights hereinabove provided for a segregated subsidiary or affiliate.

FIFTEENTH: This Trust shall be known as the "_____
_____TRUST."

SIXTEENTH: This Agreement shall be executed in any number of counterparts, each one of which shall be deemed to be the original although the others shall not be produced.

IN WITNESS WHEREOF, this instrument has been executed as of the day and year first above written.

TABLE
OF CASES

INDEX